W0232046

Solar Photovoltaic Technology and Systems
A Manual for Technicians, Trainers and Engineers

Chetan Singh Solanki

Associate Professor
Department of Energy Science and Engineering
Indian Institute of Technology Bombay

PHI Learning Private Limited
Delhi-110092
2025

In fond memory of **Shri Asoke K. Ghosh** *(October 1942 – February 2024), Founder Chairman and Managing Director of PHI Learning, whose vision endlessly inspires.*

The Legacy Continues....

Published by Pushpita Ghosh, PHI Learning Private Limited, Rimjhim House, 111, Patparganj Industrial Estate, Delhi-110092 and Printed by Mudrak, C-55, Sector 65, Noida, U.P.-201301.

₹895.00

SOLAR PHOTOVOLTAIC TECHNOLOGY AND SYSTEMS: A manual for technicians, trainers and engineers
Chetan Singh Solanki

© 2025 by PHI Learning Private Limited, Delhi.

All right reserved. This publication is protected by copyright and may not be reproduced, in whole or in part, in any form or by any electronic, mechanical, or other means, now known or hereafter invented, including photocopying, recording, or any information storage and retrieval system, OR to train artificial intelligence systems without permission in writing from the publisher.

iSBn-978-81-203-4711-3 (Print Book)
ISBN-978-93-90544-91-2 (e-Book)

The export rights of the book are vested solely with the publisher.

To

Ministry of New and Renewable Energy (MNRE), Govt. of India
for its efforts to promote solar PV installations in India

Contents

Preface

India has launched the Jawaharlal Nehru National Solar Mission (JNNSM) in 2009–10 with the ambitious target of installing 20,000 MW of solar power, solar Photovoltaic (PV) as well as solar thermal, in the country by year 2022. The JNNSM provides incentives that promote solar PV system installations both at grid-connected PV system and off-grid PV system levels. There are several state Governments in India that are also making and implementing their own plans for promoting solar PV systems by incentivising the installations. Also, in last 1 to 2 years, the prices of PV modules have fallen significantly. Considering the scenario of favourable Government policies and reduction in prices of PV modules, there is a huge interest for the installation of solar PV systems. In order to enable the deployment of solar PV systems in India, there is a need for a large number of trained people in the solar PV area. As per MNRE, Govt. of India, the requirement is of 100,000 people but my own estimates suggest the requirement of 300,000 people. The trained manpower is required at various levels ranging from researcher, engineer to technician or PV system installers. This PV manual targets the training of people who installs or going to install solar PV systems in future.

This book will be useful for anybody who wants to work with solar PV systems. Particularly, the book will be useful for technicians, trainers and engineers (or any PV system practitioner) who are working on solar PV systems for design, installation and maintenance of solar PV systems of all types.

The objective of writing this book is to prepare a text for PV system practitioner covering various aspects of Solar PV technologies and systems in simplified, easy-to-understand way. The content of the training manual is chosen to cover the basics of each topic and it is written in a manner to make it self-explanatory. The text is written in simple language so that anybody, even without having a prior background in this area, can understand the concepts explained in the book. There are a lot of illustrations on all topics covered in the book. Practical tips on the various topics are provided wherever it is required. There are a large number of solved examples included in the text that convey and clarify the various concepts covered in the manual. Using this manual, a solar PV practitioner should be able to perform operations like identifying solar PV system components, designing solar PV systems, installing solar PV systems and repairing faults in the PV systems.

The Introductory Chapter gives the basics of electricity and related concepts. It also gives details about using multimeter for measuring various electrical quantities. Basics of energy, its units, quantities of energy etc. are covered in Chapter 2. Chapter 3 details out the concept of solar cells. It describes the various parameters of solar cells and their relationship with efficiency. The interconnection of solar cells in PV modules is then described in Chapter 4. The design of PV modules, number of cells in PV modules, the size of cells, power rating, etc. are discussed. For large PV systems, we need to connect several PV modules in the form of PV arrays. Chapter 5 discusses the design of PV array. It includes inter-connection of PV modules in series and parallel, the addition of voltages and currents of PV modules in given configuration, the estimation of number of PV modules required, etc. Batteries are important component of off-grid PV systems. Understanding of batteries is very important for proper design and operation of off-grid PV systems. Chapter 6 gives the fundamentals of batteries and relates them to the parameters of battery like voltage and Ah capacity of a battery. Chapter 7 discusses the inter-connection of batteries, series and parallel combination of batteries, etc. Chapter 8 describes the electronics that are used in PV systems, particularly, off-grid PV systems. This chapter gives details about the characteristics of various electronics components like charge controller, inverter, MPPT etc. It also discusses the rated capacities of various electronic components. Wires, particularly in DC part of PV system, plays an important role in terms of resistive losses. Appropriate sizing of wires is required. The details about wires, their physical sizes as well as sizing of wire for a given system are described in Chapter 9. Chapter 10 describes the design of standalone solar PV system for providing specified quantity of electricity on daily basis. Simple methodology of design and sizing of various components of PV system is described. Chapter 11 discusses the grid-connected PV systems. Various arrangement of grid-connected PV system with design of grid-connected PV systems is discussed. Chapter 12 discusses the various aspects related to troubleshooting and maintenance of PV system components and PV system as a whole.

Chetan Singh Solanki

Basics of Electricity

We use electricity for our daily needs. Without using electricity, it is difficult to live even for a single day. Therefore, it is important for us to know some basics about electricity, its terminology, how to measure electricity, etc. All the readers of this manual are expected to be a technician on solar electricity, and therefore, as a technician of the solar energy, it is very important that one are well aware of the basic concepts of electricity. In this chapter, we will explore the basic concepts and terminologies related to it. At the end of the chapter, we will get introduced to multimeter which is the most essential tool to measure electricity and its related parameters.

1.1 Introduction to Electricity

Despite using electricity in our daily life, many of us do not understand its basic terms and people find it difficult to learn about electricity. The main terms associated with electricity are as follows:

- Current
- Voltage
- Power
- Energy
- AC and DC power

As a technician, one should know all the above terms related to electricity. Also, it is important to know not only the terms but also understand the difference between these terms. In addition, one should have a good sense of values of these terms and significance of values, i.e., whether the value is small or large.

We can easily understand electricity and its related terms, such as voltage, current, and power by considering an analogy with the flow of water from a water tank. The flow of current in a circuit and the flow of water from a tank have several similarities. When a tank is filled and a tap is opened, water flows out from the tank. Water flows out faster if a tank is fully filled as compared to the case when the tank is partially filled. Similarly, in an electrical circuit, the current flows when there is a voltage. The greater amount of current flows when the voltage is higher. Therefore, the height of the water in a tank is similar to the voltage in the electrical circuit.

In an electrical circuit, the current flows only when there is a voltage source.

1

Water flows in terms of the flow of water molecules, i.e. the flow of water molecules is the flow of water. Similarly, current flows due to the flow of electrons as shown in Figure 1.1. Thus, the flow of current is the flow of electrons in an electrical circuit. Electrons are charged particles. Therefore, in electrical terms, the flow of charged particles is defined as current-flow.

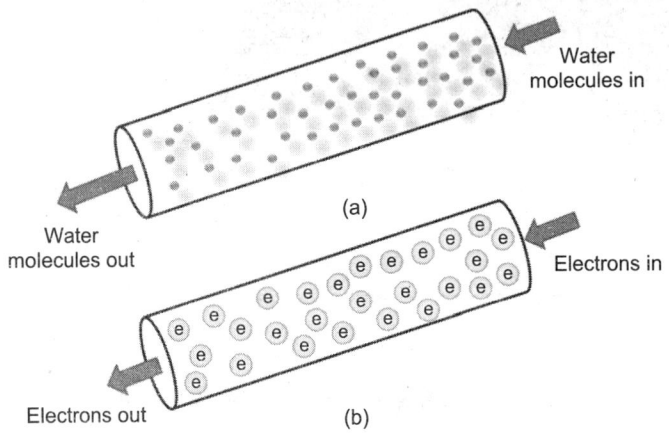

FIGURE 1.1

Schematic showing flow of (a) water particles and (b) charged particles (electrons).

Consider a water tank at a certain height from the ground and a pipe of certain diameter as shown in Figure 1.2. The flow of electrons through a wire is similar to the flow of water through the pipe. If we look into a pipe at a given point, we can see a certain amount of water passing that point each second. This flow of water through a pipe per second is called water current. Similarly, the flow of charge (electrons) through a wire per second is called electric current.

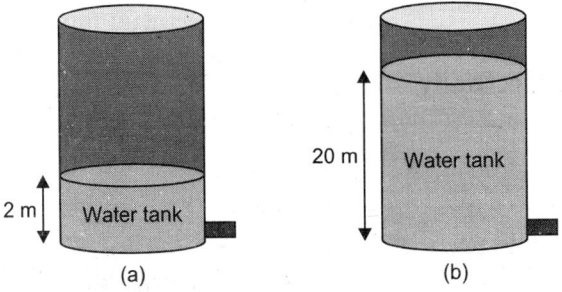

FIGURE 1.2

Water tank analogy for electric voltage.

The amount of water flowing through the pipe depends on the following two things:

1. How hard the water is being pushed, i.e., how much pressure is being applied.
2. It also depends on the diameter of the pipe which indicates the resistance to the flow of water. Higher diameter means lower resistance to the flow of water.

In a similar way, the amount of current flows through a wire depends on the following two things:

1. How much electrical pressure is being applied. This electrical pressure is called "Voltage" in electrical terminology.
2. It also depends on the diameter of the wire, which indicates the resistance to the flow of current. Higher diameter means low resistance to current flow.

Electrical voltage is equivalent of pressure in water tank.

From the above discussion, we can say that for higher pressure of water and larger diameter of water pipe, larger would be the amount of water passing through the pipe each second. Similarly, for the larger electrical pressure (the voltage) and for larger diameter of the wire (less resistance), larger will be the current passing through the wire.

The greater the height, the more the pressure on water. The more the pressure, the more the water current. Similarly, the more the voltage, the more the electric current.

1.2
Voltage

The pressure that pushes charge (electrons) in a wire is called Voltage. The symbol used for voltage is '*V*'. Consider a water tank as shown in Figure 1.2. If a tank of water were suspended 2 metres above the ground with a one centimetre pipe coming out of the bottom, the water pressure would be very small, might be similar to the force of a shower. If the same water tank were suspended 20 metres above the ground, the force of the water would be much greater. In this way, water at 2 metres height will cause lower pressure than the water at 20 metres height. In an another example, if a ball falls on your head from 2 metres height it will hurt you less as compared to the case when ball falls on your head from 20 metres height. This means that the ball falling from greater height creates more pressure and hurts you more.

In electrical terms, the term Voltage signifies the pressure on electrons to flow in the circuit. Voltage (electrical pressure) is very similar to water pressure. If voltage is more, the pressure on electrons would be more and the resultant current will be more. If the voltage is less, the resultant pressure on electrons is less and, therefore, current will be less.

Voltage is measured in 'volt' and the symbol for unit volt is V. Note that, the symbol used for voltage is also *V*. Just as 20 metres high tank will apply more pressure than a 1 metre tank; similarly, a voltage source of 10 V would apply more pressure than a voltage source of 1 V. In practice, we deal with a wide range of voltage levels; from very small voltage level to very large voltage level. For instance, small pencil batteries that we get in the market provide voltage level of 1.5 V. There are car batteries provides voltage levels of 12 V. In our homes' electrical circuit, we get voltage level of 230 V. In the industries, normally, the voltage levels are 440 V. In the sub-stations, the voltage levels are about 11,000 V and at the power plants, the voltage levels are about 66,000 V. From the above numbers, we can see that in electrical circuits around us we use large range of voltage levels.

The Voltage levels in an electrical circuit can be small like 1–2 V or it can be very large like 10,000 V.

Small voltage levels can run small electrical appliances and large voltage levels can run large electrical appliances. For example, small pencil batteries provide 1.5 V. This is small voltage or electrical pressure that would be sufficient for lighting small bulbs, for instance, in flash lights or torches. On the other hand, a car usually has a 12 V battery and it applies more voltage to push current through the wire and can run large lamps in the car.

Unit of voltage is volts (V) and the unit of current is ampere (A).

Problem 1.1: The pressure that pushes water in a tube is water pressure. What is the pressure that pushes the electrons in a wire? Consider two batteries, a 5 V battery and a 10 V battery. Which of these two batteries can push the elctrons with more pressure?

1.3
Current

The symbol used for electrical current is '*I*'. The flow of electrons through a wire is similar to the flow of water through a pipe. The water current is the number of molecules flowing past a fixed point. Similarly, electrical current is the amount of charge (electrons) flowing past a fixed point. Current is measured in ampere, and the symbol used for ampere is 'A'. One ampere current flow is actually the flow of large number of electrons per second. One ampere current is the flow of about 1,000,000,000,000,000,000 electrons per second through a wire.

We should note here that the current flow is possible only when voltage is available. If the voltage is zero, the current flow will also be zero.

For small electrical circuits or for small electrical appliances, 1 A current is very large current. Therefore, people use smaller unit of current like 0.001 A. The term 0.001 represents one thousandth fraction of one and referred as 'milli' and represented by symbol 'm'. Therefore, 0.001 A current is 1 mA current.

As the diameter of the pipe increases the amount of water that can flow through it also increases as shown in Figure 1.3. A wire having large diameter indicates lower resistance to current flow. As the cross-sectional area of the wire increases, so does the amount of electric current that can flow through it for the same voltage level. Thus, whenever we need to conduct large current, a wire of large diameter should be chosen.

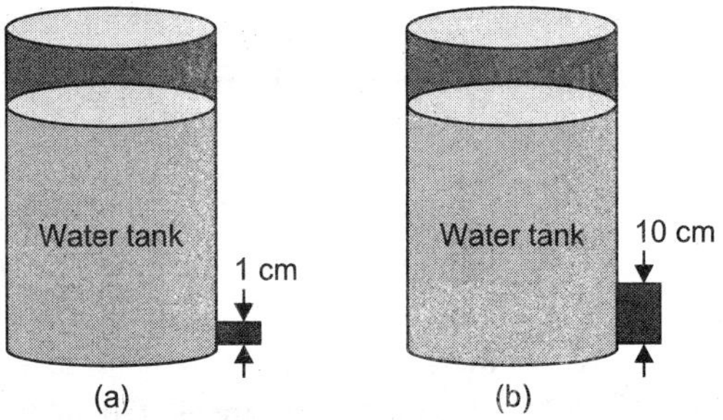

FIGURE 1.3
Water tank analogy for electric current. The more the diameter of the pipe, the more the current of water. Similarly, the more the diameter of wire, the more the electric current.

Electric current is the flow of electrons in a circuit. Large current flows when the resistance to current flow is less.

There are various possible voltage levels and similar to this, there are various possible current levels. In an electrical circuit, there can be very small current flown like 0.001 A or 1 mA, or there can be very large current flow like 1000 A. Small current is required for running small electrical appliances and large current level is required for running large electrical appliances.

Problem 1.2: The flow of water in a pipe is called water current. What is the flow of electrons in a wire called? Consider two wires, a 0.1 cm diameter and a 0.2 cm diameter. Which of these two wires can allow more flow of electrons. Given the voltage applied is same for both?

1.4

Danger with High Voltage and Current Levels

The voltage level represents the electrical pressure that is available for flow of current. It is important to note that large voltage levels are dangerous for human beings. If we come in contact with electrical wire with high voltage levels, due to large voltage levels or large pressure, the current can flow through human body and results in damages. The voltage across the human body results in current flow through the body and depending on the level of current, the body can get damaged. The results of current flow through the human body could be just painful sensation, but it can be much worse as well. The current flow through human body can also results in paralysis, respiratory paralysis, disorder of the cardiac rhythm, and burnings resulting in death. The effect of current flow depends on the level of current. Large amount of voltage and current can be dangerous for life, therefore, one must take precaution while working with electrical circuit.

1.5
Resistance to Electrical Current

The flow of current requires a medium. In the case of electrical current, the medium is conducting wires like copper and aluminium. Normally, the conducting wires are chosen to allow the smooth flow of current, but due to their material properties, all the conducting media possess some resistance to current flow. The amount of resistance in the path of current flow is given by the term Resistance, which is represented by symbol R. The resistance is measured in Ohm. Symbol of Ohm is a Greek alphabet Omega (Ω).

The property of the resistance is to resist or impedes the current flow. Normally, in electrical circuit, we would like to have as small resistance as possible, because we do not want any resistance to current flow. One of the side effects of the resistance of a wire is the voltage drop across it when current flows. The voltage drop means drop of electrical pressure to drive the current. The amount of voltage drop depends on resistance and current flowing through the wire. It is represented by the following equation:

$$\text{Voltage} = \text{Resistance} \times \text{Current}$$

or

$$V = R \times I$$

For instance, if the resistance of a wire is 0.1 Ω and the current flowing through the wire is 10 A, then the voltage drop across the wire will be $0.1 \times 10 = 1$ V. Normally, we should try to keep the voltage drop across the wire to less than 1% or 2% of the source voltage.

1.6
Electric Power

Consider, a water tank with the capacity of 100 litres which is to be emptied. Can we ask the question; what is the power of water flow? Yes, we can ask this question. So, what is the power of water flow from a tank? The power of the water flow will depend on how fast the tank can be emptied. Tank can be emptied in 10 minutes or in 1 minute. If the tank is emptied in 10 minutes, it indicates less power because the speed of work done is small. But, on the other hand, if the same 100 litres tank is emptied in 1 minute, then it indicates the large power as in this case, the speed of work done is high.

Power depends not only on the speed of flow of water but it also depends on the height of the tank (water pressure). Both higher water level (water pressure) and higher speed of water flow (water current) determine the power of water flow as shown in Figure 1.4. So, in the case of water tank,

$$\text{Power} = \text{Water Pressure} \times \text{Water Current}$$

In this example, depicted in Figure 1.4, in which case, the flow of water will be maximum and why?

FIGURE 1.4

Water tank analogy for electric power. The more the height of tank (b) and/or diameter of the pipe (c) the more the pressure and/or current of water. Similarly, the more the voltage and/or current the more the electric power.

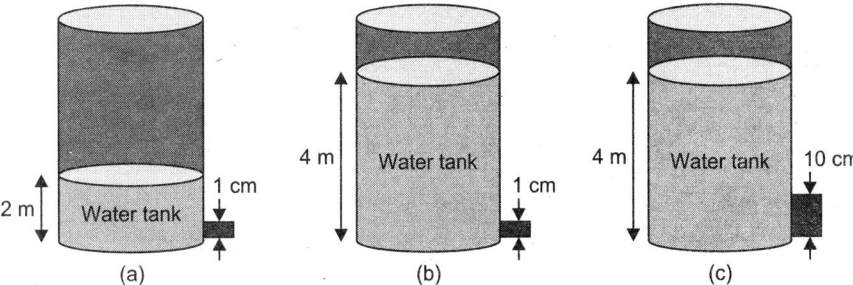

In electricity also, besides voltage and current, the next important term is Power. The term "Power" incorporates both current and voltage in it. When electricity flows in an electrical circuit, it results in some work done. For instance, when electricity flows in fan, the blade of fan rotates, when electricity flows in TV, the TV runs, and when the electricity flows in a refrigerator, it cools the things inside. Thus, when electricity flows through an appliance, it results in some work done. What is the speed of electrical work being done? What is the rate of electrical work being done? How can we represent it? The term, Power (P), is a measure of the rate of or speed of electrical work done. In this way, the more power means the electrical work is done at high speed and less power means the electrical work is done at low speed.

> The Electrical power is the rate or speed of electrical work done. The unit of power is watt.

Thus, in electrical terms, how fast the electrical work is done is called Power. Power of electrical work done or power of electricity depends on electric pressure (electrical voltage) and electron flow rate (electrical current) as shown in Figure 1.4. So, in the case of electricity,

$$\text{Electrical Power} = \text{Voltage} \times \text{Current}$$

or

$$\text{Power (watt)} = \text{Voltage (volt)} \times \text{Current (ampere)}$$

Power is measured in watts (W). Therefore, the above expression for electrical power can also be written in the following forms:

$$P \text{ (W)} = V \text{ (V)} \times I \text{ (A)}$$

In this way, the high power of electrical appliances indicates that either appliance is using high current or high voltage or it is using both high current and high voltage. Another example to understand the power would be two bulbs with different power ratings as shown in Figure 1.5. When compared to a 60 W bulb, a 100 W bulb gives more light. It means that 100 W bulb is working more than the 60 W bulb. Thus, the speed of work for 100 W bulb is more than 60 W bulb and hence 100 W bulb is more powerful.

(a)   (b)

FIGURE 1.5

Concepts of power. The more the power of bulb, the more the energy dissipated per second. This implies 100 W bulb would give more light than 60 W bulb.

In many practical applications, one watt is a small unit, and therefore, people use larger unit of power by multiplying it with 1000, i.e., 1000 W. Since 1000 represents 1 kilo, therefore, the large unit of power is kilowatt (kW). In power plants, 1 kW is also small unit of power and people use even larger unit of power. When we multiply 1 W with 1,000,000 we get 1,000,000 W. Since 1,000,000 represent 1 Million or 1 Mega, in brief, the power is called 1 MW (see Table 1.1).

Problem 1.3: What does electric power depend on? An electrical appliance is connected to 50 V which results in 3 A current through the load. What is the power consumed by the load?

Problem 1.4: For a 100 W lamp, a voltage of 240 V is applied. What is the value of resultant current?

WORKSHEET 1.1: Complete the following table (Table 1.1)

TABLE 1.1 To Obtain Missing Quantities

Voltage (V)	Current (A)	Power (W)
300	2	–
–	4	–
400	–	–
–	10	1000

1.7
Electrical Energy

Energy is another important terminology related to the use of electricity. There is very clear difference between energy and power but many people, even well educated, mix the term energy and power. Some people use term energy in place of power and power in place of energy. When it comes to solar energy, it is even more important to understand the difference. Therefore, as a technician, in solar energy, it is very important to understand the difference between these two terms; energy and power. From Section 1.6, we would have understood what electrical power is. Now, let us try to understand, what is electrical energy?

If the electrical power represents the rate or speed of work done, then the term 'electrical energy' presents the total amount of work done. Let us take an example of electric bulb. Let's say there are two bulbs, Bulb *A*, and Bulb *B*, each of them are of 100 W power as shown in Figure 1.6. Now, Bulb *A* is used to give us light for 5 hours and bulb *B* is used to give us light for 10 hours. What is the difference in both cases? In both cases, the bulb have same power, each is of 100 W. The difference is that one bulb is used for 5 hours and other bulb is used for 10 hours. Since, both the bulbs are of same power, we expect that both the bulb will give same light. This means that both bulbs are working with same speed or rate and giving us same amount of light. So, the difference in both scenarios is only duration of use. Bulb *A* is used for 5 hours and Bulb *B* is used for 10 hours. This effect of time duration in electrical terms is incorporated in terms of electrical energy. In this way, an electrical appliance of same power, if it runs for long hours, it consumes more energy, and if it runs for less hours, it will consume less energy. In this example, since bulb *B* is running for 10 hours, it will consume more energy as compared to the same bulb which runs only for 5 hours.

> Electrical energy is the total amount of electrical work done during a given time period. It is product of power of electrical appliance and duration of its usage.

100 W   100 W × 5h = 500 Wh

100 W   100 W × 10h = 1000 Wh

FIGURE 1.6
Energy consumed by an electrical appliance depends on power and time for which the power is used.

Now, suppose there are two bulbs one of 50 W and other is of 100 W, and both of them are used for 10 hours. Which one will consume more energy? In this case, since the duration of usage is same for both the cases, the bulb with higher power will consume more energy because it provides more light, which means that it works more.

From the above discussion, we can see that the amount of electrical energy consumed by an appliance depends on two factors: power of an appliance and duration of usage. The power of electrical appliances is given in terms of watt and duration of usage can be given in terms of hour. Therefore, the electrical energy can be given in following way:

$$\text{Electrical Energy} = \text{Power} \times \text{Duration of usage}$$

or

$$\text{Energy } (E) = \text{Power (watt)} \times \text{Time (hour)}$$

or

$$E \text{ (Wh)} = P \text{ (W)} \times T \text{ (h)}$$

Since the electrical energy is the product of power and time, the unit of electrical energy is the product of unit of power and time, that is, watt × hour or Watt-hour. There are other abbreviations used for energy units as well, these are WH or Wh or WHr or Whr. For many practical applications, one Wh is small unit, and therefore, people use larger unit of energy by multiplying it with 1000, i.e., 1000 Wh. Since 1000 represents 1 kilo, therefore, the large unit of energy is kWh.

The electrical energy represents total electrical work done while the electrical power represents the rate or speed of work done. Thus, in order to calculate energy we should multiply power with time, and in order to find the power, we should divide energy with time.

$$\text{Energy} = \text{Power} \times \text{Time}$$

$$\text{Power} = \frac{\text{Energy}}{\text{Time}}$$

The summary of all electrical terms, their symbols, the units used for measuring these terms and symbols of the units is given in Table 1.2.

TABLE 1.2 Summary of Electrical Terms and Their Units

Name of electrical term	Symbol of electrical term	Measured in units	Symbol of unit	Alternative units
Voltage	V	volt	V	mV
Current	I	ampere	A	mA
Power	P	watt	W	kW, MW
Energy	E	watt-hour	Wh	kWh

One watt-hour is a small amount of electrical energy. Usually, we measure electrical energy in larger units called kilowatt-hours (kWh) or 1,000 watt-hours (kilo means thousand). A kilowatt-hour is the unit that electricity utilities use when billing in our homes. The average cost of a kilowatt-hour of electricity for residential customers is about ₹2.

To find the cost of heating water using a 2000 W water heater for 2 hours, we would change the watt-hours into kilowatt-hours, then multiply the kilowatt-hours used by the cost per kilowatt-hour, as shown below:

$$\text{Electrical energy consumed} = 2000 \times 2 \text{ Wh divided by } 1{,}000 = 4 \text{ kWh} = 4 \text{ units}$$

$$\text{Cost} = 4 \text{ kWh} \times ₹2/\text{kWh} = ₹8$$

It would cost about 4 rupees to cook the food for 2 hours using a 1000 W cooker.

Problem 1.5: An energy of 100 Wh is consumed in 1 hour. What is consumed power?

Problem 1.6: An electrical bulb consumes energy at the rate of 100 W and is used for 10 hours. What is the consumed energy?

Problem 1.7: An energy of 10 kWh is consumed in 2 hours. What is consumed power?

Problem 1.8: An electrical heater consumes energy at the rate of 1000 W and is used for 30 minutes. What is the consumed energy?

Problem 1.9: An energy of 100 kWh is consumed in 2 hours. What is consumed power?

Problem 1.10: Consider two bulbs A and B with same power of 100 mW from same manufacturer. Bulb A is used for 5 hours while bulb B is used for 10 hours. Which bulb will glow more brightly? Which bulb will consume more energy? Assuming utility charges of ₹2 per unit, what would be the cost of electricity consumed by the bulbs?

Problem 1.11: Consider two bulbs A and B with same power of 200 mW from same manufacturer. Bulb A is used for 3 hours while bulb B is used for 5 hours. Which bulb will glow more brightly? Which bulb will consume more energy? Assuming utility charges of ₹2 per unit, what would be the cost of electricity consumed by the bulbs?

1.8
DC Power and AC Power

In the application of electricity, several components are required to be connected together to get desired function. The interconnection of the various electrical components can be called electrical circuit. In electrical circuit, power flows in two forms; these forms are referred as follows:

1. Direct current or DC power
2. Alternating current or AC power

Let us now learn more about the AC power and DC power, their characteristics, difference between them, and their measurement, etc.

1.8.1
DC Power

You might have read already that a photovoltaic (PV) module produce DC power or DC voltage or DC current. Also, DC current flows in DC loads or DC circuits. So, let us first explore what is DC power or a DC load or a DC circuit? A DC circuit is a circuit in which current flows in only one direction as shown in Figure 1.7(a). The direction of current does not change with time. In the circuit, a battery of voltage V_{dc} is connected with a load of R. In this figure, it is shown that the current is flowing in clockwise direction. In the circuit shown in Figure 1.7(a), the current can flow in anti-clockwise direction if the battery is connected in reverse way as shown in Figure 1.7(b), but again the direction of current will not change with time. The value of DC current is mostly constant with respect to time as shown in Figure 1.7(c). DC voltage is also constant with respect to time as shown in Figure 1.7(d). A PV module produces DC current means that the current flows in only one direction in DC circuit in which DC loads are operating on DC power of PV modules.

Direction and value of DC current and DC voltage do not change with time.

On the basis of DC current flowing through the load and DC voltage that appears across the load, the DC power consumed by the load can be estimated. The DC power (P_{dc}) is the product of DC (I_{dc}) current and DC voltage (V_{dc}).

$$P_{dc} = I_{dc} \times V_{dc}$$

A DC load is a load that operates on DC power, or a DC circuit is a circuit which works on DC current. LED (Light Emitting Diode) type light source is an example of DC load. Similarly, several other types of load like motor, refrigerator, fan, TV etc., are available that works on DC power.

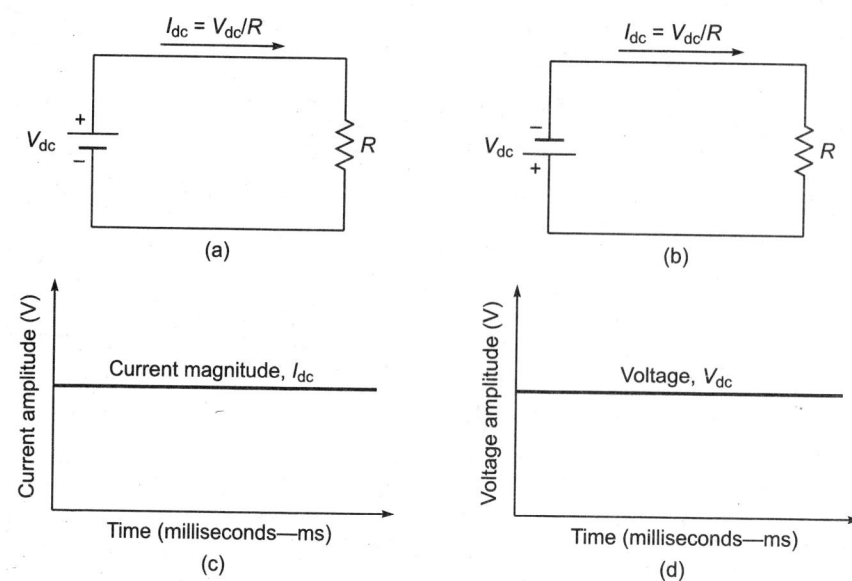

FIGURE 1.7

DC circuit showing (a) DC current direction, (b) DC current direction reverses with battery polarity, (c) DC current definition and (d) DC voltage definition.

In DC circuit, power delivered to the load is the product of current and voltage across the laod.

EXAMPLE 1.1

A DC fan works on 24 V and while running it takes 3 A current. Calculate the DC power consumed by the fan.

Solution

The fan is a DC fan, the curent flowing through fan, I_{dc}, is 3 A. The voltage of the fan, V_{dc}, is 24 V. Then the DC power consumed by the fan is:

$$P_{dc} = I_{dc} \times V_{dc}$$
$$= 3 \times 24 = 72 \text{ watt}$$

Problem 1.12: A DC TV operates at 24 V and consumes 120 watt power. Estimate the DC current required to run the TV?

 WORKSHEET 1.2: Fill in Table 1.3 given below for various DC loads.

TABLE 1.3 Table for various DC Load

Name of DC Load	Voltage across load, V_{dc} (volts)	Current through the load, I_{dc} (ampere)	Power consumes by the load, P_{dc} (watt)
Fan	12	2.5	–
LED	–	0.5	1.5
TV	–	3.3	80
Refrigerator	48	–	500
Motor	36	–	746

1.8.2
AC Power

We have discussed DC circuits, DC current, DC voltage and DC load in Section 1.8.1. One other form of circuit is called AC circuit or alternative current (AC) circuit. In AC circuit, current (I_{ac}) flows in both the directions; clockwise and counter-clockwise. The variation of AC current with respect to time is shown in Figure 1.8(c). For time period 0 to $T/2$, the current flows in clockwise direction as shown in Figure 1.8(a). For time period $T/2$ to T charge flow reverses as counter-clockwise direction as shown in Figure 1.8(b). It is not only the direction but the value of current that keeps changing with time (in the case of DC current, the value of current remains constant with time). The AC current changes its direction 50 times in one second (in this situation it is called that current has 50 Hertz frequency). Since the value of current is changing all the time, how can we say how much current is flowing? In AC circuits, there are two values of current that are normally used:

1. Peak or maximum value of current, I_m,
2. Average value of current, calculated as root of average of squares. It is called root mean square (RMS) value.

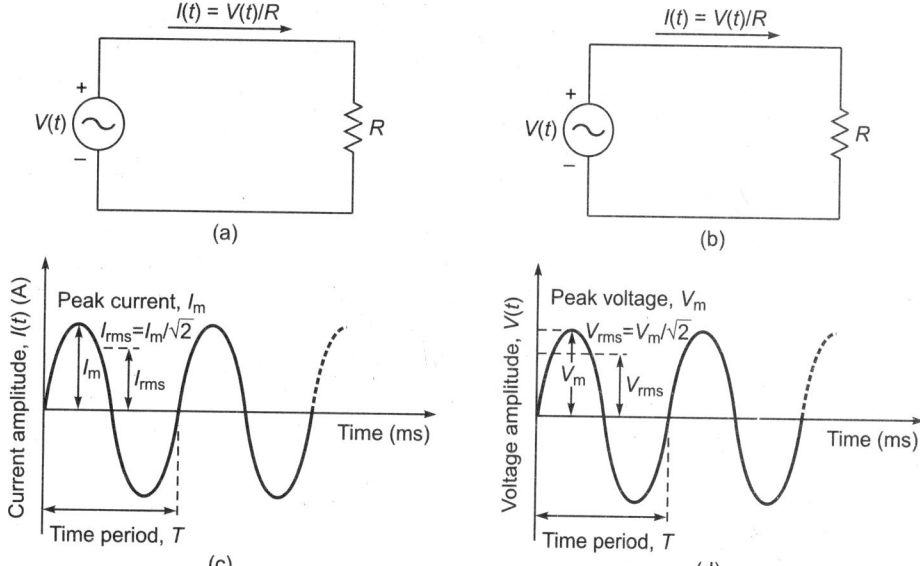

FIGURE 1.8

AC circuit showing (a) AC current direction during 0 to T/2 seconds, (b) AC circuit showing AC current direction during T/2 to T seconds, (c) AC current definition and (d) AC voltage definition.

When we say 'X' ampere AC current is flowing in a circuit, we refer to RMS value of current. Normally, with reference to AC circuits, we use RMS value of current. When we use digital ammeter to measure the value of AC current, it measures the RMS value of current.

There is a relationship between the RMS value and peak value of current. This relationship is given by the following equation:

$$I_{rms} = \frac{I_m}{\sqrt{2}}$$

Similar to AC current, the AC voltage also varies in direction and in value with time as shown in Figure 1.8(d). Similar to AC current, AC voltage also has a peak value (V_m) and RMS value (V_{rms}). When we use digital voltmeter to measure the value of voltage in the AC circuit, it measures the RMS value of voltage.

There is a relationship between the RMS value and peak value of current. This relationship is given by the following equation:

$$V_{rms} = \frac{V_m}{\sqrt{2}}$$

The direction and value of AC current and AC voltage keep changing all the time.

In this way, a circuit where AC current is flowing is called AC circuit. When a load (like TV, Fan, motor, etc.) works on AC current, then it is called an AC load.

Power in AC circuit

If AC current is flowing through the load and AC voltage appears across the load, then the AC power is consumed by the load. The AC power consumed by the load can be estimated. The AC power or RMS power of the load (P_{rms}) is the product of AC (I_{rms} current and AC voltage (V_{rms}).

$$P_{rms} = I_{rms} \times V_{rms} \text{ watt}$$

This RMS power of AC circuit is also called the **Apparent power**. This is called apparent power because it has been observed that in the AC circuit, the actual power delivered to the load is normally less than the apparent power.

> For the same power flow in wires, when the voltage is high, current that flows in the wires is small.

The actual power or real power delivered to the load depends on the power factor (PF) of AC circuit. The power factor of the AC circuit should be close to 1 and ideally, it should be one. The power factor depends on the phase difference between AC current and AC voltage. If there is no phase difference between AC current and AC voltage then PF is 1 (highest possible value), on the other hand, larger the phase difference smaller will be PF value. The smaller value of PF decreases the power delivered to the load as compared to the apparent power. The actual delivered power to the load can be given in following way:

> In AC circuits, actual power delivered to the load is lower than the apparent power because the power factor is normally not 1 but little less than one.

$$\text{Actual power } (P_{real}) = \text{Apparent power } (P_{rms}) \times \text{PF watt}$$

EXAMPLE 1.2

If V_{ac} in Figure 1.8(a) is 10 V_{rms} and resistance R is 2 kΩ, find the RMS AC current. Also, find AC power generated by generator and AC power absorbed by resistor.

Solution

The RMS voltage is $V_{rms} = 10$ V.

$$\text{RMS current, } I_{rms} = \frac{V_{rms}}{R} = \frac{10}{2} = 5 \text{ mA}.$$

$$\text{AC power, } P_{rms} = I_{rms} \times V_{rms} \text{ watt} = 10 \times 5 = 50 \text{ mW}.$$

Also, PF of resistor is 1

So, actual power $(P_{real}) = P_{rms} \times \text{PF} = 50 \times 1 = 50$ mW

EXAMPLE 1.3

If apparent power of a load is 100 mW. Find actual power or real power absorbed by the load if the power factor is 0.8.

Solution

Actual power $(P_{real}) = P_{rms} \times \text{PF} = 100 \times 0.8 = 80$ mW

 WORKSHEET 1.3:   Consider the circuit shown in Figure 1.8. Now, complete the following table (Table 1.4).

TABLE 1.4 To Obtain Missing Quantities

Voltage (V_{rms})	Resistance (R)	Current (I_{rms})	Power generated by voltage source	Power absorbed by resistor
5 V	5 Ω	–	–	–
10 V	–	2 A	–	–
20 V	–	–	60 W	–
–	3 Ω	3 A	–	–
10 V	–	–	–	100 W

 WORKSHEET 1.4:   Consider an AC circuit. Now, complete Table 1.5.

TABLE 1.5 To Obtain Missing Quantities

P_{rms} (W)	P_{real} (W)	PF
5	5	–
10	8	–
20	–	0.7
–	20	0.9
10	–	0.85

Normally, electrical power is generated as AC power in alternators or generators in remote locations and is transmitted to load centres in AC form. This is the major reason why we use AC loads rather than DC loads. We use AC power in our houses to power up AC loads like fan, light etc. We also use DC power to charge our cell phone batteries, laptop batteries etc.

1.9
Measurements of Electrical Quantities

After understanding the meaning of various electrical terms, let us now understand how these electrical quantities are measured. There are many types of meters available which can measure voltage, current, power and energy. Among these, one of the most versatile measuring tool is called Multimeter. As the name suggest, there are many meters built in one meter, called multimeter. With one multimeter, one can measure current and voltages. The multimeter can also measure the value of resistances. This section introduces you multimeter and its usage.

1.9.1
What is a Multimeter?

A multimeter is a measuring instrument that combines several measurement functions in one unit. A typical multimeter may include features, such as the ability to measure voltage, current and resistance. Multimeters can be of two type; viz., analog and Digital. The analog multimeter is one which consists of a needle which points at the scale built on it for giving the measured value. And digital multimeters are electronic meters which display the measured values in digital form. It is a portable handy device which runs on a small battery inside it. Nowadays, digital multimeters are used instead of analog multimeters, as they are easily available in market and also, digital multimeters are cheaper than analog multimeters. So, hereafter, we will see the use of digital multimeters only. Note here that multimeters discussed in this chapter are digital multimeter.

> Digital multimeters are commonly used because of easy availability and low cost.

A multimeter consists of the following parts:

1. **Display:** The measured values are displayed on this LCD display.

2. **Parameter and Range Selector Knob:** As it is known, a typical multimeter can measure the electrical parameters like voltage, current and resistance. This knob is used for selecting the parameter to be measured with the help of this multimeter. In a single parameter like (say) voltage, one can use this knob for selecting the range of measurements like 200 mV, 20 V, 200 V, etc. In the same way, one can also select the ranges for current and resistance as well.

3. **Probes:** A multimeter has two probes (as shown in Figure 1.9); one is black and other is red. The probe works as a link between the multimeter and points in electrical circuit where electrical quantities are to be measured. Usually, the black probe is used as common probe for measuring both current and voltage. Therefore, the black probe is referred as COM (or Common) probe and the red probe is used for current or voltage probe terminals.

4. **Buzzer:** The multimeter can also be used for detecting faults or broken wires in a circuit. For this, one has to put the knob of multimeter on continuity mode. If in a circuit you are measuring the continuity, then, if the buzzer gives sound, it indicates that the circuit is working fine or wire is not broken. And if the buzzer doesn't give sound it means the circuit is faulty or the wire is broken.

> A simple multimeter can be used for measuring voltage, current and resistance.

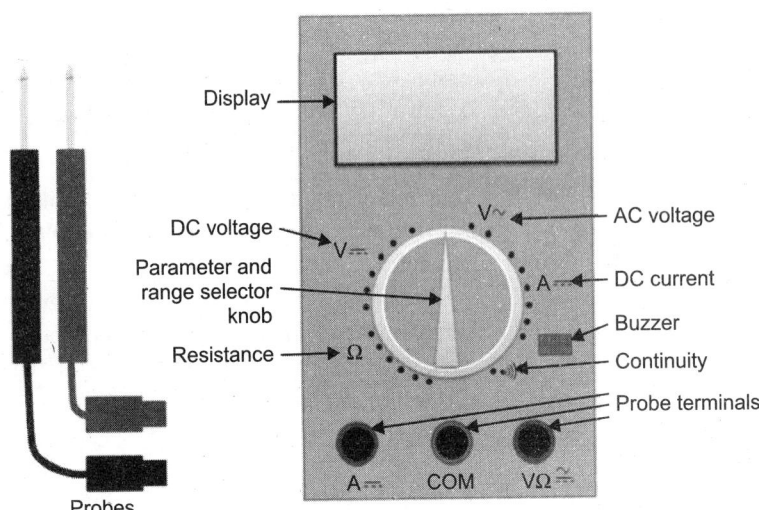

FIGURE 1.9
Illustration of a simple multimeter.

1.9.2
Use of Multimeter

A simple multimeter can be used for measuring voltage, current and resistance; and also one can make its use for fault detection in small circuits or to find out the broken wires in a circuit. Usually, a standard multimeter can measure the following electrical quantities:

1. DC voltage
2. AC voltage
3. DC current
4. AC current
5. Resistance
6. Electrical power
7. Electrical energy

1.9.3
Measurement of DC Voltage

Voltage (both DC and AC) can be measured by directly connecting the voltage meter (voltmeter) or the multimeter (in voltage mode) to the terminals of the voltage source (battery, PV module, single phase AC power supply, etc.). Voltage can also be measured between any two points in an electrical circuit by connecting the probes of multimeter at those points.

In order to measure the voltage using multimeter, it should be used in voltmeter mode, i.e., the 'range selector knob' of the meter should be kept to point towards sign volts or 'V'. Again, appropriate precaution should be taken to position the knob or probe properly for:

- Expected range of voltage level
- AC or DC form of voltage
- Position of the red probe for AC or DC voltage measurement.

Thus, the position of 'range selector knob' and position of probe should be selected properly before the measurements. Figure 1.10 shows the connection of a voltage meter (voltmeter) in a simple circuit having the voltage source and load connected to it and the voltage is measured. Hence looking at the figure, it should be remembered that to measure voltage, the voltmeter or the multimeter (in voltage mode) should be connected in parallel to the voltage source terminals.

Note 1: In order to measure the voltage, the position of 'range selector knob' and position of probe should be selected properly before the measurements.

Note 2: For measuring the voltage, the probes of the multimeter should be connected in parallel with the source or at points between which the voltage is to be measured.

Note 3: While measuring the current or voltage using multimeter, the red probe should be connected to positive terminal or point and black probe should be connected to negative terminal or negative point.

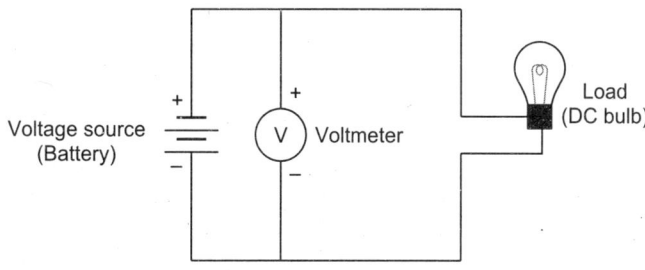

FIGURE 1.10

Arrangement for measurement of voltage using a voltmeter.

Figure 1.11 shows how to measure the voltage of the same circuit using a multimeter.

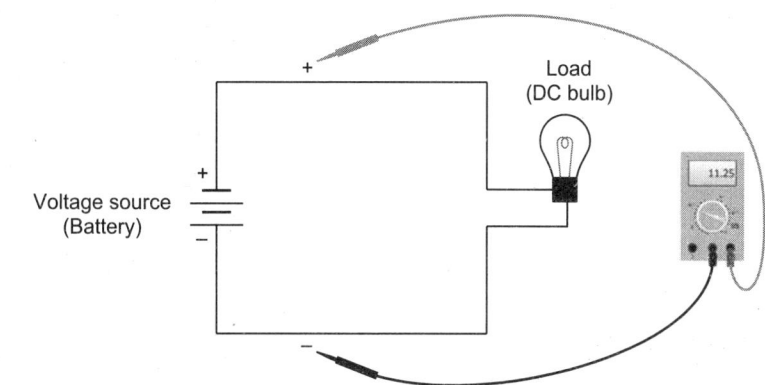

FIGURE 1.11

Measurement of DC voltage using a multimeter.

Note: The position of the probes for voltage measurement in the probe terminal of the multimeter and also the polarity for measurement.

1.9.4
Measurement of AC Voltage

For measurement of AC voltage using a multimeter, it is essential to select the AC form (~) with the range selector knob on the multimeter. It is also essential to check the position of the red probe as it should be kept in voltage mode in the multimeter. The red and black probes are to be connected to phase and neutral points in the circuit respectively as shown in Figure 1.12.

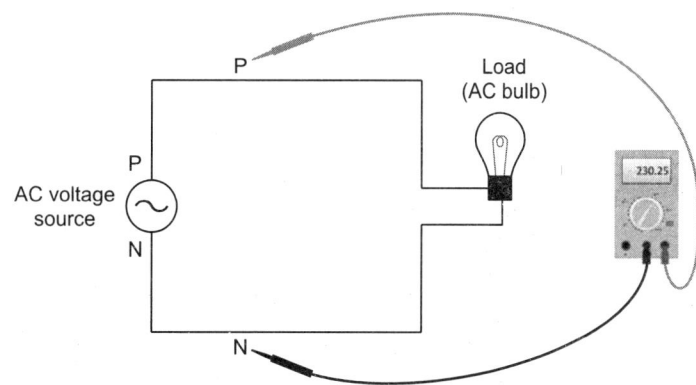

FIGURE 1.12

Measurement of AC voltage using multimeter.

Note: In AC voltage measurement using a multimeter, the phase should be considered as positive terminal and neutral as negative terminal. Again note the position of the probes and the selector knob position on the multimeter for AC voltage measurement using multimeter.

1.9.5
Measurement of DC Current

Current (both DC and AC) can be measured by connecting the current meter (ammeter) or the multimeter (in current mode) to the terminals of the voltage source (battery, PV module, single phase AC power supply etc.), provided the current is controlled by appropriate value of resistance or load in path (as shown below in Figure 1.13). Directly (without load) connecting meter across battery for measuring current or AC power source can be dangerous, as the ammeter or multimeter in ammeter mode offers very low resistance, and directly connecting ammeter across voltage source, like battery, will short its terminal. This will result in large current flow which can damage battery as well as ammeter.

An ammeter should never be connected across battery or AC supply without connecting load in the circuit.

In order to measure the current using multimeter, it should be used in current mode, i.e., the 'range selector knob' of the meter should be kept to point towards sign amperes or 'A'. Again appropriate precaution should be taken to position the knob or probe properly for:

- Expected range of current level
- AC or DC form of current
- Position of the red probe for AC or DC current measurement.

Thus, the position of 'range selector knob' and position of probe should be selected properly before the measurements. Figure 1.13 shows the connection of a current meter (ammeter) in a simple circuit having the voltage source and load connected to it. Hence looking at the figure, it should be remembered that to measure current, the ammeter or the multimeter (in current mode) should be connected in series to the voltage source terminals and load. The measurement of DC current with ammeter is shown in Figure 1.13 and the measurement of DC current with multimeter is shown in Figure 1.14.

FIGURE 1.13

Measurement of DC current using an ammeter.

In order to measure the current the position of 'range selector knob' and the position of probe should be selected properly before the measurements.

For measuring the current the probes of the multimeter should be connected in series with the source and the load.

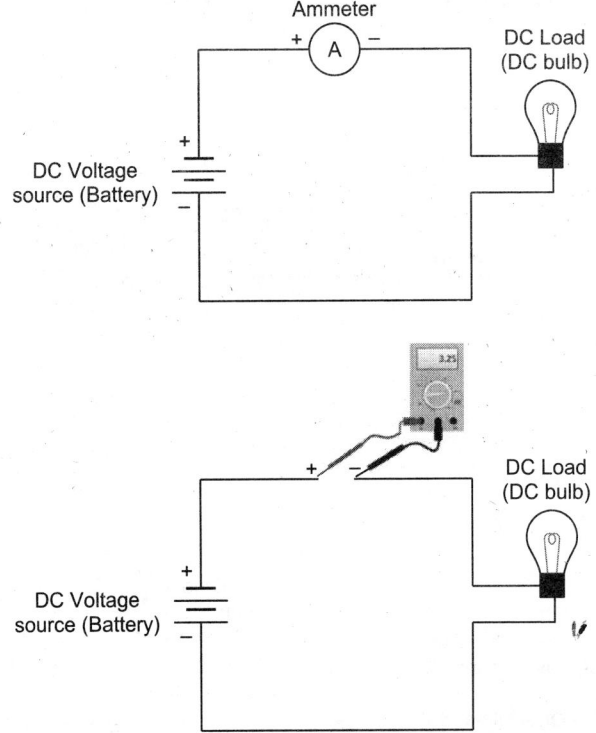

FIGURE 1.14

Measurement of DC current using a multimeter.

Note: The position of the probes for current measurement in the probe terminal of the multimeter and also note the polarity for measurement.

Negative sign in DC current and voltage measurements

While measuring current or voltage, if the red probe is connected to negative terminal and black probe is connected to positive terminal then multimeter will show the reading with negative sign.

Usually, a multimeter senses the flow of current through its probes, and convention is that current flows from positive to negative terminal is considered as positive. For measuring voltage or current, the positive probe (Red probe) should be connected to positive terminal of the voltage source and black probe should be connected to negative terminal. If the terminals are reversed, i.e., if positive terminal of multimeter is connected to negative terminal of voltage source (while voltage or current measurement) and vice versa, the display of multimeter will show negative reading, i.e. there will be a negative sign with the value of the voltage or current. This is illustrated in Figures 1.15 and 1.16.

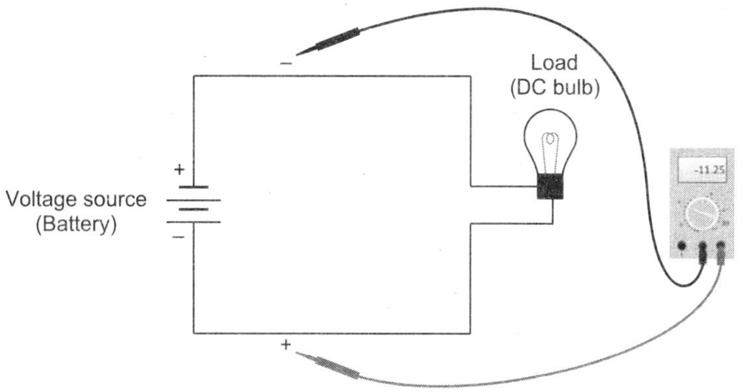

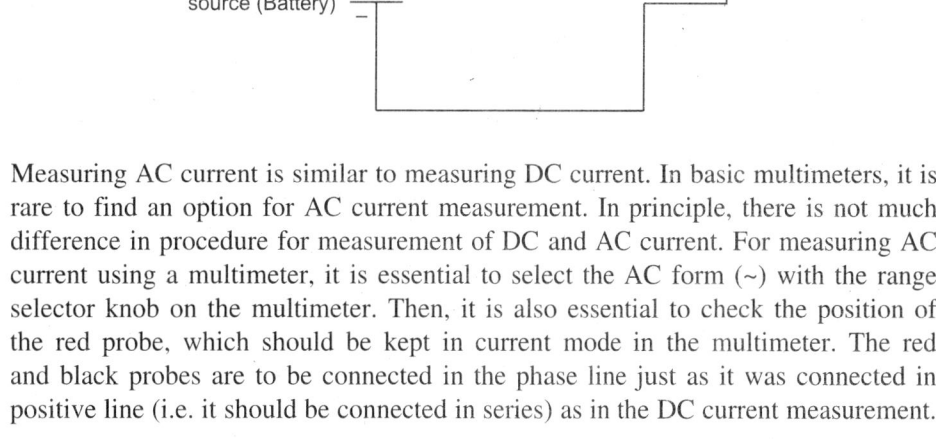

FIGURE 1.15

Figure illustrating the negative sign when probes are reversed while measuring voltage.

Note: The negative value of measured voltage (in the display of multimeter) due interchanging the position of the probes and also note the polarity for measurement.

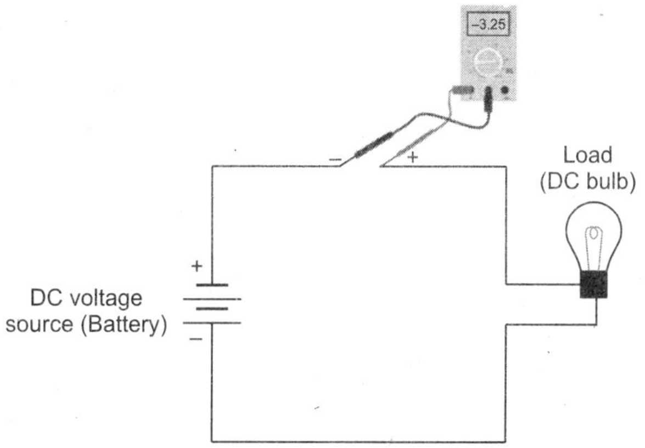

FIGURE 1.16

Figure illustrating the negative sign when probes are reversed while measurement current.

Note: The negative value of measured current (in the display of multimeter) due interchanging the position of the probes; and also note the polarity for measurement.

1.9.6
Measurement of AC Current

Measuring AC current is similar to measuring DC current. In basic multimeters, it is rare to find an option for AC current measurement. In principle, there is not much difference in procedure for measurement of DC and AC current. For measuring AC current using a multimeter, it is essential to select the AC form (~) with the range selector knob on the multimeter. Then, it is also essential to check the position of the red probe, which should be kept in current mode in the multimeter. The red and black probes are to be connected in the phase line just as it was connected in positive line (i.e. it should be connected in series) as in the DC current measurement.

1.9.7
Measurement of Resistance

Resistance measurement is an important part in the field of electricity, as resistance is the value on which the flow of current depends, it is very essential to know the value of resistance in a circuit or to measure the resistance of a resistor that needs to be connected in circuit. Hence, the basic multimeters are provided with the function for measurement of resistance as well.

For measurement of resistance using multimeter, the range selector knob should be firstly placed on the 'Resistance' mode or Ohms mode which is normally shown on multimeter with Ω symbol. The knob should be placed at appropriate range. The resistors come with colour codes printed on them, by knowing the colour code scheme an idea about the range of resistance can be made. As the resistance is measured in absence of the current flow, the position of red and black probes on quantity doesn't matter. Figure 1.17 shows the measurement of resistance of a 1 ohm resistor.

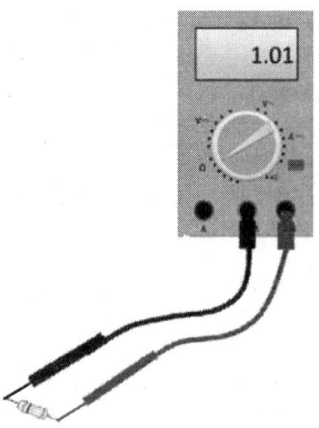

FIGURE 1.17

Measurement of resistance using a multimeter.

1.9.8

Measurement of Electrical Power

Power is the product of voltage and current in a circuit. Hence in any electric circuit, if the voltage and current is known, the power can be obtained by simply using the following formula for power.

$$\text{Power} = \text{Voltage} \times \text{Current}$$

Using ammeter and voltmeter we can mesaure current and voltage, and by multiplication we can measure the power in a circuit. This arrangement is shown in Figure 1.18. Figure 1.18 shows the ammeter and voltmeter connected in the electrical circuit in order to find out the power using formula. Note the way the connection is made for voltmeter and ammeter.

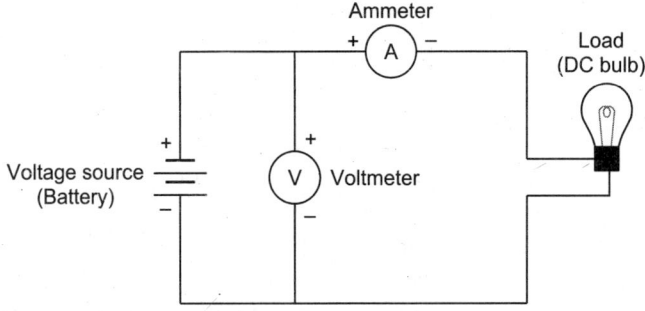

FIGURE 1.18

Measurement of current and voltage in an electrical circuit in order to find out the power.

From above description, it is clear that power in an electrical circuit can also be measured using two multimeters with following steps:

- Firstly the current value can be measured using the multimeter by properly selecting the range using the 'range selector knob' and also by properly selecting the probe position for current measurement.
- Voltage can be measured using another multimeter by properly selecting the range using the 'range selector knob' and also by properly selecting the probe position for voltage measurement.
- Once the values of current and voltage are known, power can be calculated by simply using the formula for power (i.e Power = Voltage × Current).

Note that, as the current and voltage levels can vary in the circuit with time, hence power consumed in the circuit will also vary with time.

Measuring power using two multimeters requires some calculation but it is possible to measure the power directly. The meter which is available for the measurement of power direclty is called "*wattmeter*". As the unit of power is "*watt*", the meter for its measurement is termed *wattmeter*. A wattmeter is an electrical meter which actually measures both current and voltage with the same unit and gives the value of power.

As in Figure 1.19, the wattmeter is shown in dotted line, it can be clearly seen that the wattmeter coil in series measures the current and the wattmeter coil in parallel measures the voltage in the circuit. Since the wattmeter has to measure both current and voltage there should be at least three terminals. The first terminal is for current measurement, second terminal is for voltage measurement and third terminal acts as a common terminal. Usually, wattmeters available have four terminals called Mains (*M*), Load (*L*), Common (*C*) and Voltage (*V*), and hence, for power measurement, it is for sure that the terminals *M* and *C* should be shorted (as in Figure 1.19) to get three terminals out of the wattmeter.

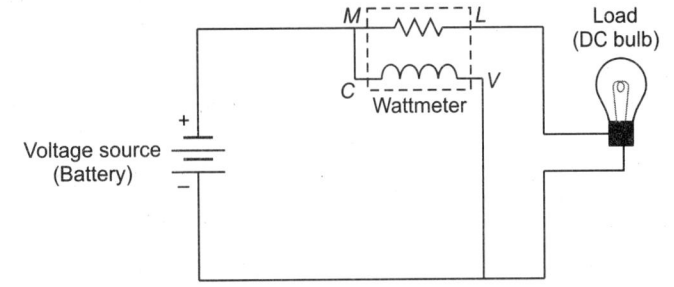

FIGURE 1.19

Power measurement in an electrical circuit using wattmeter.

Note: In a wattmeter, the terminals *M* and *C* should be shorted for power measurement.

Figure 1.20 shows an illustration of a wattmeter.

FIGURE 1.20

Illustration of a wattmeter.

1.9.9

Measurement of Electrical Energy

Electrical energy is nothing but the power consumed by a load during a specified time period. The product of Power (in watt) and Time (in hour) gives the value of Electrical Energy consumed by the load in *watt-hour*. Hence in any electric circuit, if the power and time is known, the energy can be calculated by simply using the following formula for Energy.

$$Energy = Power \times Time$$

The meters available for measurement of energy are called "*Energy Meters*". As the unit of energy is "*watt-hour*", the meters are also called *watt-hour meter*.

As it is already seen to measure the power using a multimeter, the value of power obtained can be multiplied with the time to find out energy consumption by the load or energy generation by PV module or energy provided by the source like battery or power source. Measuring power and then multiplication of duration of power requires some calculation to find out energy. In market, energy meters are available which do all such measurements internally and give us output in terms of energy or watt-hour or kilo-watt-hour. You must have seen energy meter in your house. An illustration of a basic household single phase energy meter is shown in Figure 1.21. These days, digital energy meters are also available which can be used in the solar PV system circuit. These energy meters can be used to measure energy generated by PV modules during certain period or energy consumed by the load during ceratin period.

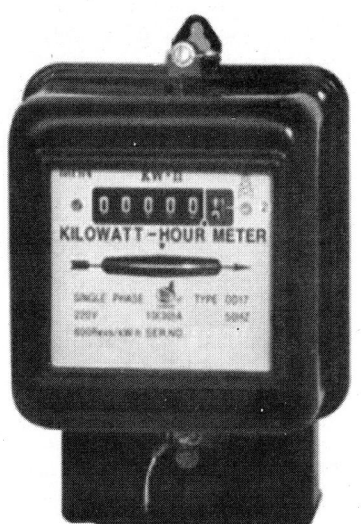

FIGURE 1.21

Illustration of a household energy meter.

Introduction to Energy and Solar Photovoltaic Energy

In this modern world energy has become an integral part of our daily life. One cannot think of living a single day without the use of energy in one form or other. We use energy in cooking our food, cooling our spaces, travelling from one point to other, transportation of goods, watching TV, using our mobile phones, running machines in an industry, water pumping, and so on.

The energy we use must come from somewhere. Normally, the energy we use is supplied to us in the form of diesel, petrol, coal, LPG, CNG and electricity (mostly derived from other fuels like coal and petroleum). These sources of energy are finite in nature and cause environmental pollution. In India, every citizen does not get sufficient amount of energy that he/she requires. There is a huge shortage of energy supply. There are 5,90,000 villages in India and 700 million people live in rural India. Most households in rural India do not get sufficient electricity, which hinders the growth of rural India both at social and economic front. There is either lack of sufficient infrastructure to supply energy to all or sufficient fuel is not available at reasonable cost. Therefore, there are efforts to use infinite or renewable energy sources such as solar radiation, wind and biomass energy. These energy sources are also available in distributed manner which means that the required energy can be generated where there is a need.

Solar photovoltaic (PV) technology converts sunlight into electricity directly without any other additional energy conversion step. India is blessed with a large amount of sunlight. We receive solar radiation in a range of 4 to 7 kWh/m^2/day. Such amount of radiation is good enough to generate electricity to fulfill our entire electricity requirement using solar PV technology. Importantly, the energy can be generated in any area, where there is need, by installing the solar PV modules. Considering the importance of the solar PV technology in needful energy supply, this training manual is focused on solar PV technology only.

In this chapter, idea of 'energy' is explored in detail which includes various forms, energy units and their conversion. An estimation of energy need is given in the following section. Practical examples are given for estimation of energy. Then, introduction to solar PV technology for supplying electrical energy is given. At the end, brief discussion is presented about other renewable energy technology including solar thermal, wind and biomass energy technologies.

Many parts of India do not get sufficient electricity.

2.1
Basic Concepts about Energy and Its Use

2.1.1
What is Energy?

In our daily life we use energy for many activities throughout the day. It has become an integral part of our daily life, and it is difficult to even think of a day without consuming any energy. Due to this reason we should have good idea about; what is energy? From where it comes? What are the different forms of energy? Etc. This section deals with basic concepts about energy and related to its use.

Energy is a concept, which, in a simple term, can be described as "an ability of an object to do work". Work is done by our body when we move, work is done by a fan when it runs, work is done by a vehicle when it moves, work is done by stove when it heats water, work is done by a horse when it carries a person, work is done by a bulb when it illuminates a room and so on. Thus, all the objects which have ability to work are said to possess energy and by doing work the objects transfer energy. For instance, a piece of wood can be burned, which can boil water and can generate steam. The generated steam can be used to move an object (as in steam engine). It implies that the piece of wood posses some energy.

We use energy to get work done. There are always numerous examples around us wherein we get the work done by using energy. Use of light bulb, heating of water, cooking of food, driving a vehicle, running a fan, etc. are examples of the use of energy. The use of energy to get our work done has become one of the necessity of our modern life. Without using energy, it is difficult to live even a single day. Energy in the form of the food is a fundamental need of a living organism. We need energy for our body to maintain it, to do the physical work and to do the mental thinking. The food, our energy source is provided to us by our mother nature. But apart from the food energy, we use energy to get several other works done. Some of these works are required for running our lives, for example cooking of food while many other works are required to provide comfort to our body such as the use of air conditioner, cooler, etc. Overall, energy is required for a wide range of applications like transportation, industrial application, agricultural application, household requirements, office applications etc.

> We use energy to get work done.

2.1.2
Forms of Energy

The energy can have many forms like heat energy, electrical energy, light energy, etc. Heat energy is used for cooking, drying and heating applications. Electrical energy is used for running fan, TV, cooler, water pumps etc. The light energy is used for illumination of our rooms. The other forms of energy include chemical energy, nuclear energy, radiation energy (for example solar energy), gravitational energy, kinetic energy, potential energy, etc. Each of these energy forms are used either directly to get our work done or we convert energy from one form to other form before utilizing it to get work done. For instance, when we drive motor vehicle, chemical energy of the petrol (or any fuel) is converted into mechanical energy used for transportation. Similarly, when we switch on a fan, electrical energy gets converted into mechanical energy to provide air flow. Thus, energy gets converted from one form to other and in this process of energy conversion we get work done of our choice.

In pre-industrial era, fuel wood was the major source of energy. After the discovery of steam engine, coal has become a choice of energy source. The discovery of internal combustion engine (used in motor cycle and cars) resulted in the use of energy of the petroleum products (petrol, diesel, natural gas) to fulfill our energy requirements. The energy of the fossil fuels like coal, oil and gas are used directly for heat by burning them. The fossil fuels are also get converted into electricity in power plants and then electricity is used to get our work done in industries, agriculture and at houses.

Electrical energy is one of the most convenient forms of energy. Almost all equipments around us can work on electrical energy. Running of fan, TV, computers, bulbs, trains, machines in industry, water pumps, etc. are the examples of the use of electrical energy. Also, cooking and heating can be done using electrical energy and even cars can run on electrical energy. Thus, electrical energy is very versatile and commonly used form in our daily life. This versatility comes from the fact that the flow of electrical energy can easily be controlled, many times just by switching a simple 'on' and 'off'. Also, the transmission and distribution of electrical energy is simple. The transmission and distribution of other forms of energy like coal, petrol, wood, etc. is quite cumbersome.

The conversion and use of solar energy into electrical energy is the topic of this training manual. Both the forms of energy; solar energy and electrical energy are very important in today's world where global warming is a concern and where there is increasing demand for electrical energy. Thus, in present world context, this manual will be a useful tool to have.

> There are several forms in which we use energy. We use sometimes in electrical form, sometime in thermal form, some time in solar radiation form, etc.

2.1.3
Renewable Energy and Non-renewable Energy Sources

The energy sources can be divided in two broad categories; Renewable and Non-renewable energy sources. Both of them are derived from the nature but they are different from the perspective of availability.

The natural energy sources, such as coal, petroleum, oil and natural gas take thousands of years to form naturally, meaning their rate of production is low. In the present world, the rate of consumption of these resources is quite high as compared to their production. These fuels cannot be produced as fast as they are being consumed. Therefore, in practical terms, we can assume that the fossil fuels are available in limited amount and continuous use of these fuels will result in their depletion from the earth. Thus, due to limited availability, the fossil fuels are considered non-renewable energy sources.

In contrast, the natural energy sources which are called renewable energy sources are continuously produced by natural processes and forces occurring in our environment. These renewable energy sources include solar radiation, wind, biomass, hydro, etc. These sources are available intermittently in cycles and can be harnessed during any number of cycles. For instance, solar radiation energy is available in cycle of 24 hours of day-night cycle. Any amount of solar energy can be harnessed without affecting the availability of solar energy for the next day, and therefore, it is termed renewable energy source. Similarly, wind energy (movement of wind) and hydro energy (movement of water) are renewable energy sources, can be harnessed in any amount and cannot be depleted. If the balance is made between consumption of biomass energy (plants energy) and growth of biomass then biomass energy can also be considered renewable energy.

> A source of energy can be exhaustible (like coal) or in-exhaustible (like solar energy).

2.1.4
Amount of Available Solar Radiation Energy

The sun is the main source of energy at the earth. The energy from the sun reaches to the earth in the form of electromagnetic radiation. On the earth, the solar radiation energy gets converted in various other forms of renewable energy. On reaching, some of the radiation energy is reflected back, some energy gets absorbed in the atmosphere, some part reaches to the earth's surface without any conversion, some part is converted into wind energy, some part is converted into biomass energy, and some part of energy is used in water evaporation causing rain and becomes available in the form of hydro energy.

The amount of energy that reaches to the earth is very large as compared to what we are using from fossil fuels. This can be seen from Table 2.1. In 2010, the annual world energy consumption from all possible sources including electricity, coal, gas, diesel, petrol, biomass, etc. was 580 Exa joule (1 Exa Joule = 1 000 000 000 000 000 000 joule) and the total electricity consumption was about 70 Exa joules. The availability of annual solar energy sources is 3,850,000 Exa joules which is many thousand times more than what we are consuming annually. Thus, in principle, solar energy alone can fulfill all the energy requirements of the world if harvested in cost-effective manner. Solar photovoltaic technology is one such means of harvesting solar radiation energy and converting into electricity. Solar thermal technology harvests solar energy in the form of heat energy.

> Solar energy is available in great quantity to fulfill all the energy needs of the whole world.

TABLE 2.1 Annual Available Renewable Energy and Annual World Energy Requirements

Annual available renewable energy (in Exa joules = 10^{18} J)	
Solar energy	3,850,000
Wind energy	2250
Biomass energy	3000
World's annual energy consumption (in Exa joules)	
Total energy consumption (including biomass, coal, diesel, petrol, electricity, etc.)	580
Electricity consumption	70

2.1.5
Energy and Its Units

'Energy' as quantity can be represented in several units. One of the basic units of energy is called 'joule' and it is abbreviated as 'J'. One joule of energy is equal to energy expended (or work done) in applying a force of one newton through a distance of one metre. In terms of electrical energy, one joule energy is equal to energy expended in 1 watt of power running for 1 second. One joule represents a very small amount of energy. For instance, energy consumed by a 100 watt bulb in one hour is 360000 joules. The energy content of the food that a normal person eats daily is about 10000 joules.

Other than joules, there are many other units of energy that we usually hear in our daily context. The other energy units normally represent higher amount of energy. For instance, energy content of food is given in terms of calorie and one calorie represents 4.182 joule of energy. Our monthly electricity bill is given in terms of number of electrical energy units consumed by us. One 'electrical energy unit' is equal to 1 kilo-watt-hour (or kWh) and 1 kWh represents 3,600,000 joules of energy. The energy content of a metric ton of crude oil is given in terms of Tons of Oil equivalent (ToE).

> There are several units of energy. The 'joule' and 'kWh' units are commonly used to measure electrical and solar radiation energy.

Unit conversion factors

The different energy units are related with each other through different constants. Table 2.2 gives relationship between different energy units. Normally, in order to represent larger units, prefix are added to the unit. For instance, joule is a small amount of energy, and in order to write a large amount of energy in term of joule, only prefix 'kilo' which represents 1000 is added to make 1000 joules or 1 kJ. This is similar to write 1000 grams of weight as 1 kg. Similarly, prefix 'mega', which represents 1000,000 (or 1 million) is added to make it 1000000 joules or 1 MJ. Also, if we multiply 1 MJ with 1000, we will get 1000 MJ. In brief, 1000 MJ is written as 1 giga joule or 1 GJ. Here, giga represents 1,000,000,000 or 1000 million.

One can notice from the above discussion that 1 kJ is 1000 times larger energy than 1 J, 1 MJ is 1000 times larger energy than 1 kJ and 1 GJ is 1000 times larger energy than 1 MJ. This can be represented in the following way:

1 kJ = 1000 J

1 MJ = 1000 kJ

1 GJ = 1000 MJ

Large energy numbers can be represented by putting appropriate prefix with energy unit.

This conversion factors are not used only in application to energy units, but they are also used in the application to other units like unit of power (watt or W). Applying these unit conversion factors to power unit we will get; W, kW, MW and GW.

Some commonly used prefix and conversion among them is given in Table 2.2.

TABLE 2.2 Commonly used Prefix, Their Value and Symbols for Representing Large Values

Prefix	Value of prefix	Alternate way of writing prefix	Symbol	Example
kilo	1000	10^3	k	1 kg = 1000 grams
				1 kJ = 1000 joule
Mega	1,000,000	10^6	M	1 MJ = 1,000,000 J
				1 MJ = 1000 kJ
Giga	1,000,000,000	10^9	G	1 GJ = 1000 MJ
				1 GJ = 1,000,000,000 J
Tera	1,000,000,000,000	10^{12}	T	1 GJ = 1,000,000,000,000 J
Peta	1,000,000,000,000,000	10^{15}	P	1 PJ = 1,000,000,000,000,000 J
Exa	1,000,000,000,000,000,000	10^{18}	E	1 EJ = 1,000,000,000,000,000,000 J

Various units of electrical energy

In this training manual, we are mainly concerned with electrical energy. One joule of electrical energy is equal to energy expended in 1 watt of power in duration of 1 second. From the above discussion, we can write the following expression for energy:

$$\text{Energy (joule)} = \text{Power (watt)} \times \text{Time (second)}$$

or
$$1 \text{ J} = 1 \text{ W} \times 1 \text{ s} \tag{2.1}$$

Thus, energy in joule is obtained if we multiply power (in watt) by time (in second). Alternatively, power can be in kilowatt (kW) and time can be in hour (h). In this way, kilowatt (kW) × hour (h) also represent energy unit.

We know that
$$1 \text{ kW} = 1000 \text{ watt}$$

and
$$1 \text{ hour (h)} = 3600 \text{ seconds}$$

Thus,
$$1 \text{ kW} \times \text{h} = 1000 \text{ W} \times 3600 \text{ s} = 3,600,000 \text{ Ws}$$

From Eq. (2.1), we know that 1 Ws = 1 J

Therefore, 1 kWh = 3,600,000 Ws = 3,600,000 J = 3,600 kJ

or, using prefix kilo for 1000, we can write as follows:
$$1 \text{ kWh} = 3,600,000 \text{ J} = 3,600 \text{ kJ}$$

In this way, energy unit 'J' can be converted into kWh or vice versa. Both of these units are commonly used to represent electrical energy as well as solar radiation energy. These units and their conversion from one unit to other units are important and one should understand these units carefully and thoroughly.

1 kWh energy (1 unit of electricity) is equivalent to 3600 kJ of energy.

The commonly used electrical energy units and their conversion from each other are presented in Table 2.3.

TABLE 2.3 Energy Units and Their Conversion

Energy unit	Equivalent energy unit
1 Joule	= 1 Ws (watt-second)
1 Wh	= 3,600 Ws
	= 3,600 J
1 kWh (kilowatt-hour)	= 3,600 kJ
	= 3,600,000 J
1 kilo Joule (kJ)	= 1,000 J
1 Mega Joule (MJ)	= 1,000,000 J
1 Mega Joule (MJ)	= 278 kWh
1 Giga Joule (GJ)	= 1000 MJ

EXAMPLE 2.1

A 200-watt fan runs for 12 hours every day. How much electrical energy it consumes in one day? Give your answer in kWh.

Solution

It is given that the power of the fan = 200 watt

The number of hours of usage per day = 12 hour

Now, electrical energy can be obtained by multiplying watt by hours.

Therefore, Electrical energy = watt × hours = 200 × 12 = 2400 watt-hour or Wh

The answer is asked in kWh. It means that we need to prefix 'kilo' for this, and therefore, we should divide the answer by 1000 as the value of prefix 'kilo' is 1000.

Hence electrical energy consumed = 2400/1000 = 2.4 kWh

Thus, the answer is 2.4 kWh.

EXAMPLE 2.2

A household in Mumbai received the monthly electricity bill of 130 units (or 130 kWh). Calculate the electricity bill in terms of joules.

Solution

Monthly bill of household is 130 units = 130 kWh

From Table 2.3, we can use the conversion between kWh and joules as follows:

$$1 \text{ kWh} = 3{,}600{,}000 \text{ J}$$

Therefore,   130 kWh = 130 × 3,600,000 J = 468,000,000 J

WORKSHEET 2.1: Fill the following table (Table 2.4) on energy units and their conversion from one unit to other unit:

TABLE 2.4 Energy Units and Their Conversion

1 MJ	= .... kJ
10 kWh	= .... J
1000 J	= .... kWh
1 kWh	= .... Wh
.... kWh	= 10,000 kJ
1 MWh	= .... kWh
.... kJ	= .... MJ
.... kWh	= 5000 Wh
10 kWh	= .... units of electricity

WORKSHEET 2.2: Fill Table 2.5 on estimation of electrical energy consumed by electrical appliances.

TABLE 2.5 Estimation of Electrical Energy Consumed

Type of appliance	Power of the appliance	Daily duration of usage of appliance	Electrical energy consumed
Tube light	40 W	4 hours	= .... Wh
Tube light	40 W	.... hours	= 400 Wh
Fan1	60 W	12 hours	= .... Wh
Fan2	30 W	12 hours	= .... kWh
TV	150 W	2 hours	= .... Wh
Cooler	200 W	10 hours	= .... kWh
Computer	.... W	2 hours	= 400 Wh
LED light	.... W	.... hours	= 20 Wh
AC	1.5 kW	10 hours	= .... kWh
AC	1.5 kW	.... hours	= .... 7.5 kWh
Unknown appliance	........W	10 hours	= 500 Wh
Unknown appliance	........W	5 hours	= 10 kWh

When we multiply the wattage of appliance with hours of usage in a day, we get energy used by appliance in a day.

2.1.6
Power and Its Units

Power is not same as energy. Many times, there are misconceptions and people tend to believe that energy and power are same and they use these two different terms for same meaning. One good place to identify the difference between these two terms is our own house. We pay electricity bill for the energy that we have consumed during the month. But when we talk about our appliances in terms of power; 10-watt bulb, 50-watt bulb, 1000-watt water heater, etc.

Power is the rate at which energy is used. The unit of power is watt and it is abbreviated as 'W'. When one joule of energy is consumed in one second, it is referred as one watt of power consumption. The definition of the power can be presented in terms of the following equation:

$$\text{Power (watt)} = \frac{\text{Energy (joule)}}{\text{Time (second)}} \tag{2.2}$$

or

$$\text{Power (watt)} = \frac{\text{Energy (watt-hour)}}{\text{Time (hour)}} \tag{2.3}$$

Let us take an example of two CFLs; a 20-Watt CFL and a 10-watt CFL. Since the power consumption of a 20-watt CFL is double than a 10-watt CFL, it implies that a 20-watt CFL consumes energy twice as fast as a 10-watt CFL. Thus, if both the CFLs are used for 1 hour, a 20-watt CFL will consume double energy (20 watt × 1 hour = 20 watt-hour) as compared to energy consumed by a 10-watt CFL (10 watt × 1 hour = 10 watt-hour). In this way, when we multiply watt (power unit) by hour (time unit), we get energy unit or when we divide energy unit by time we get power unit.

> Power is defined as the rate of energy usage. Large amount of energy used in small time indicates large power, and large amount of energy used in large time indicates small power.
>
> Powers rating of appliances are given in terms of watt (W).

In practice, power plants capacities are mentioned in terms of MW (Megawatt = 10^6 watt) and the energy contents of the fuels like petrol, diesel, coal, etc. are mentioned in terms of MJ or kWh). The electricity bill is made in terms of kWh and the ratings of our appliances are given in terms of watt.

TABLE 2.6 Different Power Units and Their Equivalent Units

Power unit	Equivalent unit
1 watt	= 1 joule-second = 1 W
1 kilowatt (kW)	= 1000 watt or 1000 W
1 megawatt (MW)	= 1,000,000 W
1 Gigawatt (GW)	= 1,000,000,000 W

> Large power numbers can be represented by putting appropriate prefix with power unit.

EXAMPLE 2.3

Solution

A tube light consumes 320 watt-hours of electrical energy when used for 8 hours. Estimate the power rating of the tube light.

Given, energy consumption of tube light = 320 watt-hour

Time duration of usage of tube light = 8 hours

Therefore,

$$\text{Power} = \frac{\text{Energy}}{\text{Time}}$$

or

$$\text{Power} = \frac{320 \text{ watt-hour}}{8 \text{ hours}} = 40 \text{ watt}$$

Thus, power rating of tube light is 40 watt.

WORKSHEET 2.3: Fill the following table (Table 2.7) on power units and their conversion from one unit to other unit.

TABLE 2.7 Power Units and Their Conversion

1 kW	= ...... W
1 MW	= ...... kW
2.4 kW	= ...... W
200 W	= ...... kW
0.5 kW	= ...... W
...... kW	= 5000 W
...... W	= 0.3 kW

2.2

Estimating Energy Requirement

One of the skills that a trainee should develop while dealing with solar PV system design and installation is to be able to estimate the energy requirement of client. The client may need small amount of energy for household applications or he/she may need energy for large industrial applications. In any case, the estimation of energy required is the first and important step for stand alone PV system. In the case of grid connected PV systems (typically in range of megawatt or MW), estimation of annual energy potentially generated by the power plant is made.

Based on the above discussion, it should be easy now for anybody to estimate the energy requirement for a given application, for a given period of time. The energy requirement can be estimated on daily basis, monthly basis or yearly basis.

It can be seen from discussion in Section 2.1.5 that the energy consumed by an appliance is the product of its power rating (in watt) and duration of usage (in hour). Energy is then presented in the units of watt-hour or Wh or kWh. Therefore, in order to estimate the energy requirement, one needs to collect the information about the power ratings of various appliances that are used in a given premises and number of hours of operation or use of those appliances.

Power ratings of appliances used at home and in industry are always mentioned on the product. Typical power rating (in watt) of some of the appliances are given in Table 2.8. But one should try to get the actual power rating or what is called the 'name-plate rating' of the appliances.

> Power rating of appliances we use in our daily lives can vary significantly; from few watt to few kW.

TABLE 2.8 Typical Power Ratings of Electrical Appliances

Name of the appliances	Range of available power rating (in watts)
Incandescent light (bulb)	5 to 100
Tube light	30 to 50
Compact fluorescent lamp (CFL)	3 to 30
Ceiling fan	30 to 70
Air conditioner (room)	1000 to 1500
Air conditioner (central)	2000 to 5000
CD player	15 to 30
TV	60 to 300
Laptop computer	50 to 75
Desktop computer	80 to 200
Printer	100 to 250
Washing machine	500 to 1000
Refrigerator	50 to 300

The next step is to find out the duration of usage of each appliance for which you are designing a PV system. Let us say that we are trying to estimate daily energy requirement for a person. There may be daily variation in hours of usage for an appliance. A TV may be used for more number of hours on Sunday than any other day of the week. Therefore, one should try to estimate the average of daily hours of usage. There may be seasonal variation in the daily usage of an appliance as well. For instance, a cooler will be used mainly in summer but not in winter. Such seasonal variation should also be considered while estimating annual energy consumption.

 WORKSHEET 2.4: Fill the typical daily duration of usage of appliances listed in Table 2.9.

TABLE 2.9 Appliances and Their Daily Consumption

Name of the appliance	Typical daily duration of usage (in hours)
Incandescent light (bulb)	....
Tube light	....
Compact fluorescent lamp (CFL)	....
Ceiling fan	....
Air conditioner	....
CD player	....
TV	....
Laptop computer	....
Desktop computer	....
Printer	....
Washing machine	....

2.2.1
Daily Energy Consumption

After collecting the above two information (power ratings and average daily hours of usage), one can make a table (like Table 2.10) where you can fill up the information regarding the power rating and hours of usage. Also, there should be one more column added for the number of appliances of same kind. For example, in a household, there can be several CFLs and several ceiling fans. Then, for instance, in order to estimate total energy consumed by all fans, energy consumed by one fan needs to be multiplied with the number of fans in the house. This needs to be repeated for all appliances in the house having more than one unit. An example for estimating total daily energy requirement of household using 3 CFLs, 2 ceiling fans, 1 TV and 1 computer is given in Table 2.10.

Table 2.10 Example Table for Estimating Total Daily Energy Requirement of a House

Name of appliances	Power rating (in watts)	Average daily hours of usage (in hour/day)	Number of appliances (in numbers)	Daily energy requirement (watt × hour × number) or Wh
CFL	12	6	3	216
Fan	50	8	2	800
TV (21")	150	2	1	300
Computer	250	3	1	750
–	–	–	–	–
–	–	–	–	–
Total daily energy requirement of household (Wh/day)				2066

Calculation of energy consumption is easy; multiply power with duration of usage of all appliances and add them.

The daily energy requirement from Table 2.10 is 2066 Wh. This daily energy requirement in terms of kWh will be 2.066 kWh. If you are designing a solar PV system, the system must supply this daily requirement of household.

WORKSHEET 2.5:   A household is using a number of electrical appliances for daily purpose. Fill in Table 2.11 on the estimation of daily energy requirement of appliances and total energy requirement of a household.

TABLE 2.11   Electrical Appliances and Their Daily Consumption

Name of appliances	Power rating (in watts)	Average daily duration of usage (in hour/day)	Number of appliances (in numbers)	Daily energy requirement (watt × hour × number) or Wh
CFL	12	....	5	....
Fan	....	8	3	....
TV	....	2	....	....
Computer	50	....	1	....
Washing machine	....	....	....	....
Total daily energy requirement of household (Wh/day)				....

2.2.2 Monthly Energy Consumption and Electricity Bill

Once you know the daily energy requirement for a given application, it is easy to find out monthly energy requirement. The monthly energy requirement can be obtained by multiplying daily energy requirement by the number of days in that month. Therefore, we can write:

Monthly energy requirement = monthly energy requirement × number of days in month

For the above example given in Table 2.10

Monthly energy requirement = 2066 (Wh/day) × 30 (days/month)
= 61980 Wh or 61.98 kWh

Cost of electricity or monthly electricity bill

The 'one unit of electricity' is equal to 1000 Wh or 1 kWh of energy. People get their monthly electricity bill based on the number of electricity units they consume in a month. Once you know the monthly energy requirement of your client, and if you know the rate/cost of a unit of electricity (in terms of ₹ per kWh), you can calculate monthly electricity bill for consuming a certain amount of energy. Keep in mind that besides the cost of electricity, the government also adds tax to monthly electricity bill. The government declares the cost of electricity for 1 kWh or one unit of electricity. The cost of one unit of electricity in current situation varies between 2 to 8 ₹/kWh, depending on the sector (domestic or commerical), depending on the state you live in, etc. Based on above discussion, one can estimate monthly electricity bill in the following way:

> Our monthly electricity bill is given in terms of kWh (1 kWh = 1 unit of electricity).

Monthly electricity bill = monthly energy requirement × rate per unit of electricity

EXAMPLE 2.4

Let us assume that the cost of electricity is ₹6/kWh, then estimate the monthly electricity bill for energy consumption represented in Table 1.6.

Solution

Reading from Table 2.10, the daily electricity requirement is = 2066 Wh = 2.066 kWh (or one can say 2.066 units of electricity is consumed every day).

Therefore, monthly energy requirement = monthly energy requirement × number of days in month = 2.066 (kWh/day) × 30 (days/month) = 61.98 kWh per month or 61.98 units of electricity consumed per month.

The rate of electricity given in problem = ₹6/kWh

Therefore, the monthly electricity bill = 61.98 (kWh/month) × 6 (₹/kWh)
= 371.88 ₹/month

Problem 2.1: Based on daily energy estimation done in Worksheet 2.5, estimate the monthly energy requirement, and also, estimate the monthly electricity bill if the cost of electricity is ₹5/kWh.

2.3
Energy from Solar Photovoltaic (PV) Conversion

A solar cell is a fundamental block of solar photovoltaic (PV) technology. The solar cell is a device that converts sunlight into electricity directly without any other intermediate conversion steps. Input to solar cells is energy in the form of solar radiation and output from the solar cells is energy in the form of electricity. In this way, a solar cell is radiation energy to electrical energy conversion device as shown in Figure 2.1.

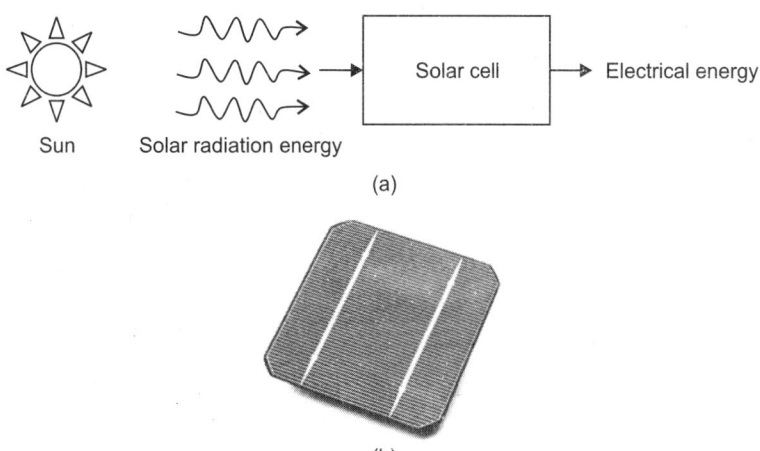

FIGURE 2.1

(a) Solar cell as radiation energy to electrical energy conversion device and (b) picture of a solar cell.

It has been discussed in Section 2.1.4 that the amount of solar energy reaching the Earth surface in the form of solar radiation is extremely large in amount; many thousands times more than our energy consumption from all other resources. Using solar cells, the solar radiation energy can be converted into electrical energy which is the most desirable form of energy. Therefore, if we manufacture a large number of solar cells, a huge amount of electricity can be generated to fulfill all our energy requirements. However, there are several challenges that needs to overcome before solar PV electricity can become our main supply of electricity.

Solar cells are made using different types of materials. A solar cell technology gets its name from the type of material used for solar cell fabrication. The types of materials include mono-crystalline silicon, multi-crystalline silicon, amorphous silicon, cadmium telluride, etc. and therefore, the names of solar cell technologies are mono-crystalline silicon cell, multi-crystalline silicon solar cells, amorphous silicon solar cells, cadmium telluride solar cells, etc. More discussion about solar cells is given in Chapter 3.

> Solar cell converts sunlight energy into electrical energy.

2.3.1
Solar PV Modules

A solar cell is a small device in terms of area, and the electricity a single solar cell can generate is also small as compared to our electricity needs. For example, a single solar cell can generate daily electricity in rage of 6 Wh to 10 Wh while our daily requirements are much higher. Therefore, in order to generate more electricity, many solar cells are connected together in the form of PV module. The number of solar cells to be connected together and the way they are connected together determine current and voltage that we can get from the modules, and average energy it can produce every day. The connection of solar cells in the form of PV module and actual picture of a PV module is given in Figure 2.2.

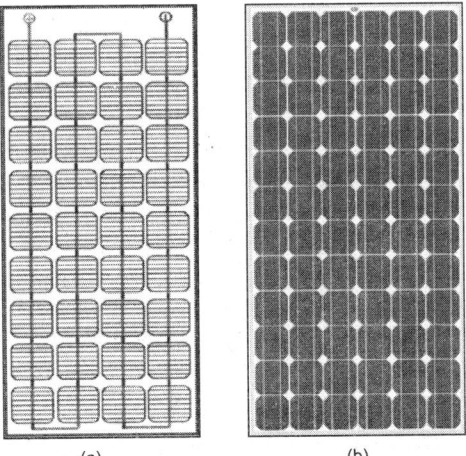

(a) (b)

FIGURE 2.2

(a) Schematic of solar PV module and (b) picture of a solar PV module.

PV modules are very important part of PV systems. It is very important to understand the characteristics of PV modules. Some important features of the PV modules are listed here:

- A solar cell converts radiation energy into electrical energy when sunlight falls on it. Since PV module is made using solar cells, a PV module generates electricity only when sunlight falls on it. Thus, in non-sunshine hours or in night, the energy output from PV module is zero.

- The amount of electricity generated from a PV module depends on the physical size of the module, larger is the size of the module, higher will be the amount of electricity generated from it.

- PV modules are mainly characterized in terms of their power rating, which is known as 'peak power' rating. The unit of power is watt and to emphasize the 'peak' power a subscript 'p' is added. Therefore, the symbol for 'peak power' of a PV modules is 'W_p'. The W_p rating is maximum power rating that a PV module can provide under best condition, called standard test condition (STC). The PV modules are available in W_p rating starting from 1 W_p to 300 W_p. Commonly available W_p rating of PV modules are 3 W_p, 10 W_p, 18 W_p, 36 W_p, 50 W_p, 75 W_p, 150 W_p, 175 W_p, 220 W_p, and 300 W_p.

- Electricity that is generated from a PV module is DC (direct current) in nature. The conventional electricity supply available to us is AC (alternating current) in nature. All our appliances like TV, CFL, tube light, refrigerator, washing machine, etc. runs on AC electricity. Therefore, if we want to use solar PV electricity, it must be first converted into AC electricity. An additional device called 'inverter' is used to convert DC electricity into AC electricity. It means we have to use an additional device in the PV system.

- Since the PV modules generate electricity only during day time, therefore for night time applications, the storage of electrical energy in batteries are required. One advantage of DC electricity generated from the PV modules is that the batteries store and supply electricity in the form of DC electricity. In addition, there are several devices that can directly be operated using DC electricity like LEDs, DC fan, DC water pumps, etc. Even other devices like mobile phone, computer, refrigerator etc. can also be run directly on DC. So, if we are using DC appliances, the use of inverter can be avoided. But the use of DC appliances is not very common.

- Similar to different types of solar cells, the solar PV modules also get different names based on type of solar cells used in making solar PV modules. The names of commonly available PV modules are: mono-crystalline silicon solar PV module, multi-crystalline silicon solar PV module, amorphous silicon solar PV module, cadmium telluride solar PV module, CIGS solar PV modules, etc. For each of these types of PV modules, there are many manufacturer in the world, but mono-crystalline silicon solar PV module and multi-crystalline silicon solar PV module are the most commonly manufactured and used.

- When large energy generation, larger than what one PV module can produce is required, many PV modules are connected together. This interconnection of PV modules is called 'PV module array'.

Several cells are connected together in solar PV modules. The solar PV modules are available in many wattage ratings.

PV modules are very important part of PV system and a detailed discussion about the solar PV modules is given in Chapter 3.

2.3.2
Solar PV Systems

The function of a solar PV system is to supply reliable electricity to the appliances when required or in case of large PV power plants to supply electricity to the grid. It has been discussed in Section 2.3.1 that the solar PV modules produce electricity only when sunlight shines on modules and for night time applications, electrical energy storage in the form of batteries may be required if there is no other supply. Batteries are also used when the demand of electricity by appliances is more than the generation of electricity in day time. In some cases, the PV modules supply electricity directly to the existing electricity grid in which the use of batteries can be avoided. Also, the electricity produced by PV modules are DC in nature while most of our appliances are AC in nature, and therefore, inversion of DC into AC is required before making use of solar PV electricity. Therefore, in all, as per above discussion, for the generation of solar PV electricity and reliable supply of electricity to the appliances, not only PV modules are required, but also, several other components are required. The other components include the following:

1. *Battery:* For storing electrical energy for night time applications and for time when demand of electricity is more than the generation of electricity. Batteries are not required in grid-connected PV systems.

2. *Inverter:* For converting DC electricity to AC electricity, the DC electricity may either come from PV modules or it can come from batteries.

3. *Charge controller:* For protecting the batteries from overcharge and over-discharge conditions which reduce the life of batteries.

4. *Maximum power point tracker (MPPT):* For extracting maximum available power from solar PV modules under given solar radiation input. Many times, charge controller or inverter (in case of grid connection) performs the function of charge controller and MPPT.

PV modules together with other components that are put connected with PV modules to supply reliable energy to appliances is referred collectively as 'solar PV system'. A solar PV system can be of several types (discussed in detail in Chapter 10) depending on the way the energy is generated and used. Broadly, PV system is divided in three categories:

1. Standalone solar PV systems,

2. Grid-connected solar PV system, and

3. Hybrid solar PV system.

The PV systems which are not connected to the grid are called standalone PV systems, and the PV systems which are connected to the grid are called grid connected PV systems.

Standalone PV systems: These systems are self-sufficient in themselves. They do not depend on any other source of energy to supply electricity to planned appliances or load. The example of standalone solar PV systems include a solar lantern, a solar PV home lighting system, a solar PV water pumping system, etc. Since the standalone solar PV systems do not depend on any other energy sources, they invariably use means to store energy, typically in the form of batteries. And since batteries are used, it is important to use to protect electronics. Also, for conversion of DC electricity from PV modules and from battery, inverter will have to be used. A typical standalone solar PV system and the flow of energy in the system (denoted by arrows) is shown in Figure 2.3.

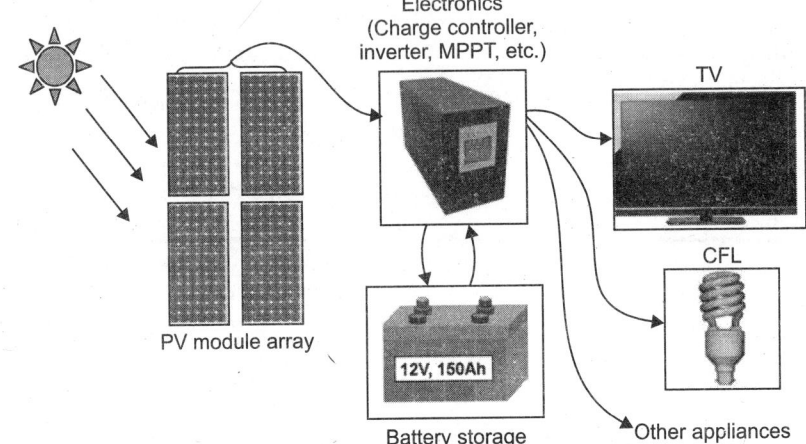

FIGURE 2.3

Stand alone solar PV system with battery storage, electronics and appliances.

A standalone PV system stores energy in batteries for night time application when there is no sunlight.

Grid-connected solar PV systems: As the name suggests, a grid-connected solar PV system is connected with nearby available electricity grid. In this way, the generated electricity is feed into the grid. No battery storage is used in this case. But conversion of DC electricity generated by solar PV modules into AC electricity is required before feeding to the grid. A typical arrangement of grid-connected solar PV systems is shown in Figure 2.4. This type of PV system configuration is used in India for large scale (MW level) solar PV power plants. Electricity grid voltage and frequency are well defined and, therefore, the PV electricity can be fed to electricity grid only after proper power conditioning, i.e., converting PV generated electricity to appropriate voltage and frequency level. Therefore, in the case of grid-connected solar PV system, the inverter not only performs the function of DC to AC conversion but also performs the function of grid synchronization which is related to bringing generated PV energy to appropriate voltage and frequency level.

FIGURE 2.4

PV system connected with electricity grid.

A grid connected PV system does not store energy in battery; it takes energy from the grid when there is no sunlight.

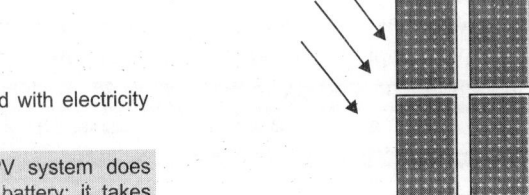

Hybrid solar PV system: In some cases, an auxiliary source of energy like diesel generator is used in addition to solar PV modules and/or grid. This need to be done when solar PV modules are not designed to supply the full required energy by the load (may be due to cost reason). In such case of use of auxiliary source a solar PV systems is called 'hybrid solar PV system'.

2.3.3 Advantages and Challenges of Solar Photovoltaic Energy Conversion

Advantages

Like other technologies, the solar PV technology also has its positive and negative aspects or has its advantages and challenges. These are discussed as follows:

Advantages of the solar PV technology is listed below:

- *Abundant source:* Solar cell uses solar radiation energy as input, which is a renewable energy source. Solar radiation energy is available in huge quantity as it is abundant. We will not run in the shortage of solar radiation energy in future. On the other hand, the world is already facing the shortage of fossil fuels based energy sources.

- *Environmentally benign:* The conversion of solar radiation energy into electrical energy does not emit any polluting products and, therefore, it does not cause damage to the environment like the smoke from use of diesel, petrol and coal does.

- *Decentralized electricity generation:* Since solar radiation energy is available everywhere, the solar PV electricity can be generated everywhere in decentralized manner in small quantities as per the need, unlike the coal based power plant where electricity can be generated only in centralized manner in large quantities. Decentralized electricity generation results in less losses occurring due to transmission of electricity. In the case of solar PV technology, one can have a small solar lantern, a solar PV system for lighting house, a solar PV system for running water pump, or a solar PV system for lighting whole village or even solar PV system for pumping MW of power into grid.

- *Modular implementation:* Implementation of solar PV technology can be modular. Size of a solar PV system for electricity generation can be increased as per the increase in need of electricity. In the case of a diesel generator or a coal based power plant, size once fixed cannot be changed. If we need to increase electricity, we need to buy another diesel generator or set up another coal based power plant.

> Solar cell uses sunlight as an input fuel source, which is abundant, sustainable and environmentally friendly energy source.

Challenges

In principle, solar PV electricity can be generated to fulfill our entire energy requirement. But there are significant challenges to be overcome in order to make wider use of electricity generated using solar PV technology. These challenges are listed below:

- *PV electricity cost:* The conventional energy sources have always been the most cost-effective way to supply the large amount of electricity needed for modern life. Producing electricity using solar PV technology is more expensive. However, the cost of solar PV electricity has been decreasing rapidly, there is further need to reduce the cost in order to make solar PV electricity affordable by all.

- *Energy fluctuation:* In the case of coal based power plants, companies can easily stockpile coal to meet the ever-changing demand for electricity, especially during peak demand hours. While the solar radiation energy can't be stored to provide energy for future use. Solar radiation is not available in the night time but there is electricity need in night. Also, during the day time peak radiation availability may not match with peak electricity demand. Therefore a mechanism for effective energy storage and efficient recovery is required.

- *Location dependency:* Fossil fuel power plants can be placed almost anywhere, as long as a railroad or pipeline can reach the site for bringing coal and gas. In contrast, solar PV electricity generation depends on the availability of solar radiation. The availability of solar radiation varies from place to place. At some places it is more and at some other places it is less. Therefore, solar electricity generation is dependent on location where system needs to be installed.

> The challenge to use PV technology is to generate electricity to bring down the cost of PV systems to affordable level.

2.4
Other Renewable Energy Technologies

> Other than solar PV technology, there are several other renewable energy technologies that use renewable energy sources.

Solar Photovoltaic is one way of converting renewable energy sources into useful energy. There are several other technologies that convert renewable energy sources like solar radiation, wind energy, biomass energy, etc. into useful energy. There are many people who are also working on other renewable energy technologies and there are many installations for energy generation which uses different types of renewable energy sources. A detailed discussion of the other renewable energy technologies is not in the scope of this manual but for the completeness of the information, brief discussions are given in the following paragraphs.

2.4.1
Solar Thermal Energy

There are two categories of solar energy technologies; one is solar PV technology (for which this manual is dedicated) and other is solar thermal technology. In solar thermal technology, the solar radiation energy is converted into heat energy while in solar PV technology, the solar radiation energy is converted into electrical energy directly.

In solar thermal technology, a device called solar collectors is used for converting solar radiation into heat energy. The sunlight is captured by different types of solar collectors which provide heat. This heat is then used for various applications, such as heating water for domestic applications (bathing, washing clothes, etc.). Water is heated up to temperatures of about 50°C–60°C. For applications which require higher temperatures (more than 100°C), special type of solar collectors, called concentrator collectors, are used. The concentrator collectors collect light from large area and concentrate it in small area. Due to such light concentration, higher temperatures (from few hundred up to 1000°C) are obtained. The solar thermal heating could also be used for industrial applications for steam generation which is used in industry for many process applications.

One of the important applications of concentrator solar thermal energy is for electricity generation. The technology is normally known as **Concentrator Solar Power (CSP)** technology. The CSP plants for electricity generation is similar to coal based power plants except that in the CSP technology, the steam is generated using solar radiation while in coal based plants steam is generated by burning coal. The rest of the processes used in steam based power generation are same. The steam is used for rotating the turbines which, in turn, rotates the electrical generator in order to generate electricity. Large megawatt scale CSP solar thermal power plants are being built at various places in the world. In 2010, the worldwide installed capacity of solar thermal power plant for electricity generation was above 190 GW (thermal power). Under Jawaharlal National Nehru Solar Mission (JNNSM), launched by Ministry of New and Renewable Energy in 2010, there will be large installations of solar thermal power plants in India as well.

2.4.2
Wind Energy

A moving object possesses energy due to its motion; this energy is called the kinetic energy. Similarly flow of air or wind, around the earth possess kinetic energy. The kinetic energy of the blowing wind is called the wind energy. The flow of wind in our atmosphere is mainly caused by uneven heating of the earth's surface by the sun. Thus wind energy is indirect manifestation of sun's energy. The wind energy has a good potential to be a source of renewable and pollution free power. About 1 to 3% of the solar energy falling on earth surface gets converted into wind energy. The solar energy to wind energy conversion is about 50 to 100 times higher than the solar energy to biomass energy conversion through photosynthesis. Though, similar to solar radiation energy, the wind energy is also dilute in nature and its availability varies considerably over a day and over one season to other season.

The wind energy can be used in many ways. Historically wind energy is used for sailing ships. The energy contained in the wind can be converted to the useful energy through wind mills. Wind energy can be converted into mechanical energy for grinding or water pumping. Alternatively the wind energy can be converted to electrical energy (the most desired form of energy) by converting wind energy into mechanical energy (rotary motion of wind turbine), which is then converted to electrical energy using generators. Some important applications of wind energy are the generation of electricity and to some extent for water pumping.

The conversion of wind energy to electrical energy is one of the most successful renewable energy technologies. It has already proven to be economical in many parts of the world where wind resources are good. All over the world, large amount of wind machines for electrical energy generation have been installed. In 2010 the worldwide installed capacity of wind machine was about 200,000 MW. In India the installed capacity of wind machine is about 13000 MW.

2.4.3
Biomass Energy

Biomass refers to the mass of biological material produced from the living processes. This includes the materials derived from the plants as well as from animals. Chemically, biomass refers to the materials containing hydrogen, carbon and oxygen. We extract biomass from numerous sources like; plants, trees, agricultural crops, raw material from the forest, household waste and wood. The contribution of the biomass to our energy requirement comes in the form of food and fuel. There are several other requirements that are being served by the use of biomass, namely shelter preparation, fodder for animals, nutrient for soil, etc. The earliest inhabitants on the earth burned wood in their campfires for heat and since then it has been a source of energy for meeting human needs.

Biomass grows in the presence of sunlight only. Therefore, the biomass can be considered as 'solar energy stored in organic matter'. As trees and plants grow, the process of photosynthesis uses energy from the sun to convert CO_2 of the atmosphere into carbohydrates (sugar, starch and cellulose). The process of photosynthesis can be written as follows:

$$6CO_2 \text{ (gas)} + 6H_2O \text{ (liquid)} + \text{light} \rightarrow C_6H_{12}O_6 \text{ (solid)} + 6O_2 \text{ (gas)}$$

The biomass has been used extensively in the development of societies since the beginning of civilizations. It has played a very important role in the development of societies. Many people in the developing countries still depend on the use of biomass for their daily livelihood. They use it for food, fuel as well as a source of income. It is estimated that biomass contributes to about 14% of the world's total energy requirement. In many developing countries, the contribution to total energy requirement is as high as 90%. As a renewable energy source, biomass should be able to meet all its requirements in various forms, provided the balance between production and consumption of biomass is maintained.

Energy can be generated from bio degradable items, such as plants, cow dung, leaves, etc. These items are rich in hydrocarbons and release energy when burned. The main application of biomass energy is fuel generation which is used for cooking as well as for vehicular transport applications. Biodiesel is one of the most important products of the biomass. Cooking gas from biomass, also called biogas, is also an important source of energy. Using a process, called gasification, biomass can also be converted into fuel gas, which can be used in engine in place of diesel.

2.4.4
Hydro Energy

An object, kept at a height, is said to possess some energy called potential energy, because a falling object can provide some energy. For instance, in hydro power plants, energy of water falling from a certain height is used to generate electrical energy. Water falling from a height has stored potential energy. This energy could then be utilized to rotate the hydro turbines for generation of electricity. Large hydro projects make use of huge tanks or dams to store water in their catchment areas. This water is then allowed a free passage through pipes or channels to water turbines that are placed at the bottom of the tank. The potential energy of water is then used to rotate the turbine for electricity generation. Around the world, large amount of electricity is generated using this method. The total installed capacity of hydro power plant in the world is about 800,000 MW. In India also the total installed capacity for hydro electricity is about 40,000 MW.

The energy of running water in small water streams, rivers and canals is called kinetic energy of water (similar to energy of blowing wind). Similar to wind energy technology, kinetic energy of water can also be converted into electricity. A small water turbine is placed in the movement of water. The turbine converts kinetic energy water into electrical energy. There are water turbines of small capacity in the range of few kW to few tens of kW are available. Thus wherever there is moving water some electrical energy can be generated.

2.4.5
Geothermal Energy

The Earth is a large sphere. The surface of this sphere is cold but its center is still very hot. Core of the earth is plasma (materials in molten form) which is at very high temperatures about 5000°C while the earth surface is at temperatures less than 100°C. Due to the temperature gradient, there is always heat conduction from the earth crust to the surface. The heat flow due to conduction could be used for heat and electricity generation. Special types of heat exchangers are used for conversion of the heat generated in the earth to the end applications, such as steam generation for process heat or for electricity generation.

REFERENCES

www.kajul.org (This website gives introduction about energy at beginners level)

www.ren21.net/gsr (This website gives globle renewable energy status report for 2011)

3

Solar Cells

A solar cell is a semiconductor device that converts sunlight energy into electrical energy directly without going through any intermediate energy conversion steps. It is a fundamental block of solar photovoltaic (PV) technology. Many solar cells are connected together to form solar PV modules. Several solar PV modules are connected together to make PV array in small power applications as well as in big power plant applications. Therefore, it is important to understand how does a solar cell work, how to identify a solar cells, what are its parameters, how much power a solar cell can generate, how the generated power depends on sunlight falling on it, etc. This chapter focuses on providing the fundamental understanding of solar cells, its parameters and how the variation in parameter and ambient conditions affect the performance of solar cells of different technologies.

3.1

How Solar Cells are Better than any Conventional Sources of Electricity?

The electricity is conventionally generated by using coal energy, hydro energy or nuclear energy. One of the most common ways of generating electricity is using coal energy. In India, about 55% of electricity is generated using coal energy. A typical coal power plant, shown in Figure 3.1, involves several steps before the energy of coal gets converted into useful energy form, the electricity. The power plant process starts from the burning of coal and ends with the generation of electricity by generators. In the whole process, only fraction of coal energy is eventually used in running our appliances. Most of the coal energy is wasted in the conversion process and transmission of electricity from power plant to our homes. Other than the waste of energy, there is also environmental pollution caused of coal based power plants. Also, coal as a source of energy is not available in infinite quantity, which means that sooner or later we will run in the shortage of coal. Considering these facts, one must look for alternate source of energy.

One of the modern ways of generating electricity is using solar cells or solar Photovoltaics (PV); a technology that converts sunlight into electricity. Solar cell and its technology have drawn lots of attention of engineers, researchers, industries and governments in recent times. Therefore, in this chapter, we will focus on solar cells. So, let us see what is a solar cell? How is current generated by it and what are its applications?

In conventional energy conversion process, several steps are involved in converting fuel energy (like coal, diesel, hydro energy, etc.) into electricity.

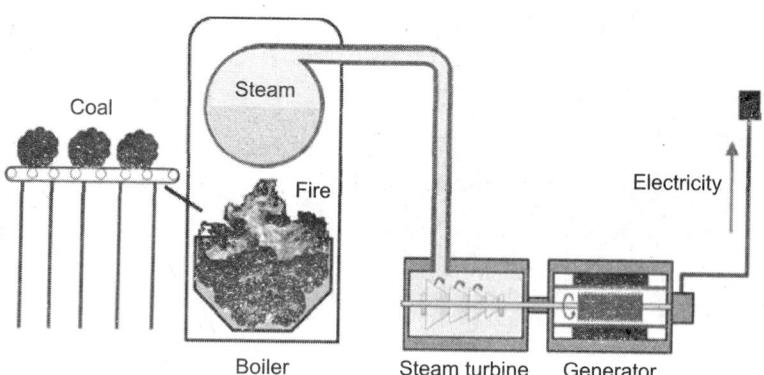

FIGURE 3.1

A typical coal power plant generating electricity using coal.

3.2

What is a Solar Cell?

A solar cell converts sunlight into electricity directly, without any intermediate conversion steps.

FIGURE 3.2

Front side and back side of a typical solar cell.

Solar cell is a semiconductor device which directly converts sunlight into electricity. Solar cell converts sunlight into electricity by photovoltaic effect. Hence, they are also called photovoltaic cell. A typical commercial silicon solar cell is shown in Figure 3.2.

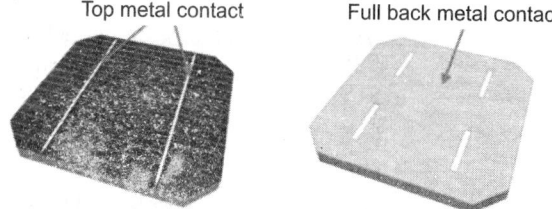

The solar cell generates current and voltage at its terminals when sunlight falls on it. The amount of electricity generated by a solar cell depends on the amount of sunlight incident on it. The electricity generated by solar cell depends upon the intensity (amount) of light, the area of a cell and the angle at which light falls on it. The higher is the intensity of sunlight, the more is the electricity generated by solar cell. If area of a solar cell is increased, the current generated by it increases. The power generated by the solar cell is optimum when sunlight falling is perpendicular to the front side of solar cell.

In common, all solar cells, irrespective of the technology and material used have only two terminals (positive and negative terminals) as output. Typically solar cells have front contact at the top, emitter-base junction or p-n junction in the middle and the back contact at the bottom. At the emitter-base junction, the separation of negative and positive charge takes place. Electricity is supplied to a load by connecting its terminals to the front and back contacts of a solar cell or solar module or solar panel as shown in Figure 3.3.

A solar cell is a two terminal power generating device, one is a positive (anode) terminal and another is a negative terminal (cathode).

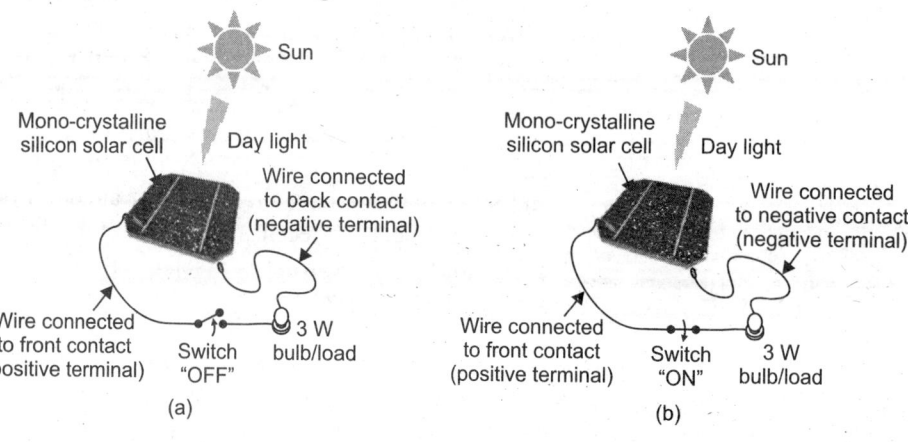

FIGURE 3.3

Solar cell converting day light into electricity; front and back terminals connected to torch bulb, (a) switch is OFF and (b) switch is ON.

3.3
How Solar Cell Generates Electricity?

The sunlight falling on the earth is basically the bundles of photons or bundles of small energy. Each photon in a bundle has a finite amount of energy. In solar spectrum, there are many photons of different energy. For generation of electricity, photons must be absorbed by solar cell. The absorption of photon depends upon the energy of photon and the band-gap energy of semiconductor material of a solar cell. The photon energy and the band-gap energy of semiconductor is expressed in terms of Electron-volt (eV). The eV is a unit of energy.

So, the working of a solar cell can be explained as follows:

1. Photons in the sunlight falling on the solar cell's front face are absorbed by semiconducting materials.
2. Free electron-hole pairs are generated. Electrons are considered as negative charge and holes are considered as positive charge. When solar cell is connected to a load, electron and holes near the junction are separated from each other. The holes are collected at positive terminal (anode) and electrons at negative terminal (cathode). Electric potential is built at the terminals due to the separation of negative and positive charges. Due to the difference between the electric potentials at the terminals we get voltage across the terminals.
3. Voltage developed at the terminals of a solar cell is used to drive the current in the circuit. The current in the circuit will be direct current or DC current.

So, the solar cell with day light falling on it can directly drive DC electrical appliances. But, the amount of electricity generated is proportional to the amount of light falling. So, the amount of electricity generated throughout the day is not constant. The current generated also depends on several other parameters. In the following section, we will now see why the generated current is not constant?

3.4
Parameters of Solar Cells

A solar cell converts the sunlight into electricity. How nicely a solar cell does the conversion of sunlight into electricity is determined the parameters of solar cells. There are several parameters of solar cells that determine the effectiveness of sunlight to electricity conversion. The list of solar cell parameters is following:

- Short circuit current (I_{sc}),
- Open circuit voltage (V_{oc}) and
- Maximum power point
- Current at maximum power point (I_m)
- Voltage at maximum power point (V_m)
- Fill factor (FF)
- Efficiency (η),

These parameters can be best understood by Current-Voltage curve (*I-V* curve) of a solar cell. The representation of *I-V* curve is plotted in Figure 3.4. The Y-axis is normally plotted as current axis and X-axis is plotted as voltage axis.

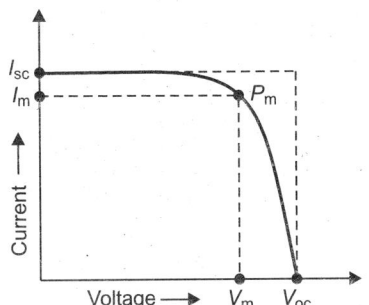

FIGURE 3.4

Schematic of solar cell *I-V* curve and its parameters.

Using Figure 3.4, the cell parameters are defined here. Normally, the value of the cell parameters are given by a manufacturer or scientist at standard test conditions (STC) which is corresponding to 1000 W/m^2 of input solar radiation and 25°C cell operating temperature.

- *Short circuit current* (I_{sc}): It is the maximum current a solar cell can produce. The higher the I_{sc}, better is the cell. It is measured in Ampere (A) or milli-ampere (mA). The value of this maximum current depends on cell technology, cell area, amount of solar radiation falling on cell, angle of cell, etc. Many times, people are given current density rather than current. The current density is obtained by dividing I_{sc} by the area of solar cell (A). The current density is normally referred by symbol, 'J', therefore, the short circuit current density, J_{sc} is given by I_{sc}/A.

- *Open circuit voltage* (V_{oc}): It is the maximum voltage that a solar cell produce. The higher the V_{oc}, the better is the cell. It is measured in volts (V) or sometimes milli-volts (mV). The value of this maximum open circuit voltage mainly depends on cell technology and operating temperature.

- *Maximum power point* (P_m or P_{max}): It is the maximum power that a solar cell produces under STC. The higher the P_m, the better is the cell. It is given in terms of watt (W). Since it is maximum power or peak power, it is sometimes also referred as W_{peak} or W_p. A solar cell can operate at many current and voltage combinations. But a solar cell will produce maximum power only when operating at certain current and voltage. This maximum power point is denoted in Figure 3.4 as P_m. Normally, the maximum power point for a *I-V* curve of solar cells occurs at the 'knee' or 'bend' of the curve. In terms of expression P_m is given as:

$$P_m \text{ or } P_{max} = I_m \times V_m$$

- *Current at maximum power point* (I_m): This is the current which solar cell will produce when operating at maximum power point. The I_m will always be lower than I_{sc}. It is given in terms of ampere (A) or milli-ampere (mA).

- *Voltage at maximum power point* (V_m): This is the voltage which solar cell will produce when operating at maximum power point. The V_m will always be lower than V_{oc}. It is given in terms of volt (V) or milli-volt (mV).

- *Fill factor* (FF): As the name suggests, FF is the ratio of the areas covered by I_m-V_m rectangle with the area covered by I_{sc}-V_{oc} rectangle (both shown by dotted line in Figure 3.4), whose equation is given below. It indicates the square-ness of *I-V* curve. The higher the FF, the better is the cell. The FF of a cell is given in terms of percentage (%). Cell with squarer *I-V* curve is a better cell.

$$FF = \frac{I_m \times V_m}{I_{sc} \times V_{oc}}$$

or

$$FF = \frac{P_m}{I_{sc} \times V_{oc}}$$

Here the expression for P_{max} or P_m can alternatively be written in terms of I_{sc}, V_{oc} and FF as:

$$P_m = I_{sc} \times V_{oc} \times FF$$

- Efficiency (η): The efficiency of a solar cell is defined as the maximum output power (P_{m} or P_{max}) divided by the input power (P_{in}). The efficiency of a cell is given in terms of percentage (%), which means that this percentage of radiation input power is converted into electrical power. P_{in} for STC is considered as 1000 W/m^2. This input power is power density (power divided by area), therefore, in order to calculate the efficiency using P_{in} at STC, we must multiply by solar cell area. Thus, efficiency can be written as:

$$\eta = \frac{P_{\text{m}}}{P_{\text{in}}} = \frac{I_{\text{sc}} \times V_{\text{oc}} \times \text{FF}}{P_{\text{in}} \times A}$$

> A solar cell performance depends on its parameters or the cell parameters and determines the performance of a solar cell under the sunlight, particularly the amount of power it will produce in a given condition.

Let us now see what the possible values of solar cell parameters and how the values that depend on the various solar cell technologies.

WORKSHEET 3.1: Fill below in Table 3.1, the various solar cell parameters and their units by which they are presented.

TABLE 3.1 Solar Cell Parameters and their Units

S. No.	Name of parameter	Unit of parameter
1		
2		
3		
4		
5		
6		
7		

EXAMPLE 3.1

The current density of a solar cell having an area of 100 cm^2 at Standard Test Condition (STC) is given as 35 mA/cm^2. Find out the output current of the solar cell.

Solution

First, we write the formula for current density of a solar cell given by

$$\text{Current density } (J_{\text{sc}}) = \frac{I_{\text{sc}}}{A} \ (\text{mA/cm}^2)$$

where,

J_{sc} = Current density (mA/cm^2)

I_{sc} = Output current (mA)

A = Area (cm^2)

Given that, J_{sc} = 35 mA/cm^2

So, the expression for solar cell current can be written as:

$$\text{Output current } (I_{\text{sc}}) = J_{\text{sc}} \times A \ (\text{mA})$$

Now, given that area of solar cell is 100 cm^2, then

$$\text{Output current } (I_{\text{sc}}) = 35 \text{ mA/cm}^2 \times 100 \text{ cm}^2 = 3500 \text{ mA or } 3.5 \text{ A}$$

Similarly, we calculate output current for different values of solar cell area in the Table 3.9.

EXAMPLE 3.2

A solar cell gives a current of 0.6 A and voltage of 0.5 V at maximum power point. What is the maximum power point of the solar cell?

Solution

First, we write formula for the maximum power point of a solar cell, given by

$$P_m \text{ or } P_{max} = I_m \times V_m$$

Given that, $I_m = 0.6$ A

$$V_m = 0.5 \text{ V}$$

Therefore, the maximum power point, $P_m = 0.6 \text{ A} \times 0.5 \text{ V} = 0.3 \text{ W}$

EXAMPLE 3.3

A solar cell having an area of 100 cm² gives 3.1 A current at maximum power point and 0.5 V at maximum power point at STC. The cell gives 3.5 A short circuit current and 0.6 V open circuit voltage. What is the maximum power point of the solar cell? Also, find out the efficiency of the cell.

Solution

First, we write the formula for the maximum power point of a solar cell, given by

$$P_m \text{ or } P_{max} = I_m \times V_m$$

Given that,

$$I_{sc} = 3.5 \text{ A}$$
$$I_m = 3.1 \text{ A}$$
$$V_{oc} = 0.6 \text{ V}$$
$$V_m = 0.5 \text{ V}$$

Maximum power point, $P_m = 3.1 \text{ A} \times 0.5 \text{ V} = 1.55 \text{ W}$

Now, we write the formula for efficiency of a solar cell given by

$$\eta = \frac{P_{max}}{P_{in} \times A}$$

where,

η = Efficiency in per cent (%)

P_{max} = Output power in watt (W)

P_{in} = Light input power per unit area in watt/square meter (W/m²)

A = Solar cell area in square meter (m²)

η = ?

We know, $P_m = 1.55$ W and at STC, $P_{in} = 1000$ W/m²

First, we convert the unit of area from square centimetre (cm²) to square metre (m²) by dividing area in cm² by 10000.

Here, $A = 100 \text{ cm}^2 = 100 \times 10^{-4} \text{ m}^2 = 0.01 \text{ m}^2$

Now, putting the number we can calculate the efficiency of the cell.

$$\eta = \frac{P_{max}}{P_{in} \times A} = \frac{1.55 \text{ watt}}{1000 \text{ W/m}^2 \times 0.01 \text{ m}^2} \times 100 = 15.5\%$$

From an *I-V* curve of a solar cell, all solar cell parameters can be derived.

Thus, efficiency of the solar cell is 15.5%.

EXAMPLE 3.4

Refer the characteristic curve (Figure 3.5) and find out the Fill Factor for the solar cell.

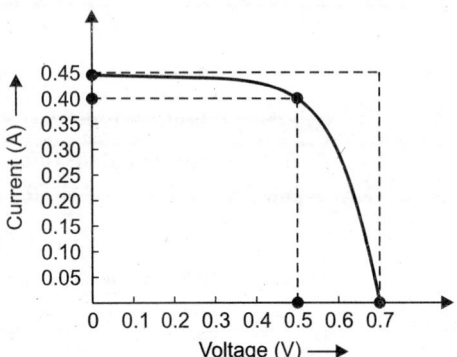

FIGURE 3.5

Figure for Example 3.4.

Solution

Short circuit current (I_{sc}) = 0.45 A
Open circuit voltage (V_{oc}) = 0.7 V
Current at maximum power point (I_m) = 0.40 A
Voltage at maximum power point (V_m) = 0.5 V
Now,

$$\text{Maximum power point, } P_m \text{ or } P_{max} = I_m \times V_m = 0.40 \times 0.5 = 0.2 \text{ W}$$

$$\text{Fill Factor, FF} = \frac{I_m \times V_m}{I_{sc} \times V_{oc}}$$

or $$\text{FF} = \frac{P_m}{I_{sc} \times V_{oc}} = \frac{0.2}{0.45 \times 0.7} \times 100 = 63.49\%$$

Note: In order to represent the FF value in 'percentage', multiply by 100.

EXAMPLE 3.5

A solar cell having an area of 25 cm^2 gives a current of 0.85 A and voltage 0.55 V at maximum power point. The short circuit current is 0.9 A and open circuit voltage is 0.65 V. What is the Fill Factor, maximum power point and efficiency of the solar cell? Consider STC.

Solution

Given, Short circuit current (I_{sc}) = 0.9 A
Open circuit voltage (V_{oc}) = 0.65 V
Current at max power point (I_m) = 0.85 A
Voltage at maximum power point (V_m) = 0.55 V
Light input power (W/m^2) = 1000 W/m^2

$$\text{Area} = A = 25 \text{ cm}^2 = 25 \times 10^{-4} \text{ m}^2 = 0.0025 \text{ m}^2$$

Now,
Maximum power point, P_m or $P_{max} = I_m \times V_m = 0.85 \times 0.55 = 0.4675$ W

$$\text{Fill Factor, FF} = \frac{I_m \times V_m}{I_{sc} \times V_{oc}}$$

or $$\text{FF} = \frac{P_m}{I_{sc} \times V_{oc}} = \frac{0.4675}{0.9 \times 0.65} \times 100 = 79.91\%$$

$$\text{Efficiency } (\eta) = \frac{P_{max}}{P_{in} \times A} = \frac{0.4675}{1000 \times 0.0025} \times 100 = 18.7\%$$

Note: In order to represent the FF and efficiency values in 'percentage', multiply by 100 in both cases.)

EXAMPLE 3.6

A solar cell having Fill Factor (FF) 60% gives 2.5 A current at maximum power point at STC. The cell gives 3 A short circuit current and 0.5 V open circuit voltage. What is the voltage at maximum power point of the solar cell?

Solution

Given that,

I_{sc} = 3 A
I_m = 2.5 A
V_{oc} = 0.5 V
V_m = ?
FF = 60%

First, we write formula for Fill Factor of a solar cell given by

$$\text{Fill Factor (FF)} = \frac{I_m \times V_m}{I_{sc} \times V_{oc}}$$

where,

I_{sc} = Short circuit current (A)

I_m = Current at maximum power point (A)

V_{oc} = Open circuit voltage (V)

V_m = Voltage at maximum power point (V)

FF = Fill Factor (%)

We know, FF = 60%

First, we convert Fill Factor (FF) from per cent to decimal by dividing it by 100.

Therefore,
$$FF = \frac{60}{100} = 0.6$$

Now, we rewrite the formula for Fill Factor of a solar cell to get the value of V_m given by expression below.

$$\text{Voltage at maximum power point, } V_m = FF \times \frac{I_{sc} \times V_{oc}}{I_m}$$

Now, putting the value, we can calculate the voltage at maximum power point.

$$V_m = FF \times \frac{I_{sc} \times V_{oc}}{I_m} = 0.6 \times \frac{3 \times 0.5}{2.5} = 0.36 \text{ V}$$

Thus, the voltage at maximum power point is 0.36 V.

EXAMPLE 3.7

A solar cell having Fill Factor (FF) 68% gives 0.6 V voltage at maximum power point at STC. The cell gives 3 A short circuit current and 0.7 V open circuit voltage. What is the current at maximum power point of the solar cell?

Solution

Given that,

I_{sc} = 3 A

I_m = ?

V_{oc} = 0.7 V

V_m = 0.6 V

FF = 68%

First we write formula for Fill Factor of a solar cell given by expression below

$$\text{Fill Factor (FF)} = \frac{I_m \times V_m}{I_{sc} \times V_{oc}}$$

where,

I_{sc} = Short circuit current (A)

I_m = Current at maximum power point (A)

V_{oc} = Open circuit voltage (V)

V_m = Voltage at maximum power point (V)

FF = Fill Factor (%)

We know, FF = 68%

First, we convert Fill Factor (FF) from per cent to decimal by dividing it by 100.

$$FF = \frac{68}{100} = 0.68$$

Now, we rewrite formula for Fill Factor of a solar cell to get the value of I_m given by expression below.

Current at maximum power point, $I_m = \text{FF} \times \dfrac{I_{sc} \times V_{oc}}{V_m}$

Now, putting the value, we can calculate the current at maximum power point.

$$I_m = \text{FF} \times \frac{I_{sc} \times V_{oc}}{V_m} = 0.68 \times \frac{3 \times 0.7}{0.6} = 2.38 \text{ A}$$

Thus, current at maximum power point is 2.38 A.

EXAMPLE 3.8

A solar cell has maximum power point of 0.3 W. The cell voltage at maximum power point at STC is 0.65 V. What is the current at maximum power point of the solar cell?

Solution

Given that,

$P_m = 0.3$ W

$I_m = ?$

$V_m = 0.65$ V

First, we write the formula for maximum power point P_m or P_{max} of a solar cell given by

Maximum power point $(P_m) = I_m \times V_m$

where,

P_m = Maximum power point (W)

I_m = Current at maximum power point (A)

V_m = Open circuit voltage (V)

Now, we rewrite formula for maximum power point P_m of a solar cell to get the value of I_m given by expression below.

Current at maximum power point, $I_m = \dfrac{P_m}{V_m}$

Putting the value, we can calculate the current at maximum power point.

$$I_m = \frac{P_m}{V_m} = \frac{0.3}{0.65} = 0.46 \text{ A}$$

Thus, the current at maximum power point is 0.46 A.

 WORKSHEET 3.2: Current and voltage of a solar cell has been measured under STC at various points of cell operation. These values are given in Table 3.2 below. For this solar cell, calculate the maximum power that can be extracted from solar cell.

TABLE 3.2 Current and Voltage of a Solar Cell Under STC at Different Points of Operation

S. No.	Current, I (A)	Voltage, V (V)	Power, P (W) = I × V
1	0.00	0.58	
2	0.01	0.58	
3	0.39	0.57	
4	0.79	0.57	
5	1.19	0.56	
6	1.58	0.55	
7	1.99	0.54	
8	2.39	0.53	
9	2.79	0.52	
10	3.19	0.51	
11	3.58	0.46	
12	4.33	0.00	

The solar cell parameters can be extracted by measuring several current-voltage data points from short circuit to open circuit condition.

WORKSHEET 3.3: A solar cell's current and voltage at various operating has been given in Worksheet 3.2. Using that *I-V* data, fill in estimate and fill in the parameters of solar cell given in Table 3.3 below.

TABLE 3.3 Problem to Find Various Solar Cell Parameters Based on Table 3.2

S. No.	Parameters	Reading or calculating from Table 3.2	Values
1	Short circuit current (I_{sc})	Current value when voltage is zero	
2	Open circuit voltage (V_{oc})	Voltage value when current is zero	
3	Maximum power point, P_m	Value of maximum power	
3	Current at max power point (I_m)	Current value at maximum power point	
4	Voltage at max power point (V_m)	Voltage value at maximum power point	
5	Fill Factor (FF)	$= \dfrac{I_m \times V_m}{I_{sc} \times V_{oc}}$	
6	Efficiency	$= \dfrac{V_{oc} \times I_{sc} \times FF}{P_{in} \times A}$	

WORKSHEET 3.4: *I-V* characteristic of a solar cell is given below (Table 3.4). Fill in the blank spaces.

TABLE 3.4 To Obtain the Missing Quantities

S. No.	Current, I (A)	Voltage, V (V)	Power, P (W)
1	0.00	0.58	–
2	0.01	0.58	–
3	0.39	–	0.22
4	0.79	0.57	–
5	1.19	0.56	–
6	–	0.55	0.88
7	1.99	0.54	–
8	2.39	0.53	–
9	2.79	–	1.47
10	3.19	0.51	–
11	–	0.46	1.65
12	4.33	–	

3.5
Solar Cell Technologies

In market, a wide variety of solar cells are available. These cells are made of using different materials. The name of a particular solar cell or solar cell technology depends on the name the material used in that particular technology. The properties of materials used in different type of solar cells are different. Hence, different types of solar cells have different values of solar cell parameters like efficiency (η), short circuit current density (J_{sc}), open circuit voltage (V_{oc}) and Fill Factor (FF). The list of commercial solar cells technology, materials and efficiency is given in Table 3.5. The commonly available commercial solar cells along with η, A, J_{sc}, V_{oc} and FF are mentioned in Table 3.6.

TABLE 3.5 Commercial Solar Cells Technology, Materials and Efficiency

Solar photovoltaic technologies	Solar cell type	Materials used	Efficiency (η in per cent)
Crystalline Silicon (c-Si) solar cell	Mono-crystalline silicon	Mono-crystalline silicon	14–16
	Poly or multicrystalline Si (mc-Si)	Multi-crystalline silicon	14–16
Thin film solar cell	Amorphous Si (a-Si)	Amorphous silicon	6–9
	Cadmium telluride (CdTe)	Cadmium and tellurium	8–11
	Copper-Indium-Gallium-Selenide (CIGS)	Copper, Indium, Gallium, Selenium	8–11
Multi-junction solar cell	GaInP/GaAs/Ge Gallium indium phosphide/Gallium arsenide/ Germanium	Gallium (Ga), Arsenic (Ar), Indium (In), Phosphorus (P), Germanium (Ge)	30–35

There are many commercially available solar cell technologies. The name of technology comes from the materials used in making solar cells.

TABLE 3.6 Typical Solar Cell Parameters (η, J_{sc}, V_{oc} and FF) of Commercial Solar Cells with Available Cell Areas

Solar cell type	Efficiency (η) (in %)	Cell area (A) (in cm^2)	Output voltage (V_{oc}) (in V)	Output current (J_{sc}) (in mA/cm^2)	Fill factor (FF) (in %)
Mono-crystalline silicon	14–17	5–156	0.55–0.68 V	30–38	70–78
Poly or multi-crystalline Si (mc-Si)	14–16	5–156	0.55–0.65 V	30–35	70–76
Amorphous Si (a-Si)	6–9	5–200	0.70–1.1 V	8–15	60–70
Cadmium telluride (CdTe)	8–11	5–200	0.80–1.0 V	15–25	60–70
Copper-Indium-Gallium-Selenide (CIGS)	8–11	5–200	0.50–0.7 V	20–30	60–70
Gallium indium phosphide/Gallium arsenide/Germanium (GaInP/ GaAs/Ge)	30–35	1–4	1.0–2.5 V	15–35	70–85

The efficiency of solar cell varies from one technology to other technology and from one manufacturer to other manufacturer.

3.6
Factors Affecting Electricity Generated by a Solar Cell

There are five common factors that affect the power generated by solar cells. They are as follows:

1. The conversion efficiency (η),
2. The amount of light (P_{in}),
3. The solar cell area (A),
4. The angle at which day light falls (θ), and
5. The operating temperature (T)

3.6.1
Effect of Conversion Efficiency (η)

Of the total light energy falling on a solar cell, only some fraction of the light energy gets converted into electrical energy by the solar cells. The ratio of electrical energy generated to the input light energy is referred as conversion efficiency of solar cells. The conversion efficiency of solar cell is fixed, based on material and the manufacturing process. Once a solar cell of given material is manufactured, its efficiency value becomes fixed and it cannot be changed.

Efficiency of a solar cell is given in terms of maximum power that solar cell can generate for a given input solar radiation. The maximum power output (P_{max} or P_{out}) of solar cells depends on voltage developed across cell terminal and current it can supply. The cell area also affects the power output. If the instantaneous solar radiation or power density is P_{in}, the expression for the efficiency (η) of solar cell can be given as:

$$\eta = \frac{P_{out}}{P_{in} \times A} \quad \text{or} \quad P_{out} = P_{in} \times \eta \times A$$

For given input power, the value of the output power is directly determined by the value of solar cell's conversion efficiency and solar cell area. The solar cells with higher efficiency values will always give better performance. The unit of solar cell efficiency is percentage (%), the unit of P_{out} is normally watt, the unit of P_{in} is normally W/m^2 or W/cm^2 and unit of cell area is in m^2 or cm^2. The solar cell efficiency is given for standard test condition (STC) and under the STC, the value of input power density, P_{in} is taken as 1000 W/m^2 or 0.1 W/cm^2.

> More efficient solar cell produces more power from the same area.

EXAMPLE 3.9

Calculate the output power from a solar cell if its efficiency (in %) is 30, 24, 19, 16 and 12, input power density is 1000 W/m^2, and area of the solar cell is 100 cm^2.

Solution

First, we write formula for efficiency of a solar cell given by

$$\eta = \frac{P_{out}}{P_{in} \times A} \quad \text{or} \quad P_{out} = P_{in} \times \eta \times A$$

where,

η = Efficiency in per cent (%)

P_{out} or P_{max} = Output power in watt (W)

P_{in} = Light input power per unit area in watt/metre^2 (W/m^2)

A = Solar cell area in metre^2 (m^2)

η = 30%, 24%, 19%, 16%, 12%

P_{in} = 1000 W/m^2

P_{max} = ?

First, we convert cell area from cm^2 to m^2.

It is given that cell area A = 100 cm^2 = 100 × 10^{-4} m^2

Now, we solve for solar cell of efficiency 30%

Above equation can be written as:

$$P_{max} = \eta \times P_{in} \times A$$

We put the respective terms values and we get,

$$P_{max} = \left(\frac{30}{100}\right) \times 1000 \times 100 \times 10^{-4} = 3 \text{ W}$$

Similarly, we calculate output power for other efficiencies in the table form as shown in Table 3.7.

TABLE 3.7 Table for Example 3.9

η (%)	P_{in} (W/m^2)	A (cm^2)	A (m^2)	$\eta/100$	$P_{max} = (\eta/100) \times P_{in} \times A$ (W)
30	1000	100	0.01	0.30	3
24	1000	100	0.01	0.24	2.4
19	1000	100	0.01	0.19	1.9
16	1000	100	0.01	0.16	1.6
12	1000	100	0.01	0.12	1.2

> A solar cell with double efficiency will give double power output from same area.

From the above table, it clear that when efficiency of a solar cell reduces the output power generated is also reduces. The output power of solar cell directly depends on the efficiency of solar cell as shown in Figure 3.6.

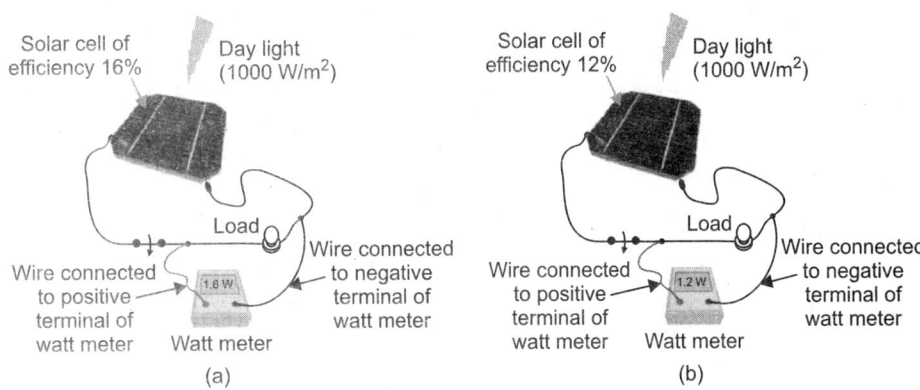

FIGURE 3.6

The effect of solar cells conversion efficiency on the output power for solar cell of 100 cm² area.

3.6.2
Change in the Amount of Input Light (P_{in})

We should keep in mind that the amount of sunlight (intensity of sunlight) falling on solar cells keeps changing from morning to evening. The current and voltage output of a solar cell depends on the amount of light falling on it. The electric current generated by solar cell is directly proportional to the amount of light falling on it. Suppose, a solar cell produce 1 A current under 1000 W/m² input solar radiation, then under 500 W/m² input solar radiation, the cell will only produce ½ A current (because input radiation is half). As the amount of sunlight falling on the solar cell increases from morning till afternoon, the current output of a solar cell also increases from morning till afternoon. From afternoon, till evening, the amount of sunlight falling on the solar cell decreases, and hence, the current output of a solar cell also decreases from afternoon till evening. The output voltage of a solar cell is not affected strongly by change in the amount of light. If a solar cell produces 1 V at noon time, its voltage will roughly remain same in the morning as well as in evening hours.

The solar cell current output is proportional to the amount of solar radiation and voltage is relatively not affected by the variation in sunlight intensity. Therefore, the amount of power generated (*Current × Voltage*) by solar cell is proportional to the amount of light falling on it. The amount of power generated by the solar cells throughout the day keeps changing (i.e., it is not constant). So, a solar cell gives high power when the intensity of light falling is high. Similarly, less power is generated when the intensity of light falling is low.

Large amount of light falling means high generated power, less amount of light falling means low generated power.

EXAMPLE 3.10

Calculate the output power for solar cells of efficiencies 16%. When the input power is say, 1000, 800, 600 and 400 W/m² and area of solar cell is 100 cm².

Solution

First we write formula for efficiency of a solar cell given by

$$\eta = \frac{P_{max}}{P_{in} \times A}$$

where,

η = Efficiency in per cent (%)

P_{max} = Output power in watt (W)

P_{in} = Light input power per unit area in watt/meter (W/m²)

A = Solar cell area in square metre (m²)

η = 16%

P_{in} = 1000, 800, 400 W/m²

P_{max} = ?

It is given that cell efficiency is 16% and cell area is A = 100 cm².

First, we convert area unit from square centimetre (cm^2) to square metre (m^2) by dividing area in cm^2 by 10000.

$$A = 100 \text{ cm}^2 = 100 \times 10^{-4} \text{ m}^2$$

Now, we solve for light input power = 1000 W/m^2

Above equation can be written as:

$$P_{max} = \eta \times P_{in} \times A$$

We put the respective terms values and we get,

$$P_{max} = \left(\frac{16}{100}\right) \times 1000 \times 100 \times 10^{-4} = 1.6 \text{ W}$$

Similarly, we calculate output power for other efficiencies in table form as shown in Table 3.8.

TABLE 3.8 Table for Example 3.10

η (%)	P_{in} (W/m^2)	A (cm^2)	A (m^2)	$\eta/100$	$P_{max} = (\eta/100) \times P_{in} \times A$ (W)
16	1000	100	0.01	0.16	1.60
16	800	100	0.01	0.16	1.28
16	600	100	0.01	0.16	0.96
16	400	100	0.01	0.16	0.64

A solar cell with double light power input will produce double electrical power output from same area.

The amount of power generated by solar cell depends on the amount of light falling on a solar cell is shown in Figure 3.7. From above table, it clear that when amount of light falling on a solar cell reduces, the output power generated also reduces.

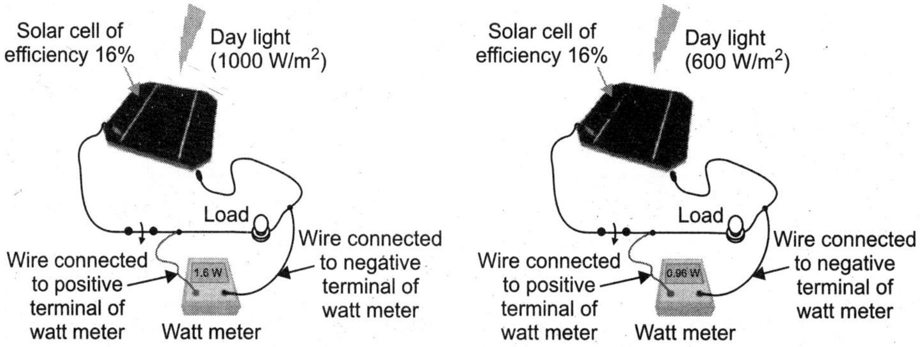

FIGURE 3.7
The effect of amount of light (light intensity) falling on solar cell on the output power for solar cell of 100 cm^2 area and 16% efficiency.

3.6.3
Change in Solar Cell Area (A)

The amount of maximum output current (I_{sc} or short circuit current) of a solar cells depends on the area of a solar cells. The current output is directly proportional to the cell area. So, when solar cell area is large, the amount of electric current generated by it will be large. Similarly, less amount of electric current will be generated when the cell area is small. For a given amount of input sunlight if 100 cm^2 cell produces 2 A current, then a 200 cm^2 cell will produce 4 A current, and a 50 cm^2 cell will produce 1 A current under same input sunlight intensity. When we divide the generated current by area of solar cells, we get current/area or current per unit area, which is also referred as current density. The current density is given in units of A/cm^2 or mA/cm^2. The current density of solar cell does not depend on area and for a given sunlight intensity the current density of solar cell is also fixed.

Current density (J_{sc}) of a solar cell is always fixed or constant.

Large solar cell area means high current, small solar cell area means low current.

The output voltage of solar cells does not change with the change in solar cell area (A). The output voltage is independent of cell area. Thus, at a given input sunlight intensity, if a 100 cm² cell produces 0.5 V, then cell of 100 cm², or 200 cm² or 50 cm² or 10 cm², etc. will produce same 0.5 V.

EXAMPLE 3.11

Calculate new value of output current for solar cells of area 20, 30, 50, 80 and 100 cm², when current density of cell is 35 mA/cm².

Solution

The current density of a solar cell is its current divided by cell area. The current density is given by the expression

$$\text{Current density } (J_{sc}) = \frac{I_{sc}}{A} \; (\text{mA/cm}^2)$$

Here, J_{sc} = 35 mA/cm²

So, the expression for the solar cell current can be written as:

$$\text{Output current } (I_{sc}) = J_{sc} \times A \; (\text{mA})$$

Now, say, the area of solar cell is 20 cm², then

$$\text{Output current } (I_{sc}) = 35 \text{ mA/cm}^2 \times 20 \text{ cm}^2 = 700 \text{ mA}$$

Similarly, we calculate output current for different values of solar cell area in the table form shown in Table 3.9.

TABLE 3.9 Table for Example 3.11

Current density J_{sc} (mA/cm²)	Solar cell area A (cm²)	Output Current $I_{sc} = J_{sc} \times A$ (mA)	Output Current I_{sc} (A)
35	20	700	0.70
35	30	1050	1.05
35	50	1750	1.75
35	80	2800	2.80
35	100	3500	3.50

So, from above table, it is clear that with increase in area of a solar cell, the amount of output current also increases. Figure 3.8 shows the effect of solar cell area on the amount of electric current generated by it.

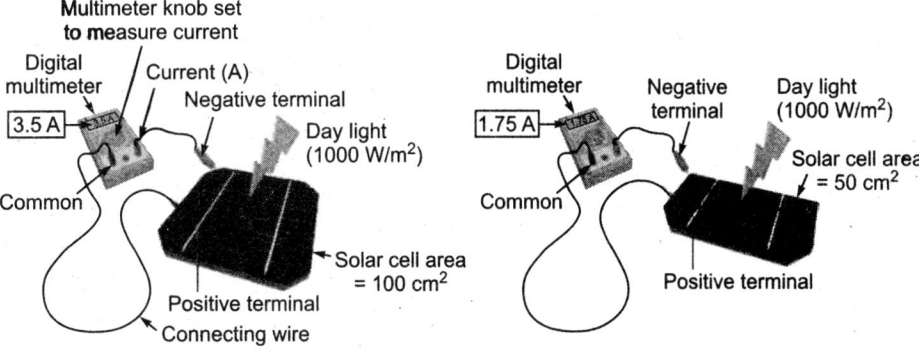

FIGURE 3.8
The effect of cell area on the output current for same light intensity and efficiency of the cell.

3.6.4
Change in Angle of Light Falling on Solar Cell (θ)

The angle of sunlight with respect to solar cell greatly affects the output power. Solar cell produces maximum power (for given light intensity) when sunlight falls perpendicular to the surface of solar cells. When the light does not perpendicular to solar cells, it always gives less output power than maximum possible output power. This is because when light falls at some angle, some part of light falling on solar cell is reflected. Hence, the actual light utilized by a solar cell is less than the amount of light falling on it. So, the output power generated is less when light is not falling perpendicular to solar cell as shown in Figure 3.9. Therefore, one should always try to install a solar cell or module in such a way that most of the time sunlight is close to perpendicular, especially in the afternoon time when the intensity of sunlight is high.

Light falling perpendicular to solar cell gives maximum output power.

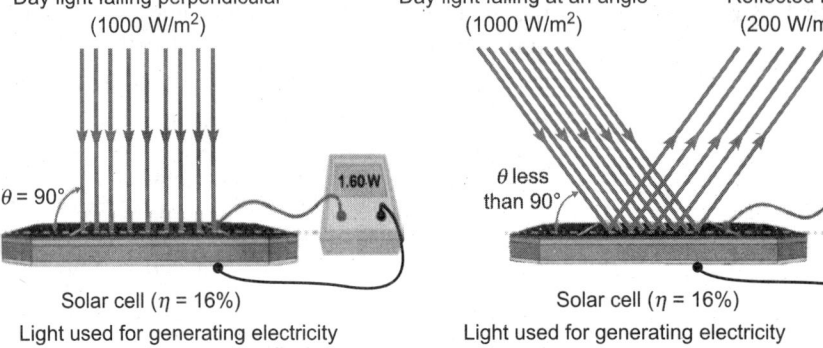

FIGURE 3.9
The effect of the angle of sunlight falling on a solar cells on output power of cells.

For any solar cell, the output voltage is always constant. It is independent of solar cell area, the amount and angle of light falling on solar cell.

3.6.5
Change in Solar Cell Operating Temperature (T)

The solar cells output voltage, power and efficiency ratings are given at standard test condition (STC = 1000 W/m² and 25°C). The cell output voltage, cell efficiency and output power depends on cell temperature. In practical applications, the operating temperature of solar cells may be different than 25°C. The cell temperature varies due to ambient temperature and in practice, the solar cells are encapsulated (in PV module) with glass which results in heating of solar cells. Due to encapsulation also solar cell temperature increases. The change in temperature from standard operating temperature directly affects the output voltage, efficiency and power. Normally, when a solar cell operates at temperature above 25°C temperature; the output voltage, cell efficiency and output power of a solar cell reduces.

The decrease in voltage, power and efficiency with temperature is different for different type of solar cells. For crystalline Si solar cells, for every 1°C increase in temperature above 25°C, the decrease in value of voltage, power and efficiency is given in Table 3.10.

TABLE 3.10 Decrease in Value of Parameters of Crystalline Silicon Solar Cells Per °C Rise in Cell Temperature from Standard Test Condition (STC) Value of 25°C

For a solar cell, higher temperature means lower power output.

For typical Silicon solar cell the output voltage decreases by 2.3 mV per degree centigrade increase in temperature.

Parameter of crystalline silicon solar cells	Decrease per °C rise in cell temperature from standard test condition (STC) value of 25°C
Voltage	−0.0023 V or −2.3 mV
Power	−0.45%
Efficiency	−0.45%

EXAMPLE 3.12

Solution

If the actual operating temperature of the solar cell is 40°C. The output voltage of a solar cell at standard operating temperature is, say 0.7 V. The output voltage decreases by 2.3 mV/°C. Calculate the new value of output voltage?

Let us consider, actual operating temperature = T_{actual} = 40°C

Standard operating temperature = $T_{standard}$ = 25°C

Output voltage decrease per degree Celsius = $V_{decrease}$ = 2.3 mV/°C

Output voltage at 25°C = V_{oc} (25°C) = 0.7 V

Output voltage at 40°C = V_{oc} (40°C) = ?

We know the solar cells output voltage reduces by some value when the temperature is above 25 °C.

So, the reduced output voltage = $V_{oc}(40\,°C) = V_{oc}(25\,°C) - (V_{decrease} \times \Delta T)$

$$\Delta T = T_{actual} - T_{standard}$$
$$= 40 - 25 = 15\,°C$$

Now, $\quad 0.7\,V - (2.3 \times 10^{-3}\,V/°C \times 15\,°C) = 0.7\,V - 0.0345\,V$
$$= 0.67\,V$$

So, from the above result, is clear that the solar cells output voltage decreases if operating temperature is above 25 °C. Figure 3.10 shows the change in the output voltage with the change in the operating temperature of a solar cell.

EXAMPLE 3.13

Efficiency of a crystalline silicon solar cell at STC is 15%. What would be its efficiency when cell operating temperature is 60 °C? Refer to Table 3.10.

Solution

It is given that the cell is a crystalline silicon cell,

The cell efficiency at STC is; $\eta(STC) = 15\%$,

The cell temperature at STC is 25 °C,

The operating temperature of the cell at which efficiency needs to be calculated is 60 °C, i.e. we need to calculate $\eta(60\,°C)$.

The difference in operating cell temperature and STC temperature,

$$\Delta T = 60 - 25 = 35\,°C.$$

Now considering Table 3.10, the decrease in peak power per degree centigrade is given but not for efficiency. It is safe to assume that the change in efficiency will be the same as change in peak power of the cell. Therefore, the change in efficiency (η) per degree centigrade rise in cell temperature from standard test condition (STC) value of 25°C is −45%.

Thus,

Cell efficiency at 60°C

= cell efficiency at STC − decrease in cell efficiency due to temperature

$$\eta(60\,°C) = \eta(STC) - 0.45\,\%/°C \text{ of } \eta(STC)$$
$$= \eta(STC) - 0.45\,\%/°C \times \eta(STC) \times \Delta T\,(°C)$$
$$= 15 - \frac{0.45}{100} \times 15 \times 35 = 15 - 2.36 = 12.63\%$$

It is clear from the above calculations that the cell efficiency decreases as the cell operating temperature increases. In practice, the ambient temperature can be higher than the value of temperature in STC. On top of that, in solar PV modules where cells are encapsulated, the cell temperature is normally higher than the ambient temperature. Thus, in most cases, in moderate to hot climate, cell efficiency is normally lower than the cell efficiency at STC, which means that the power generated by the cell is normally lower than power generated under STC.

In the above problem, the loss of efficiency due to increase in cell temperature was calculated. In the same way, the loss of generated power (peak power) of the cell with increase in cell temperature can be calculated.

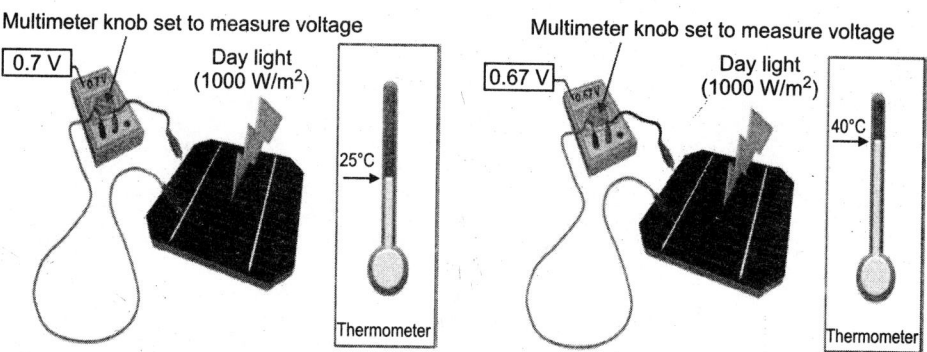

FIGURE 3.10
The effect of change in solar cell operating temperature on voltage output of a solar cell.

WORKSHEET 3.5: The maximum rated power point of a crystalline silicon solar cell is 2.5 W$_p$. Calculate the maximum power output at 45 °C, 55 °C, and 65 °C cell operating temperatures. For crystalline silicon cell decrease in maximum power per degree centigrade increase in cell temperature, (from STC value of 25 °C), is –0.45%/°C. Fill the sheet (Table 3.11).

Use following equation:

Actual P_{max} at cell operating temperature (watt)

$$= P_{max}(STC) - 0.45\,\%/°C \times P_{max}(STC) \times \Delta T\,(°C)$$

$$= P_{max}(STC) - \frac{0.45}{100} \times P_{max}(STC) \times \Delta T$$

TABLE 3.11 To Obtain Missing Quantities

Operating cell temperature (°C)	STC cell temperature (°C)	Different in temperature ΔT (°C)	P_{max} at STC (watt)	% decrease in power per °C rise in temperature	Decrease in cell power at operating temperature (watt)	Actual maximum power point at cell operating temperature (watt)
A	B	C	D	E	F = E × D × C	G = D – F
45	25	20	–	–0.45%	–	2.27
55	–	–	2.5	–	0.337	–
65	–	–	–	–0.45%	–	–

In Section 3.6, we have learned five factors affecting the power generated by solar cells. In addition to these factors, the material used for making any solar cells determines its properties and overall performance. In Chapter 4, we see the effect of different materials used for solar cells.

4
Solar PV Modules

A solar PV module is a collection of solar cells, mainly connected in series. These combinations of solar cells provide higher power than a single solar cell. The PV modules are available in the power rating range from 3 watt to 300 watt. They really form the basic building block of PV systems as power generating unit. With further connection of PV modules together, one can generate very large amount of power, in range of megawatt or MW. It is important to understand the making of a PV module. In this chapter, design PV modules, its parameters, calculation of PV module parameters and measurement of PV module parameters are discussed. Output of a PV module depends on ambient conditions, the temperature and solar radiation intensity. The PV module power variation with the ambient condition variation is also discussed.

4.1
What is a Solar PV Module?

A single solar cell can generate very less amount of power depending on the area of the cell. A single solar cell would generate power in range of a fraction of a watt (like 0.1 watt) to few watt (like 2 to 3 watt). But in practice, the power requirement by our loads, like fan, TV, refrigerator is in the range of several 100s of watts and sometimes more than 1000 watt or kilowatt (kW). When we talk about grid electricity and conventional power plants we talk about power in the range of millions of watts or MW. Therefore, a single solar cell is of no use for running the actual loads in home or supplying power to the electricity grid. We must generate solar PV power in large amounts, in several watts, kW and MW. In order to fulfill the high power requirements, the number of cells are connected together to make a Solar PV Module. In this way, the solar PV module is a device which can supply larger power, larger than what individual solar cell can supply.

A single solar cell is shown in Figure 4.1. It is shown to have typical shape of crystalline silicon solar cells, having lines across it which represent metal line of top contact. The cell is shown to have two terminals, a positive terminal and a negative terminal. When light falls on solar cells, voltage gets generated across these two terminals. In PV modules, many cells are connected together. The cells are connected in serial fashion, wherein positive terminal of one cell is connected to the negative terminal of the next cell and this is repeated to make a string of solar cells, or a solar PV module (shown in Figure 4.2).

A solar PV module is a device in which several solar cells are connected together to generate more power than a single solar cell.

FIGURE 4.1

A single solar cell.

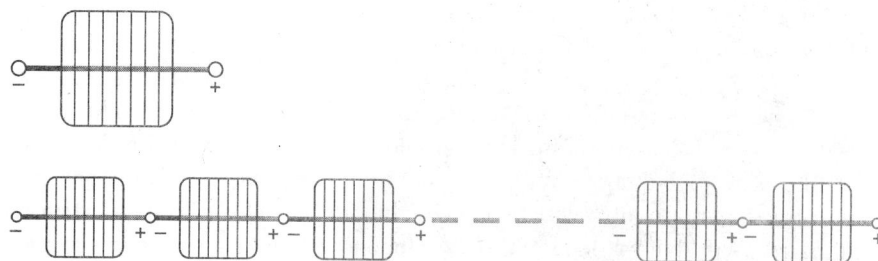

FIGURE 4.2

A single string of cells or PV module wherein many cells are connected together in series.

Voltage of cells strings connected in series

When we connect cells in series, we get a string of solar cells. The string of solar cells will also have two terminals. When we connect cells in series the voltage of solar cells gets added, therefore, the terminal voltage of a PV string (PV module) will be higher and equal to the sum of all the solar cells connected in series. Suppose, terminal voltage of a solar cell is 0.5 V under operating conditions (shown in Figure 4.3) and two such identical cells are connected in series, so, the terminal voltage of string of two solar cells will be 0.5 + 0.5 = 1 V. If 6 cells are connected in series, than terminal voltage of series of 6 cells will be 0.5 × 6 = 3 V (shown in Figure 4.3). If 36 solar cells are connected in series, then terminal voltage of series of 36 cells, or PV string of 36 cells will be 0.5 × 36 = 18 V.

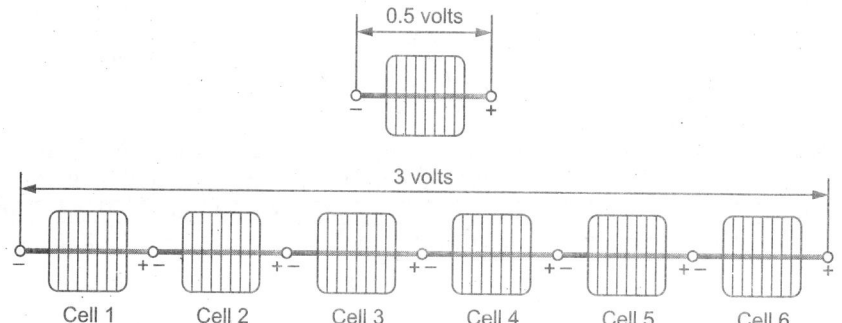

FIGURE 4.3

One cell and 6 cells in series.

EXAMPLE 4.1

Solution

When solar cells are connected in series the voltage of each cell adds up while the current in the series connected cells remain same as that of a single cell.

A solar cell has terminal voltage of 0.75 volt under operating condition. What will be the terminal voltage of a PV module in which 28 cells are connected in series?

It is given that the terminal voltage of an individual cell under operating condition is 0.75 volt.

Number of cells connected in series = 28

Total terminal voltage of the PV string of 28 cells or module = 28 × 0.75 = 21 volt.

Note: When we connect cells in series, voltage gets added and current remains nearly the same as that of individual cell and when we connect cells in parallel the current gets added but the voltage remain nearly same as that of a single cell.

4.2

Ratings of PV Module

The parameters of the solar PV modules (V_{oc}, I_{sc}, W_p), mentioned by the manufacturer are measured under some standard conditions of temperature (25°C) and solar radiation (1000 W/m^2). These test conditions are known as standard test conditions (STC). The testing condition of STC is summarized in Table 4.1.

The most important parameter of a PV module is its peak output power. The Solar PV modules are rated in terms of their peak power (W_p) output. It is the most important parameter from a user point of view. The W_p is specified by the manufacturer under so-called standard test conditions (STC). The module rating under STC is widely accepted by the manufacturers and by the users.

Table 4.1 PV Module Testing Parameter Under Standard Test Conditions (STC)

Test parameters	Values	Remarks
Solar input radiation	1000 W/m²	This solar radiation is corresponding to the condition when solar radiation travels 1.5 times the thickness of the earth's atmosphere. Therefore, this radiation value is called Air Mass 1.5, and also referred as AM1.5 global solar radiation.
Temperature	25°C	This is cell temperature in the PV modules and not the PV module surface temperature. Normally, cell's temperature in a PV module is much higher than PV module's surface temperature.
Wind speed	1 m/s	The flow of winds cools the PV module and that is why sometimes wind speed is also specified.

Departure from STC

The conditions specified in the STC do not occur for most of the time and locations. This happens mainly because of two reasons; the real solar irradiation is normally less than 1000 W/m² and the module temperature under real operation is more than the STC specified temperature of 25°C. Both of these reasons result in lower module power output than the expected under the STC condition. The variation in output power of PV module with variation in input solar radiation and temperature is discussed in detail in Section 4.3.

4.3
Standard PV Module Parameters

A PV module is made up of many cells connected together, and the electrical behaviour of PV module is similar to PV cells. Therefore, the PV module parameters are also similar to solar cell parameters. In Chapter 3, solar cell parameters have been discussed, which include; open circuit voltage (V_{oc}), short circuit current (I_{sc}), maximum power point (P_m), voltage at maximum power point (V_m), current at maximum power point (I_m), fill factor (FF) and efficiency (η) of the cells. A solar PV module also has same set of parameters. Most of the times all above parameters are mentioned in the datasheet of the modules supplied by a manufacturer. These electrical parameters of the PV modules are discussed here with the help of current-voltage curve or *I-V* curve and power-voltage curve or *P-V* curve.

4.3.1
I-V and *P-V* Characteristic of SPV Module

The *I-V* characteristic of a SPV module is a graph of current (I) and voltage (V) in which values of different current for different voltages is plotted on Y-axis and X-axis respectively. A typical *I-V* curve of a PV module is shown in Figure 4.4. A *P-V* curve is plotted between power of a PV module on Y-axis and voltage of a PV module on X-axis. A typical *P-V* curve of a PV module is shown in Figure 4.4.

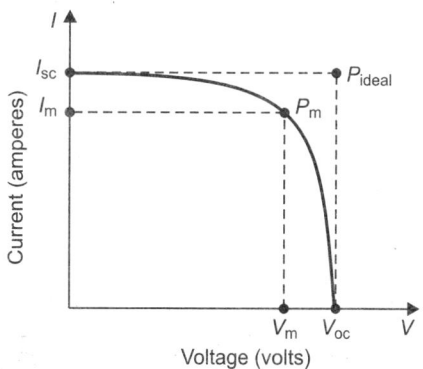

FIGURE 4.4

A typical *I-V* curve of a solar PV module.

Short circuit current (I_{sc})

It is the maximum current a solar PV module can produce. It happens when two terminals of a PV module is shorted, hence the name short circuit current. For a given solar cell area used in module, the higher the I_{sc}, the better is the PV module. It is measured in ampere (A). The value of this maximum current depends on PV module technology, PV module area, the amount of solar radiation falling on PV module, angle of PV module with respect to the sun's rays, etc. Many times, people

Short circuit current is the maximum current that a solar PV module can produce under STC.

are given current density rather than current. The current density is obtained by dividing the I_{sc} by the area of solar PV module (A). The current density is normally referred by symbol, 'J', therefore, the short circuit current density, J_{sc} is given by I_{sc}/A.

Open circuit voltage (V_{oc})

Open circuit voltage is maximum voltage that a solar PV module can produce under STC.

It is the maximum voltage that solar PV modules produce. It happens when two terminals of the PV module left open, and hence name is open circuit voltage. For a given number of cells in series in a PV module, higher the V_{oc} better is the PV module. It is measured in Volts (V). The value this maximum open circuit voltage mainly depends on PV module technology and operating temperature.

Maximum power point (P_m or P_{max})

It is the maximum power that a solar PV module produces under STC. For a given PV module dimensions, the higher the P_m, the better is the PV module. It is given in terms of watt (W). Since it is maximum power or peak power, it is sometimes also referred as W_{peak} or W_p. A solar PV module can operate at many current and voltage combinations. But a solar PV module will produce maximum power only when operating at certain current and voltage. This can be seen from the *P-V* curve of a PV module shown in Figure 4.5. In Figure 4.5, the power axis is corresponding to current axis in *I-V* curve of module (Figure 4.4). For comparison, *I-V* curve of the module is shown as dotted line on the *P-V* curve. Figure 4.5 indicates that at small voltages and current power output of a PV module is small. As the voltage increases, the power output increases and reaches a peak value corresponding to I_m and V_m of a PV module. This maximum power point is denoted in Figure 4.5 as P_m. If a PV module operates at voltage higher than V_m, the module output power decreases again (due to decrease in current) and at open circuit voltage (V_{oc}), PV module power decreases to zero. Normally, the maximum power point for *I-V* curve of the solar PV modules occurs at the 'knee' or 'bend' of the curve. In terms of expression, P_m is given as:

The maximum power point is the maximum power that a solar PV module can produce under STC. This peak power is written as W_p.

$$P_m \text{ or } P_{max} = I_m \times V_m \qquad (4.1)$$

FIGURE 4.5

A typical *P-V* curve of a solar PV module. For comparison, *I-V* curve is also shown as dotted line on the same graph. A solar PV module must operate at P_m (and corresponding voltage and current) to get maximum power output.

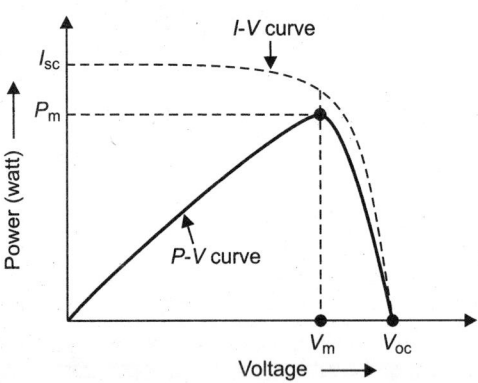

Please note here that W_p or P_m or P_{max} is the maximum power output under standard test condition. The maximum PV module power output P_{max} is obtained only when solar PV module operates at certain current (I_m) and voltage (V_m) in STC solar radiation condition of 1000 W/m². If PV module operates at any other combination of current and voltage under STC, we will not get the maximum possible output power from the PV module as shown in Table 4.2. Similarly, at solar radiation condition other than STC (solar radiation lower than 1000 W/m²), there will be only one combination of current and voltage at which the PV module output power will be maximum (but lower than W_p under STC). Thus, there exists a maximum power point corresponding to each input solar radiation condition, and not only for STC condition.

TABLE 4.2 Measured Current-voltage Data Points of a PV Module Corresponding to Figure 4.6

S. No.	Current (A)	Voltage (V)	Power (W)
1	1	2.5	$P_1 = 2.4$
2	0.9	6	$P_2 = 5.4$
3	0.85	13.5	$P_3 = 11.475$
4	0.65	15	$P_4 = 9.75$
5	0.45	16	$P_5 = 7.2$

Current at maximum power point (I_m)

This is the current which solar PV module will produce when operating at maximum power point. Sometimes, people write I_m as I_{mp} or I_{mpp}. The I_m will always be lower than I_{sc}. It is given in terms of A. Normally, I_m is equal to about 90% to 95% of the I_{sc} of the module.

Voltage at maximum power point (V_m)

This is the voltage which solar PV module will produce when operating at maximum power point. The V_m will always be lower than V_{oc}. Sometimes, people write V_m as V_{mp} or V_{mpp}. It is given in terms of V. Normally, V_m is equal to about 80% to 85% of the V_{oc} of the PV module.

Fill factor (FF)

As the name suggests, the FF is the ratio of the areas covered by I_m-V_m rectangle with area covered by I_{sc}-V_{oc} rectangle (both shown by dotted line in Figure 4.4). It indicates the squareness of the I-V curve. The higher the FF, the better is the PV module. The FF of PV module is given in terms of percentage (%). PV module with squared I-V curve is a better PV module.

$$\text{FF} = \frac{I_m \times V_m}{I_{sc} \times V_{oc}} \quad \text{or} \quad \text{FF} = \frac{P_m}{I_{sc} \times V_{oc}} \tag{4.2}$$

Here, the expression for P_{max} or P_m can alternatively be written in terms of I_{sc}, V_{oc} and FF as:

$$P_m = I_{sc} \times V_{oc} \times \text{FF} \tag{4.3}$$

Efficiency (η)

The efficiency of a solar PV module is defined as the maximum output power (P_m or P_{max}) divided by the input power (P_{in}). The efficiency of a PV module is given in terms of percentage (%), means that this percentage of radiation input power is converted into electrical power. P_{in} for STC is considered as 1000 W/m². This input power is power density (power divided by area), therefore, in order to calculate the efficiency using P_{in} at STC, we must multiply by the solar PV module area. Thus, efficiency can be written as:

$$\eta = \frac{P_m}{P_{in}} = \frac{I_{sc} \times V_{oc} \times \text{FF}}{P_{in} \times A} \tag{4.4}$$

PV module efficiency determines the power output per unit area. Higher efficiency means higher power output from the same area.

A module manufacturer provides most of the above module parameters in the form of their datasheets.

EXAMPLE 4.2

A solar PV module is fabricated using 36 solar cells of 155 cm² connected in series. The cells have 35 mA/cm² current density at Standard Test Condition (STC). Estimate the maximum current produced by the module at STC.

Solution

It is given that all the solar cells are connected in series, therefore, current generated by one solar cell will be the current flowing in the string of 36 solar cells, which will be the current of the PV module. Therefore, in order to calculate the module current, we must calculate the maximum current (I_{sc} at STC) of one solar cell. Current density of a solar cell is given by

$$\text{Current density } (J_{sc}) = \frac{I_{sc}}{A} \text{ (A/m}^2)$$

where,

J_{sc} = Current density (A/m^2)

I_{sc} = Output current (A)

A = Area (cm^2)

It is given that J_{sc} = 35 mA/cm^2, and cell area is 155 cm^2.

So, the expression for solar cell current can be written as,

$$\text{Output current } (I_{sc}) = J_{sc} \times A = 0.035 \text{ A/cm}^2 \times 155 \text{ cm}^2 = 5.42 \text{ A}$$

Thus, the maximum PV module current, that is I_{sc} (at STC) will be 5.41 A.

EXAMPLE 4.3

A small PV module having an area of 0.094 m^2 gives a current of 0.71 A and voltage of 16.5 V at maximum power point under STC. What is the maximum power point of the SPV module? Also, find out the efficiency.

Solution

First, we write formula for the maximum power point of a solar cell given by expression

$$P_m \text{ or } P_{max} = I_m \times V_m$$

Given that, I_m = 0.71 A

$$V_m = 16.5 \text{ V}$$

Therefore, maximum power point, P_m = 0.71 A × 16.5 V = 11.71 W

Now, we write formula for efficiency of a solar cell given by the expression

$$\eta = \frac{P_{max}}{P_{in} \times A}$$

where,

η = Efficiency in per cent (%)

P_{max} = Output power in watt (W)

P_{in} = Light input power per unit area in watt/square metre (W/m^2)

A = Solar cell area in square meter (m^2)

η = ?

We know, P_m = 10.06 W and at STC, P_{in} = 1000 W/m^2

Now, we solve for efficiency,

$$\eta = \frac{P_{max}}{P_{in} \times A}$$

$$\eta = \left(\frac{11.71}{1000 \times 0.0945} \right) \times 100 = 12.39\%$$

Note: We need to multiply FF and Efficiency with 100 in order to present the result in percentage.

Reading PV module parameters from I-V curve

In the preceding sections, the parameters of solar PV modules are defined using *I-V* and *P-V* curves. Therefore, if we have measured *I-V* curve of a PV module, we should be able to extract all parameters of PV module. A measured *I-V* curve of a crystalline Si PV module of 0.1 square metre area is given in Figure 4.6 and the measured data points (P_1, P_2, P_3, P_4, P_5) are given in Table 4.2.

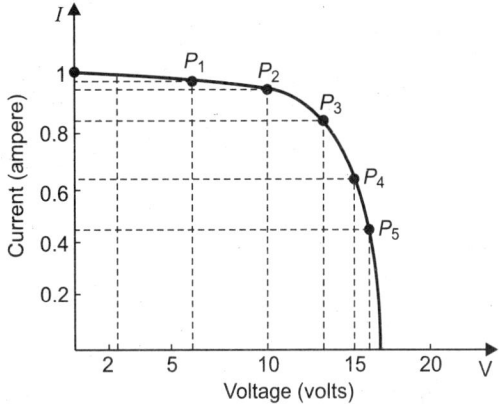

FIGURE 4.6

Measured *I-V* curve of a solar PV module of 0.1 m² PV module.

PV modules parameters can be extracted from *I-V* curve of a PV module.

- From Figure 4.6 and Table 4.2, estimate the main parameters of solar PV module.
- Short circuit current (I_{sc}): At 0 V (short circuit), the current of a module is 1 A (from Figure 4.6), therefore, I_{sc} = 1 A.
- Open circuit voltage (V_{oc}): At 0 A (open circuit), the voltage of the module is about 18 volt, therefore, V_{oc} = 18 V.
- Maximum power point (P_m): From Table 4.2, the value of maximum power is 11.47 watt.
- Current at maximum power point (I_m): From Table 4.2, the current at maximum power point is 0.85 A.
- Voltage at maximum power point (V_m): From Table 4.2, the voltage at maximum power point is 13.5 V.
- Fill factor (FF): It can be calculated using the expression for FF:

$$\text{FF} = \frac{I_m \times V_m}{I_{sc} \times V_{oc}} = \frac{0.85 \times 13.5}{1 \times 18} = 63.4\%$$

- Efficiency (η): It can be calculated from the given parameters.

$$\eta = \frac{P_m}{P_{in}} = \frac{I_{sc} \times V_{oc} \times \text{FF}}{P_{in} \times A}$$

Here, the P_{in} is input power corresponding to STC, which is 1000 W/m². Thus, feeding the parameters in above equation, we get.

$$\eta = \frac{1 \times 18 \times 63.4}{1000 \times 0.1} = 11.41\%$$

In this way, one can estimate all parameters of PV module from its *I-V* curve.

WORKSHEET 4.1: Comment on the values of V_{oc}, FF and Efficiency of the PV module given in Figure 4.6 (whether the values are as per your expectations, smaller or larger, etc.)

Comments:

_____

_____

_____

_____

_____

_____

_____

4.3.2
How Many Cells in Module?

The module manufacturing technology was developed aggressively in the 1980s. At that time, the PV modules were designed for charging batteries of 12 V terminal voltages. Therefore, one of the module's requirements is to provide the sufficient voltage to be able to charge 12 V batteries under typical daily solar radiation. Now, voltage source will be able to charge battery if the source voltage is higher than the battery voltage. It means that the module voltage, under daily radiation conditions should be higher than the battery voltage. Generally, it is expected that the PV module must provide about 15 volts (or around this value) in all operating conditions, meaning low solar radiation (like in morning and evening) and high temperatures (like in summer).

PV module design for 12 V battery level has now become standard. For large power module, the design is done for 24 V battery level (two batteries in series), 36 V battery level (three batteries in series), etc. or, we can say the PV modules are designed to provide voltages in a multiple of 12 V battery level, that is 12 V, 24 V, 36 V, 48 V, etc. We must note here that for 12 V batteries voltage level, PV module (V_m) should be around 15 V, and for 24 V battery voltage level, PV module voltage should be around 30 V. Similarly, for 36 V battery voltage level, PV module voltage should be around 45 V. Also, note here that when we refer to the module voltage level, we refer to the module voltage at maximum power point. Table 4.3 shows the possible voltage level of batteries and corresponding voltage levels of PV modules. Considering this, the other electronics devices used in PV system also follow the similar voltage levels. For instance, charge controller, MPPT and inverter are designed in such a way that they can take input voltage in multiples of 12 V, i.e., 12 V, 24 V, 36 V, etc. battery voltage levels or 15 V, 30 V, 45 V, etc. PV module voltage level (V_m).

> PV modules and other electronic devices, used in PV system, are compatible to work with voltage levels multiple of 12 V, like 12 V, 24 V, 36 V (battery voltage level) and 15 V, 30 V, 45 V, etc. for PV module voltage level.

TABLE 4.3 Voltage Levels for Combination of Batteries and Corresponding Voltage Level (V_m) Required from Combination of PV Modules

Battery voltage (single battery or series combination of batteries)	Corresponding PV module voltage levels, at maximum power point condition (single module or series combination of modules)
12 V	15 V
24 V	30 V
36 V	45 V
48 V	60 V

Since single solar cell provides smaller voltage, it is required to connect many solar cells in series to get higher PV module voltage to charge a battery. As mentioned earlier, there are different technologies of Solar PV cells. Depending upon each technology, the number of cells to be connected in series is decided. The decision of 'how many cells to connect in series in a PV module' is determined by V_{oc}

of the cell. V_{oc} of a single solar cell for various solar cell technologies has been mentioned in Table 3.4 in Chapter 3.

For crystalline silicon solar cell technology, required voltage for charging 12 V battery can be obtained by the series connection of 36 solar cells. Why 36 cells in series? Commercial Si solar cells generally have a V_m of about 0.5 volts at 25 °C. We also know that due to higher operational temperature (higher than specified by STC, 25°C), the voltages (V_m and V_{oc}) decrease. The solar cell under encapsulation operates at higher temperature resulting in loss of voltage (as discussed in Chapter 3) by about 0.08 V.

Thus available cell terminal voltage

$$V_m = V_m \text{ (STC)} - \text{loss of voltage due to higher temperature}$$
$$= 0.50 - 0.08 = 0.42 \text{ V}$$

Now, we want about 15 volt module output voltage in all conditions, and each solar cell will give us about 0.42 V. Now, in order to calculate number of cells to be connected in series, required voltage must be divided by possible operating voltage from one cell.

$$\text{Number of cell in series} = \frac{15}{0.42} = 35.71 \text{ or approximately 36 cells.}$$

> Number of cells to be connected in series in PV modules depends on the output voltage requirement of the module. Typically, a PV module should provide enough output voltage to charge a 12 V battery (or other battery) in all operating conditions.

Note: Estimation of the number of cells in a module depends on the V_m and loss of voltage due to temperature, both of these depend on the cell technology. Thus, with the technology, the number of cells to be connected in series to get desired voltage can change. If V_m (STC) is higher, we need less number of solar cells in series and if V_m (STC) is lower, we need more number of solar cells in series to get desired operating voltage.

A schematic diagram and actual photograph of a typical crystalline Si PV module having 36 cells is connected in series is shown in Figure 4.7. The symbol of module is given in Figure 4.8 and it shows positive and negative terminals, peak power, and current and voltage at peak power.

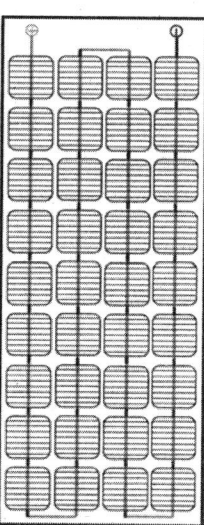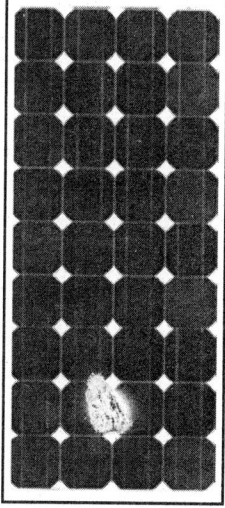

FIGURE 4.7

Schematic diagram and actual photograph of a crystalline silicon PV module having 36 cells connected in series.

In this way, one can estimate the number of cells in series for any PV module voltage requirement and for any PV technology.

Nowadays, solar PV modules are also available to charge 6 V and 3 V batteries. Since the battery terminal voltage is lower, the module voltage requirement will also be lower and the number of cells one must connect in series will also be lower.

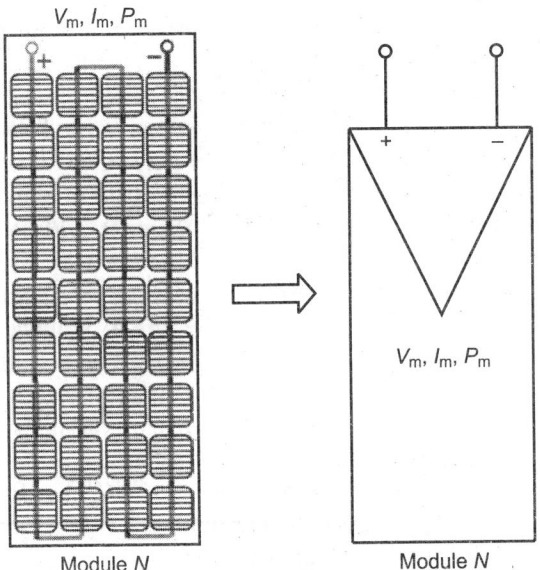

V_m, I_m, P_m

Module N Module N

FIGURE 4.8

Typical module representation.

Procedure to estimate or design number of cells in a module

Thus, in order to estimate the number of cells in a PV module, one can use following steps:

Step 1: Find out the V_m (at STC) of a solar cell of given technology (if V_m is not given, it can be estimated by V_{oc}); the PV module parameters V_m and V_{oc} are discussed in the next section.

Step 2: Find out loss of voltage (loss of V_m) under operating conditions.

> The solar cell voltage decreases with temperature. Loss of voltage of solar cell should be taken into account in order to estimate number of cells to be connected in series in a PV module.

Step 3: Available voltage at operating conditions = V_m(STC) – Loss of voltage.

Step 4: Note down the required PV module voltage.

Step 5: Divide the required module voltage by available operating voltage to get the number of cells connected in series.

EXAMPLE 4.4

A PV module of new solar cell technology is to be designed to charge a battery of 12 V. The V_{oc} and V_m of the cell of new technology under STC are 0.90 and 0.80 respectively. The cell's voltage decreases by 1 mV every degree centigrade rise in temperature. How many cells should be connected in series in this PV module, if cell temperature under operation is 60°C. Make a drawing of PV module with this new technology.

Solution

Let us estimate the number of cells as per the procedure given above.

Following parameters are given:

V_m of new solar cell = 0.80 volt

Battery voltage = 12 V

Cell operating temperature = 60°C

Per degree centigrade decrease in voltage = 1 mV or 0.001 V

Step 1: Find out the V_m (at STC) of a solar cell of given technology V_m (at STC) = 0.8 V.

Note: If V_m is not given, it can be estimated using V_{oc}, typically, V_m is about 80% to 85% of V_{oc} for all technologies.

Step 2: Find out loss of voltage (loss of V_m) under operating conditions.

The temperature corresponding to STC is 25 °C, the cell is operating at 60 °C, therefore, the cell is operating 60 – 25 = 35 °C above STC.

Loss in voltage per degree centigrade rise in temperature is 0.001 V,

Therefore, loss of voltage due to 35°C rise in temperature = 0.001 × 35 = 0.035 volt

Step 3: Available voltage at operating conditions = V_m(STC) – Loss of voltage

Available voltage at operating conditions = 0.8 – 0.035 = 0.765 V

Step 4: Note down the required PV module voltage.

The battery to be charged is 12 V, therefore, the PV module voltage in all operating conditions should be about 15 V.

Required PV module voltage = 15 V

Step 5: Divide the required module voltage by available operating voltage to get number of cells connected in series.

Number of new type of cells to be connected in series = $\dfrac{15}{0.765}$

$$= 19.6 \text{ or about } 20 \text{ cells.}$$

Thus, 20 new type of cells must be connected in series to get sufficient voltage to charge 12 V battery in all operational conditions (draw 20 cells connected in the series in space shown below).

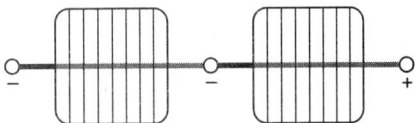

EXAMPLE 4.5

A manufacturer using advanced crystalline silicon cell technology produces the solar cells with V_{oc} of 0.620 V and V_m of 0.510 V at STC. Cell temperature reaches to about 60 °C in operating conditions. The modules are designed to connect in grid connected PV plant. If required operating voltage of module is 13.5 V, then estimate the number of cells to be connected in series.

Solution

Let us estimate the number of cells as per the procedure given above.

Following parameters are given:

V_m of new solar cell = 0.510 volt

Cell operating temperature = 60°C

Per degree centigrade decrease of voltage for crystalline silicon cell = 0.0023 V

Step 1: Find out the V_m (at STC) of a solar cell of given technology.

$$V_m \text{ (at STC)} = 0.510 \text{ V}$$

Note: If V_m is not given, it can be estimated using V_{oc}, typically V_m is about 80% to 85% of V_{oc} for all technologies.

Step 2: Find out loss of voltage (loss of V_m) under operating conditions.

The temperature corresponding to STC is 25 °C, the cell is operating at 60 °C, therefore, the cell is operating (60 – 25) °C = 35 °C above the STC.

Loss in voltage per degree centigrade rise in temperature is 0.0023 V.

Therefore, loss of voltage due to 35 °C rise in temperature is = 0.0023 × 35 = 0.080 volt.

A PV module designed to charge 12 V battery must provide about 14 V to 15 V in all operating conditions.

A PV modules made of solar cells of different technologies will have different number of cells connected in series (as compared to crystalline Si PV module) to get same output voltage levels.

Step 3: Available voltage at operating conditions = V_m (STC) – Loss of voltage
Available voltage at operating conditions = 0.510 – 0.080 = 0.430 V

Step 4: Note down the required PV module voltage.
Required PV module voltage = 13.5 V (given)

Step 5: Divide the required module voltage by available operating voltage to get number of cells connected in series.

Number of new type of cells to be connected in series = $\dfrac{13.5}{0.430}$ = 31.39 or about 32 cells.

Thus, in this case, only 32 cells must be connected in series to get sufficient voltage.

Note: Sometime when we need to get higher output voltage from a PV module, higher than 15 V or so, we need to connect more cells in series. When we need lower output voltage we connect fewer cells in series. These days high power modules (more than 100 W_p) with 60 to 70 cells connected in series are also available in the market. Sometime less wattage modules (<10 W_p) will have only 18 cells in series.

> A crystalline silicon PV module will have about 32 to 36 cells connected in series for 12 V batteries, and about 60 to 72 cells for 24 V batteries charging level.

4.3.3
Estimating or Designing Wattage of a PV Module

Wattage of PV module is one of the most important parameter from user perspective. When a user buy a PV module from a market, the cost of the PV module is given in terms of Wattage that a PV module can generate. Normally, the PV module output power changes with the solar radiation intensity, which changes throughout the day, therefore, all manufacturers rate the PV module power output under one certain condition, which is known as Standard Test Condition (STC). The STC is corresponding to 1000 W/m^2 of solar radiation at 25 °C of cell temperature. Under this condition, if the PV module is operating at maximum power point, the output power of the module is known as 'Peak power' and written as watt$_{peak}$ or W_p. Normally, the solar radiation intensity is lower than 1000 W/m^2 and cell temperature under operation is higher than 25 °C; both of these effects decreases the power output of module. Thus, in almost all operating condition, the actual output power of PV module is less than the rated peak power or W_p of PV module given by manufacturer. Anyway, the question is how to estimate the peak power or W_p of a PV module?

The output power of a PV module depends on the voltage and current at which the module is operating. As discussed earlier, if the module operates at current I_m and voltage V_m, then the power generated (P_m) by the PV module is maximum. The estimation of V_m of the module is discussed already in Section 4.3.1 of this chapter. Let us now learn to estimate the I_m of a PV module. In Chapter 3 about solar cells, it is mentioned that the current generated by a solar cell depends on area of the cell. Smaller area solar cell produce small current and large area solar cell produces large current. A parameter called current density, which is current divided by area, is independent of the cell area. In chapter 3, Table 3.4, the typical current density of solar cells of different technology is given. For instance, for crystalline silicon solar cell technology, the current densities (J_{sc}) of commercial cells are in range of 30 to 35 mA/cm^2 (given under STC), and the size of solar cells can vary from small 5 cm^2 cells to large 225 cm^2 cells. Thus, knowing cell area and current density of cell of given technology, we can estimate the current that a cell produces under STC condition, that is, $J_{sc} \times A$, and this current will be nothing but I_{sc}.

> Wattage of a PV module depends on the current and voltage of a PV module at peak power condition.
>
> Total current produced by a solar cell is obtained by multiplying the current density of a cell with its area. Current density of cell depends on a technology and manufacturer. For the same technology cells, large area cells produce more current.

In the module, since cells are connected in series, normally, in the module designed for 12 volt operation, the current produced by a single solar cell is the current of the PV module. Thus, if a large area cell is producing 5 A (I_{sc}) current, if there are 36 identical cells connected in series, the I_{sc} of the PV module will also be 5 A.

EXAMPLE 4.6

A manufacturer of crystalline silicon solar cell guarantees 33 mA/cm^2 current density of his solar cells. If the cell area is 144 cm^2, then estimate the I_{sc} of solar cell.

Solution

It is given that:

Cell area is = 144 cm^2

Current density J_{sc} = 33 mA/cm^2 or 0.033 A/cm^2

Therefore,

$$I_{sc} = J_{sc} \times A$$
$$= 33 \text{ mA/cm}^2 \times 144 \text{ cm}^2$$
$$= 0.033 \text{ A/cm}^2 \times 144 \text{ cm}^2 = 4.75 \text{ A}$$

EXAMPLE 4.7

A manufacturer of cadmium telluride solar cell guarantees 25 mA/cm^2 current density of his solar cells. If the cell area is 100 cm^2, then estimate the I_{sc} of solar cell.

Solution

From the above calculation, one can estimate the I_{sc} of the module. But in order to calculate the P_m of the module, we need to estimate I_m. Normally, I_m is equal to about 90% to 95% of the I_{sc} of the module, and normally V_m is equal to about 80% to 85% of the V_{oc} of the PV module.

EXAMPLE 4.8

A cell mentioned in Section 4.1 is used to make a solar PV module wherein 36 cells are connected in series. The PV module has the V_m of 15 volt. Estimate the P_m of the module.

Solution

It is given that:

V_m of the module: 15 volt

I_{sc} of single cell = 4.75 A

Assuming that I_m = 95% of I_{sc} = 0.95 × 4.75 = 4.51 A

Thus, the P_m of the module will be:

$$P_m = I_m \times V_m = 4.51 \times 15$$
$$= 67.7 \text{ watt}$$

WORKSHEET 4.2: Some PV module parameters are given in Table 4.4. Fill in the blanks by estimating the other PV module parameters. Assume $V_m = 0.85 \times V_{oc}$ and $I_m = 0.93 \times I_{sc}$. All the parameters are given at STC.

TABLE 4.4 PV Modules Parameters

V_{oc} (volts)	V_m (volts)	I_{sc} (ampere)	I_m (ampere)	Cell area (cm^2)	P_m (watt)
21	–	5.0	–	145	–
–	13.5	2.0	–	55	–
–	14.5	–	0.8	30	–
19	–	–	1.5	50	–
–	14.2	–	3.2	100	–
–	15	5.7	–	160	–

Problem 4.1: A *I-V* curve of PV module is given in Figure 4.9. Read and note down in Table 4.5 the main parameters of PV module from the graph (Figure 4.9). Write down appropriate units of the parameter as well.

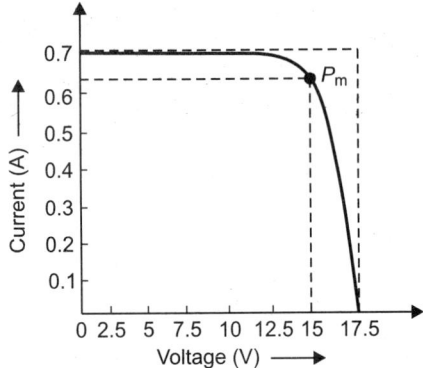

FIGURE 4.9

I-V curve of a PV module.

TABLE 4.5 Table of Problem 4.1

S. No.	Parameters	Reading or calculating from Figure 4.9	Values of parameter	Unit of parameter
1	Short circuit current (I_{sc})	Current value when voltage is zero		
2	Open circuit voltage (V_{oc})	Voltage value when current is zero		
3	Maximum power point, (P_m)	Value of maximum power		
3	Current at maximum power point (I_m)	Current value at maximum power point		
4	Voltage at maximum power point (V_m)	Voltage value at maximum power point		
5	Fill factor (FF)	$= \dfrac{I_m \times V_m}{I_{sc} \times V_{oc}}$		
6	Efficiency (η)	$= \dfrac{V_{oc} \times I_{sc} \times FF}{P_{in} \times A}$		

WORKSHEET 4.3: Current and voltage of a PV module is measured at various operating points. Estimate the power that can be produced at each operating point. Using these calculations, fill the solar PV module parameter in Table 4.6.

TABLE 4.6 To Obtain Power

S. No.	Current I (A)	Voltage V (V)	Power P (W) = I × V
1	0	37.72	—
2	0.25	37.58	—
3	0.44	37.15	—
4	0.46	37.04	—
5	0.53	36.77	—
6	0.60	36.53	—
7	0.69	35.97	—
8	0.86	35.02	—
9	1.06	33.77	—
10	1.37	29.32	—
11	1.48	16.73	—
12	1.50	00.00	—

The solar PV module parameters can be extracted from the table of Current-Voltage points measured between short circuit conditions to open circuit condition.

Fill in the parameter of PV module (Table 4.7) using the measured I-V points given in Table 4.6.

TABLE 4.7 Parameters of PV Modules

S. No.	Parameters	Values of parameter	Unit of parameter
1	Short circuit current (I_{sc})		
2	Open circuit voltage (V_{oc})		
3	Maximum power point, P_m		
4	Current at maximum power point (I_m)		
5	Voltage at maximum power point (V_m)		
6	Fill factor (FF)		
7	Efficiency		

4.4
Factors Affecting Electricity Generated by a Solar PV Module

Let us now discuss how in practical applications the PV module power output varies with variation in ambient conditions like temperature, solar radiation, angle of sunrays, etc. The change in PV module parameter output power with change in ambient condition is important to understand. This will be useful in estimating the possible generation of electricity using solar PV modules and possible performance of PV systems in a given condition.

There are five common factors affecting the power generated by solar modules. These factors are listed below and discussed in detail in the following sections:

1. The conversion efficiency (η)
2. The amount of light (P_{in})
3. The operating temperature (T)
4. The solar cell area (A), and
5. The angle at which day light falls (θ)

4.4.1
Effect of Conversion Efficiency (η)

The modules consist of several cells electrically interconnected to each other in series or/and parallel. A solar cell converts some fraction of light energy falling on it into electrical energy. In this way, a PV module also converts only some portion of the total light falling on it into electrical energy. The ratio of electrical energy generated to the input light energy is referred as conversion efficiency of PV modules. The efficiency of modules is always less than the efficiency of solar cells used in it.

All solar cells used in PV modules may not be perfectly identical, that is, all the parameters of solar cells may not be exactly identical. Difference in solar cells used in PV modules results in less power generation when connected in modules (as compared to the case when all cells work individually, as discussed in Section 4.1). Also, the module area is always larger than the total cells area as the spacing area between the cells is considered (shown in Figure 4.10). The area considered for the calculation of efficiency affects the conversion efficiency. The conversion efficiency of module basically depends on the solar cells used and the method used for interconnecting them. In a module, the cells can be inter-connected in series or parallel combination. Once a module is assembled, its efficiency value becomes fixed and it generally does not change.

The efficiency of a module is given in terms of maximum power (P_{max}) or peak power (P_m) that module can generate for a given input solar radiation. The P_{max} output or P_m output of module depends on voltage developed across module terminal and current it can supply. In a module, the type of cells inter-connection greatly affects the output power. If the instantaneous solar radiation or power density is P_{in}, the expression for the efficiency (η) of module can be given as:

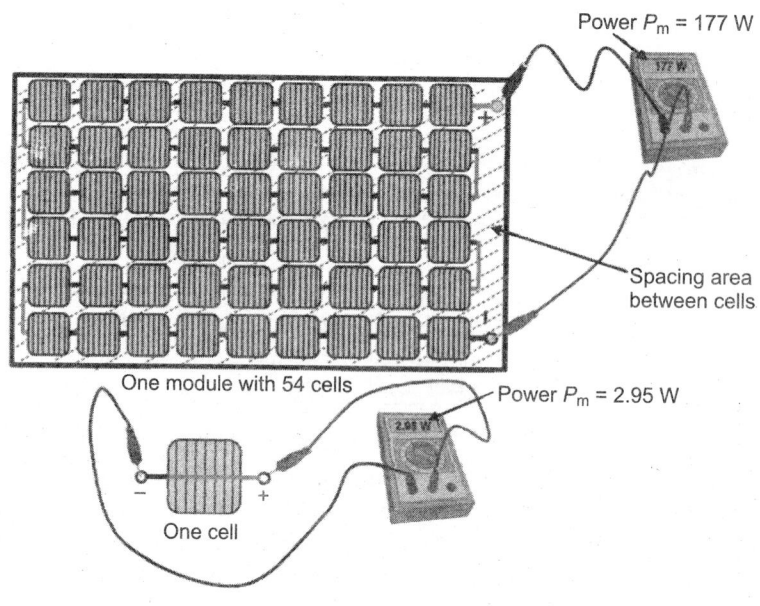

Power P_m = 177 W

Spacing area between cells

One module with 54 cells

Power P_m = 2.95 W

One cell

FIGURE 4.10

Showing solar cell area and spacing area between cells in a module.

$$\eta = \frac{P_m}{P_{in} \times A} \quad \text{or} \quad P_m = P_{in} \times \eta \times A \tag{4.5}$$

For given input power, the value of the output power is directly determined by the value of module's conversion efficiency and module area. The modules with higher efficiency values will always give better performance. Similar to solar cells, the unit of module efficiency is percentage (%), the unit of P_m is normally watt, the unit of P_{in} is normally W/m^2 or W/cm^2 and the unit of module area is m^2 or cm^2. The module efficiency is given for standard test condition (STC) and under the STC, the value of input power density, P_{in} is taken as 1000 W/m^2 or 0.1 W/cm^2.

EXAMPLE 4.9

Solution

Calculate the output power from a module if its efficiency (in %) is 22, 17, 16 and 12, input power density is 1000 W/m^2 and area of module is 58.7 inch by 39.0 inch.

First, we write formula for efficiency of a solar cell given by the expression

$$\eta = \frac{P_m}{P_{in} \times A} \; (\%)$$

where

η = Efficiency in percent (%)

P_m or P_{max} = Output power in watt (W)

P_{in} = Light input power per unit area in watt/metre^2 (W/m^2)

A = Solar cell area in metre^2 (m^2)

η = 22, 17, 16, 12 (in %)

P_{in} = 1000 W/m^2

A = 58.7 × 39.0 (inch)^2

P_m = ?

First, we convert cell area from (inch)^2 to m^2

We know, 1 inch = 0.0254 metres

58.7 inch = 1.49 metre and 39.0 inch = 0.99 metre

Therefore, module area (A) = 1.49 × 0.99 = 1.475 m^2

Now, we solve for solar cell of efficiency 22 %.

Above equation can be written as:

$$P_m = \eta \times P_{in} \times A$$

We put the respective terms values and we get,

$$P_m = \left(\frac{22}{100}\right) \times 1000 \times 1.475 = 324.5 \text{ W}$$

Similarly, we calculate output power for other efficiencies in the table form as shown in Table 4.8.

TABLE 4.8 Table for Example 4.9

η (%)	P_{in} (W/m^2)	A (inch)^2	A (m^2)	$\eta/100$	$P_m = (\eta/100) \times P_{in} \times A$ (W)
22	1000	2289.3	1.475	0.22	324.50
17	1000	2289.3	1.475	0.19	250.75
16	1000	2289.3	1.475	0.16	236.00
12	1000	2289.3	1.475	0.12	177.00

From the above table it clear that when efficiency of a module reduces the output power generated also reduces. The output power of module directly depends on the efficiency of module as shown in Figure 4.11.

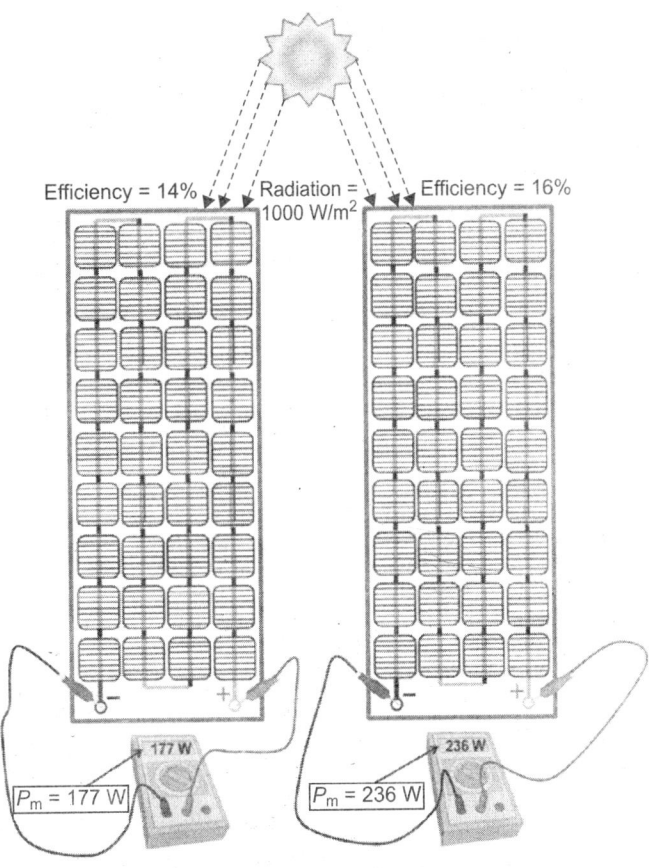

FIGURE 4.11

The effect of module conversion efficiency on the output power for module of 1.475 m^2 area.

4.4.2
Change in the Amount of Input Light (P_{in})

We should keep in mind that the amount of sunlight (intensity of sunlight), falling on solar PV module keeps changing from morning to evening. The current and voltage output of a solar PV module depends on the amount of light falling on it. The electric current generated by solar PV is directly proportional to the amount of light falling on it. Suppose, a solar PV module produces 5 A current under 1000 W/m² input solar radiation, then under 500 W/m² input solar radiation, the PV module will only produce 2.5 A current (because input radiation is half). As the amount of sunlight falling on solar PV module increases from morning till afternoon, the current output of a solar PV module also increases from morning till afternoon. From afternoon till evening, the amount of sunlight falling on a solar PV module decreases, and hence the current output of a solar PV module also decreases from afternoon till evening. The output voltage of a solar PV module is not affected strongly by change in the amount of light. If a solar PV module produces 20 V at noon time, its voltage will roughly remain same in the morning as well as evening hours.

The solar PV module current output is proportional to the amount of solar radiation and voltage is relatively not affected by variation in the sunlight intensity. Therefore, the amount of power generated (Power = Current × Voltage) by solar PV module is proportional to the amount of light falling on it. The amount of power generated by the solar PV modules throughout the day keeps changing (i.e., it is not constant). So, a solar PV module gives high power when the intensity of light falling is high. Similarly, less power is generated when the intensity of light falling is low. An example of a 75 W_p (or 75 W_{max} or 75 W_m) PV module is shown in Figure 4.12. The expected power output of the 75 W_p PV module under various input solar radiation intensity is given, including the PV module power output under STC. The corresponding *I-V* characteristics of the same PV module, for 25 °C cell temperature and for various solar radiation intensity (1000 W/m², 800 W/m², 600 W/m², 400 W/m² and 200 W/m²) are also given in Figure 4.12. Please note here that the power output under various solar radiation conditions given in Table 4.9 and in Figure 4.12 are the peak power output in that condition. Peak

> Large amount of light falling means high generated power, less amount of light falling means low generated power by the solar PV module.

power or maximum power point is shown by '×' in Figure 4.12. The actual power output from a PV module may be lower than the maximum power point, if the PV module is not operating at current and voltage corresponding to maximum power point (as discussed in Section 3.2.1).

FIGURE 4.12

I-V characteristics of a 75 W_p (STC condition) PV module under various input solar intensities (The peak power of the module under various solar radiation intensities is also mentioned).

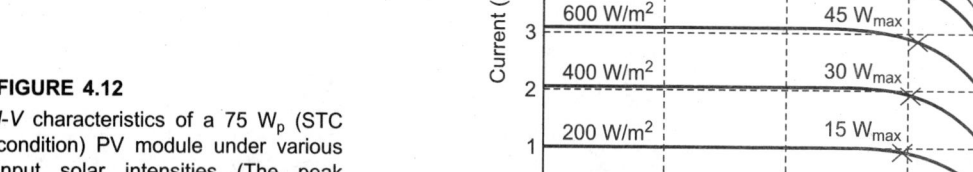

TABLE 4.9 Expected Output Power of a 75 W_p PV Module Under Various Solar Radiation Intensity. (Temperature of the PV Module is Assumed to be Constant in all Conditions)

Amount of light input or sunlight intensity (P_{in}) (W/m²)	Peak power output of a PV module (W_p) (watt)
1000 (STC)	75 (STC)
800	60
600	45
400	30
200	15

A solar PV module with double light power input will produce double electrical power output.

EXAMPLE 4.10

A W_p rating of a PV module is 230 W_p (or 230 W_{max}) under STC. What will be the output power of the PV module if the solar radiation intensity is only 400 W/m²? Assume the temperature of the cells module remain the same in both conditions.

Solution

It is given that peak power rating is 230 W_p.

Given, solar radiation condition is STC, which is equivalent to 1000 W/m² input power.

Now, we know that the PV output power varies linearly with the input sunlight intensity (when cell temperature is constant, which is given). In this way, at 1000 W/m² input power, if the peak output power is 230 W_p, then at 1000 W/m² input power, the peak output power will be

$$\frac{230 \ W_p}{1000 \ W/m^2} \times 400 \ W/m^2 = 92 \ W_p$$

EXAMPLE 4.11

A solar PV module's maximum power output at 300 W/m² and 700 W/m² is 42 watt and 98 watt respectively. What will be the PV W_p rating of the module under STC? Assume the temperature of the cells module remain the same in both conditions.

Solution

It is given that at 300 W/m², maximum output power is 42 watt, and at 700 W/m², maximum output power is 98 watt.

Since the cell temperature is constant, the PV module's maximum power output at any solar radiation condition will linearly depend on the solar radiation power input.

We need to find out the peak power output of the PV module under STC, which means under 1000 W/m² solar radiation condition.

We can write; at 300 W/m² input power, the peak output power is 42 W_p, then at 1000 W/m² input power, the peak output power will be

$$\frac{42 \ W_p}{300 \ W/m^2} \times 1000 \ W/m^2 = 140 \ W_p$$

Also, we can write; at 700 W/m² input power, the peak output power is 98 W_p, then at 1000 W/m² input power, the peak output power will be

$$\frac{98 \ W_p}{700 \ W/m^2} \times 1000 \ W/m^2 = 140 \ W_p$$

4.4.3
Effect of Change in PV Module Temperature

The solar PV modules output voltage, power and efficiency ratings are given at standard test condition (STC = 1000 W/m² and 25 °C). The PV module output voltage, PV module efficiency and output power depends on cell temperature in PV module. In practical applications, the operating temperature of solar cells in PV modules may be different than 25 °C. The cell temperature varies due to ambient temperature. In many cases, the ambient temperature is higher than the STC temperature of 25 °C. Moreover, in practice, the cells in a PV module are encapsulated with glass cover. The presence of glass cover has a greenhouse effect, which results in heating of solar cells and increase in their temperature. The change in temperature from standard operating temperature directly affects the output voltage of a PV module. With increase in cell temperature in PV modules, the voltage output of PV module decreases, which results in decrease in PV module efficiency and PV module output power.

The change in PV module parameters with increase in cell's operating temperature (or temperature coefficient of PV module parameters) in PV module is given in Table 4.6. The different values of module output at different temperatures. The short circuit current of PV module increases with increase in cell temperature, while the other parameters like open circuit voltage, efficiency and output power decreases with increase in cell temperature in PV modules. Change in parameters value with temperature for crystalline silicon, cadmium telluride and amorphous silicon is given in Table 4.10.

TABLE 4.10 Typical Value of Change in Parameter Value Per °C Rise in Cell Temperature From Standard Test Condition (STC) Value of 25 °C (The PV module parameters of various commercially available technologies are given)

PV Technology name	Typical value of change in parameter value per °C rise in cell temperature from standard test condition (STC) value of 25 °C (+ indicates increase, – indicates decrease)			
	Temperature coefficient of current (I_{sc})	Temperature coefficient of voltage (V_{oc})	Temperature coefficient of fill factor (FF)	Temperature coefficient of power (P_m)
Crystalline silicon	+0.08%/°C	−0.35%/°C	−0.15%/°C	−0.45%/°C
Cadmium telluride	+0.04%/°C	−0.25%/°C	−0.035%/°C	−0.25%/°C
Double junction amorphous silicon	+0.07%/°C	−0.3%/°C	−0.095%/°C	−0.25%/°C

Note: The temperature coefficient of parameters are given as percentage of parameter value at STC. The values given in this table are typical values of the parameter, the actual value may be different from one manufacturer to other.

Normally, the W_p rating of PV module is one of the most important parameters. In real-life situation, due to higher cell operating temperature than the STC temperature, the actual maximum output power of modules is lower than STC value. Using the temperature coefficient of the module parameter, the change in value of parameter with increase in temperature can be estimated. In this way, if we know the temperature coefficient of power, we can calculate how much will be drop in peak power output of a PV module in real-life operating condition.

The temperature coefficient of parameters is given in percentage of parameter value at STC. Thus, following formulae can be written to find out the change in parameter value as compared to STC value due to increase in temperature:

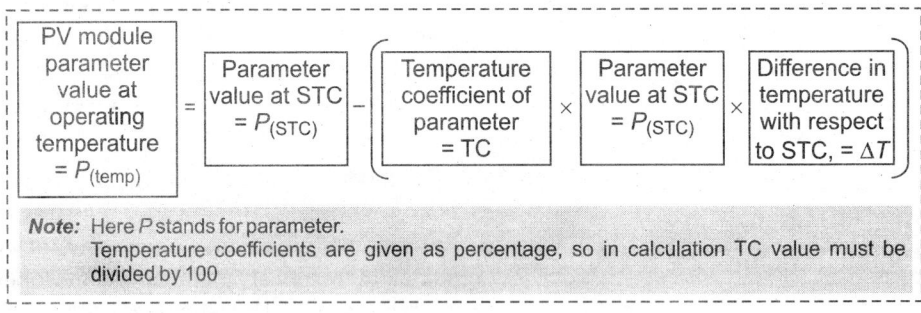

Note: Here P stands for parameter.
Temperature coefficients are given as percentage, so in calculation TC value must be divided by 100

In terms of formula, we can write as:

$$P_{(temp)} = P_{(STC)} - TC \times P_{(STC)} \times \Delta T$$

Using the above formulae, one can find the change in any parameter value for any given cell operating temperature. The above formula can be written for any parameter. For instance, the formulae for change in maximum module voltage due to increase in cell temperature in PV module will be given as:

$$V_{m,(temp)} = V_{m,(STC)} - TC_{voltage} \times V_{m,(STC)} \times \Delta T$$

For a solar PV module, higher temperature means lower power output. For a typical crystalline silicon PV module, the output voltage decreases by 0.35% per degree centigrade rise in temperature.

The change in module's maximum power output due to increase in cell temperature in PV module will be given as:

$$P_{max,(temp)} = P_{max,(STC)} - TC_{power} \times P_{max,((STC)} \times \Delta T$$

TABLE 4.11 Different Values of Module Output at Different Temperatures

S. No.	Temperature (°C)	Wattage (watts)
1	25 (STC)	75.0
2	30	73.3
3	40	69.9
4	50	66.6
5	60	63.2
6	70	59.8

 WORKSHEET 4.4: The maximum rated power point of a crystalline silicon solar cell is 75 W_p. Calculate the maximum power output at 45 °C, 55 °C, and 65 °C cell operating temperature. For crystalline silicon, cell decrease in maximum power per degree centigrade increase in cell temperature, (from STC value of 25 °C), is −0.45%/°C. Fill Table 4.12.

Use the following equation:

Actual P_{max} at cell operating temperature (watt)

$$P_{max,(temp)} = P_{max,(STC)} - TC_{power} \times P_{max,(STC)} \times \Delta T$$

TABLE 4.12 Change in Wattage of Module due to Change in Temperature

Operating cell temperature (°C)	STC cell temperature (°C)	ΔT (°C)	$P_{max,(STC)}$ (watt)	TC (%)	$TC_{power} \times P_{max,(STC)} \times \Delta T$ (watt)	$P_{max,(temp)}$ (watt)
45	25	20	–	−0.45	–	–
55	–	–	75	–	–	64.87
65	–	–	–	−0.45	–	–

EXAMPLE 4.12

Voltage at maximum power point (V_m) of a crystalline silicon solar PV module at STC is 17 V. What would be the voltage when PV module operating temperature is 60 °C? Refer to Table 4.10.

Solution

It is given that the PV module is a crystalline silicon PV module.

The PV module voltage at maximum power point at STC is

$$V_{m,(STC)} = 17 \text{ V}$$

The PV module temperature at STC is 25 °C.

The operating temperature of the PV module at which V_m needs to be calculated is 60 °C, i.e., we need to calculate V_m, (60 °C).

The difference in operating PV module temperature and STC temperature

$$\Delta T = 60 - 25 = 35 °C$$

Now, considering Table 4.10 the decrease in voltage per degree centigrade rise in PV module temperature from standard test condition (STC) value of 25 °C is −0.35%.

Now, using the formulae for estimating change in the voltage due to temperature increase

$$V_{m,(temp)} = V_{m,(STC)} - TC_{voltage} \times V_{m,(STC)} \times \Delta T$$

$$= 17 - \frac{0.35}{100} \times 17 \times 35 = 17 - 2.08 = 14.91 \text{ V}$$

4.4.4
Change in PV Module Area (A)

Large number of cells in a module means large module area; Small number of cells in a module means small module area.

Generally, the modules of a large area give high power compared to the modules of a small area. It is very important to understand the reason behind it. When we say the area of a module has increased or decreased, it means the area of module increases or decreases with the increase or decrease in the number of cells in a module. For example in a module there are 36 cells and the area of each cell is 156 cm^2 then total area of 36 cells = 36 × 156 = 562 cm^2 = 0.562 m^2. Now, if the number of cells in same module is increased to say 72 cells then the total area of cells becomes 1.12 m^2 (i.e., double of 0.562 m^2).

Now, we need to understand how change in area of a module is related to the change in maximum output power (P_m) of a module. We have learned in the Section 4.3.3 of this chapter that the maximum output power of a module depends on the maximum output current (I_m) and the maximum output voltage (V_m). For example, if at STC module of area 1.475 m^2 having V_m = 26 V and I_m = 6.73 A gives P_m = 175 W then a module of area 2.950 m^2 having V_m = 52 V and I_m = 6.73 A will give P_m = 350 W under same input sunlight intensity (shown in Figure 4.13).

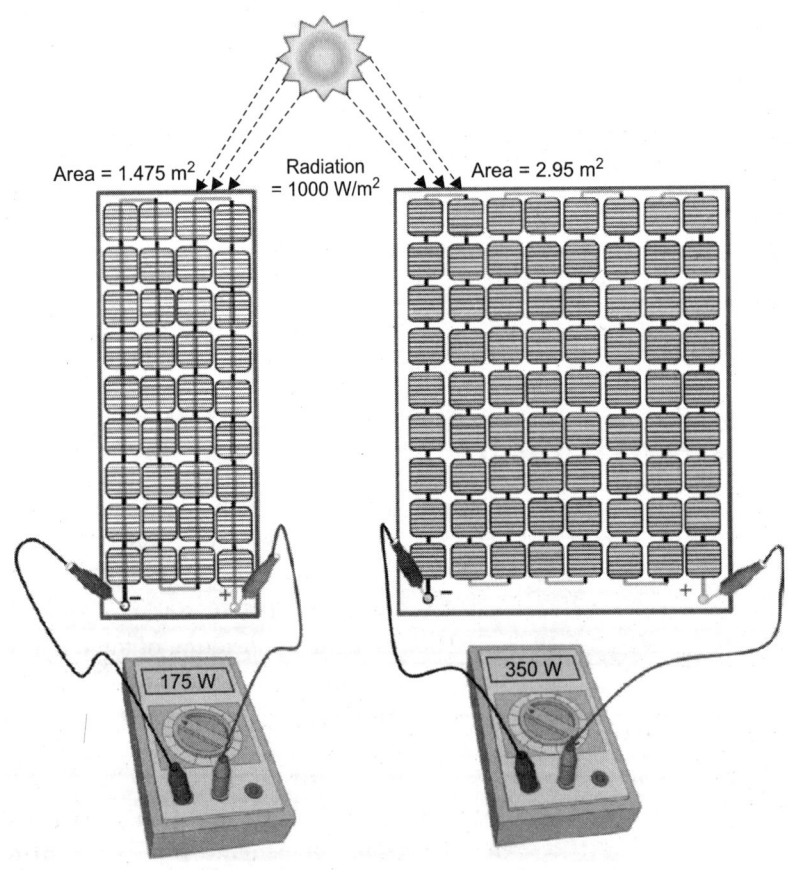

FIGURE 4.13

The effect of module area on the output current for same light intensity and efficiency of the module.

From above example, the question arises; why has the output voltage and output power doubled with the increase in module area? This is because V_m and I_m of modules depend on the series or parallel types of cells inter-connectivity used. When strings of cells are connected in series, the voltage is additive and current is fixed (i.e., current of a single string of cells). When the strings of cells are connected in parallel, the current is additive and voltage is fixed (i.e., voltage of a single string of cells). So, when the strings of cells in a module are inter-connected in series, high output voltage is obtained. When the strings of cells in a module are inter-connected in parallel, high output current is obtained. Let us consider a module of area 2.95 cm^2 that consists of two units of 1.475 m^2 area in which the cells are connected in series to give high $V_m = 26$ V and $I_m = 6.73$ A at STC ($P_m = 175$ W) as shown in Figure 4.13). These units of 1.475 m^2 are connected in parallel to give $V_m = 26$ V and high current $I_m = 13.46$ A at STC ($P_m = 350$ W) as shown in Figure 4.14. So, for practical applications, it doesn't matter in which way the cells or the strings of cells are inter-connected in a module. Here, change in area is mainly due to increase or decrease in the number of cells in a module. It is important to understand that with the change in the area of module, the output power of the modules also changes.

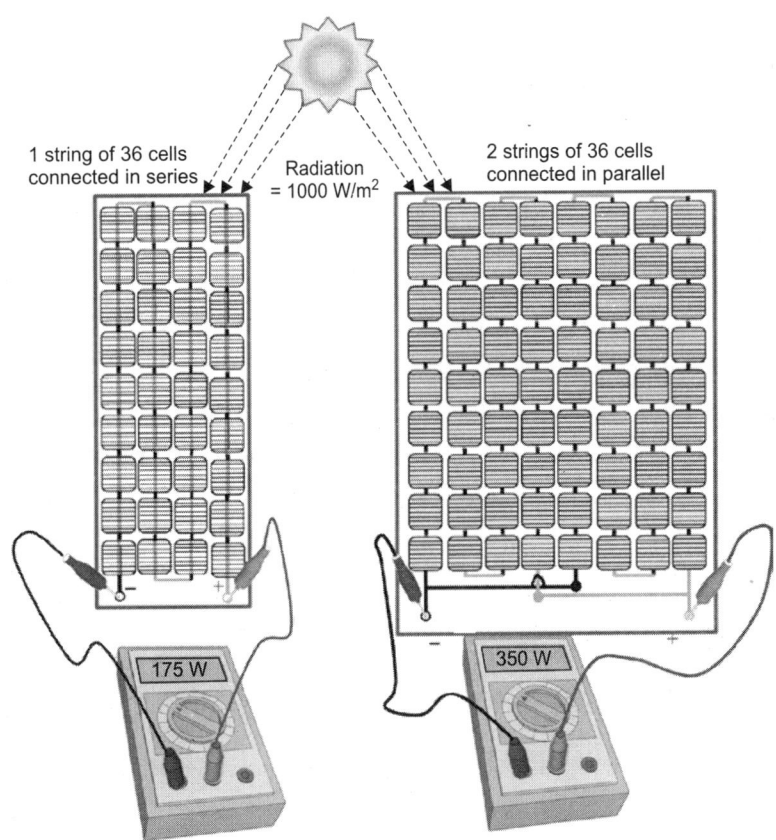

FIGURE 4.14

(a) Module with single string of cells and (b) Module with two strings of cells connected in parallel type of connection.

Large module area means high power and small module area means low power.

In Table 4.13, it can be seen that as the area of module (i.e., no. of cells in module) increases the power of the modules also increases.

TABLE 4.13 Comparison of Commercially Available Modules of Different Wattages at STC Along with A, I_m, V_m and n Respectively

	Module 1	Module 2	Module 3	Module 4
Power (P_m)	115 W$_p$	175 W$_p$	230 W$_p$	230 W$_p$
Area (A)	0.882 m^2	1.476 m^2	1.646 m^2	1.646 m^2
Maximum current (I_m)	6.76 A	6.73 A	7.93 A	13.64 A
Maximum Voltage (V_m)	17 V	26 V	29 V	17 V
Number of cells (n)	36	54	60	72

4.4.5

Change in Angle of Light Falling on PV Module (θ)

Similar to the solar cells discussed in Chapter 3, the angle of sunlight with respect to module greatly affects the output power. The modules produce maximum power (for given light intensity) when sunlight falls perpendicular to the surface of a module. When the light does not fall perpendicular on the module, it always gives less output power than maximum possible output power. This is because when light falls at some angle, some part of light falling on module is reflected. Hence, the actual light utilized by a module is less than the amount of light falling on it. So, the output power generated is less when light is not falling perpendicular to module as shown in Figure 4.15. Therefore, one should always try to install a module in such

Light falling perpendicular to modules gives maximum output power.

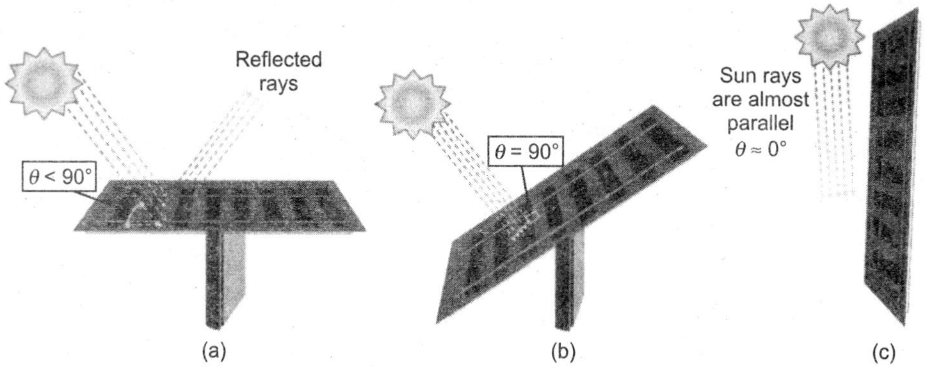

a way (i.e., angle of module inclination) that most of the time sunlight is close to perpendicular, especially in the afternoon time when the intensity of sunlight is high.

FIGURE 4.15
The effect of the angle of sunlight falling on a module on output power of module (a) light is at an angle less than 90°, (b) light is at an angle of 90° and (c) light is falling parallel.

4.5

Measuring Module Parameters

The module parameters mentioned in Section 4.3 can also be measured or calculated based on some measured parameters. The parameters that can be measured by means of the measuring devices like open circuit and maximum voltage, short circuit and maximum current and parameters which can be calculated using measured parameters are Fill Factor, maximum power point and efficiency. For measuring the module parameters, following equipments are required:

1. Ammeter or a multimeter
2. Voltmeter or a multimeter
3. Rheostat
4. Connecting wires

4.5.1

Measuring V_{oc} and I_{sc}

The open circuit voltage (V_{oc}) and short circuit current (I_{sc}) can be directly measured with multimeter. For measuring V_{oc}, multimeter in voltmeter mode or a voltmeter can be used. For measuring I_{sc}, a multimeter in DC current mode or an ammeter can be used.

V_{oc} measurement

When you are measuring V_{oc} or open circuit voltage of a module, there should not be any load connected to the module, and it should be in open circuit condition. For measuring V_{oc}, first set the multimeter knob to voltage measurement and set the range of voltage according to the given module (normally 6 V, 12 V, 24 V, etc.). Then connect the two terminals of multimeter/voltmeter across two terminals of a SPV module directly as shown in Figure 4.16. Ensure that the terminals of same polarity of multimeter and module are connected together. In this arrangement, the reading shown by the multimeter/voltmeter is open circuit voltage of the given SPV module. If a negative sign is shown in the meter with reading, it indicates that the appropriate polarity of the module terminal and meter terminal is not connected. Reverse the connection and then measure again.

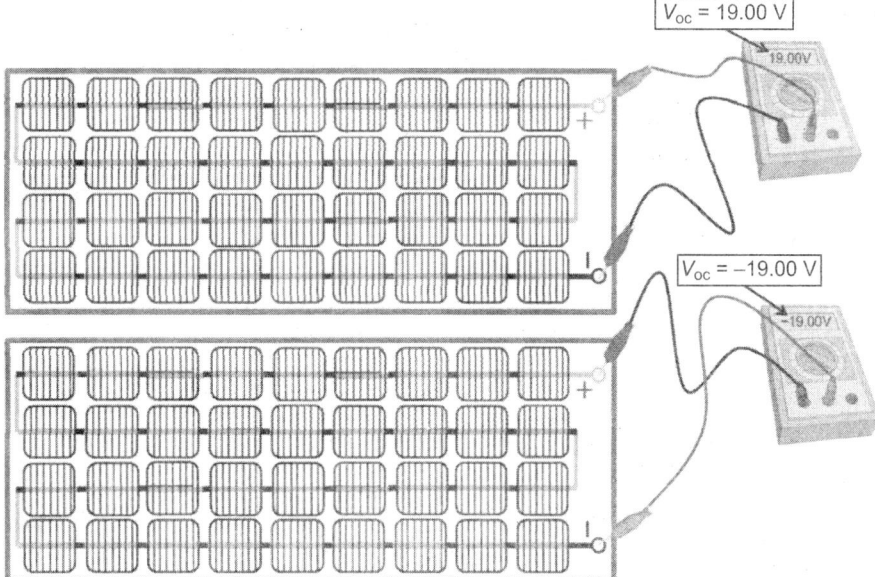

FIGURE 4.16

Multimeter connection to solar PV module for measuring open circuit voltage (V_{oc}).

I_{sc} *measurement*

When you are measuring I_{sc} or short circuit current of a module, there should not be any load connected to the module, it should be in short circuit condition. For measuring I_{SC} using a multimeter, first put the probes of multimeter into the current measurement slots given in multimeter, and then set the multimeter knob to appropriate current range according to the module rating. The typical I_{sc} values of modules could be in range starting from 0.1 A to 10 A. Then connect the opposite polarity terminal of multimeter/ammeter and SPV module directly as shown in Figure 4.17. The reading shown by multimeter/ammeter in this case is short circuit current of the given SPV module. If a negative sign is shown in the meter with some reading, it indicates that the appropriate polarity of the module terminal and meter terminal is not connected. Reverse the connection and then measure again.

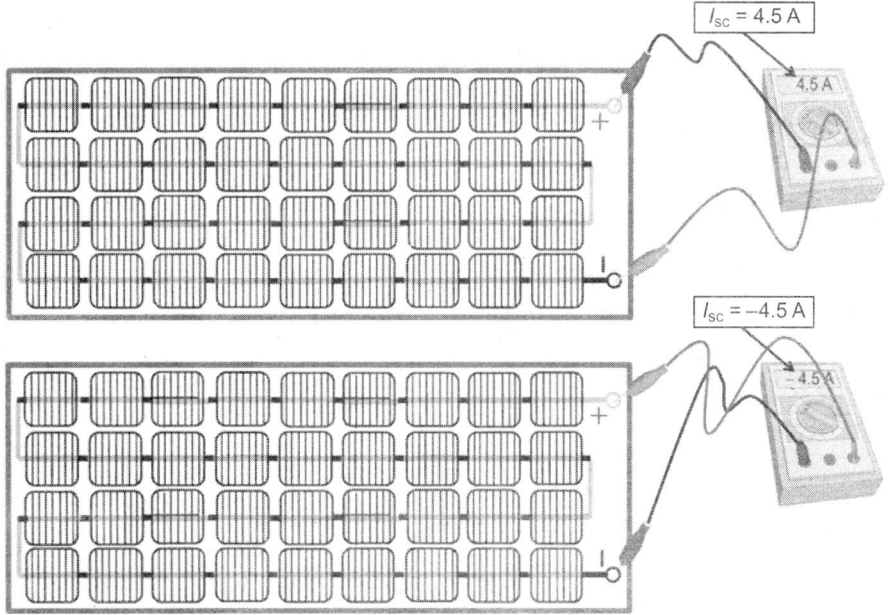

FIGURE 4.17

Ammeter connection to solar PV module for measuring short circuit current (I_{sc}).

It is easy to measure open circuit voltage and short circuit current using multimeter.

Measuring *I-V* curve (*V*$_m$ and *I*$_m$)

This is the very useful measurement for any solar PV module to measure its performance in the laboratory as well as on the field in real time. The measurement would require two multimeters (or a voltmeter and an ammeter) and a rheostat. Make the electrical connections as shown in Figure 4.18. For measuring *I-V* curve, the solar PV module has to be connected in series with the Rheostat, i.e., negative terminal of a solar PV module to the one end of rheostat and other end of rheostat should be connected to the positive terminal of the multimeter/ammeter. The negative terminal of the multimeter/ammeter should be connected to the positive terminal of the SPV module. The voltmeter or multimeter for voltage measurement is directly connected across the SPV module. If, by mistake, the connection of positive and negative terminals of voltmeter and ammeter is not done properly, it is not a problem, the difference however would be that the meters will show readings with negative sign. If the signs of reading are negative, make changes in connections.

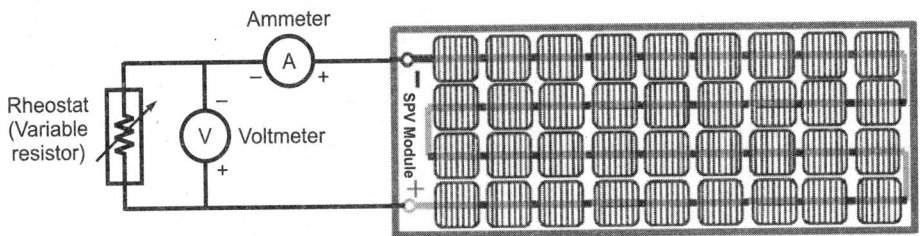

FIGURE 4.18
Connection diagram for *I-V* measurement.

After making the connections, now you are ready to make the measurements. Make a Table as shown in Table 4.14 to note down the readings. Make the table with three columns one for serial number, one for noting down the voltage and one column for noting down the current. One extra column should be kept empty to make calculations for power (Current × Voltage). After doing all the connections, in order to start the measurement, slide the rheostat at one side where the voltage should be maximum and current should be minimum, and note down the values of current and voltage at that instant, and note the readings in table. Now, slightly slide the rheostat, readings of current and voltage will change. Note down the readings again. Keep on sliding the rheostat (and noting the readings) until knob of the rheostat reaches the other end.

> Using two multimeter and rheostat (variable resister) complete current-voltage characteristics of a PV module and its parameters can be measured.

TABLE 4.14 Table for Noting the Current and Voltage Values from *I-V* Curve Measurement of PV Modules

S. No.	Current (A)	Voltage (V)	Power (W) = Current × Voltage
1			
2			
3			
4			
5			
–			
–			
–			

Noting and calculating module parameters

From the measured data point for *I-V* curve, all the parameters related to PV module can be calculated. Using Table 4.14 one can make a table of parameters of PV modules by noting the values in Table 4.15.

TABLE 4.15 Calculating Module Parameters

S. No.	Parameters	Reading or calculating from Table 4.14	Values
1	Short circuit current (I_{sc})	Current value when voltage is zero	
2	Open circuit voltage (V_{oc})	Voltage value when current is zero	
3	Maximum power point (P_m)	Value of maximum power	
3	Current at maximum power point (I_m)	Current value at maximum power point	
4	Voltage at maximum power point (V_m)	Voltage value at maximum power point	
5	Fill factor (FF)	$= \dfrac{I_m \times V_m}{I_{sc} \times V_{oc}}$	
6	Efficiency (η)	$= \dfrac{V_{oc} \times I_{sc} \times FF}{P_{in} \times A}$	

Note: I_m is normally 90% to 95% of I_{sc} and V_m is normally 80% to 85% of V_{oc} for nearly all technologies.

EXAMPLE 4.13

Count the number of cells connected in series in the module shown in Figure 4.19 and calculate the open circuit voltage (V_{oc}) and voltage at maximum power point (V_m). It is given that open circuit voltage of a single cell is 0.6 V.

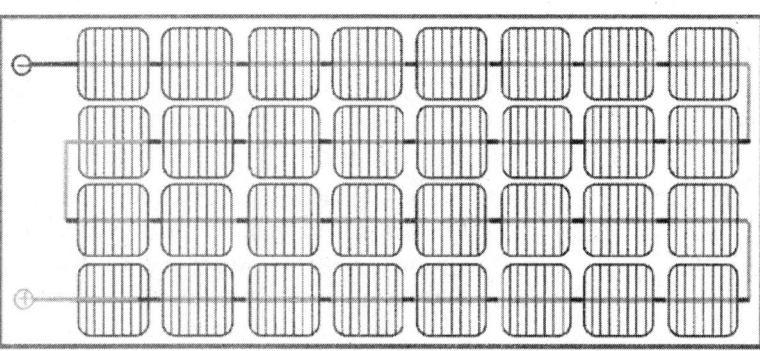

FIGURE 4.19
Series connected cells in PV module for Example 4.14.

Solution

Number of cells to be connected in series (n) = _____

Total series open circuit voltage (V_{oc}) = V_{oc} (single cell) × number of cells in series

V_{oc} (module) = _____ × _____

V_{oc} (module) = _____ volts

V_m is normally 80% to 85% of V_{oc}. Let us assume that V_m = _____ V_{oc} = _____ V

Therefore, V_m (module) = _____ volts.

**4.5.2
Higher Wattage Modules**

The crystalline Si cell technology is the most commonly used technology. For this technology, the large area solar cells are available in either size 12.5 × 12.5 cm² or 15 × 15 cm². These size of solar cells are commonly used, particularly, in all modules which are used in grid-connected PV plants. Crystalline silicon cells with larger than this area are not available. How much peak power or W_p these modules can provide? What to do if we want more power output per module?

We now know that the PV modules are typically designed to produce about 15 volt (V_m) under operating conditions. And in order to get this voltage, there are about 32 to 36 cells connected in series (depending on V_m of individual cells and operating temperature). The current produced by the cells depends on the area and current density. The current density of commercially available crystalline Si solar cell is about 30 mA/cm² to 35 mA/cm². Let us take 35 mA/cm² here for estimation, relatively towards bit higher side. Thus, the maximum possible short circuit current (I_{sc}) that we can get from modules with large area solar cells is:

$$I_{sc} = J_{sc} \ (mA/cm^2) \times Area \ (cm^2)$$
$$= 35 \times 12.5 \times 12.5$$
$$= 5468 \ mA = \mathbf{5.46} \ A$$

$$I_{sc} = J_{sc} \ (mA/cm^2) \times Area \ (cm^2)$$
$$= 35 \times 15 \times 15$$
$$= 7875 \ mA = \mathbf{7.87} \ A$$

We know that I_m is normally about 90 to 95% of the I_{sc}. Let us assume 90% here for calculations.

Therefore, $I_m = 0.09 \times I_{sc}$

$$I_m = 0.90 \times 5.46 = \mathbf{4.91} \ A \ (for \ 12.5 \times 12.5 \ cm^2 \ cells)$$
$$I_m = 0.90 \times 7.87 = \mathbf{7.08} \ A \ (for \ 15 \times 15 \ cm^2 \ cells)$$

Now, the maximum wattages (W_p) that we can get using these two types of cells are:

$$W_p = I_m \times V_m$$
$$W_p = 4.91 \times 15 = \mathbf{73.65} \ watt$$
$$W_p = 7.08 \times 15 = \mathbf{106.2} \ watt$$

Using the best available crystalline Si cell technology with large area solar cells, the maximum possible wattages possible are **73.65** watt (15 V, 4.91 A, $12.5 \times 12.5 \ cm^2$ cell) and **106.2** watt (15 V, 7.87 A, $15 \times 15 \ cm^2$ cells).

The modules designed above can be used for 12 volts system voltages. In order to get higher voltages, two or more modules are connected in series. In order to get more current, two or more modules are connected in parallel. In this way, by making series and parallel connection, voltage and current of a PV system as well as power of a PV system can be increased.

We can increase the power output of crystalline silicon PV modules more than what we have just calculated in this section. A single solar cell provide V_m of about 0.5 V, the modules of 15 V (V_m) are obtained by connecting many individual cells in series. We can extend the same logic further. Higher voltage modules (higher than 15 V) can be designed by connecting a large number of cells in series, in this case, larger than 30 to 36 cells normally connected in the case of crystalline silicon cell technology. Thus, by connecting more cells in series we can get higher voltage, and thus, higher power from the module. In similar way, if we connect more cells or string of cells in parallel, we can get more current and in this way, more power from the modules.

Higher wattage PV modules, higher than 100 W_p, have larger area solar cells and more number of cells in series.

EXAMPLE 4.14

Design a Solar PV module for providing voltage at maximum power point of V_m 30 V (STC), and 28.5 V (under operating conditions, 55 °C cell temperature). Use the cells with open circuit voltage of 0.62 V, and 0.002 V decrease in V_m per degree centigrade rise in temperature.

Solution

We can use step by step method (refer to Section 5.1) to estimate the number of cells required in a module.

Step 1: Find out V_m (at STC) of a solar cell of given technology.

If V_m (at STC) is not given; we can estimate V_m using V_{oc} value.

Assume V_m is about 80% to 85% of the V_{oc}. Let us assume $V_m = 0.80 \times V_{oc}$

V_m (cell) $= 0.80 \times V_{oc}$ (cell) $= 0.80 \times 0.62 = 0.496$ volts

Step 2: Find out loss of voltage (loss of V_m) under operating conditions.

The temperature corresponding to STC is 25 °C, the cell is operating at 60 °C, therefore the cell is operating $55 - 25$ °C $= 35$ °C above the STC.

Loss in voltage per degree centigrade rise in temperature is 0.002 V

Therefore loss of voltage due to 35 °C rise in temperature $= 0.002 \times 30 = 0.06$ volt

Step 3: Available voltage at operating conditions $= V_m$ (STC) – Loss of voltage

Available voltage at operating conditions $= 0.496$ V $- 0.06$ V $= 0.49$ V

Step 4: Note down the required PV module voltage.

Required PV module voltage $= 28.5$ V (given).

Step 5: Divide the required module voltage by available operating voltage to get the number of cells connected in series.

Number of new type of cells to be connected in series: $= \dfrac{28.5}{0.49}$

$$= 58.16 \text{ or about 59 cells.}$$

Normally, in the commercially available PV modules of large power, there are 60 cells connected in series as shown in Figure 4.20.

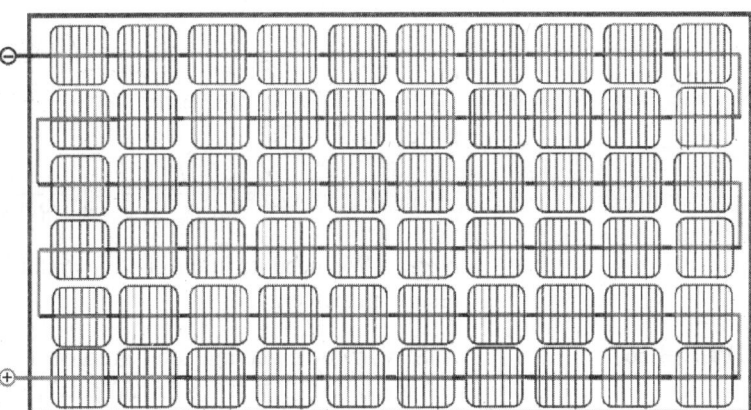

FIGURE 4.20
Higher open circuit voltage solar PV module.

Amount of peak power generated from large modules?

Now let us estimate how much power these modules with 60 cells connected in series (as shown in Figure 4.20) can generate under STC condition. Thus, now considering V_m (STC) of 30 V and considering the same values of I_m for two size of solar cells as (shown in previous calculations):

$I_m = 4.91$ A (for 12.5×12.5 cm^2 cells) and

$I_m = 0.90 \times 7.87 = 7.08$ A (for 15×15 cm^2 cells)

In this way, peak power output of a solar PV module will be:

$$W_p = 4.91 \times 147.3 = 723.24 \text{ watt}$$

$$W_p = 7.08 \times 212.4 = 1503.79 \text{ watt}$$

Thus, depending on the size of the solar cell, significantly large power can be generated using single PV module. Again, depending on the requirement of even larger power (as in big PV plants), these modules can again be connected in series and parallel to get more power output. However since the power output of these modules are large, fewer connection would be required to get a given power output. These types of large PV modules are normally used in PV power plants of MW scale or of several MW sizes.

EXAMPLE 4.15

A SPV high power module is having an area of 1.62 m^2 gives a current at maximum power point of 7.83 A and voltage at maximum power point of 29.4 V. The short circuit current of the module is 8.52 A and open circuit voltage is 36.7 V. What is the fill factor, maximum power point and efficiency of the solar cell? Consider STC.

Solution

Following parameters of the module are given:

Short circuit current (I_{sc}) = 8.52 A

Open circuit voltage (V_{oc}) = 36.7 V

Current at maximum power point (I_m) = 7.83 A

Voltage at maximum power point (V_m) = 29.4 V

Light input power (W/m^2) = 1000 W/m^2

Area (m^2) = 1.62 m^2

Now,

Maximum power point

$$P_m \text{ or } P_{max} = I_m \times V_m = (8.52 \times 29.4) = 250.48 \text{ watt}$$

Fill factor

$$FF = \frac{I_m \times V_m}{I_{sc} \times V_{oc}}$$

or

$$FF = \frac{P_m}{I_{sc} \times V_{oc}} = \left(\frac{250.48}{8.52 \times 36.7} \right) \times 100 = 80.106\%$$

Efficiency

$$\eta = \frac{P_{max}}{P_{in} \times A} = \left(\frac{250.48}{1000 \times 1.62} \right) \times 100 = 15.46\%$$

Note: We need to multiply FF and Efficiency with 100 in order to present the results in percentage.

EXAMPLE 4.16

A SPV module having total area of 1.646 m^2 and gives a current of 8.08 A and voltage of 29.72 V at maximum power point. The short circuit current of the module is 8.48 A and open circuit voltage is 37.34 V. What is the fill factor, maximum power point and efficiency of the solar cell? Consider STC.

Solution

Following parameters of the module are given:

Short circuit current (I_{sc}) = 8.48 A

Open circuit voltage (V_{oc}) = 37.34 V

Current at maximum power point (I_m) = 8.08 A

Voltage at maximum power point (V_m) = 29.72 V

Light input power (W/m^2) = 1000 W/m^2

Area (m^2) = 1.646 m^2

Now,

Maximum power point

$$P_m \text{ or } P_{max} = I_m \times V_m = (8.08 \times 29.72) = 240.13 \text{ watt}$$

Note that, the power of the module is very high, i.e., 240.1 W$_p$. Such modules are available these days in the market.

Chapter 4: Solar PV Modules | 87

Fill factor

$$FF = \frac{I_m \times V_m}{I_{sc} \times V_{oc}}$$

or $\qquad FF = \frac{P_m}{I_{sc} \times V_{oc}} = \left(\frac{240.13}{8.48 \times 37.34} \right) \times 100 = 75.83\%$

Efficiency

$$\eta = \frac{P_{max}}{P_{in} \times A} = \left(\frac{240.13}{1000 \times 1.646} \right) \times 100 = 14.58\%$$

Note: We need to multiply FF and Efficiency with 100 in order to present the results in percentage.

Bypass diode

In solar PV modules, in almost all cases, all the solar cells, identical in nature, are connected in series. When light falls on a PV module, same current is generated in all solar cells which flow through PV module. Now, due to some reason, if one of the solar cells gets shaded (no light falling on one cell), then the current generated by that cell will be lower than the rest of the solar cells. Since the cells are connected in series, the shaded solar cell (generating low or no current) will resist the current flow generated by non-shaded solar cells generating full current. In this case, the shaded solar cell becomes a load for the other cells, and the power generated by other solar cells may get dissipated in the shaded solar cells. Due to this, the shaded solar cell can become very hot, forming hot spots in the PV module. The hot spots sometimes can give rise to breaking of glass cover in PV module or in a worst case, it can cause fire. Therefore, local heating of solar cells in a PV module due to shading should be avoided.

Bypass diode is used to avoid the destructive effect of hot spots or local heating in series connected cells in PV modules. A diode, called bypass diode, is connected in parallel with solar cells with opposite polarity to that of a solar cell as shown in Figure 4.21. Thus, in normal condition (no shading), the bypass diode is operated in reverse bias condition, effectively in open circuit. But if a series connected cell is shaded, reverse bias will appear across it. This reverse bias will act as a forward bias voltage for bypass diode since it is connected with opposite polarity. In this way, the bypass diode will carry the current, rather than shaded cell (meaning bypassing the current from shaded cell). By bypassing the current, the solar cell gets protected by heating and causing permanent damage to the PV module.

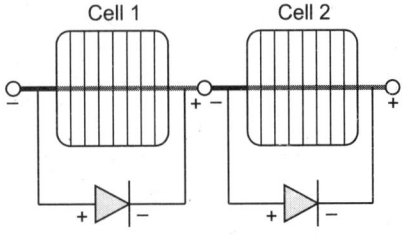

FIGURE 4.21

A bypass diode connected in parallel but with reverse polarity to solar cells.

Ideally, there should be each diode for the each solar cell in the solar PV module, but practically, due to cost reason, there are few bypass diodes which are connected in PV module. It is recommended that practically, there should be at least one diode for each series combinations of 10–15 cells. This connection is shown in Figure 4.22.

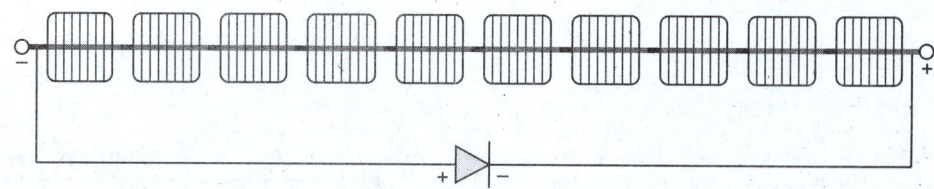

FIGURE 4.22

10 cells connected in series with one bypass diodes.

Bypass diodes are added in parallel to solar cells to avoid the formation of hot spots and damage to PV modules.

Blocking diode

In standalone PV systems, PV modules are used to either supply the load during day time or to charge a battery. In day time, energy is generated by PV module and supplied to battery. When there is no sunlight, like in the night, the SPV modules stop producing the energy and become idle. During night, charged batteries start supplying energy to the SPV modules. This is loss of energy and should be avoided. In order to avoid the flow of current from battery to solar PV modules, a diode, called blocking diode is used to block the current flow. Thus, the blocking diode prevents the discharging of battery into the SPV module. The connection of blocking diode with a solar PV module is shown in Figure 4.23.

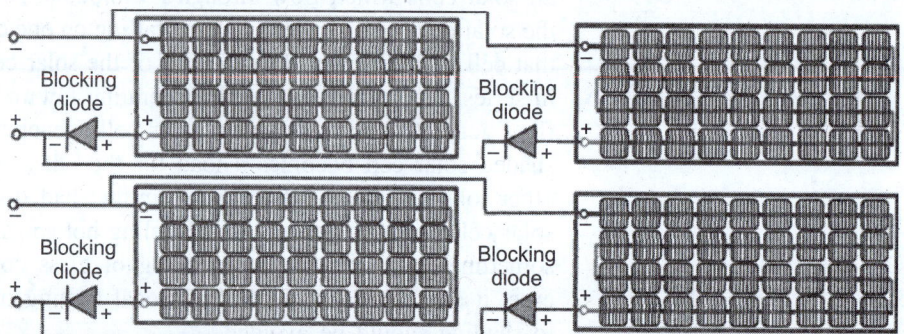

FIGURE 4.23

Blocking diode with the SPV modules to prevent reverse current flow.

Blocking diodes are added in PV system to avoid reverse flow of current into the PV modules.

How to identify diode?

The diode by appearance is cylindrical in shape with a silver ring on it, and other part is black in colour. The diode has two pins; one is positive and other one is negative. The silver ring (as shown in Figure 4.24) represents the negative terminal and other terminal is positive.

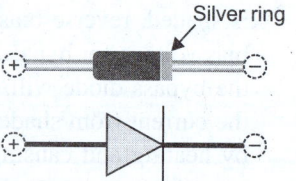

FIGURE 4.24

Diode representation.

Typical diode ratings

The diodes used for bypass and blocking are different for the different modules/cells depending on their current and voltage ratings. There are various ratings of diodes available. The rating of a bypass diode, which is used for 16–19 cells in series, is the total current flowing through the series connected cells in a string. That means, the one module of 36 cells contains 2 bypass diodes and a module with 72 cells contains 4 bypass diodes. Typically, the rating of bypass diode is of order 5–10 ampere and 30–50 volts (depending on the number of cells which are connected in series and their current and voltages). The blocking diode ratings depend on the array current and the voltage because main function of these diodes is to block the current coming from the battery during night when modules do not produce any power. Typical rating of the blocking diode ranges from small current like 10s of amperes to the large current like 100s of amperes for SPV arrays.

Solar PV Module Arrays

A single solar cell does not produce enough power (voltage and current) to operate the load and, therefore, many cells are connected together to make a PV module. The PV modules are available in wattage rating of 3 W_p to 300 W_p. A PV module is characterized by several parameters including I_{sc}, V_{oc}, I_m, V_m, W_p (P_{max} or P_m), FF and η. The main parameters useful for the practical application are I_m, V_m and P_m. While showing a large number of modules, a representative symbol of module is used. The symbol of a PV module is shown in Figure 5.1.

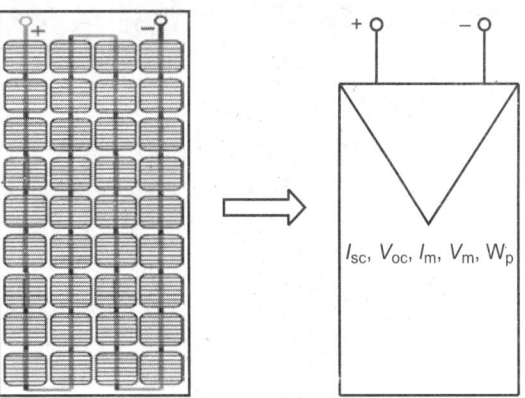

FIGURE 5.1

Schematic representation of a PV module (module parameters may or may not be mentioned).

Many times, in practice, we need power in large quantity, like in several hundred watts, kW and in MW. In order to have a large power generations (larger than a single PV module can produce), these solar PV modules are connected in series and/or parallel combinations.

PV module string: When many PV modules are connected in series, a single row of series connected PV modules is referred as PV module string. The series connection of PV modules is used for increasing the voltage in PV systems. A schematic representation of series connected PV modules or a PV module string is shown in Figure 5.2.

In a PV power plant, the PV modules connected in series are referred as PV modules string.

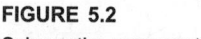

FIGURE 5.2

Schematic representation of series connected PV modules or a PV module string.

PV modules array: In order to increase the current in PV system, the PV individual PV modules or PV module strings are connected in parallel. Such series and parallel combination of PV modules is referred as 'solar PV array'.

A schematic diagram of a solar PV array is shown in Figure 5.3, and a photograph of a installed solar PV array is shown in Figure 5.4. When the number of modules are connected in series and/or parallel combination, the symbol of PV module (Figure 5.3) can be used for the representation of the modules.

Note that, in both series and parallel combination of PV modules, the power of the PV modules always gets added.

A solar PV array is a combination of PV modules in series and parallel.

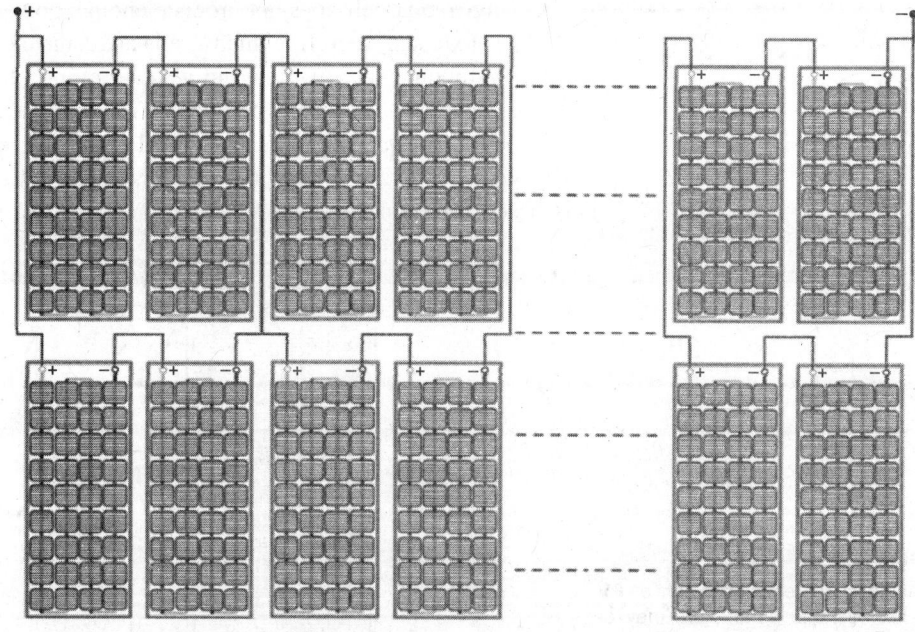

FIGURE 5.3

A schematic of solar PV array.

In order to get power output larger than a single PV module can generate, many PV modules are connected in series and/or parallel in the form of PV array.

FIGURE 5.4

Photo of a solar PV array.

5.1

Connection of Modules in Series

Do you remember from Chapter 4, why solar cells are connected in series in a PV module? If you recall, the main reason for connecting cells in series is to increase the output voltage of a PV module up to certain level, for instance, up to 15 V at maximum power point. Normally, the standard maximum voltages of modules are 15 V, 30 V and 45 V. There are possibilities when the PV system voltage requirement may be higher than what a single PV module can provide. Thus, in the case when PV system (a PV power plant and standalone PV system) voltage requirement is more than the maximum voltage delivered by a single PV module, two or more PV modules are connected in series. The series connection of PV modules is similar to the series connection of solar cells in a PV module. Note that, in making a series connection of PV modules, it is not only the PV module voltage that increases but also the total PV power generated also increases.

> If PV modules are connected in series, then their voltage gets added up.

Series combination of the PV modules is achieved by connecting the opposite polarity terminals of modules together as shown below in Figure 5.5. The negative terminal of one module is connected with the positive terminal of the other module. When two modules with open circuit voltage of V_{oc1} and V_{oc2} are connected in series, the voltage of series combination is the addition of two voltages, which is $V_{oc1} + V_{oc2}$ (as shown in Figure 5.5(a)). Here, the description is given for open circuit voltages. The concept of addition of voltages in series connected PV modules is also applicable for other voltages, like V_m, the voltage at maximum power point. An example of two PV modules with series connection is given in Table 5.1.

> Series connection of PV modules is obtained by connecting positive terminal of one module to negative terminal of the next module.

When PV modules are connected in series, the voltage of the series connected PV modules is the sum of the voltages of individual PV modules.

In the same way (as in Table 5.1), the voltage at maximum power point, V_m, of the PV modules can also be added.

TABLE 5.1 An Example of Summation of Open Circuit Voltages of Two Series Connected PV Modules (*Note:* Combination of Current Remains Same as that of Single Module)

Open circuit voltage of module 1	V_{oc1}	18 V
Open circuit voltage of module 2	V_{oc2}	18 V
Open circuit voltage of modules connected in series	V_{oc}	$= V_{oc1} + V_{oc2} = 18 + 18 = 36$ V

When three modules with open circuit voltage of V_{oc1}, V_{oc2} and V_{oc3} are connected in series, the total voltage of series combination will be the sum of these three voltages, i.e., $V_{oc1} + V_{oc2} + V_{oc3}$ [as shown in Figure 5.5(b)].

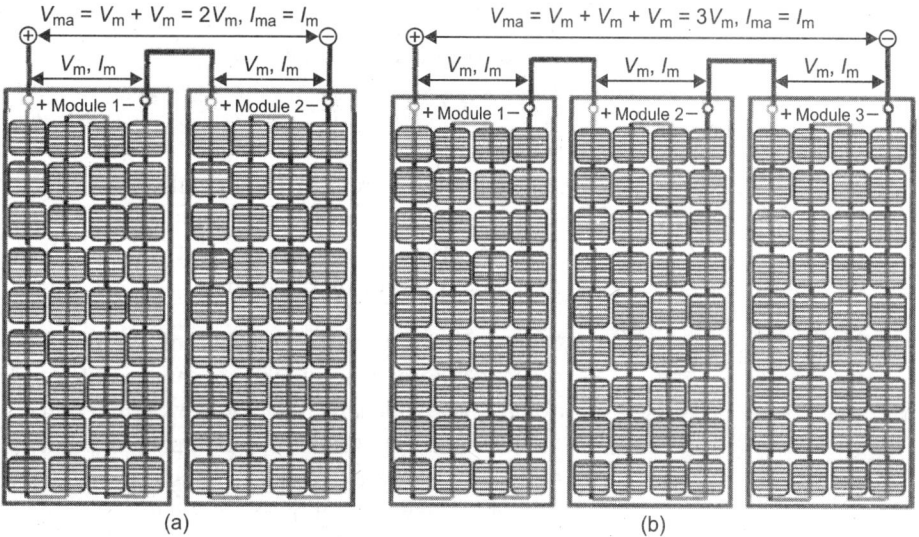

FIGURE 5.5

Series connection of (a) two modules, and (b) three modules.

(a)   (b)

WORKSHEET 5.1: Find out the total open circuit voltage of three PV modules connected in series. Open circuit voltage of individual module is specified in Table 5.2.

TABLE 5.2 Open Circuit Voltage Modules

Open circuit voltage of module 1	V_{oc1}	18 V
Open circuit voltage of module 2	V_{oc2}	17.5 V
Open circuit voltage of module 3	V_{oc3}	17.9 V
Open circuit voltage of modules connected in series	V_{oc}	$= V_{oc1} + V_{oc2} + V_{oc3}$
		$= 18 + \rule{1cm}{0.15mm} + \rule{1cm}{0.15mm} = \rule{1cm}{0.15mm}$ V

5.1.1
Estimating Number of PV Modules Required in Series and Their Total Power

It is mentioned in the earlier sections that PV modules are connected in series in order to increase the voltage. The series connection of PV modules is called 'PV module string' or if, in a PV system, the modules are connected only in series, then we can call the series connection of PV modules as 'PV modules array'. In the series connection, the voltage of the PV modules gets added while the current of the series connected modules remain the same as that of an individual module. This is assuming that all the PV modules are identical, having identical parameters like V_{oc}, V_m, I_{sc} and I_m.

Now, let us calculate the number of modules which are required to be connected in a series if the requirement of voltage of PV modules array is known. Also, we should be able to estimate the total power that the series connected PV modules will be generating. This exercise can be done in three steps:

Step 1 Note down the voltage requirement of series connected PV modules: Since the idea is to connect PV modules in series to increase the voltage of array. How much voltage is required from PV module array should be noted as follows:

PV module parameter	Symbol	Value	Unit
PV module array open circuit voltage	V_{oca}		volt
PV module array at maximum power point	V_{ma}		volt

Step 2 Note down the parameter of a PV module that is to be connected in series: Since in operation, it is expected that a PV module operates under maximum power point condition, therefore, current and voltage at maximum power point, that is, V_m and I_m of the available PV module (or PV module specified by client) must be noted. Other PV module information like V_{oc}, I_{sc} and P_m can also be noted in the following table:

PV module parameter	Symbol	Value	Unit
Open circuit voltage of module	V_{oc}		volt
Short circuit current of PV module	I_{sc}		ampere
Voltage at maximum power point	V_m		volt
Current at maximum power point	I_m		ampere
Maximum power of PV module	P_m		watt

Step 3 Estimating the number of PV modules to be connected in series: In order to find out the number of PV modules to be connected in series, total array voltage is divided by the voltage of individual modules. Since in real time, PV modules are supposed to work under maximum power point condition, the ratio of V_{ma} to V_m (array module voltage to module voltage at maximum power point) should be taken as follows:

PV module parameter	Symbol	Value	Unit
Required PV array voltage at maximum power point	V_{ina}		volt
Voltage at maximum power point of single PV module	V_m		volt
Number of PV modules in series, N_s	$N_s = (V_{ma}/V_m)$		number
Current at maximum power point of PV array	$I_{ma} = I_m$		

The number of PV modules connected in series depends on the amount of voltage required from a PV module string.

Current of a PV module string is the same as the current of individual PV module of a string, assuming all PV modules are identical.

If the ratio of V_{ma} to V_m is not an integer, then the next integer value should be taken. For instance, if the ratio is 3.5. We know that number of modules cannot be 3.5, it can be either 3 or 4. Therefore, in this case, the next integer number, i.e., 4 should be taken.

Also note in the above table that the current at maximum power point of PV array remains the same as that of current of individual PV module, i.e., $I_{ma} = I_m$.

In this step, the calculations for finding out the number of modules to be connected in series is done using voltage at maximum power point, but similar calculations can also be done using open circuit voltage of PV modules. Please note that voltage at maximum power point of a PV module is normally in range of 75% to 85% of open circuit voltage.

Step 4 Estimating the total power of the series connected PV modules: The total power of the PV array in series connected PV modules is the sum of the maximum power of individual PV modules. Thus, if N_s PV modules are connected in series and maximum power of one PV module is P_m, then the total power output of the PV array (P_{ma}) would be $N_s \times P_m$. Thus, by connecting PV modules in series, not only the voltage but the total power of the series connected PV modules also increases, depending on the number of PV modules connected in series. The PV array power output can also be calculated from PV array voltage and current at maximum power point, V_{ma} and I_{ma}. The PV module array power is the product of V_{ma} and I_{ma}, that is, $P_{ma} = V_{ma} \times I_{ma}$. This can be tabulated (Table 5.3) in following way:

TABLE 5.3 Calculation of PV Modules Array

PV module parameter	Symbol	Value	Unit
PV array voltage at maximum power point (note actual PV voltage, this can be higher than the required voltage, because we have to take integer value of V_{ma}/V_m)	$V_{ma} = V_m \times N_s$		volt
PV array current at maximum power point	I_{ma}		volt
Maximum power of single PV module	P_m		watt
Number of PV modules in series, N_s	N_s		number
Maximum power of PV module array[#]	$P_{ma} = P_m \times N_s$ $= V_m \times I_m \times N_s$ or $P_{ma} = V_{ma} \times I_{ma}$		watt

[#] Because of approximating N_s value to the next higher integer value in Step 3, the value of V_{ma} will be higher than the initial desired value noted in Step 1.

EXAMPLE 5.1

Calculate the number of modules to be connected in series to obtain the open circuit voltage of the array as 40 V and/or maximum power point voltage of 32 V. The modules available for connection are having the following parameters:

$$V_{oc} = 20 \text{ V}, \ V_m = 16 \text{ V}, \ I_{sc} = 4 \text{ A and } I_m = 3 \text{ A}$$

Solution

Step 1 Note down the voltage requirement of series connected PV modules:

PV module parameter	Symbol	Value	Unit
PV module array open circuit voltage	V_{oca}	40	volt
PV module array at maximum power point	V_{ma}	32	volt

Step 2 Note down the parameter of a PV module that is to be connected in series:

PV module parameter	Symbol	Value	Unit
Open circuit voltage of module	V_{oc}	20	volt
Short circuit current of PV module	I_{sc}	4	ampere
Voltage at maximum power point	V_m	16	volt
Current at maximum power point	I_m	3	ampere
Maximum power of PV module	$P_m = V_m \times I_m$	48	watt

Step 3 Estimating the number of PV modules to be connected in series:

PV module parameter	Symbol	Value	Unit
Required PV array voltage at maximum power point	V_{ma}	32	volt
Voltage at maximum power point of single PV module	V_m	16	volt
Number of PV modules in series, N_s	$N_s = (V_{ma}/V_m)$	(32/16) = 2	number
Current at maximum power point of PV array	$I_{ma} = I_m$	3	ampere

Figure 5.6 shows two modules connected in series to make array.

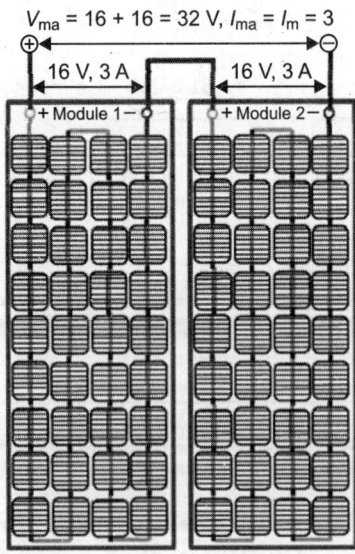

FIGURE 5.6

Two modules connected in series to make array.

Total power of number of PV modules connected in series is sum of powers of individual PV modules, assuming all modules are identical.

Step 4 Estimating the total power of the series connected PV modules:

PV module parameter	Symbol	Value	Unit
PV array voltage at maximum power point	V_{ma}	32	volt
PV array current at maximum power point	I_{ma}	3	amperes
Maximum power of single PV module	P_m	48	watt
Number of PV modules in series (N_s)	N_s	2	number
Maximum power of PV module array	$P_{ma} = P_m \times N_s$ or $P_{ma} = V_{ma} \times I_{ma}$ or $P_{ma} = V_m \times I_m \times N_s$	48×2 or 32×3 or $16 \times 3 \times 2 = 96$	watt

EXAMPLE 5.2

Calculate the number of modules to be connected in series to obtain maximum power point voltage of 70 V. The modules available for connection are having following parameters.

$$V_{oc} = 20 \text{ V}, \ V_m = 15 \text{ V}, \ I_{sc} = 5 \text{ A and } I_m = 3.5 \text{ A}$$

Solution

Step 1 Note down the voltage requirement of series connected PV modules:

PV module parameter	Symbol	Value	Unit
PV module array open circuit voltage	V_{oca}	(not given)	volt
PV module array at maximum power point	V_{ma}	70	volt

Step 2 Note down the parameter of a PV module that is to be connected in series:

PV module parameter	Symbol	Value	Unit
Open circuit voltage of module	V_{oc}	20	volt
Short circuit current of PV module	I_{sc}	5	ampere
Voltage at maximum power point	V_m	15	volt
Current at maximum power point	I_m	3.5	ampere
Maximum power of PV module	$P_m = V_m \times I_m$	52.5	watt

Step 3 Estimating the number of PV modules to be connected in series:

PV module parameter	Symbol	Value	Unit
Required PV array voltage at maximum power point	V_{ma}	70	volt
Voltage at maximum power point of single PV module	V_m	15	volt
Number of PV modules in series, N_s	$N_s = (V_{ma}/V_m)$	70/15 = 4.66 ≈ 5	4.66 modules can not be connected in series, we have to connect 5 modules
Current at maximum power point of PV array	$I_{ma} = I_m$	3.5	ampere

Figure 5.7 shows five identical modules connected in series (a PV module string).

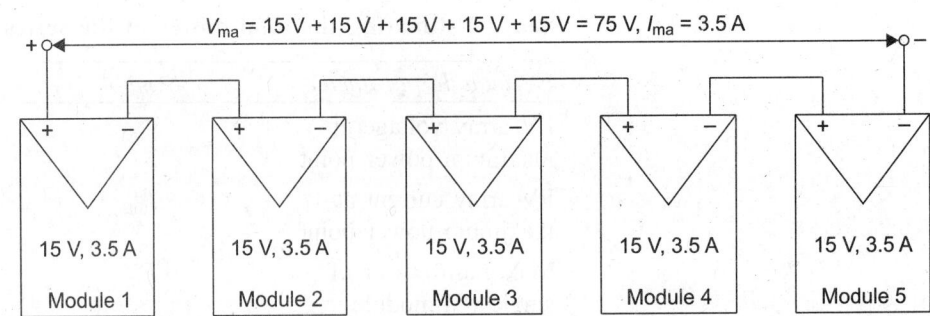

$V_{ma} = 15\,V + 15\,V + 15\,V + 15\,V + 15\,V = 75\,V$, $I_{ma} = 3.5\,A$

15 V, 3.5 A	15 V, 3.5 A	15 V, 3.5 A	15 V, 3.5 A	15 V, 3.5 A
Module 1	Module 2	Module 3	Module 4	Module 5

FIGURE 5.7
Five identical modules connected in series (a PV module string).

Step 4 Estimating the total power of the series connected PV modules:

PV module parameter	Symbol	Value	Unit
PV array voltage at maximum power point (note here the designed array voltage, 75 V, is higher than the required voltage, 70 V)	$V_{ma} = V_m \times N_s$	$15 \times 5 = 75$	volt
PV array current at maximum power point	I_{ma}	15	volt
Maximum power of single PV module	P_m	52.5	watt
Number of PV modules in series (N_s)	N_s	5	number
Maximum power of PV module array	$P_{ma} = P_m \times N_s$ or $P_{ma} = V_{ma} \times I_{ma}$ or $P_{ma} = V_m \times I_m \times N_s$	52.5×5 or 75×3.5 or $15 \times 3.5 \times 5$ $= 262.5$	watt

EXAMPLE 5.3

In a PV power plant of 1 MW capacity, a large number of PV modules are connected in series. In such plants, 1 MW inverter can take input voltage in range of 600 V to 800 V. Design the number of PV modules to be connected in a single series (PV module string) to obtain voltage at maximum power point of 700 V. Also, estimate the peak power that will be supplied by one such PV module string. The parameters of PV modules to be used are:

$$V_{oc} = 36\,V,\ V_m = 30\,V,\ I_{sc} = 8.2\,A\ \text{and}\ I_m = 7.4\,A.$$

Solution

Step 1 Note down the voltage requirement of series connected PV modules:

PV module parameter	Symbol	Value	Unit
PV module array open circuit voltage	V_{oca}	(not given)	volt
PV module array at maximum power point	V_{ma}	700	volt

Step 2 Note down the parameter of a PV module that is to be connected in series:

PV module parameter	Symbol	Value	Unit
Open circuit voltage of module	V_{oc}	36	volt
Short circuit current of PV module	I_{sc}	8.2	ampere
Voltage at maximum power point	V_m	30	volt
Current at maximum power point	I_m	7.4	ampere
Maximum power of PV module	$P_m = V_m \times I_m$	$30 \times 7.4 = 222$	watt

Step 3 Estimating the number of PV modules to be connected in series:

PV module parameter	Symbol	Value	Unit
Required PV array voltage at maximum power point	V_{ma}	700	volt
Voltage at maximum power point of single PV module	V_m	30	volt
Number of PV modules in series (N_s)	$N_s = V_{ma}/V_m$	$700 \div 30$ $= 23.333$ ≈ 24	23.33 modules can not be connected in series, therefore, we have to connect 24 modules
Current at maximum power point of PV array	$I_{ma} = I_m$	7.4	ampere

Figure 5.8 shows 24 modules connected in series (a PV module string).

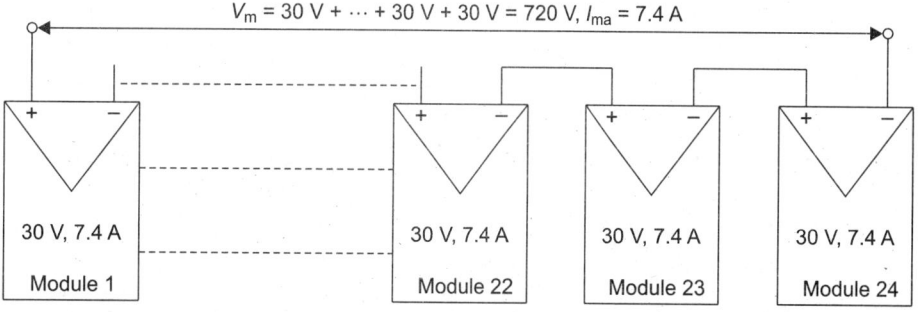

$V_m = 30\ V + \cdots + 30\ V + 30\ V = 720\ V,\ I_{ma} = 7.4\ A$

FIGURE 5.8

24 modules connected in series (a PV module string).

Step 4 Estimating the total power of the series connected PV modules:

PV module parameter	Symbol	Value	Unit
PV array voltage at maximum power point (note here the designed array voltage, 75 V, is higher than the required voltage, 70 V)	$V_{ma} = V_m \times N_s$	$30 \times 24 = 720$	volt
PV array current at maximum power point	I_{ma}	7.4	volt
Maximum power of single PV module	P_m	222	watt
Number of PV modules in series, N_s	N_s	24	number
Maximum power of PV module array	$P_{ma} = P_m \times N_s$ or $P_{ma} = V_{ma} \times I_{ma}$ or $P_{ma} = V_m \times I_m \times N_s$	222×24 or 720×7.4 or $30 \times 7.4 \times 24$ $= 5328$	watt

WORKSHEET 5.2: In a PV power plant of 1 MW capacity, a large number of PV modules are connected in series. In such plants, 1 MW inverter can take input voltage in range of 400 V to 500 V. Design the number of PV modules to be connected in a single series (PV module string) to obtain voltage at maximum power point of 450 V. Also, estimate the peak power that will be supplied by one such PV module string. The parameters of PV modules to be used are: $V_{oc} = 45$ V, $V_m = 35$ V, $I_{sc} = 8.2$ A and $I_m = 7.8$ A.

Step 1 Note down the voltage requirement of series connected PV modules:

PV module parameter	Symbol	Value	Unit
PV module array open circuit voltage	V_{oca}	(not given)	volt
PV module array at maximum power point	V_{ma}	450	volt

Step 2 Note down the parameter of a PV module that is to be connected in series:

PV module parameter	Symbol	Value	Unit
Open circuit voltage of module	V_{oc}		volt
Short circuit current of PV module	I_{sc}		ampere
Voltage at maximum power point	V_m		volt
Current at maximum power point	I_m		ampere
Maximum power of PV module	$P_m = V_m \times I_m$	____ × ____ = ____	watt

Step 3 Estimating the number of PV modules to be connected in series:

PV module parameter	Symbol	Value	Unit	
Required PV array voltage at maximum power point	V_{ma}		volt	
Voltage at maximum power point of single PV module	V_m		volt	
Number of PV modules in series (N_s)	$N_s = V_{ma}/V_m$	____ ÷ ____ = ____ ≈ ____	23.33 modules cannot be connected in series, we have to connect 24 modules	
Current at maximum power point of PV array	$I_{ma} = I_m$		ampere	

Step 4 Estimating the total power of the series connected PV modules:

PV module parameter	Symbol	Value	Unit
PV array voltage at maximum power point (note here the designed array voltage, 75 V, is higher than the required voltage, 70 V)	$V_{ma} = V_m \times N_s$	____ × ____ = ____	volt
PV array current at maximum power point	I_{ma}		volt
Maximum power of single PV module	P_m		watt
Number of PV modules in series (N_s)	N_s		number
Maximum power of PV module array	$P_{ma} = P_m \times N_s$ or $P_{ma} = V_{ma} \times I_{ma}$ or $P_{ma} = V_m \times I_m \times N_s$	____ × ____ or ____ × ____ or ____ × ____ × ____ = ____	watt

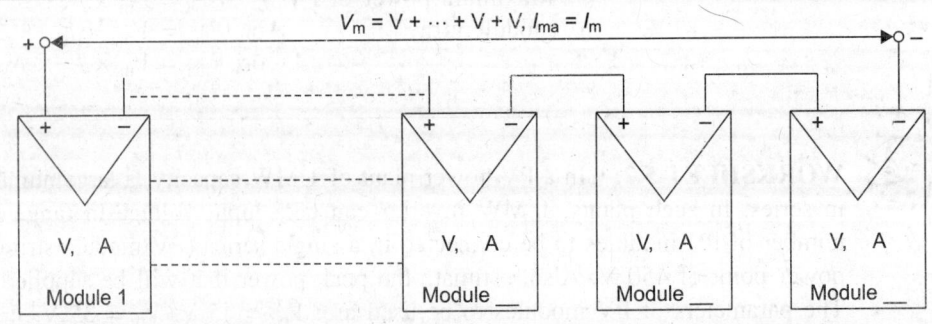

$V_m = V + \cdots + V + V, I_{ma} = I_m$

FIGURE 5.9

____ modules connected in series (a PV module string).

5.1.2
Mismatch in Voltage in Series Connected PV Modules

Maximum power or the peak power output of a PV module (under STC) is the product of current at maximum power point (I_m) and voltage at maximum power point (V_m). When PV modules are not connected with each other, the total peak power produced by PV modules is the sum of the total peak power produced by individual modules. An example of total power produced by three individual PV modules is given in Table 5.4.

TABLE 5.4 Total Power Produced by PV Modules When Working Independently

	V_m (V)	I_m (A)	P_m (watt) = $V_m \times I_m$
Module 1	17	5.1	86.7
Module 2	16.5	5.1	84.15
Module 3	16.3	5.1	83.13
Total wattage produced by three modules when not connected with each other			253.98 watt

Now, let us take the case when the three PV modules mentioned in Table 5.4 are connected in series. In series connection, only voltage gets added but current in series combination remains the same, provided all the modules are with identical current values. For example, in Table 5.4, all the PV modules have I_m of 5.1 A each. Therefore, the current, when three modules are connected in series will be 5.1 A. An example of calculation of P_m of three series connected PV modules is given in Table 5.5. Compare the total power output of these three series connected PV modules (Table 5.5) with the power output of three individual PV modules (Table 5.4). One can notice that the difference in V_m of three series connected PV modules does not affect the total power output of series connected PV modules. But the differences in current of series connected PV modules do affect the power output of series connected PV modules (as discussed in Section 5.1.3).

Mismatch in voltages of series connected PV modules is not an issue, mismatch in currents is.

The difference in the voltages of series connected PV modules does not affect the total power generating capacity of the combination.

TABLE 5.5 Calculation of P_m of Three PV Modules Connected in Series with Identical Current

	V_m (V)	I_m (A)	P_m (watt)
Module 1	17	5.1	86.7
Module 2	16.5	5.1	84.15
Module 3	16.3	5.1	83.13
	Total voltage of series combination	Total current of series combination	Total power of series combination
	49.8	5.1	49.8 × 5.1 = 253.98 watt
Total wattage produced by three PV modules when connected with each other in series.			

5.1.3
Mismatch in Current in Series Connected PV Modules

In series connection, only voltage gets added but current remains the same, provided all the modules are with identical current values. If the current producing capacity of the PV modules is not same, then the current flowing in the series connected modules will be equal to the current of the module with the lowest current producing capacity. Thus, the lowest current producing module determines the current in series connected modules. For examples, if there are three modules having I_m of 5.1 A, 4.9 A and 5.0 A, then the current of the series combination of these modules will be 4.9 A (which is smallest of three currents). Due to this mismatch in current, the power generation from the series combination of three modules will be less than the case when the three modules are working independently. An example of mismatch in series connected PV modules and its effect of total power generation is given in Table 5.6. It can be noticed that the total power generation capacity of three individual modules is 249.05 watt but when connected in series, the power generation capacity of combination is reduced to 244.02 watt. Due to such power generation losses, it is advised that PV modules with difference in I_m should not be connected in series.

PV modules with difference in I_m should not be connected in series. It results in loss of power output.

TABLE 5.6 Total Power Produced by PV Modules When They are Connected with Each Other in Series (STC Conditions)

	V_m (V)	I_m (A)	P_m (watt)
Module 1	17	5.1	86.7
Module 2	16.5	4.9	80.85
Module 3	16.3	5.0	81.5
Total power of modules when not connected in series		249.05 watt	
Total voltage of series combination	Total current of series combination		Total power of series combination
49.8	4.9		49.8 × 4.9 = 244.02 watt
Total wattage produced by three PV modules when connected with each other in series			244.02 watt

5.2

Connection of Modules in Parallel Combination

When solar PV system power requirement is higher than the available single module power, then the solar PV modules are connected in series or parallel. A series connection of PV modules is discussed in Section 5.1. Sometimes, instead of series connection of PV modules, a parallel connection is done to increase the power output. In parallel combination of PV modules, the voltage of the combination remain the same as that of individual module voltage (provided all modules have identical voltage) where as the current of the parallel combination is the sum of currents of all PV modules. The parallel configuration is achieved by connecting same polarity terminals together. In this way, the positive terminal of one module is connected to the positive terminal of the other module and similarly, negative terminal of one module is connected to the negative terminal of other PV module. The parallel combination of the PV modules is shown in Figure 5.10.

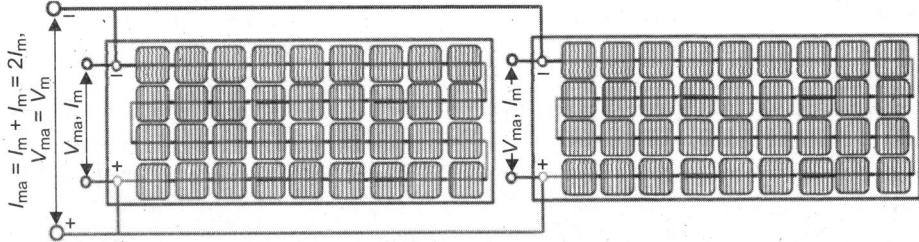

FIGURE 5.10
Two modules in parallel combination.

As shown in Figure 5.10, two modules are connected in parallel configuration by connecting their same polarity terminals to each other (positive terminal to positive and negative terminal to negative). In the parallel combination, individual currents of each module gets added up. Suppose, the short circuit current of two PV modules is I_{sc1} and I_{sc2}, then the total current of parallel connection will be $= I_{sc1} + I_{sc2}$. As the number of modules is added, the current keeps on adding but voltage remains the same. An example of parallel combination of two PV modules, each having 2 A current is given in Table 5.7. The above description is given for short circuit current, but it is applicable for any other current component of PV modules. Thus, if current at maximum power point of two PV modules is I_{m1} and I_{m2}, then the total current at maximum power point of parallel connection will be $I_{m1} + I_{m2}$.

The PV modules are connected in parallel in order to obtain higher currents in PV systems. Module currents in parallel combination get added up.

In parallel combination of PV modules, currents get added while the voltage of combination remains the same as that of a single PV module.

TABLE 5.7 An Example of Summation of Currents when PV Modules Connected in Parallel

Short circuit current of module 1	I_{sc1}	2 A
Short circuit current of module 2	I_{sc2}	2 A
Short circuit current of modules connected in series	I_{sc}	$I_{sc1} + I_{sc2} = 2 + 2 = 4$ A

> The PV modules with different wattages should not be connected together in series or parallel combination.
>
> **Note:** Voltage of combination remains same as that of single module.

EXAMPLE 5.4

What will be the current of three modules connected in parallel as shown in Figure 5.11.

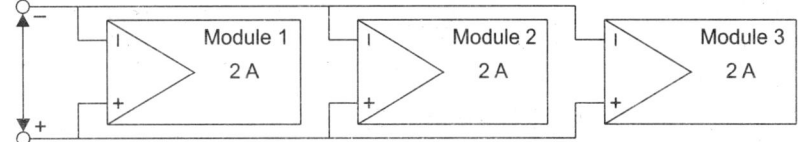

FIGURE 5.11
Three modules in parallel connection.

Solution

In Figure 5.11, positive terminals of all modules are connected together and negative terminals of all modules are connected together. It indicates that the PV modules are connected in parallel configuration.

It is given that the current produced by all PV modules is 2 A. Now, in parallel combination, the total current is the sum of current of individual PV modules. Therefore, the total current of the combination will be

$$= I_{\text{module } 1} + I_{\text{module } 2} + I_{\text{module } 3}$$

$$= 2 + 2 + 2 = 6 \text{ A}.$$

 WORKSHEET 5.3: Find out the total current at maximum power point, I_m, of parallel combination of three PV modules. Current at maximum power point of individual modules is given in Table 5.8.

TABLE 5.8 Current at Maximum Power Point

Current at maximum power point of module 1	I_{m1}	7.8 A
Current at maximum power point of module 2	I_{m2}	7.7 A
Current at maximum power point of module 3	I_{m3}	7.9 A
Current at maximum power point of parallel combination of PV modules	I_m	$I_{sc1} + I_{sc2} + I_{sc3} = $ ____ + ____ + ____ = ____ A

5.2.1
Power Generated by Parallel Connected PV Modules

The P_m of a PV module (under STC) is the product of current at maximum power point (I_m) and voltage at maximum power point (V_m). When PV modules are not connected with each other, the total peak power produced by the PV modules is the sum of the peak power produced by individual modules. An example of total power produced by three individual PV modules (having same V_m but different I_m) is given in Table 5.9. The total power produced by three individual PV modules is 255 watt. When these modules are connected in parallel, the V_m of the parallel combination is same as V_m of individual PV modules which is 17 V (from Table 5.9). Now, the total I_m of the parallel combination will be the sum of I_m of each PV modules, which is 15 A (from Table 5.9). The total power produced by the parallel combination of PV modules is 255 watt which is same as power produced by individual modules. It indicates that while making parallel connection, the voltages of modules should be same and the difference in current is acceptable.

TABLE 5.9 Total Power Produced by Three Individual PV Modules and by Parallel Combination of Same PV Modules (STC Conditions)

	V_m (V)	I_m (A)	P_m (watt) = $V_m \times I_m$
Module 1	17	5.1	86.7
Module 2	17	4.9	83.3
Module 3	17	5	85
Total power of modules when not connected with each other			255.0 watt
Total voltage of parallel combination	Total current of parallel combination		Total power of series combination
17	15		17 × 15 = 255.0 watt
Total wattage produced by three PV modules when connected with each other in parallel			255.0 watt

Total power of PV modules connected in parallel is the sum of powers of individual PV modules, assuming all modules are identical.

5.2.2

Estimating the Number of PV Modules to be Connected in Parallel and Their Total Power

When PV modules are connected in parallel, the current of individual PV module gets added while the voltage of the parallel combination remains the same. Therefore, the main purpose of parallel combination of PV modules is to increase the current of combination. In a PV array, either individual PV modules can be connected in parallel or PV module strings (series connected PV modules) can be connected in parallel. In this section, we will learn to calculate the number of PV modules or PV module strings to be connected in parallel if the requirement of total current of PV system is known. Also, we should be able to estimate the total power that the parallel connected PV modules will be generating. Here it is assumed that all PV modules are identical, having identical parameters like V_{oc}, V_m, I_{sc} and I_m. This exercise can be done in the following steps:

Step 1 Note down the current requirement of parallel connected PV modules or PV array: Since the idea is to connect PV modules or PV module strings in parallel (to form a PV module array) to increase the current of PV array. How much current is required from PV module array should be noted as follows:

PV module parameter	Symbol	Value	Unit
Short circuit current of PV module array	I_{sca}		ampere
Current at maximum power point of PV module array	I_{ma}		ampere

Step 2 Note down the parameter of a PV module or PV module string that is to be connected in parallel: Since in operation, it is expected that a PV module or a PV module string operates under maximum power point condition, therefore, current and voltage at maximum power point, that is, V_m and I_m of available PV module or PV module strings must be noted. Other PV module informations like V_{oc}, I_{sc} and P_m can also be noted in the following table:

PV module or PV module string parameter	Symbol	Value	Unit
Open circuit voltage of module or string	V_{oc}		volt
Short circuit current of PV module or string	I_{sc}		ampere
Voltage at maximum power point or string	V_m		volt
Current at maximum power point or string	I_m		ampere
Maximum power of PV module or string	$P_m = V_m \times I_m$		watt

Step 3 Estimating the number of PV modules or strings to be connected in parallel: In order to find out the number of PV modules to be connected in parallel, total array current (I_{ma}) is divided by the current of individual modules or

module string (I_{ma}). Since in real time, PV modules are supposed to work under maximum power point condition, the ratio of I_{ma} to I_{m} (PV array current to module current at maximum power point) should be taken as follows:

PV module parameter	Symbol	Value	Unit
Required PV array current at maximum power point	I_{ma}		ampere
Current at maximum power point of single PV module or PV module string	I_{m}		ampere
Number of PV modules to be connected in parallel, N_{p}	$N_{\text{p}} = I_{\text{ma}}/I_{\text{m}}$		number
Voltage at maximum power point of PV array	$V_{\text{ma}} = V_{\text{m}}$		volts

If the ratio of I_{ma} to I_{m} is not an integer, then the next integer value should be taken. For instance, if the ratio is 4.7, then we know that number of modules in parallel cannot be 4.7, therefore, it can be either 4 or 5. Hence, in this case, the next integer number, that is 5 should be taken. It means that the number of modules or PV strings to be connected in parallel is 5.

In parallel connection, the voltage of the PV array, remains the same as that of voltage of individual PV module or PV module string. Therefore, note here, in the above table that the voltage at maximum power point of PV array remains same as that of voltage of individual PV module or module string, i.e. $V_{\text{ma}} = V_{\text{m}}$.

In this step, the calculations for finding out the number of modules to be connected in parallel is done using current at maximum power point, but similar calculations can also be done using short circuit current of PV modules. Please note that module current at maximum power point is normally in range of 85% to 95% of current of short circuit point.

> The number of PV modules connected in parallel is obtained by dividing the desired current from the parallel combination with current of individual PV module.

Step 4 Estimating the total power of the series connected PV modules: The total power of the PV array in parallel connected PV modules is the sum of the maximum power of individual PV modules or the total power of the PV array in parallel connected PV module strings is the sum of the maximum power of individual PV modules strings. Thus, if N_{p} PV modules or strings are connected in parallel and maximum power of one PV module or string is P_{m}, then the total power output of the PV array is $P_{\text{ma}} = N_{\text{p}} \times P_{\text{m}}$. The PV array power output can also be calculated from PV array voltage and current at maximum power point, that is, V_{ma} and I_{ma}. The PV module array power is the product of V_{ma} and I_{ma}, that is, $P_{\text{ma}} = V_{\text{ma}} \times I_{\text{ma}}$. This can be tabulated in the following way:

PV module parameter	Symbol	Value	Unit
PV array voltage at maximum power point	$V_{\text{ma}} = V_{\text{m}}$		volt
PV array current at maximum power point[#]	$I_{\text{ma}} = N_{\text{p}} \times I_{\text{m}}$		volt
Maximum power of single PV module	P_{m}		watt
Number of PV modules to be connected in parallel (N_{p})	N_{p}		number
Maximum power of PV module array	$P_{\text{ma}} = P_{\text{m}} \times N_{\text{p}}$ or $= V_{\text{m}} \times I_{\text{m}} \times N_{\text{p}}$ or $= V_{\text{ma}} \times I_{\text{ma}}$		watt

[#] Because of approximating N_{p} value to the next higher integer value in Step 3, the value of I_{ma} will be higher than the initial desired value noted in Step 1.

EXAMPLE 5.5

Estimate the number of SPV modules to be connected in parallel to achieve the current at peak power point of 42 A. The system voltage requirement is 16 volts. The modules to be connected are having parameters V_m = 16 V, I_m = 7 A, V_{oc} = 20 V, I_{sc} = 8.5 A.

Solution

Step 1 Note down the current requirement of parallel connected PV modules or PV array:

PV module parameter	Symbol	Value	Unit
Short circuit current of PV module array	I_{sca}	(not given)	ampere
Current at maximum power point of PV module array	I_{ma}	42	ampere

Step 2 Note down the parameter of a PV module or PV module string that is to be connected in parallel:

PV module or PV module string parameter	Symbol	Value	Unit
Open circuit voltage of module or string	V_{oc}	20	volt
Short circuit current of PV module or string	I_{sc}	8.5	ampere
Voltage at maximum power point or string	V_m	16	volt
Current at maximum power point or string	I_m	7	ampere
Maximum power of PV module or string	$P_m = V_m \times I_m$	= 7 × 16 = 112	watt

Step 3 Estimating the number of PV modules or strings to be connected in parallel:

PV module parameter	Symbol	Value	Unit
Required PV array current at maximum power point	I_{ma}	42	ampere
Current at maximum power point of single PV module or PV module string	I_m	7	ampere
Number of PV modules to be connected in parallel (N_p)	$N_p = I_{ma}/I_m$	= 42 ÷ 7 = 6	number
Voltage at maximum power point of PV array	$V_{ma} = V_m$	16	volts

Step 4 Estimating the total power of the series connected PV modules:

PV module parameter	Symbol	Value	Unit
PV array voltage at maximum power point	$V_{ma} = V_m$	16	volt
PV array current at maximum power point	$I_{ma} = N_p \times I_m$	= 6 × 7 = 42	volt
Maximum power of single PV module	P_m	112	watt
Number of PV modules to be connected in parallel (N_p)	N_p	6	number
Maximum power of PV module array	$P_{ma} = P_m \times N_p$ or = $V_m \times I_m \times N_p$ or = $V_{ma} \times I_{ma}$	= 112 × 6 = 16 × 7 × 6 = 16 × 42 = 672	watt

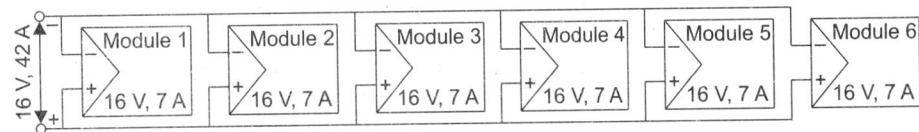

FIGURE 5.12

Six modules connected in parallel combination.

WORKSHEET 5.4: Find out the number of modules to be connected in parallel and series combination for voltage and current requirement of 40 V and 60 A respectively (at maximum power point). The modules available for this power plant are with parameters $V_m = 40$ V, $I_m = 6$ A. Also, calculate the total power rating of the power plant.

Step 1 Note down the current requirement of parallel connected PV modules or PV array:

PV module parameter	Symbol	Value	Unit
Short circuit current of PV module array	I_{sca}	(not given)	ampere
Current at maximum power point of PV module array	I_{ma}	60	ampere

Step 2 Note down the parameter of a PV module or PV module string that is to be connected in parallel:

PV module or PV module string parameter	Symbol	Value	Unit
Open circuit voltage of module or string	V_{oc}		volt
Short circuit current of PV module or string	I_{sc}		ampere
Voltage at maximum power point or string	V_m		volt
Current at maximum power point or string	I_m		ampere
Maximum power of PV module or string	$P_m = V_m \times I_m$	___ × ___ = ___	watt

Step 3 Estimating the number of PV modules or strings to be connected in parallel:

PV module parameter	Symbol	Value	Unit
Required PV array current at maximum power point	I_{ma}		ampere
Current at maximum power point of single PV module or PV module string	I_m		ampere
Number of PV modules to be connected in parallel (N_p)	$N_p = I_{ma}/I_m$	___ ÷ ___ = ___ ≈ ___	number
Voltage at maximum power point of PV array	$V_{ma} = V_m$	35	volts

Step 4 Estimating the total power of the series connected PV modules:

PV module parameter	Symbol	Value	Unit
PV array voltage at maximum power point	$V_{ma} = V_m$		volt
PV array current at maximum power point	$I_{ma} = N_p \times I_m$	___ × ___ = ___	volt
Maximum power of single PV module	P_m		watt
Number of PV modules to be connected in parallel (N_p)	N_p		number
Maximum power of PV module array	$P_{ma} = P_m \times N_p$	___ × ___	watt
	or $= V_m \times I_m \times N_p$	___ × ___ × ___	
	or $= V_{ma} \times I_{ma}$	___ × ___ = ___	

FIGURE 5.13
_____ modules connected in parallel combination (to be drawn by the readers).

EXAMPLE 5.6

Estimate the number of modules required to fulfill the maximum power point current of 96 A, with maximum voltage of 35 V. The modules available are having the following parameters:

$$V_{oc} = 40 \text{ V}, \ V_m = 36 \text{ V}, \ I_{sc} = 8.5 \text{ A}, \ I_m = 7.5 \text{ A}$$

Also, find out the total power of the plant designed.

Solution

Step 1 Note down the current requirement of parallel connected PV modules or PV array:

PV module parameter	Symbol	Value	Unit
Short circuit current of PV module array	I_{sca}	(not given)	ampere
Current at maximum power point of PV module array	I_{ma}	96	ampere

Step 2 Note down the parameter of a PV module or PV module string that is to be connected in parallel:

PV module or PV module string parameter	Symbol	Value	Unit
Open circuit voltage of module or string	V_{oc}	40	volt
Short circuit current of PV module or string	I_{sc}	8.5	ampere
Voltage at maximum power point or string	V_m	36	volt
Current at maximum power point or string	I_m	7.5	ampere
Maximum power of PV module or string	$P_m = V_m \times I_m$	36×7.5 = 270	watt

Step 3 Estimating the number of PV modules or strings to be connected in parallel:

PV module parameter	Symbol	Value	Unit
Required PV array current at maximum power point	I_{ma}	95	ampere
Current at maximum power point of single PV module or PV module string	I_m	7.5	ampere
Number of PV modules to be connected in parallel (N_p)	$N_p = I_{ma}/I_m$	$96 \div 7.5$ = 12.8 ≈ 13	number
Voltage at maximum power point of PV array	$V_{ma} = V_m$	36	volts

Step 4 Estimating the total power of the series connected PV modules:

PV module parameter	Symbol	Value	Unit
PV array voltage at maximum power point	$V_{ma} = V_m$	36	volt
PV array current at maximum power point	$I_{ma} = N_p \times I_m$	$13 \times 7.5 = 97.5$	volt
Maximum power of single PV module	P_m	270	watt
Number of PV modules to be connected in parallel (N_p)	N_p	13	number
Maximum power of PV module array	$P_{ma} = P_m \times N_p$	270×13	watt
	or $\quad = V_m \times I_m \times N_p$	$36 \times 7.5 \times 13$	
	or $\quad = V_{ma} \times I_{ma}$	36×97.5	
		$= 3510$	

WORKSHEET 5.5: Estimate the number of SPV modules to be connected in parallel to achieve the current requirement of 100 A. The system voltage requirement is 35 Volts. The modules to be connected are having parameters $V_m = 36$ V, $I_m = 8$ A, $V_{oc} = 45$ V, $I_{sc} = 8.75$ A.

Step 1 Note down the current requirement of parallel connected PV modules or PV array:

PV module parameter	Symbol	Value	Unit
Short circuit current of PV module array	I_{sca}	(not given)	ampere
Current at maximum power point of PV module array	I_{ma}	100	ampere

Step 2 Note down the parameter of a PV module or PV module string that is to be connected in parallel:

PV module or PV module string parameter	Symbol	Value	Unit
Open circuit voltage of module or string	V_{oc}		volt
Short circuit current of PV module or string	I_{sc}		ampere
Voltage at maximum power point or string	V_m		volt
Current at maximum power point or string	I_m		ampere
Maximum power of PV module or string	$P_m = V_m \times I_m$	____ × ____ = _____	watt

Step 3 Estimating the number of PV modules or strings to be connected in parallel:

PV module parameter	Symbol	Value	Unit
Required PV array current at maximum power point	I_{ma}	100	ampere
Current at maximum power point of single PV module or PV module string	I_m	8	ampere
Number of PV modules to be connected in parallel (N_p)	$N_p = I_{ma}/I_m$	____ ÷ ____ = _____ $\approx$ ____	number
Voltage at maximum power point of PV array	$V_{ma} = V_m$		volts

Step 4 Estimating the total power of the series connected PV modules:

PV module parameter	Symbol	Value	Unit
PV array voltage at maximum power point	$V_{ma} = V_m$		volt
PV array current at maximum power point	$I_{ma} = N_p \times I_m$	___ × ___ = ___	volt
Maximum power of single PV module	P_m		watt
Number of PV modules to be connected in parallel (N_p)	N_p		number
Maximum power of PV module array	$P_{ma} = P_m \times N_p$	___ × ___	watt
or	$= V_m \times I_m \times N_p$	___ × ___ × ___	
or	$= V_{ma} \times I_{ma}$	___ × ___ = ___	

FIGURE 5.14

____ modules connected in parallel combination (to be drawn by the readers).

5.2.3
Mismatch in Module Voltages Connected in Parallel

Mismatch in currents of PV modules connected in parallel is not an issue, mismatch in voltages is.

It has been mentioned that the voltage of parallel combination of PV modules is equal to the voltage of a single module, if the module voltages are identical. If there is difference in PV module voltages, then the voltage of the parallel combination is determined by the PV module with lowest voltage. Normally, the effect of difference in modules voltages in parallel combination is not as severe as the difference in module currents in series combination. In general, as a practice, care should be taken to avoid series or parallel connection of the PV modules of different power ratings (means different current and voltage rating). Or, if, there is need to connect PV modules of different power ratings together, efforts should be made to put PV modules of same current rating in series combination and PV modules of same voltage ratings in parallel combination.

5.3
Connection of Modules in Series and Parallel
(Mixed Combination)

When the PV power requirement is more than few hundred watts, the PV modules needs to be connected in both series and in parallel combination. Also, when we need to generate a very large amount of power, like in solar PV megawatt scale power plants, then the PV modules are connected in both series and parallel configuration to increase the required current as well as voltage. Just to remind you that the series connection of PV module increases the voltage levels while the parallel connection of PV modules increases the current levels. Normally, in big PV power plants, many PV modules are connected in series. The series connected PV modules may be referred as PV module 'string'. In a PV system, the number of PV modules is first connected in series (string) as per the requirement of system voltage, and then many PV module strings are connected together in parallel. An example of series and parallel combination of four PV modules is shown in Figure 5.15.

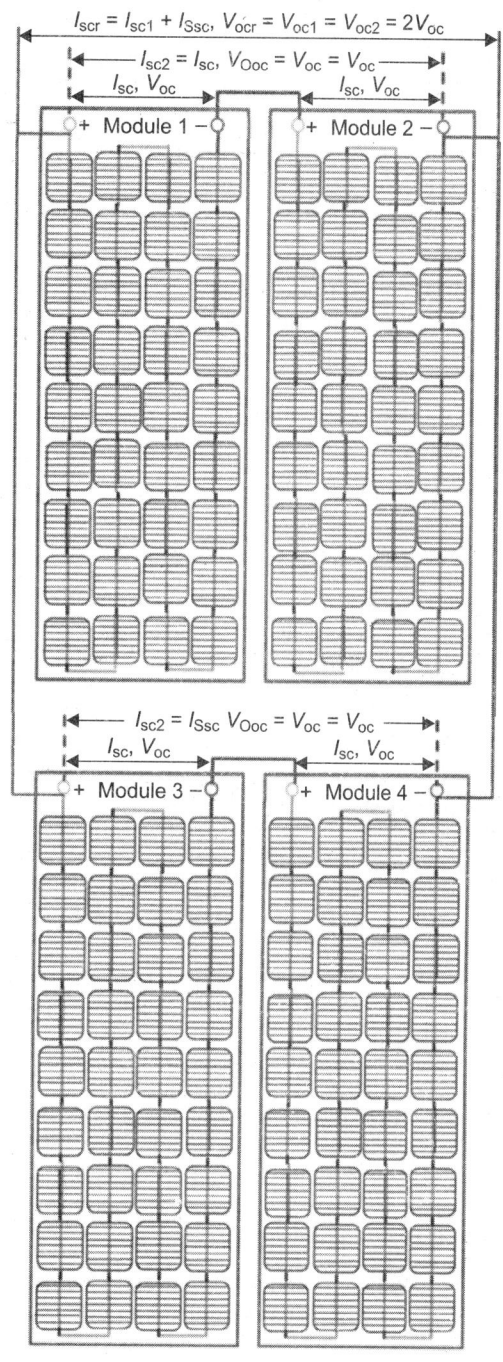

FIGURE 5.15

Series and parallel combination of PV modules.

In this example, four identical PV modules (Module 1, Module 2, Module 3 and Module 4) with open circuit voltage of V_{oc} and short circuit current of I_{sc} are used.

In Figure 5.15, the connection of four identical PV modules is shown, each PV module having short circuit current of I_{sc} and open circuit voltage of V_{oc}. A close observation of the Figure 5.15 will show that two PV modules are connected in series (a PV module string), and two such strings are connected in parallel. In series connection of PV modules, the voltage gets added while current remains the same and in parallel connection of PV modules, the current gets added and voltage remains the same. In this case, Module 1 and Module 2 (in Figure 5.15) are connected in series, let us call it string 1. Similarly, Module 3 and Module 4 are also connected in series, and let us call it string 2. Since all the PV modules are identical, the open circuit voltage of string 1 (V_{oc1}) and short circuit current of PV module string 1 (I_{sc1}) will be $2 \times V_{oc}$ and I_{sc} respectively (refer to Table 5.10). Similarly, the the open circuit voltage of PV module string 2 will be $2 \times V_{oc}$ while the short circuit current will be I_{sc}.

TABLE 5.10   Example of Summation of Currents and Voltages in Series and Parallel Combination of PV Modules (Voltage Adds up in Series Connection and Current Adds up in Parallel Connection)

Open circuit voltage of PV modules	V_{oc}
Short circuit current of PV modules	I_{sc}
Module 1 and Module 2 are connected in series (string 1)	
(voltage gets added up but current remains same)	
Open circuit voltage of PV module string 1, V_{oc1}	$V_{oc1} = V_{oc} + V_{oc} = 2V_{oc}$
Short circuit current of PV module string 1, I_{sc1}	$I_{sc1} = I_{sc}$
Module 3 and Module 4 are connected in series (string 2)	
Open circuit voltage of PV module string 2, V_{oc2}	$V_{oc2} = V_{oc} + V_{oc} = 2V_{oc}$
Short circuit current of PV module string 2, I_{sc2}	$I_{sc2} = I_{sc}$
PV module string 1 and string 2 are connected in parallel (voltage remains the same but current gets added), the combination is called array	
Open circuit voltage of PV module array (V_{ocr})	$V_{ocr} = V_{oc1} = V_{oc2} = 2V_{oc}$
Short circuit current of PV module array (I_{scr})	$I_{scr} = I_{sc1} + I_{sc2} = I_{sc} + I_{sc} = 2I_{sc}$

Now, the PV module string 1 and string 2 are connected in parallel (this combination of series and parallel PV modules is called PV module array). In parallel combination, voltage remains the same but currents get added. As given in Table 5.10, since the open circuit voltage of the both the PV strings is same ($V_{oc1} = 2V_{oc}$, and $V_{oc2} = 2V_{oc}$), the open circuit voltage of the PV module array, $V_{ocr} = V_{oc1} = V_{oc2} = 2V_{oc}$. The short circuit current of string 1 is $I_{sc1} = I_{sc}$ and that of string 2 is $I_{sc2} = I_{sc}$. Therefore the short circuit current of PV module array, I_{scr}, wherein two strings are connected in parallel is $I_{sc1} + I_{sc2} = I_{sc} + I_{sc} = 2I_{sc}$. In this case of PV module array, the array open circuit voltage will be $2V_{oc}$ and the array short circuit current will be $2I_{sc}$.

In the same way, current and voltage of any combination of series and parallel connected PV modules can be obtained. In practice, PV modules do not operate at open circuit and short circuit conditions, but they operate under maximum power point condition. Therefore, for calculations, current at maximum power point (I_m) and voltage at maximum power point (V_m) should be taken for calculations.

> In high power PV systems, PV modules are connected in series and many such series are connected in parallel.

> In a PV system, voltage increases due to series connection, current increases due to parallel connection, and power increases in both series and parallel connection.

5.3.1
Estimation Number of Modules to be Connected in Series and Parallel and their Total Power

The objective of making series and parallel combination of PV modules, to form PV array, is to increase the current as well as the voltage of combination in order to get higher power. In PV module array, modules are connected in series (to form module string) to get higher voltages and modules or module strings are connected in parallel to get higher currents. In both series and parallel combination, the power output of the combination increases.

PV array formation is required as soon as PV power requirement is higher than the individual power output. Individual PV modules are available in few watt to few hundred watt power range. Nowadays, PV arrays are installed for household application wherein the power requirement ranges from few hundred watts to few kilowatts (kW). The PV power plants are installed with power range from few hundred kW to several megawatt (MW). In this section, we will learn to calculate the number of PV modules to be connected in series, and the number of PV modules to be connected in parallel in order to get desired power output of PV module array. Here, it is assumed that all PV modules are identical, having identical parameters like V_{oc}, V_m, I_{sc} and I_m. The estimation of number of series and parallel connected PV modules can be done in the following steps:

Step 1 Note down the voltage, current and power requirement of PV module array: In PV module array, the idea is to connect PV modules in series and in parallel to increase both voltage and current in PV module array, and to increase power. The desired power of array, P_{ma}, should be noted. If the desired current of array (I_{ma}) and desired voltage of array (V_{ma}) are mentioned, then note it down. Else, if only one of the parameter (current or voltage) is given then other parameter can be estimated using $P_{ma} = I_{ma} \times V_{ma}$ relationship. All three parameters; power, voltage and current are assumed at maximum power point condition.

PV module parameter	Symbol	Value	Unit
PV array power requirement (peak power or maximum power point)	P_{ma}		watt
PV module array open circuit voltage at peak power	V_{ma} or P_{ma}/I_{ma}		volt
PV module array current at peak power	I_{ma} or P_{ma}/V_{ma}		ampere

Step 2 Note down the parameter of a PV module that is to be connected in PV array: Since in operation, it is expected that a PV module operates under maximum power point condition, therefore, current and voltage at maximum power point, that is, V_m and I_m of a PV module to be connected in PV array, must be noted. Other PV modules information like V_{oc}, I_{sc} and P_m can also be noted in the following Table:

PV module parameter	Symbol	Value	Unit
Open circuit voltage of module	V_{oc}		volt
Short circuit current of PV module	I_{sc}		ampere
Voltage at maximum power point	V_m		volt
Current at maximum power point	I_m		ampere
Maximum power of PV module	$P_m = V_m \times I_m$		watt

Step 3 Estimating the number of PV modules to be connected in series and parallel: In order to find out the number of PV modules to be connected in series (voltage addition), total array voltage is divided by the voltage of individual modules. And, in order to find out the number of PV modules or PV module strings to be connected in parallel (current addition), PV array current should be divided by the current of individual PV modules or module string. All the parameters are to be taken under maximum power point condition because PV array is assumed to work under maximum power point condition.

PV module parameter	Symbol	Value	Unit
Required PV array voltage at maximum power point	V_{ma}		volt
Voltage at maximum power point of single PV module or PV string	V_m		volt
Number of PV modules in series (N_s)	$N_s = V_{ma}/V_m$		number
Current at maximum power point of PV array	I_{ma}		ampere
Current at maximum power point of PV module or PV string	I_m		ampere
Number of PV modules in series (N_p)	$N_p = I_{ma}/I_m$		number

The value of N_s and N_p should be an integer. If the calculated ratio is not an integer, then the next higher integer value should be chosen. Thus, if N_s is 3.7, then next higher integer value, that is, 4 should be taken. It means that four PV modules should be connected in series. If N_p is 6.7, then the next higher integer value, that is, 7 should be taken. It means that the 7 PV modules or PV module strings should be connected in parallel. In this case, the PV module array will satisfy both current and voltage requirements.

In this step, the calculation for obtaining the number of PV modules to be connected in series is done using voltage at maximum power point but the same calculation can be done using open circuit voltage. Also, the calculation for obtaining the number of modules or module strings to be connected in parallel is done using current at maximum power point, but similar calculation can also be done using short circuit current of PV modules. Please note that voltage at maximum power point of a PV module is normally in the range of 75% to 85% in open circuit. And, module current at maximum power point is normally in the range of 85% to 95% of current at short circuit point.

Step 4 Estimating the total power of the series PV module array: Normally, before designing the number of PV modules in series and parallel, we should know the total PV array power for which we need to do the design. Therefore, this step is to be done in order to cross check the design. The total power of the PV array, wherein PV modules are connected in series as well as in parallel, is the sum of power of all PV modules connected in PV array. In series connection, voltage and power of modules gets added up, and in parallel connection, current and power of PV modules gets added up. Thus, if N_s PV modules are connected in series and N_p such series are connected in parallel, then the total number of PV modules connected in PV arrays is $N_s \times N_p$. Now, if maximum power of one PV module is P_m, then the total power output of the PV array (P_{ma}) would be $N_s \times N_p \times P_m$. In this process, it is assumed that all PV modules connected in series and in parallel are identical. The PV array power output can also be calculated from PV array voltage and current at maximum power point, that is V_{ma} and I_{ma}. The PV module array power is the product of V_{ma} and I_{ma} and

$$P_{ma} = V_{ma} \times I_{ma}$$

This can be tabulated in the following way:

PV module parameter	Symbol	Value	Unit
Number of PV modules in series (N_s)	N_s		number
Number of PV modules or module strings in parallel (N_p)	N_p		number
New value of PV array voltage at maximum power point[#]	$V_{ma} = V_m \times N_s$		volt
New value of PV array current at maximum power point[#]	$I_{ma} = I_m \times N_p$		volt
Maximum power of single PV module	$P_m = V_m \times I_m$		watt
Maximum power of PV module array[#]	$P_{ma} = P_m \times N_s \times N_p$ $= V_m \times I_m \times N_s \times N_p$ or $P_{ma} = V_{ma} \times I_{ma}$		watt

Design of large power PV plants can be done by designing the appropriate numbers of PV modules in series, and appropriate number of PV modules series in parallel to fulfill desired power requirements.

[#] Note that because of converting N_s and N_p ratio to next higher integer value, the new calculated value of I_{ma} and V_{ma} in above table will be higher than the desired value of I_{ma} and V_{ma} as noted in Step 1. As a result of this, the new calculated PV array power will also be higher than the desired value of power for which design is done.

EXAMPLE 5.7

Estimate the number of PV modules to be connected together in order to design a solar PV system for power generation with following requirements:

Power = 10 kW, Voltage at peak power = 200 V, Current at peak power = 50 A,

The PV modules available for this plant are having the following parameters:

V_m = 35 V, I_m = 8.5 A. Recalculate the numbers. After calculation of number of PV modules, estimate the actual peak power of the system.

Solution

Since the peak voltage and current requirement of the PV system is higher than the peak voltage and current of individual PV modules, it is required to connect the PV modules in series to get desired voltage (higher than individual module voltage) and connect the PV modules strings in parallel to get the desired current (higher than individual module current). The following procedure can be adopted to estimate the number of PV modules to be connected in series and parallel.

Step 1 Note down the voltage, current and power requirement of PV module array:

PV module parameter	Symbol	Value	Unit
PV array power requirement (peak power or maximum power point)	P_{ma}	10,000	watt
PV module array open circuit voltage at peak power (it is given here but can also be calculated if I_{ma} is known)	V_{ma} or $= P_{ma}/I_{ma}$	$=10000 \div 50$ $= 200$	volt
PV module array current at peak power (it is given here but can also be calculated if V_{ma} is known)	I_{ma} or $= P_{ma}/V_{ma}$	$= 10000 \div 200$ $= 50$	ampere

Step 2 Note down the parameter of a PV module that is to be connected in PV array:

PV module parameter	Symbol	Value	Unit
Open circuit voltage of module	V_{oc}	(not given)	volt
Short circuit current of PV module	I_{sc}	(not given)	ampere
Voltage at maximum power point	V_m	35	volt
Current at maximum power point	I_m	8.5	ampere
Maximum power of PV module	$P_m = V_m \times I_m$	$35 \times 8.5 = 297.5$	watt

Step 3 Estimating the number of PV modules to be connected in series and parallel:

PV module parameter	Symbol	Value	Unit
Required PV array voltage at maximum power point	V_{ma}	200	volt
Voltage at maximum power point of single PV module or PV string	V_m	35	volt
Number of PV modules in series (N_s)	$N_s = V_{ma}/V_m$	$= 200 \div 35$ $= 5.71$ ≈ 6	number
Current at maximum power point of PV array	I_{ma}	50	ampere
Current at maximum power point of PV module or PV string	I_m	8.5	ampere
Number of PV modules in series (N_p)	$N_p = I_{ma}/I_m$	$= 50 \div 8.5$ $= 5.88$ ≈ 6	number

Figure 5.16 shows six modules in series and six such PV modules strings in parallel.

Step 4 Estimating the total power of the series PV module array:

PV module parameter	Symbol	Value	Unit
Number of PV modules in series (N_s)	N_s	6	number
Number of PV modules or module strings in parallel (N_p)	N_p	6	number
New value of PV array voltage at maximum power point	$V_{ma} = V_m \times N_s$	$= 35 \times 6$ $= 210$	volt
New value of PV array current at maximum power point	$I_{ma} = I_m \times N_p$	$= 8.5 \times 6$ $= 51$	ampere
Maximum power of single PV module	$P_m = V_m \times I_m$	$= 35 \times 8.5$ $= 297.5$	watt
Maximum power of PV module array	$P_{ma} = P_m \times N_s \times N_p$ or $\quad = V_m \times I_m \times N_s \times N_p$ or $P_{ma} = V_{ma} \times I_{ma}$	$= 297.5 \times 6 \times 6$ or $= 35 \times 8.5 \times 6 \times 6$ or $= 210 \times 51$ $= 10710$	watt

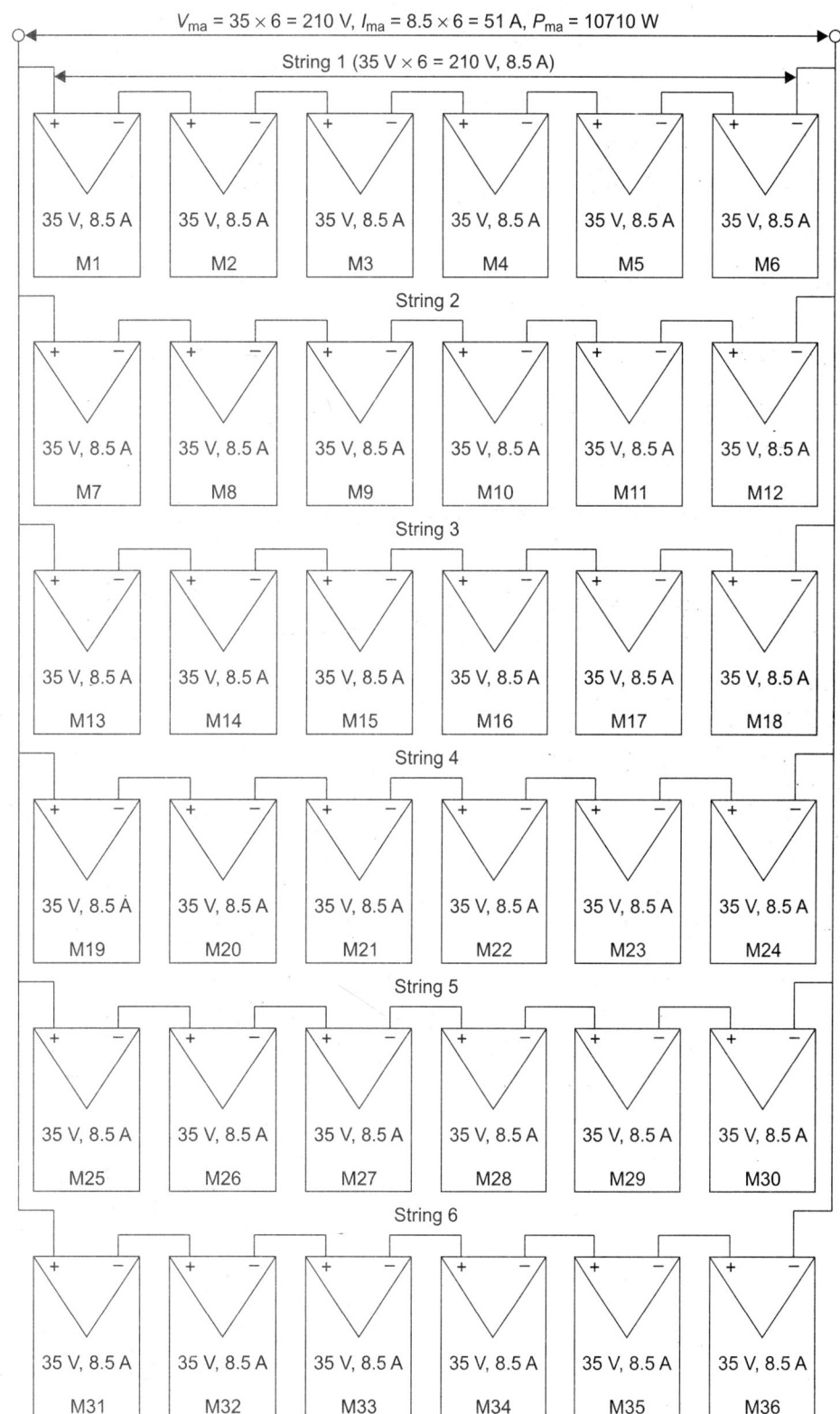

FIGURE 5.16

Six modules in series and six such PV modules strings in parallel.

In MW size PV power plants, many modules are connected in series (PV module string) and many such strings are connected in parallel.

WORKSHEET 5.6: A grid connected PV power plant is installed wherein PV modules are connected to the grid through a grid-tied inverter. The voltage range for inverter operation is 300–400 V and maximum current the inverter can handle is 150 A. Design a solar PV system for such inverter which should operate at maximum voltage of 350 V and current at 150 A. The modules available for this are having $V_m = 40$ V, $I_m = 9$ A. Also, estimate the final power of the system.

Step 1 Note down the voltage, current and power requirement of PV module array:

PV module parameter	Symbol	Value	Unit
PV array power requirement (peak power or maximum power point)	P_{ma} or $I_{ma} \times V_{ma}$	$350 \times 150 =$ _____	watt
PV module array open circuit voltage at peak power	V_{ma} or P_{ma}/I_{ma}	_____ ÷ _____ = _____	volt
PV module array current at peak power	I_{ma} or P_{ma}/V_{ma}	_____ ÷ _____ = _____	ampere

Step 2 Note down the parameter of a PV module that is to be connected in PV array:

PV module parameter	Symbol	Value	Unit
Open circuit voltage of PV module	V_{oc}	(not given)	volt
Short circuit current of PV module	I_{sc}	(not given)	ampere
Voltage at maximum power point	V_m	40	volt
Current at maximum power point	I_m	9	ampere
Maximum power of PV module	$P_m = V_m \times I_m$	= _____ × _____ = _____	watt

Step 3 Estimating the number of PV modules to be connected in series and parallel:

PV module parameter	Symbol	Value	Unit
Required PV array voltage at maximum power point	V_{ma}		volt
Voltage at maximum power point of single PV module or PV string	V_m		volt
Number of PV modules in series (N_s)	$N_s = V_{ma}/V_m$	_____ ÷ _____ = _____	number
Current at maximum power point of PV array	I_{ma}		ampere
Current at maximum power point of PV module or PV string	I_m		ampere
Number of PV modules in series (N_p)	$N_p = I_{ma}/I_m$	_____ ÷ _____ = _____ $\approx$ _____	number

Step 4 Estimating the total power of the series PV module array:

PV module parameter	Symbol	Value	Unit
Number of PV modules in series (N_s)	N_s		number
Number of PV modules or module strings in parallel (N_p)	N_p		number
New value of PV array voltage at maximum power point	$V_{ma} = V_m \times N_s$	_____ × _____ = _____	volt
New value of PV array current at maximum power point	$I_{ma} = I_m \times N_p$	_____ × _____ = _____	ampere
Maximum power of single PV module	$P_m = V_m \times I_m$	_____ × _____ = _____	watt
Maximum power of PV module array	$P_{ma} = P_m \times N_s \times N_p$	___ × ___ × ___	watt
	$= V_m \times I_m \times N_s \times N_p$ or	$=$ ___ × ___ × ___ × ___	
or	$= V_{ma} \times I_{ma}$ or	$=$ ___ × ___ = ___	

EXAMPLE 5.8

In a PV power plant of 1 MW capacity, a large numbers of PV modules are required to be connected in series and parallel combinations. Design number of PV modules to be connected in a series and in parallel for 1 MW_p PV plant. In the PV power plant, the desired voltage at maximum power point is 700 V. Estimate the current at peak power point of the plant. Estimate the peak power that will be supplied by one such PV module string. The parameters of PV modules to be used in the PV plant are following: $V_{oc} = 44$ V, $V_m = 32$ V, $I_{sc} = 8.5$ A and $I_m = 7.5$ A.

Solution

Step 1 Note down the voltage, current and power requirement of PV module array:

PV module parameter	Symbol	Value	Unit
PV array power requirement (peak power or maximum power point)	P_{ma} or $I_{ma} \times V_{ma}$	1000,000	watt
PV module array open circuit voltage at peak power	V_{ma} or P_{ma}/I_{ma}	700	volt
PV module array current at peak power	I_{ma} or P_{ma}/V_{ma}	$1000000 \div 700$ = 1428.57 ≈ 1429	ampere

Step 2 Note down the parameter of a PV module that is to be connected in PV array:

PV module parameter	Symbol	Value	Unit
Open circuit voltage of PV module	V_{oc}	(not given)	volt
Short circuit current of PV module	I_{sc}	(not given)	ampere
Voltage at maximum power point	V_m	32	volt
Current at maximum power point	I_m	7.5	ampere
Maximum power of PV module	$P_m = V_m \times I_m$	$32 \times 7.5 = 240$	watt

Step 3 Estimating the number of PV modules to be connected in series and parallel:

PV module parameter	Symbol	Value	Unit
Required PV array voltage at maximum power point	V_{ma}	700	volt
Voltage at maximum power point of single PV module or PV string	V_m	32	volt
Number of PV modules in series (N_s)	$N_s = V_{ma}/V_m$	$700 \div 32$ = 21.875 ≈ 22	number
Current at maximum power point of PV array	I_{ma}	1429	ampere
Current at maximum power point of PV module or PV string	I_m	7.5	ampere
Number of PV modules in series (N_p)	$N_p = I_{ma}/I_m$	$1429 \div 7.5$ = 190.53 ≈ 191	number

Step 4 Estimating the total power of the series PV module array:

PV module parameter	Symbol	Value	Unit
Number of PV modules in series (N_s)	N_s	22	number
Number of PV modules or module strings in parallel (N_p)	N_p	191	number
New value of PV array voltage at maximum power point	$V_{ma} = V_m \times N_s$	$32 \times 22 = 704$	volt
New value of PV array current at maximum power point	$I_{ma} = I_m \times N_p$	7.5×191 $= 1432.5$	ampere
Maximum power of single PV module	$P_m = V_m \times I_m$	$32 \times 7.5 = 240$	watt
Maximum power of PV module array	$P_{ma} = P_m \times N_s \times N_p$ $= V_m \times I_m \times N_s$ $\times N_p$	$240 \times 22 \times 191$ or $32 \times 7.5 \times 22$ $\times 191$	watt
	or $= V_{ma} \times I_{ma}$	or 704×1432.5 $= 1008480$	

WORKSHEET 5.7: In a PV power plant of 1 MW capacity, a large number of PV modules are connected in series and parallel combinations. In such plants, 1 MW inverter can take input voltage in the range of 500 V to 700 V. Design number of PV modules to be connected in a single series (PV module string) to obtain voltage at maximum power point of 600 V. Also, estimate the peak power that will be supplied by one such PV module string. The parameters of PV modules to be used are: $V_{oc} = 44$ V, $V_m = 35$ V, $I_{sc} = 8$ A and $I_m = 7$ A.

Step 1 Note down the voltage, current and power requirement of PV module array:

PV module parameter	Symbol	Value	Unit
PV array power requirement (peak power or maximum power point)	P_{ma} or $I_{ma} \times V_{ma}$	10,00,000	watt
PV module array open circuit voltage at peak power	V_{ma} or P_{ma}/I_{ma}	600	volt
PV module array current at peak power	I_{ma} or P_{ma}/V_{ma}	____ ÷ ____ = ____ ≈ ____	ampere

Step 2 Note down the parameter of a PV module that is to be connected in PV array:

PV module parameter	Symbol	Value	Unit
Open circuit voltage of PV module	V_{oc}	(not given)	volt
Short circuit current of PV module	I_{sc}	(not given)	ampere
Voltage at maximum power point	V_m	35	volt
Current at maximum power point	I_m	7	ampere
Maximum power of PV module	$P_m = V_m \times I_m$	____ × ____ = ____	watt

Step 3 Estimating the number of PV modules to be connected in series and parallel:

PV module parameter	Symbol	Value	Unit
Required PV array voltage at maximum power point	V_{ma}	600	volt
Voltage at maximum power point of single PV module or PV string	V_m		volt
Number of PV modules in series (N_s)	$N_s = V_{ma}/V_m$	___ ÷ ___ = ___ ≈ ___	number
Current at maximum power point of PV array	I_{ma}		ampere
Current at maximum power point of PV module or PV string	I_m		ampere
Number of PV modules in series (N_p)	$N_p = I_{ma}/I_m$	___ ÷ ___ = ___ ≈ ___	number

Step 4 Estimating the total power of the series PV module array:

PV module parameter	Symbol	Value	Unit
Number of PV modules in series (N_s)	N_s		number
Number of PV modules or module strings in parallel (N_p)	N_p		number
New value of PV array voltage at maximum power point	$V_{ma} = V_m \times N_s$	___ × ___ = ___	volt
New value of PV array current at maximum power point	$I_{ma} = I_m \times N_p$	___ × ___ = ___	ampere
Maximum power of single PV module	$P_m = V_m \times I_m$	___ × ___ = ___	watt
Maximum power of PV module array	$P_{ma} = P_m \times N_s \times N_p$	___ × ___ × ___	watt
	$= V_m \times I_m \times N_s \times N_p$ or	___ × ___ × ___ × ___	
		or ___ × ___ = ___	
or	$= V_{ma} \times I_{ma}$		

6

Basics of Batteries

Batteries, as electrical energy storage medium, are very important and delicate part of standalone solar PV systems. They are important because without energy storage, a solar PV system will not be able to deliver the energy to the load when there is no sunlight. In the case of standalone systems, we need electrical energy for running our appliances in non-sunshine hours, while in the case of grid connected PV systems, we do not require any energy storage. Grid, if operational, provides the energy whenever it is required. In standalone PV systems, batteries are delicate because the misuse or non-optimal use of batteries can reduce their life significantly. These days, as the cost of solar PV modules are decreasing; the cost of battery is becoming a significant part of the overall solar PV system cost. Thus, from cost perspective as well the batteries are becoming more important in solar PV systems. Due to the importance of batteries in solar PV system, significant efforts are made here to give all technical as well as practical details about batteries.

6.1

Some Basics about Batteries

The basic purpose of battery is to store charge and deliver the same when used in an application.

In our day-to-day life, we frequently use things like torch, calculator, mobile phone, radio, electronic watch, etc. All these things are portable electronic devices and they require movable supply of energy. The DC (direct current) supply is needed to run these devices. The conventional form of AC (alternating current) supply available to us cannot be applied to these devices directly. To provide the power supply to these devices, a device having electrical energy stored in it is used. These devices having stored electrical energy or stored charge is known as battery. The charge stored in the batteries can be used to supply the energy to appliances when required. A battery stores electrical energy (charge) in the form of chemical energy. When a battery is used, the chemical energy stored is converted into electrical energy.

A simple analogy can be drawn between battery as electrical energy storage medium and water tank as water storage medium. We all know the water tank is used to store large quantity of water and we can use water from tank when needed. Water storage tanks come in different shapes like cylindrical and cuboid and different storing capacities like 500 litres, 1000 litres, 10,000 litres, etc. The quantity of water to be stored determines the size of water tank to be used. Similarly, depending on the electrical energy requirement, size of the battery (charge storage capacity) and its terminal voltage is determined.

A battery is a two terminal device. One terminal is called positive (+) and the other terminal is called negative (–). In the charged condition, there is a voltage difference between two terminals. This voltage difference drives the current in appliances when connected. For giving supply to a device from battery; the positive and negative terminals of a battery is connected to the corresponding terminals of the device.

Based on the application, the type of battery to be used is decided. There are different types of batteries; which are available in various sizes, shapes, voltages and storage capacities. The types of batteries include single time use (non-rechargeable) batteries and multiple time use (rechargeable) batteries. While buying or selecting batteries; the batteries are identified by different features like the type of battery, voltage, capacity, charging-discharging cycles and shelf-life (all these are discussed later in detail). The batteries used in the torch, calculator, radio, mobile phones, etc. are of low voltage and low capacity. For applications like TV, fans, tube lights, motors, cars, train, stand-alone power supply, etc; high voltage and high capacity batteries are used.

| Batteries are the backbone of standalone PV systems. |

6.1.1
Rechargeable Batteries

| As water tank stores water, the batteries can be considered as 'charge tank' for storing charge. |

Batteries used in solar PV systems require frequent charging or refilling of charge. Again an analogy can be drawn with regular refilling of water tank in our house. The water tanks in our houses and commercial buildings need to be refilled on regular basis. As per the usage of water, the level of water decreases in the tank and after sometime the tank becomes empty. To avoid disruption to the continuous supply of water, the tank has to be refilled as soon as it gets empty. This process of emptying water from tank and refilling the tank is repeated frequently, almost on daily basis.

Similar to water tank, batteries are the tanks for storing electrical charge or electrical energy. Alternatively, batteries are 'charge storage tanks'. Also, similar to the emptying and refilling cycle of water tank, the electrical energy of batteries gets emptied (while in use) which we need to refill again. This refilling of electrical energy in batteries is technically known as "charging". Actually, during the charging process, electrical energy supplied from outside to the batteries get converted into chemical energy. The process of consumption of electrical energy from batteries is technically known as "discharging". During the discharging process, chemical energy stored in batteries gets converted into electrical energy which is supplied to appliances. In this way, the working of batteries typically consists of two processes; charging and discharging. Single charging and single discharging process together is called one *charging-discharging cycle*.

| One charging and discharging of a battery is equivalent to one charge cycle. |

Some batteries allow repeated charging-discharging cycles while others do not. The batteries which allow repeated charging-discharging cycles are known as *'rechargeable batteries'*. The rechargeable batteries are widely used in the solar PV systems. The batteries in PV system play an important role in the storage of electrical energy and providing continuous electric current supply irrespective of absence/presence of the sun and the change in weather. Without batteries, it is difficult to think of 'standalone solar PV systems'.

| Batteries which allow repeated charging-discharging cycles are known as 'rechargeable batteries'. |

6.2
How Does a Battery Work?

Generally, a battery is made of a combination of two or more units of electrochemical cells (voltaic cells) connected together in series or parallel combination. It is called electrochemical cell because it deals with the electrical and chemical energy. The electrochemical cell, in general, is also termed cell. A single unit of an electrochemical cell consists of two half-cells as shown in Figure 6.1. Each half-cell consists of an electrode and an electrolyte. The two half-cells are electrically connected to each other by salt bridge. The electrodes in the two half-cells are of different metals. In each half-cell, a chemical reaction occurs at the metal electrode. The operation of the cell involves two chemical reactions.

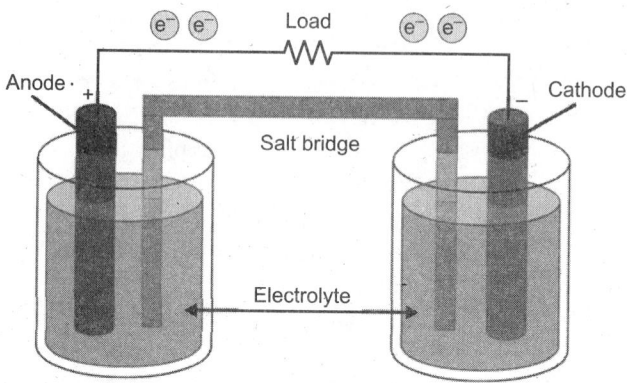

FIGURE 6.1

A typical single unit of an electrochemical cell.

One is oxidation reaction and the other is reduction reaction, commonly called the Redox reaction which converts the chemical energy into electrical energy as shown in Figure 6.1. Oxidation is a process in which electrons are lost or released, and the reduction is a process in which electrons are accepted or gained and both can be represented by the following expressions:

Oxidation: Reductant $\rightarrow$ Product $+ e^-$ (Loss of electrons)

Reduction: Oxidant $+ e^- \rightarrow$ Product (Gain of electrons)

6.2.1
Charging and Discharging of Batteries

Both oxidation and reduction reactions take place at the time of charging and discharging. While charging, the oxidation reaction takes place at negative terminal (cathode) and reduction reaction takes place at positive terminal (anode) and vice-versa during discharging (Figure 6.2). A charging process and subsequent discharging process together are defined as one charging-discharging cycle or a single cycle.

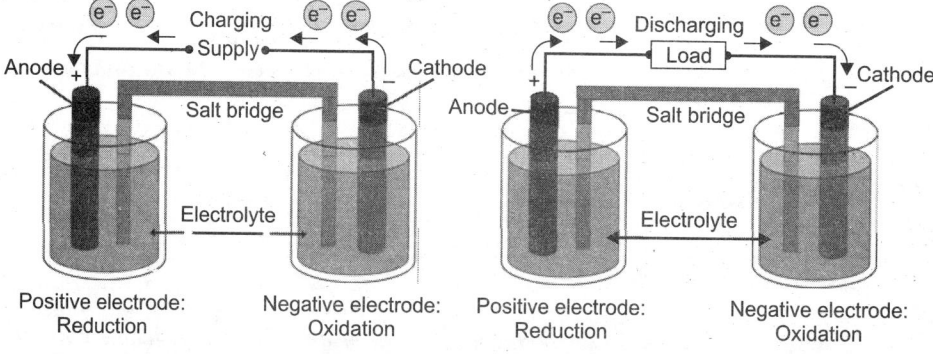

FIGURE 6.2

Shows the charging and discharging process in an electrochemical cell.

During charging and discharging chemical reactions take place at both positive and negative electrodes.

When the battery is completely filled with charge up to its maximum level, it is said to be fully charged. When the charge is completely used or finished, the battery is said to be fully discharged.

6.2.2
Components of a Battery Cell

It can be seen from the discussion in Section 6.2 that operation of a battery, that is, charging and discharging of a battery requires anode (positive electrode), cathode (negative electrode), electrolyte, and salt bridge (Figure 6.2). The role of each of these components is briefly described below:

1. **Anode:** It is generally referred as positive terminal or positive node or positive lead. It is the electrode which gives up electrons to the external circuit, as a result the electrode is oxidized during the discharging reaction.

2. **Cathode:** It is generally referred as negative terminal or negative node or negative lead. It is the electrode which gains electrons from the external circuit, as a result of which the electrode is reduced during the discharging reaction.

3. **Electrolyte:** It is a medium which provides conductivity to ions between anode and cathode. One can say that an electrolyte is a medium through which current flows internally in a battery. An electrolyte is typically a liquid, such as water or other solvents with dissolved salts, acids or alkalis.

4. **Salt bridge:** It is a porous material used to keep the two electrodes connected but yet keep them separate from each other; otherwise the chemical reaction would stop. It is also referred as a separator.

> Anode, cathode, electrolyte and separator are four important components of a battery.

6.3
Types of Batteries

There are varieties of batteries that are available in the market for several types of applications. Each battery type is more suited for one particular application. The type of battery is identified by the chemistry of materials used in making it. The batteries are broadly divided into two categories:

1. Non-rechargeable batteries or primary batteries, and
2. Rechargeable batteries or secondary batteries.

6.3.1
Non-rechargeable Batteries

In the non-rechargeable batteries, the electrochemical reaction is not reversible. This type of batteries is used for one time and once discharged, they cannot be charged again.

The non-rechargeable batteries are the most convenient, simple, easy to use and require less maintenance. These types of battery are portable and are made in various sizes and shapes. The sizes are normally referred as size A, AA, AAA, C, D, etc. and the shapes of such batteries can be of several types like coin, cylindrical, cuboid, etc. These batteries are mainly used in transistors, toys, torches, etc. These batteries have high shelf life, reasonable cost, energy and good power density. Generally, these batteries are available in small capacities, typically below 20 Ah (ampere-hour). These batteries can be operated in a wide range of temperatures; $-40\,°C$ to $70\,°C$.

FIGURE 6.3
The 1.5 V (AA) zinc chloride battery.

The most common example of non-rechargeable battery is Zinc Chloride battery, commonly known as pencil cell (shown in Figure 6.3). This battery can be used only once and it cannot be recharged. Other examples of non-rechargeable batteries are Magnesium cells, Aluminum cells, Alkaline-manganese dioxide cells, Mercuric oxide cells, etc. All of them are used for different applications. The batteries that are required in solar PV systems need to be charged and discharged regularly, therefore, non-rechargeable batteries are not used in standalone solar PV systems.

6.3.2
Rechargeable Batteries
(Secondary Battery)

The batteries in which the conversion of chemical energy into electrical energy (discharging) and the reverse process, that is, conversion of electrical energy into chemical energy (charging) can take place are called the rechargeable battery or secondary battery.

The rechargeable batteries are the most widely used batteries in the world. These batteries are used for various applications, such as starting, lighting and ignition (SLI) in automotives, standby power supply, electronic appliances like DVD player, mobile phones, camera, camcorder, laptops, etc. These batteries are available in a wide range of charge storage capacities in the market and can be easily procured.

The commonly available rechargeable batteries are listed below and their pictures are shown in Figure 6.4.

- Lead Acid
- Nickel Cadmium (NiCd)
- Nickel Metal Hydride (NiMH)
- Lithium Ion (Li-ion), and
- Lithium Ion Polymer (Li-ion polymer)

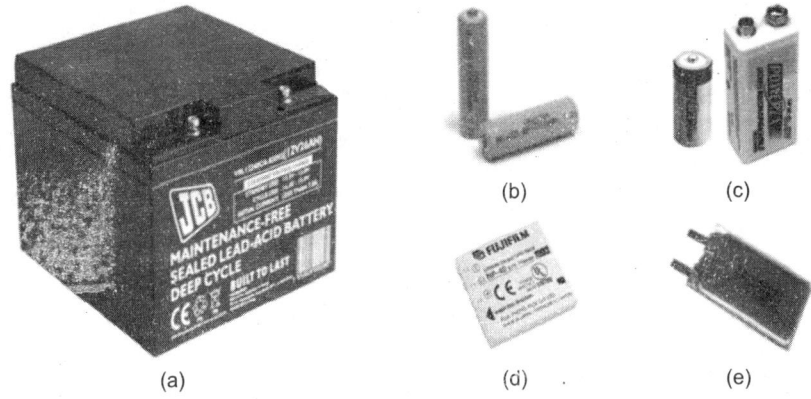

FIGURE 6.4

Images of various types of batteries (a) Lead acid, (b) NiCd, (c) NiMH, (d) Li-ion and (e) Li-ion polymer battery.

We can see in Figure 6.4, the size of each battery is different. The physical size of a battery also reflects its energy storage or charge storage capacity. The batteries of small charge capacities are small in size and high charge capacities are large in size. The lead-acid batteries are normally big in size which means that they can store large amount of charge. Due to this reason, the lead-acid batteries are commonly used for solar PV applications. The lead-acid batteries are actually one of the most widely used rechargeable batteries used for large amount energy storage application. They are also mostly used for solar PV applications.

Rechargeable batteries are used in solar PV systems.

6.4
Parameters of Batteries

One must choose appropriate batteries for application in the solar PV systems. The choice is determined by the various characteristics of batteries, suitable for given need. The characteristics of batteries are defined by a set of battery parameters. These parameters include charge storage capacity, terminal voltage, rate at which batteries can be charged and discharged, the cost of battery, the number of times the charging-discharging cycle can be carried out in a battery lifetime and so on. In practice, these parameters affect the performance of the battery. For design, installation and maintenance of the battery or group of batteries (called *battery bank*) knowing and understanding the battery parameters are very important. Ideally, we would like our battery to work for many years and should give us required energy in all conditions. On every battery casing, the important parameters are displayed by the manufacturers. Based on the parameters values mentioned by the manufacturer, the selection of a battery can be made. Various parameters related to battery are discussed in this section.

The standard parameters of a battery specified by the manufacturers are following:

- Battery terminal voltage (in volts),
- Charge storage capacity (in Coulomb or ampere-hour or Ah),
- Depth of discharge (in percentage),
- Number of useful charging-discharging cycle (in number),
- Life cycle (in years),
- Self discharge (in %), etc.

6.4.1
Battery Terminal Voltage (V)

Batteries supply electrical energy to the load by flowing current to the loads/devices connected across its terminals. The electrical energy transfer from battery to load is possible only when there is voltage difference between two terminals. Thus, a battery's terminal voltage is the voltage difference between its two electrodes.

The voltage difference between the battery terminals is driving force for current to flow. For a given appliance, an appropriate level of terminal voltage must be available, otherwise the device does not work. For instance, sometimes, you need to supply 1.5 V (volt), sometimes 3 V, sometimes 6 V and sometimes 12 V. Some devices may also need higher voltages. Thus, battery terminal voltage is one of the important parameter that determines the choice of the battery.

For solar PV system applications, there are batteries which are available with 6 V and 12 V ratings. Each battery is made up of cells. The terminal voltage of cells is determined by the material they are made up of. Normally, the cell voltage is not large to give us required 6 V or 12 V. Therefore, many cells are connected together in series to get higher voltage. In a 12 V Lead-acid batteries, 6 cells are connected together.

The battery terminal voltage changes with the condition of battery. The terminal voltage increases when battery gets charged, the terminal voltage decreases when battery gets discharged. It also depends on several other conditions.

6.4.2
Battery Open Circuit Voltage and Terminal Voltage

The terminal voltage of battery is maximum when it is fully charged and when no current is flowing. The condition of no current flow is equivalent to open circuit. Therefore, the maximum terminal voltage of battery is also referred as open circuit voltage of battery or V_0. It is also referred as e.m.f. (electromotive force) of the battery or V_{emf}.

When current flows through battery, its terminal voltage is normally lower than the open circuit voltage, V_0. This happens because of the internal resistance of the battery. Due to its own resistance, some voltage drop occurs inside the battery. This voltage drop is equal to the current flowing through the battery multiplied by the internal resistance of the battery or equal to $I \times R_i$ [as shown in Figure 6.5(a)]. The battery and its symbol used in electrical circuit diagram are shown in Figure 6.5(b). Therefore, when current is flowing, the actual available terminal voltage will be different between open circuit battery voltage (V_0) and internal voltage drop in battery $I \times R_i$. This voltage drop $I \times R_i$ occurs inside the battery.

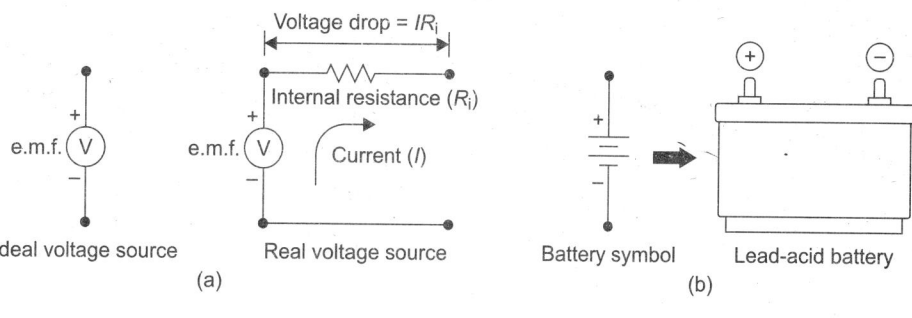

FIGURE 6.5

(a) Shows difference between ideal DC source and practical DC source and (b) battery symbol for lead-acid battery used in circuit diagrams.

In this way, the battery terminal voltage can be written as:

$$V_{\text{battery}} = V_o - (I \times R_i) \tag{6.1}$$

where,

V_{battery} = Battery voltage or terminal voltage (in volts);

V_o = Open-circuit voltage (in volts);

I = Current flow when load is connected to a battery (amperes); and

R_i = Internal resistance of battery (ohms).

The battery has its internal resistance due to many factors. A battery consists of many cells. The factors like the contacts within the cells, metal plates/electrodes and salt bridge/separator, even the electrolyte creates some internal resistance. The schematic representation of open circuit voltage and terminal voltage of battery when current is flowing is given in Figure 6.6.

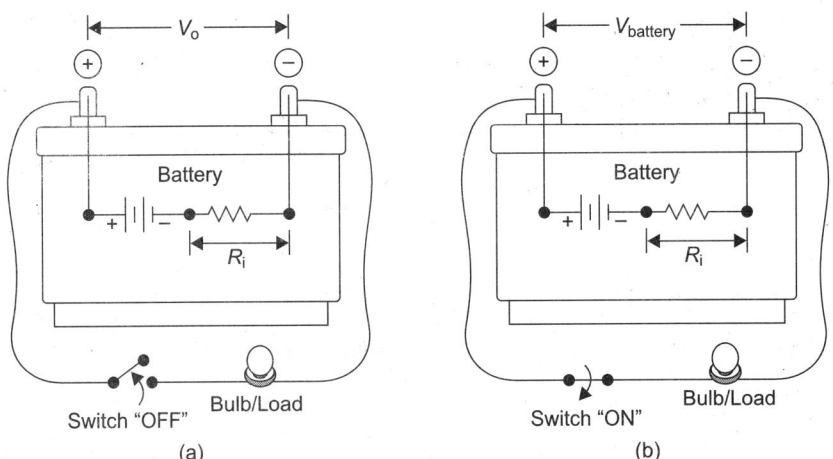

FIGURE 6.6

Voltage measurement across the battery terminals (a) terminal voltage as V_o when no load is connected and (b) terminal voltage as V_{battery} when load is connected.

Open circuit voltage of a battery is higher than the terminal voltage under usage due to internal resistance of batteries.

EXAMPLE 6.1

Solution

A battery has an internal resistance (R_i) of 0.6 Ω and an open circuit voltage (V_o) of 14 V. What is its terminal potential difference or voltage developed (V_{battery}) if it delivers current (I) of (a) 5 A, (b) 10 A and (c) 20 A?

V_o (V)	R_i (Ω)	I (A)	$V_{\text{battery}} = V_o - IR_i$ (V)
14	0.6	5	11
14	0.6	10	8
14	0.6	20	2

It can be seen from the above problem that the battery internal resistance should be very small. Otherwise when the large current flow through battery, significant voltage drop occurs inside the battery and actual terminal voltage available to the load is small.

6.4.3
Terminologies for Battery Terminal Voltage

There are various voltage terminologies associated with battery like Open-circuit voltage, Nominal or operating voltage, and Cut-off voltage, and these terminologies are briefly described here:

- **Open circuit voltage:** It is also called theoretical voltage because this is the maximum possible voltage at output terminals of battery when circuit is open.

- **Nominal terminal voltage or operating voltage:** It is actual voltage available at the output terminals of the battery on which load can operate. The standard battery nominal voltages available are 1.5 V, 3 V, 6 V, 12 V, 24 V, 48 V, etc.
- **Cut-off voltage:** It is a voltage up to which the load can be operated and below which the battery should be disconnected from the load in order to prevent it from over-discharge.

Figure 6.7 shows and points up the voltage and capacity values of sealed lead-acid battery along with the other parameters.

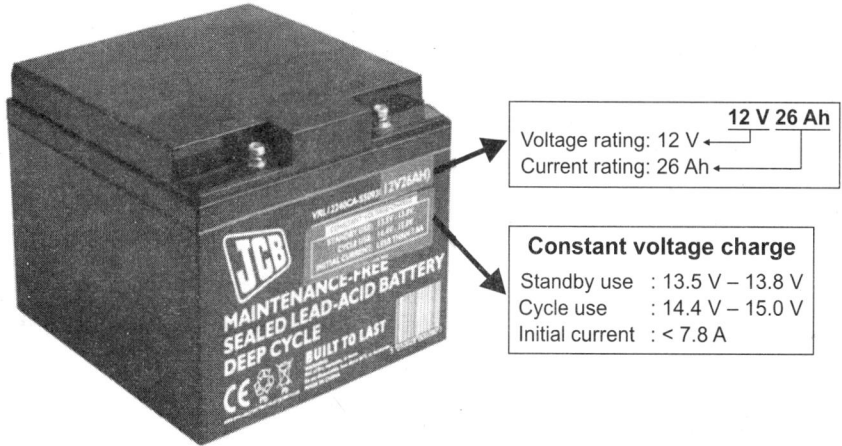

FIGURE 6.7

Shows the voltage and capacity rating of sealed lead-acid battery.

6.4.4
Battery Storage Capacity (C)

The capacity of a battery is the capacity to store the charge in the battery. It is the product of current (in amperes) it can deliver for a given time (in hours), i.e., Ampere × Hour (Ah). One ampere-hour (Ah) is the amount of charge delivered when constant current of one ampere (A) is used for one hour (h). In this chapter, we will express battery capacity in term of ampere-hour. The capacity of a battery is given by the expression shown below:

$$\text{Capacity (C)} = \text{Current (A)} \times \text{Hour (h)} \qquad (6.2)$$

The capacity of non-rechargeable batteries normally varies in few mAh (milli Ah) to several Ah range. The capacity of rechargeable batteries can vary from few Ah to thousands of Ah.

The capacity of batteries depends on temperature. The same battery will have different capacity at different temperatures. The capacity is specified at standard test conditions of 25 °C. Hence, the capacity value measured at installation sites may vary from the values given by the manufacturer because of the change in temperature at particular location. Therefore, while selecting the battery for a given purpose, temperature of the location should be taken in account.

Battery capacity is given in terms of Ah. Large size batteries have large Ah capacity.

After knowing charge storage capacity and terminal voltage of the battery, we can find out some other informations about the battery.

How much current battery can supply?

We must always remember, in practical, there is no source which can supply an unlimited amount of current. Similarly, battery is a device that can only supply fixed amount of current. The capacity rating helps in finding out how much current a battery can provide, if duration of the current drawn (or discharge duration) is given. The current drawn can be given as:

$$\text{Current (I)} = \frac{\text{Capacity (Ah)}}{\text{Discharge duration (h)}} \text{ (amperes)} \qquad (6.3)$$

The above expression suggests that, for a given battery capacity, if the discharge duration is long, we can draw small current from battery, but if our discharge duration is small, we can draw large current from battery. This is analogues to water tank, from a water tank of fixed capacity, if we draw water slowly, we can draw water for long time, but if we draw water fastly then the tank will get emptied soon. Thus, by choosing small discharge duration, it is possible to draw a large amount of current. But drawing large current from battery must be avoided. As large current cause large voltage drop inside the battery due to internal resistance and terminal voltage available outside decreases.

Here, the question is, what current is large current? Normally, for batteries used for solar PV systems, the discharge duration is 10 to 20 hours. Corresponding this discharge duration, the magnitude of current drawn will be considered normal current. But if you are discharging battery in 1 to 2 hours then the current drawn will be considered large current. The amount of current that can be drawn from a battery is discussed more in details in Section 6.4.5 and 6.4.6.

EXAMPLE 6.2

A 100 Ah capacity battery is discharged in 20 hours in one case and in 5 hours in other case. Estimate the current that can be drawn from battery in these two cases.

Solution

Case 1:

Given: capacity = 100 Ah and discharge duration = 20 hours

$$\text{Current produced by battery 1} = \frac{\text{Capacity (Ah)}}{\text{Discharge duration (h)}} = \frac{100 \text{ Ah}}{20 \text{ h}} = 5 \text{ A}$$

Case 2:

Given: capacity = 100 Ah and discharge duration = 5 hours

$$\text{Current produced by battery 2} = \frac{\text{Capacity (Ah)}}{\text{Discharge duration (h)}} = \frac{100 \text{ Ah}}{5 \text{ h}} = 20 \text{ A}$$

Therefore, the current produced by battery in Case 1 will be 5 A and in Case 2 will be 20 A.

WORKSHEET 6.1   Fill Table 6.1 on Capacity, discharge rate and current of battery.

TABLE 6.1   Current Produced by Batteries

Capacity	Discharge duration	Current produced/Available
50 Ah	10 h	5 ....
120 Ah	.... h	4 A
250	20 h	12500 mA
....	12 h	30 A
450 Ah	15 h	....
1200 mAh	.... h	10 A

How much energy is stored in battery?

If we know the terminal voltage of the battery and its charge storage capacity, we can obtain how much electrical energy is stored in the battery. The electrical energy is given in terms of the product of charge capacity and voltage. Thus, energy stored in a battery can be given by the following expression:

$$\text{Energy (watt-hour)} = \text{Capacity (Ah)} \times \text{Voltage (V)} \qquad (6.4)$$

> The amount of energy stored in a battery is the product of its terminal voltage and Ah capacity.

The above expression indicates that large capacity battery and higher terminal voltage battery stores higher amount of electrical energy.

What is the power of the battery?

Power for any device is defined as product of voltage and current. In case of battery if we multiply the terminal voltage of battery with discharge current we will get the power of the battery. Thus, battery power can be written as:

$$\text{Battery power (watt)} = \text{Terminal voltage (V)} \times \text{Current drawn (A)} \quad (6.5)$$

EXAMPLE 6.3

If we have 12 V battery of capacity 500 Ah, then calculate the power of battery and the amount of energy stored in the battery?

Solution

It is given that:

Battery terminal voltage (V) = 12 V

Battery capacity (C) = 500 Ah

Battery discharge duration is not given, here, so, we assume the battery discharge duration is 10 hours.

Since the battery is discharged in 10 hours, the current drawn from the battery is:

$$\text{Discharge current} = \frac{\text{Capacity (Ah)}}{\text{Discharge duration (h)}} = \frac{500 \text{ Ah}}{10 \text{ h}} = 50 \text{ A}$$

Now, for power calculation of the battery, we can write

Power = Voltage (V) × Current (A) = 12 × 50 = 600 watt

Thus, the power of the battery is 600 watt.

The energy stored in a battery is given by the expression,

Energy = Voltage (V) × Capacity (C)

So, Energy = 12 V × 500 Ah = 6000 Wh = 6 kWh

Therefore, energy stored in the battery is 6 kWh.

 WORKSHEET 6.2 Fill the following worksheet (Table 6.2) on Voltage, Capacity, discharge rate, current, power and energy of a battery.

TABLE 6.2 Calculation of Battery Parameters

Battery voltage	Capacity	Discharge duration	Current drawn/produced	Power of battery	Energy stored in battery
6 V	1.2 Ah	6 h	.... A	.... W	.... kWh
6 V	1200 mAh	6 h	.... mA	.... mW	.... kWh
.... V	.... Ah	.... h	100 A	600 W	12 kWh
12 V	120 Ah	.... h	.... A	180 W	.... kWh
12 V	.... Ah	10 h	50 A	.... W	.... kWh
.... V	.... Ah	15 h	60 A	720 W	.... kWh
24 V	.... Ah	.... h	30 A	.... W	10.8 kWh

6.4.5
State of Charge (SoC) and Depth of Discharge (DoD)

Depth of discharge

In practical applications, all the charge stored in a battery cannot be used for running load. Only some percentage of total charge stored can be used. The percentage of total charge that can be used for running the load is referred as Depth of Discharge (DoD). 50% DoD means that only 50% of the total stored charged can be used. 70% DoD means that only 70% of the total stored charge can be used. In general, we want higher DoD for the batteries which are used in solar PV systems. Therefore, normally, deep discharge batteries are preferred for PV applications. In practice, there is no battery for which the allowable DoD is 100%. Normally, the batteries used for SLI (starting, lighting, and ignition, for instance, our car batteries) applications have small DOD, about 10% to 20%. The batteries which are used for solar PV applications have high DoD, about 50%. The Li-ion batteries have DoD of 80% to 90%.

As the depth of discharge of battery increases (due to use of its stored charge), the terminal voltage of the battery decreases. Fully charged battery will have higher terminal voltage as compared to discharged battery. Table 6.3 shows the voltage level at different DoD level in terms of percentage.

TABLE 6.3 Depth of Discharge Along with Open Circuit Voltage for 12 V and 6 V Lead-acid Battery

Open circuit voltage for 12 V battery	Open circuit voltage for 6 V battery	Approximate DoD (%)
12.65 V	6.32 V	0%
12.45 V	6.22 V	25%
12.24 V	6.12 V	50%
12.06 V	6.03 V	75%
11.89 V	6.00 V	100%

Manufacturers specify allowable DoD level for their batteries. The battery should not be discharged below manufacturers specified level in order to prevent damage to the battery. If the batteries are discharged below their DoD rating, then the life of the batteries decreases very fast. It means that if the life of the battery is 3 years and it is continuously discharged below its DoD limit, then battery may stop functioning in 6 months only. For practical application, it is better to take batteries to 50% of the DoD specified by manufacturer. The tolerable limit of DoD is determined from the charging/discharging efficiency of a battery. The typical tolerable DoD of various types of batteries is given in Table 6.4.

TABLE 6.4 Tolerable Level of DoD of Various Types of Batteries

Battery type	Tolerable DoD (%)
Lead-acid	70–90
Nickel Cadmium	70–90
Nickel Metal Hydride	60–70
Li-ion	80–90
Li polymer	90–98

The Depth of Discharge indicates the amount of charge (in percentage) that has already withdrawn from a battery.

State of charge

Rechargeable batteries have to be often charged for reuse. For such batteries, the time of charging is decided by the present values of charge level or present State of Charge (SoC). The SoC indicates the level of charge, i.e., percentage of total charge that is stored at this time in a battery. Thus, if 60% of the total charge storage capacity is still there in the battery then the battery's SoC is 60%.

The DoD is another way of showing SoC. The DoD is the inverse of SoC. Both DoD and SoC are expressed in percentage. Present SoC when subtracted from 100% gives the present value of DoD. This can be written in the following way:

$$DoD\ (\%) = 100\% - SoC\ (\%)$$

or

$$SoC\ (\%) = 100\% - DoD\ (\%)$$

For example, suppose a battery after sometime of usage has SoC 70%. This indicates that its present DoD = 100% – 70% = 30%. As we keep using battery, its DoD percentage increases and the SoC decreases. The schematic representation in Figure 6.8 shows the different levels of SoC and DoD.

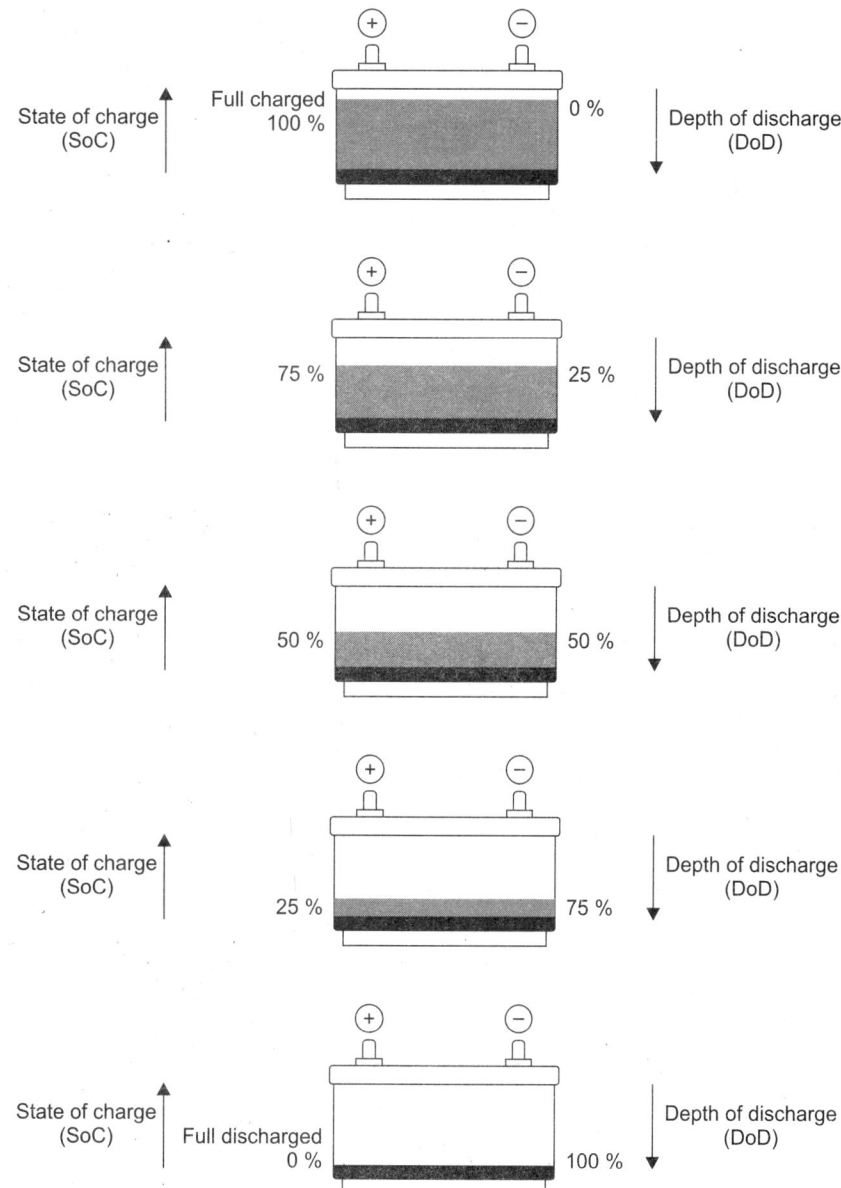

FIGURE 6.8

Schematic representation of state of charge and discharge.

It is discussed earlier that as the SoC decreases, the open circuit voltage and terminal voltage of the battery decreases. In other words, for higher SoC, the battery will have higher terminal voltage and for lower SoC, the battery will have lower terminal voltage. Thus, when a fully charged battery is utilized to supply the charge to a load, and as the amount of stored charge in the battery decreases, its terminal voltage keeps decreasing. In this way, at any stage of discharge, if we measure the terminal voltage, we can estimate the state of charge of a battery. For a Lead-acid battery, the relationship between the open circuit voltage and SoC is given in Figure 6.9.

The State of Charge indicates the amount of charge (in percentage) that is still there in the battery.

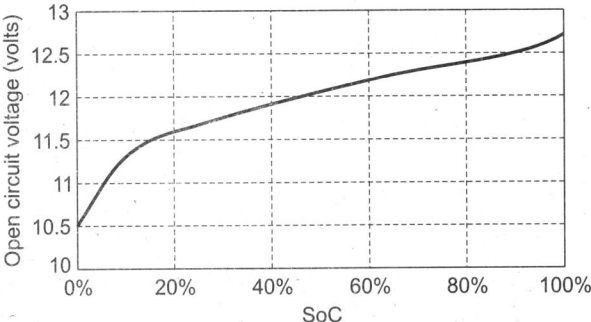

FIGURE 6.9

Relationship between State of Charge (SoC) and open circuit voltage of a Lead-acid battery.

6.4.6
Charging/Discharging Rate or C-rating

It has been discussed earlier that the terminal voltage (when current is drawn) of the battery is less than the open circuit voltage (when no current is drawn) due to voltage drop in internal resistance of the battery. The voltage drop due to internal resistance is $I \times R_i$. The large current drawn from the battery causes large voltage drop, meaning less terminal voltage is available for the load. Discharging battery at high rate (high current flow out of the battery to load) is not safe. Similarly, charging battery at high rate (high current flowing into the battery) is also not safe. The amount of current (discharge current) drawn from battery plays a very important role in service life or back-up time of the battery. As we increase the load current the battery discharges at faster rate (as shown in Figure 6.10). Over-discharging of battery leads to decrease in capacity and life span as well as it causes mechanical damage to the battery.

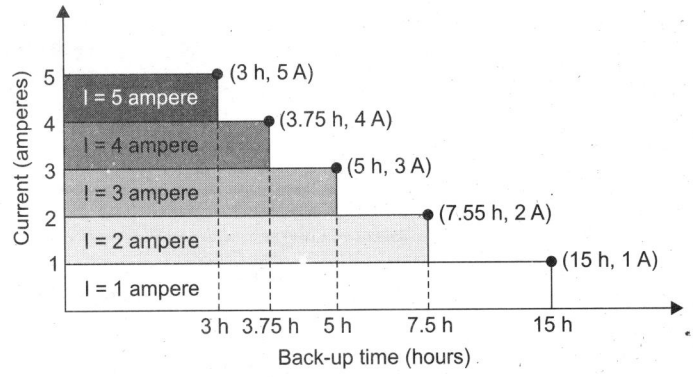

FIGURE 6.10

Possible battery discharge characteristics as function of time for 15 Ah battery (assuming 100% DoD).

One cycle of battery means one charging plus one discharging cycle. Typically, the life cycle of a lead-acid battery is 500–800 cycles. Generally, manufacturer gives the values of maximum charging-discharging current and voltage. The battery can be charged with the following three methods:

1. Constant voltage
2. Constant current or
3. Both.

A lead acid battery accepts all of these methods of charging. Proper charging of batteries increases their life. The mechanism for charging is inbuilt in the good charge controllers. Therefore, appropriate charge controllers must be used for good life of the battery.

In order to ensure proper charging/discharging of batteries, manufacturers specify the charging/discharging current rates in terms of C-rating. The C-rating specify in how many hours a given battery should be charged or discharged. The

C-rating value is obtained by dividing the battery capacity (Ah) by the suggested number of hours taken to fully charge the battery completely (or to reach 100% SoC) or time taken to reach the full tolerable DoD of the battery. The expression for C-rating is as follows:

$$\text{C-rating (amperes)} = \frac{\text{Capacity (C)}}{\text{No. of hours for full charge or discharge } (t)} \quad (6.6)$$

where, Capacity (C) is in ampere-hour (Ah), and time for full charge or full tolerable discharge (t) is in hours (h).

Consider, a battery of capacity C and time for full charge or discharge is 1 hour, then C-rating will be $C/1$ or $1C$. Similarly, If $t = 10$ hours, then C-rating is $C/10$.

EXAMPLE 6.4

The capacity of a battery is 100 Ah. Determine the C-rating of the battery for 1, 2, 5, 10 and 100 hours of charging?

Solution

The C-rating is given in Table 6.5 using the formula

$$\text{C-rating} = \frac{\text{Capacity (C)}}{\text{No. of hours for full charge or discharge } (t)} \text{ (amperes)}$$

TABLE 6.5 Table for Example 6.4

Total battery capacity (Ah)	Number of hours of charging, t (hours)	Current required (A)	C-rating
100	1	100/1 =100	C
100	2	100/2 = 50	C/2
100	5	100/5 = 20	C/5
100	10	100/10 = 10	C/10
100	20	100/20 = 5	C/20
100	100	100/100 = 1	C/100

In the above example, C-ratings are obtained for different hours of charging. From the table in the example above; it can be observed that the higher is the number of hours for full charge or discharge, the lower is the charging/discharging rate or current. Normally, fast discharging of battery is not good for battery until it is designed for fast discharging. It reduces the life of battery. A $C/10$ battery should not be charged or discharged with $C/5$ or $C/2$ rating.

 WORKSHEET 6.3 Fill the following worksheet (Table 6.6) on C-rating of a battery.

TABLE 6.6 Calculation of C-ratings

Total battery capacity (Ah)	Number of hours of charging, t (hours)	Current required (A)	C-rating
......	1	120	C
120	2	......	......
120	......	......	C/5
120	......	10	......
120	......	......	0.05C

Batteries should be charged and discharged as per the C-rating specified by the manufacturer.

6.4.7
Battery Efficiency

The charging voltage for any rechargeable battery is greater than the discharging voltage. The charging voltage is the sum of battery e.m.f. and voltage drop due to the battery's internal resistance. The discharging voltage is the difference of battery e.m.f. and voltage drop due to the battery's internal resistance. Due to the internal resistance of the battery, the discharged energy is always less than the charging energy. Typically, a lead-acid battery is 80% to 90% efficient in doing charge transfer. The expression for the *charge transfer efficiency* is given below:

$$\text{Ampere-hour/Charge transfer efficiency} = \frac{\text{Discharged energy (Ah)} \times 100\%}{\text{Charging energy (Ah)}} \quad (6.7)$$

Another way to calculate energy efficiency for a battery, in terms of watt-hours, is shown in the expression below. It is also called *watt-hour efficiency.*

$$\text{Watt-hour/Energy efficiency} = \frac{\text{Discharged energy (Wh)} \times 100\%}{\text{Charging energy (Wh)}} \quad (6.8)$$

The energy efficiency is typically 65% to 70% for a lead-acid battery. Charge transfer efficiency/ampere-hour efficiency is very useful for solar power requirement calculations because ampere-hours is usually used to calculate the panel array needed to charge the battery bank.

EXAMPLE 6.5

A discharged 12 V battery is charged for 10 hours at 12 A, the average charging terminal voltage being 14.5 V. When connected to a load for discharging current of 10 A is drawn for 10 hours at an average terminal voltage of 12 V. Calculate the ampere-hour and watt-hour efficiency?

Solution

A discharged 12 V battery is charged for 10 h at 12 A, the average charging terminal voltage is 14.5 V.

The battery is connected to load; at an average terminal voltage of 12 V battery discharges current of 10 A for 10 h.

Now, for calculations, the following expressions is used:

Ampere-hour efficiency (%)

$$= \frac{\text{Discharging current (A)} \times \text{Discharging time (h)} \times 100}{\text{Charging current (A)} \times \text{Charging time (h)}}$$

and watt-hour efficiency (%)

$$= \frac{\text{Discharging voltage (V)} \times \text{Discharging current (A)} \times \text{Discharging time (h)} \times 100}{\text{Charging voltage (V)} \times \text{Charging current (A)} \times \text{Charging time (h)}}$$

Now, Ampere-hour efficiency (%) $= \dfrac{10 \times 10}{12 \times 10} \times 100 = 83.3\%$

> The internal resistance of the battery will always affect the efficiency and hence the charging and discharging rate.

Watt-hour efficiency (%) $= \dfrac{12 \times 10 \times 10}{14.5 \times 12 \times 10} \times 100 = 68.9\%$

 WORKSHEET 6.4: Fill the following worksheet (Table 6.7) on battery efficiency in ampere-hour.

TABLE 6.7 Battery Efficiency (Ah)

S. No.	Charging current (A)	Charging time (h)	Discharge time (h)	Discharge current (A)	Ampere-hour efficiency (%)
1	7	5	3	8	......
2	10	......	9	12	75
3	12	9	15	......	60
4	......	8	6	10	68

6.4.8
Operating Temperature

The operating temperature of battery is one of the factors which affect the performance of the battery. As the temperature decreases, chemical activity and the internal resistance of the cell increases, in turn, this reduces the voltage and current capacity of the battery. As the temperature reduces, the available capacity of battery decreases but internal resistance of the battery increases which results in reducing available terminal voltage. Typically, the operating temperature range of a lead-acid battery is –15 °C to 60 °C. Note that battery ratings are given for 25 °C.

When a 100 Ah battery is discharged at 25 °C temperature, it will provide its maximum capacity, but when the same battery operates at 20 °C it gives less capacity in comparison to capacity given at 25 °C. As the temperature decreases, the battery capacity also decreases. The decrease in capacity is indicated by the SoC of a battery. If SoC of a battery (with same charging status) is measured at two different temperature, say 40 °C and 20 °C, then the battery will show different SoC in both cases, as shown in Figure 6.11. At 40 °C, the battery will show higher SoC as compared to 20 °C. This point should be taken care of while designing a SPV system. The battery capacity can also decrease at higher temperatures due to deterioration in chemical activities. Normally, the best battery performance is obtained between 20 °C to 40 °C.

Charge delivering capacity of a battery depends on the temperature. At higher temperature battery can deliver more charge then lower temperature.

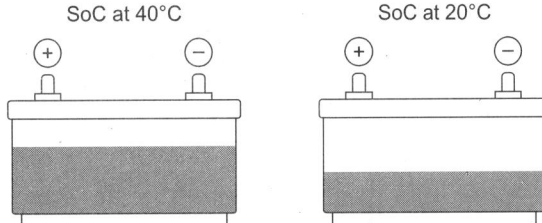

FIGURE 6.11
The difference in reading of same capacity at 40 °C and 20 °C.

6.4.9
Life Cycle

One charging and discharging operation of a battery is referred as one cycle of battery. A battery cannot be used for infinite number of charge-discharge cycles. Due to each charge-discharge cycle, the capacity of a battery decreases slightly. Therefore, depending the material and technology used for making a battery, the batteries can be used only for a certain number of cycles. The usable number of charge-discharge cycles of a battery is referred as life cycle of the battery. After the life cycle, the battery capacity decreases below acceptable level.

After each charge-discharge cycle, the battery capacity decreases by some amount. When, after certain usage, the battery capacity decreases to 80% of the initial capacity, it is considered the end of life for the battery. The life cycle of a battery is defined as the number of charging and discharging cycles it can perform when its capacity reaches below 80% of its initial nominal capacity. If battery is charged and discharged daily, then one cycle is equivalent of one day, and one year is equivalent to 365 cycles. In this way, the life of a battery can be given in terms of the number of cycles or number of years of operation.

The life cycle for non-rechargeable batteries is 1 cycle because only one time the chemical energy is converted into electricity. For typical rechargeable batteries, life cycle ranges from 500 to 1500 cycles. The degradation of performance of batteries occurs due to ageing effect which includes the shedding of active material from plates. This induces gradual decrease in performance of the battery.

Life of a battery can be given in terms of the number of charge-discharge cycle it can provide.

DoD directly affects the life cycle of a battery. In case, the batteries are discharged below the lowest DoD limit, there is a danger; the batteries may get damaged when recharged. This, in turn, will shorten the life span of batteries. As the DoD increases, the life of the battery decreases fast. For instance, a Lead-acid battery if discharged only 10% daily and then charged again, the battery may work for 5 years. But if the same battery is discharged 30% daily then it may work for 3 years only. If the same battery is discharged 80% daily, it may only work for less than one year. Allowable DoD limit depends on the types of battery material and the construction of its two electrodes (or plate) called anode and cathode. A typical life of a lead-acid battery as a function of its DoD is given in Figure 6.12. In this figure, the life of the battery is given in terms of the number of cycles of charge and discharge. It is clear from the figure that, if we discharge our batteries more on regular basis, then the life of the battery is shorter.

> The life of batteries are smaller if we discharge them deep on regular basis and the life is longer if we discharge them to small depths.

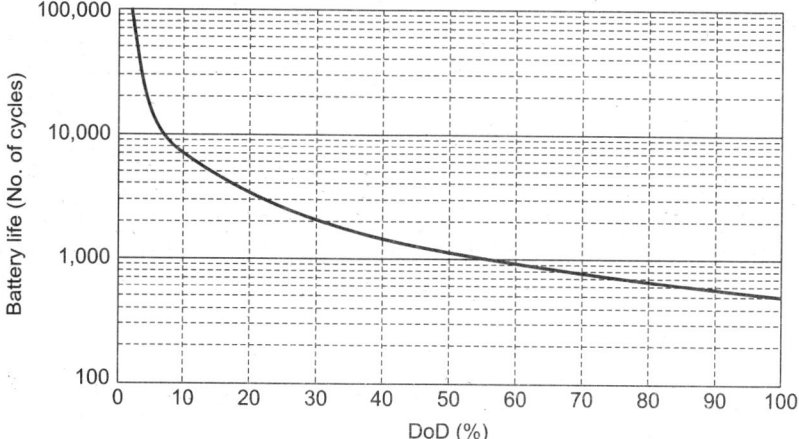

FIGURE 6.12

A typical battery life (in terms of No. of cycles) with DoD for lead-acid battery. Other batteries have similar behaviour but the scale of the curve is different.

The lead-acid batteries come in different electrode design. Depending on the design of a battery, the life of the battery can be different. The DoD of a lead-acid battery for different electrode designs and possible life time of batteries are given below in Table 6.8.

TABLE 6.8 Possible Life Time of Lead-acid Batteries for Different DoD and Electrode Designs at 25°C Temperature

S. No.	Depth of discharge (%)	Life Time of			
		Thin plate battery (Years)	Thick plate battery (Years)	Sealed gel battery (Years)	Tubular battery (Years)
1	10	3–4	5–7	6–8	>10
2	20	2–3	4–5	5–6	8–10
3	30	1.5–2	3–4	4–5	5–6
4	50	6 months–1 year	1–2	2–3	3–4
5	80	2 months	3–4 months	1–2	1.5–2

6.4.10
Self Discharge/Shelf Life

Self discharge is the charge consumed when battery is not in use for a long time, i.e., sits on the shelf. The reason for self discharge is that the electrochemical process takes place within the cell. Self discharge is equivalent to the application of a small external load. Self discharge of batteries should be as low as possible. The self discharge rate of battery increases with increase in temperature of battery. Therefore, it is recommended to store batteries at lower temperatures in order to reduce self discharge. Self discharge of a battery is directly influenced by the chemistry of battery. The charge stored stays in a battery depends on the chemistry of battery. Li-ion cells typically lose 25% of the stored charge in three months when stored at about 30°C, the lead-acid battery would lose 50% of the stored charge in 3 to 4 months, while the Ni-Cd battery would lose the same charge in just 6 weeks.

> Batteries get discharged automatically when not in use.

6.5
Comparison of Various Rechargeable Batteries

With PV System in focus, we focus more on the typical features, components and other related information of lead-acid battery. The typical values of voltage (e.m.f.), efficiency, self discharge, number of cycles and life of rechargeable batteries are tabulated in Table 6.9.

TABLE 6.9 Typical Values of a Rechargeable Cell

S. No.	Type	Voltage per cell (volts)	Efficiency charge/discharge (%)	Self discharge (per cent/month)	Cycles (number)	Life (years)
1	Lead acid	2.1	70–92	3–4	500-800	2–3
2	Nickel cadmium	1.2	70–90	20	1500	3–5
3	Nickel metal hydride	1.2	60–70	30	500–1000	2–4
4	Lithium ion	3.6	80–90	5–10	1200	3–4
5	Lithium ion polymer	3.7	80–90	5–10	500–1000	2–4

6.6
How to Select a Battery?

Knowing the different categories and the types of battery is not sufficient to select a battery for given requirement. The selection of a battery is done by seeing the battery parameters. The parameter values for voltage rating, current rating, capacity rating, number of charging-discharging cycles and shelf life differs from battery-to-battery. These values also differ from one manufacturer to another. So, we must have good understanding of the battery parameters to identify a proper battery for an application before buying or using it.

In the market, many types of batteries are available. While designing a solar PV system comprises batteries, the one problem often faced is a proper choice of battery from many available batteries. This problem can be simplified by making a list of minimum requirements, conditions and limitations:

6.6.1
Types of Battery

Based on application, the type of a battery is chosen. For example, primary batteries are used in portable devices which run on very low current, such as electronic watch, torch and radio. Primary batteries are used for one time only. They are cheap and easily disposable. Some applications require high current to run devices. In such cases, the secondary batteries or rechargeable batteries are used which provide high current as they have high capacity and can be recharged a number of times. The rechargeable batteries are costly compared to other primary batteries, but they are cost effective over long time use.

6.6.2
Voltage and Current

A battery should be selected according to the voltage and current requirements of the instrument to which it is connected. This is discussed in more detail in Chapter 7.

6.6.3
Temperature Requirement

The batteries are designed to operate at certain temperature, normally about 25 °C. In practice, the prevailing temperature or ambient temperature may be different. Sometimes, the ambient temperature can be above 45 °C and sometimes, it can be negative or at freezing temperature. The battery output current and its capacity depends on the temperature. At higher temperature, batteries can deliver higher current as compared to lower temperature. At lower temperatures, like below 20 °C, the chemical reactions in battery become slower and the battery can only deliver lower current than designed value. At higher temperatures, the battery may provide higher current but its life decreases when operating temperatures are high. At very high temperature, some batteries can be dangerous causing explosion and fire can occur. Therefore, depending on the operating temperature of battery, appropriate battery must be chosen for a given applications. The manufacturer datasheet provides the information about safe operating temperature and how the capacity and current will change with temperature for a given battery.

6.6.4
Shelf Life

Batteries shelf life is directly affected by the rate of self-discharge. Self discharge occurs all the time, even when the battery is not used. Some batteries have extremely low self-discharge rates, such as most of the lithium battery whereas, some nickel metal hydride batteries can lose up to 4% of their capacity every day.

6.6.5
Charge-Discharge Cycle
(If Rechargeable)

The number of charge-discharge cycle of a battery depends on the type of battery. Normally, for rechargeable applications, battery with large number of charge-discharge cycle should be chosen. For instance, for standalone solar PV systems, batteries with large number of charge-discharge cycles are chosen.

6.6.6
Cost

Costing is based on the type of batteries selected and it's pricing by different manufacturers. Also, it depends on the features of the battery. Generally, the maintenance free and advanced technology batteries are expensive. Normally, the efforts are made to optimize the battery requirement and reduce the cost. In some cases, it may require that system must perform in all conditions, therefore, the over sizing of the battery is done. In such cases, the cost of the battery is not important but the reliable system performance is given importance. But if the system requirement is not crucial, then we should try to minimize the battery expenses in a system.

6.6.7
Availability

Before selecting a battery, we should check its availability in the market. If a battery, rarely available, is used in a system, it may create problems while replacing or buying new one for the system. So, a battery that is readily available, easy in transportation and can be bought even in remote places, should be selected.

6.7
Batteries for Photovoltaic (PV) Systems

The batteries used for PV systems must be rechargeable, allow deep discharge, should have long life span, easily serviced and have high capacities and low self-discharge. Lead-acid batteries are rechargeable, typically, they have capacities in the range of 1 to 12000 Ah, they have 500 to 800 charge-discharge cycles and life time is of about 2 to 3 years. The lead-acid battery performs very well for a wide range of temperatures, from $-15\,°C$ to $60\,°C$. The replacement and maintenance of lead-acid batteries are simple. All these factors make lead-acid batteries a good choice for PV applications. There are varieties of lead-acid batteries available. In general, the lead-acid batteries are classified into two categories:

1. Liquid vented
2. Sealed or VRLA (Valve Regulated Lead-Acid) It is of two types:
   • Absorbed glass mat (AGM) battery
   • Gel battery (gel cell)

6.7.1
Liquid Vented

Hydrogen is a very explosive. No flames or fire should be allowed near battery. Hence it is not preferred for PV applications.

Liquid vented batteries are generally used in automobiles. When a battery is charged and discharged, the hydrogen and oxygen gas is produced due to chemical reactions. The gas produced during charging-discharging cycle must be vented out of the battery. In the process of venting out the gas, some water from the battery is lost. This loss of water must be supplied to the battery again, otherwise the battery will become dry and will not function properly. Therefore, for such batteries, some maintenance like regular water refilling is required.

6.7.2
Sealed or VRLA
(Valve Regulated Lead-acid)

Sealed or valve regulated lead-acid (VRLA) batteries do not have any caps from where the gases produced in the charge-discharge cycle can exit as in case of liquid vented batteries. The VRLA batteries are designed in a manner that hydrogen and oxygen produced in the battery are recombined again to produce water. The valve is provided in the battery to regulate the pressure inside the battery. Since during charge-discharge cycle no water is lost, no refilling of water is required for sealed or VRLA batteries. They are maintenance free. Sealed batteries have the electrolyte or acid either gelled or put into a sponge-like glass mat. They have the advantage/disadvantage of being completely liquid-tight. They can be operated in any position, even sideways or upside down, and acid will not leak.

Absorbed Glass Mat (AGM) battery

In this type of battery, the fibrous silica glass mat is used to suspend electrolyte. It forms semi solid (Gel) electrolyte along with empty pockets which helps in recombination of gas like hydrogen generated during the charging process. This decreases the risk of hydrogen explosion.

Gel battery

The Gel battery is the most preferred battery for PV applications due to its features.

The gel battery is similar to Absorbed Glass Mat battery. The only difference here is the silica gel is used instead of fibrous silica glass.

6.8
Design of Lead-acid Batteries

Lead acid batteries are manufactured based on the application requirements. The requirements can be of different types, such as large number of charging and discharging cycles (long life), deep discharge capability in each cycle (high DoD) and high current supplying capacity. The distinguishing feature from one design to other design is their structure of electrodes or plates (where chemical reactions take place in batteries). In PV systems, the batteries are very frequently charged and discharged. The batteries selected for PV systems should meet the high number of charging-discharging cycle requirement. Hence, sealed Lead-acid Deep cycle battery is the ideal choice used widely in the PV systems. Deep cycle batteries can be deeply discharged allowing to use most of its capacity (i.e., ~50% of its capacity).

Electrode design

A typical Lead-acid battery consists of electrodes, electrolyte, separator and polypropylene monoblock casing. For constructing batteries, two important techniques, **flat-plate design** and **tubular electrode design** are used.

The charge storage capacity of a battery depends on the amount of active material available at electrode and maximum current supply capacity of battery depends on the rate of chemical reactions at the electrode. The large surface area of the electrode allows more chemical reaction at electrode and hence large current supply capacity. Therefore, a battery used for SLI (starting, lighting and ignition) where high current is required for short time, flate plate design of electrode is used (shown in Figure 6.13(a)). In the case of large capacity requirement, a large volume of active material on electrodes is required in which the electrodes are made thicker. Also, when we discharge battery to deep levels (deep discharge batteries) the active material on electrode gets lose and falls off the electrode reducing the capacity of the battery. In order to avoid the loss of active material from electrode in charge-discharge cycle in deep discharge battery with tubular electrode design is used.

Flat-plate designs are mostly used for manufacturing starting, lighting and ignition (SLI) Lead-acid battery. The Tubular electrode designs are used in batteries for deep discharge cycle. Tubular positive plates are made of 20–30 tubes connected together by a connector bus as shown in Figure 6.13(b). The manufacturing steps are almost same for all batteries except electrodes design.

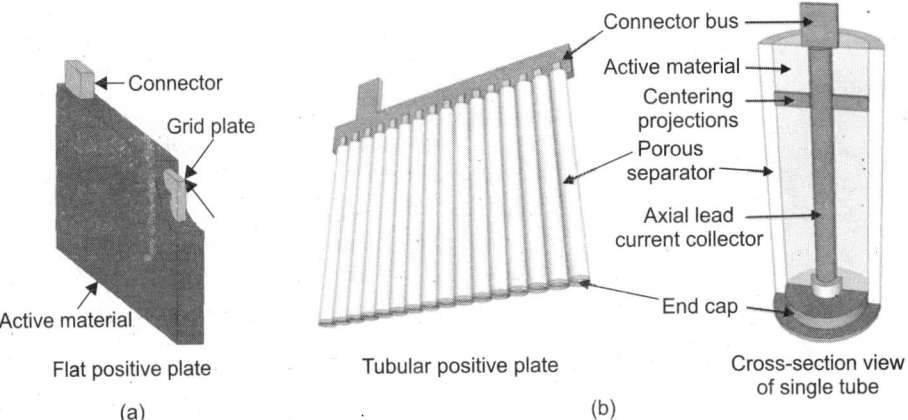

FIGURE 6.13

(a) A typical flat positive plate and (b) tubular positive plate with a cross-section view of single tube.

Electrode shape and size of battery depends on applications. Flat electrode design is used for car battery applications and tubular electrode design is used for PV applications.

Flat positive plate

(a)

Tubular positive plate

(b)

Cross-section view of single tube

Electrical design

The lead-acid batteries generally come with voltage ratings 6 V, 12 V and 24 V. Figure 6.14 shows a typical 12 V lead-acid battery configuration; the battery consists of six cells connected in series. Each cell with e.m.f is 2 V and capacity is $1C$. The cells connected in a string gives voltage 12 V and capacity $1C$.

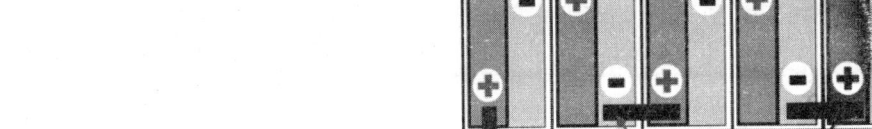

FIGURE 6.14

Schematic of a typical 12 V sealed Lead-acid battery consisting of six 2 V cells in series connection.

6.8.1
How Battery is Constructed?

To introduce the battery preparation steps, we take an example of typical 12 volt battery. The battery manufacturing process involves about 7 stages, as mentioned here:

1. Casting the positive and negative grids.
2. Applying the active material (pasting) on the grids.
3. Covering the positive plate with microporous separators.
4. Combine the positive and negative plate.
5. Arrange the plate sets and form plate blocks.
6. Forming cells and filling the acidic solution.
7. Finalizing battery: carrying out initial charge, testing the mechanical and electrical reliability, closing the vents, cleaning and sticking the label and other related cautionary information.

It must be noted that the number of stages in the line of process may differ depending on the manufacturer's adopted method. The battery manufacturing in line process in detail is as follows:

Stage 1 Casting grids: Firstly, the positive grids are casted using melting procedure and negative grids from expanded metal respectively. The grid serves the purpose of holding the active material and conduct electricity between active material and the terminal (see Figure 6.15).

Stage 2 Applying active material on grid: Secondly, a layer of lead dioxide as an active material is applied for positive plate. A layer of metallic lead as an active material is applied for negative plate. Here, by means of a Cementation process, the active material gains mechanical (structural) strength and retention properties through the grid and active mass (see Figure 6.15).

The preparation of the active material precursor involves a sequence of mixing and curing process using lead oxide (PbO + Pb), sulfuric acid, and water. Curing is a process that makes the paste into a cohesive, porous mass. This develops a bond between the paste and the grid. At the end of pasting process we get positive and negative plates.

Stage 3 Putting separator: The positive plates are put in separators with a microporous cover. The separators cover each positive plate like an envelope so as to prevent it coming into contact with a negative plate and causing internal short-circuits (see Figure 6.15).

Stage 4 Forming plate set: Positive plate with microporous separator and negative plate are arranged together to form a single unit plate set (see Figure 6.15).

Stage 5 Forming plate block: Several plate sets are placed together in a single group. Then all the positive plates in a group are connected together by a small strap which forms positive plate pack. Similary, all the negative plates in a group are connected together by a small strap which forms a negative plate pack. The number of sets in a group depends on the capacity of unit cell that is to be made. One positive plate pack and one negative plate pack form a unit plate block (see Figure 6.15). A cell consists of only one plate block. The plate packs in a plate block has cell connectors which act as cell terminals.

Stage 6 Connecting cells to form battery: The plate blocks are placed in a polypropylene monoblock casing consisting of six chambers. Each chamber with a plate block placed vertically forms a unit cell of 2 V. Each cell has one positive and one negative connector (cell connector). As shown in Figure 6.15, the red and yellow colour cell connector acts as positive and negative terminals of a cell respectively. Many 2 V cells are connected in series as shown in Figure 6.14 and described in the preceding section. The unconnected terminal of the first cell and the last cell of cells connected in series forms the terminals of a battery. A 12 V-battery is made up of 6 cells. In the end of this stage, the cells are filled with an electrolyte which is a sulfuric acid solution (35% sulfuric acid and 65% water solution). The ions required for carrying out electrochemical reactions are present in the acidic solution. The plate blocks are completely submerged in the acidic solution (see Figure 6.15).

Stage 7 Putting battery into operation: After initial battery charging, mechanical and electrical tests are done. This means that when we buy a new battery, it comes in fully charged condition. Every battery is subjected to rigorous mechanical and electrical tests in order to check and guarantee that it works correctly and is reliable. The lids are sealed by welding to ensure that electrolyte cannot escape even in critical situations (friction welding process). After this step, the external surfaces are cleaned to prevent electrical dispersion and corrosion of the contacts and connections. In the end, the company label and other details are put on a battery and the process ends by assembling the carry handle. The usage instructions and the removable contact protector are also added with the battery.

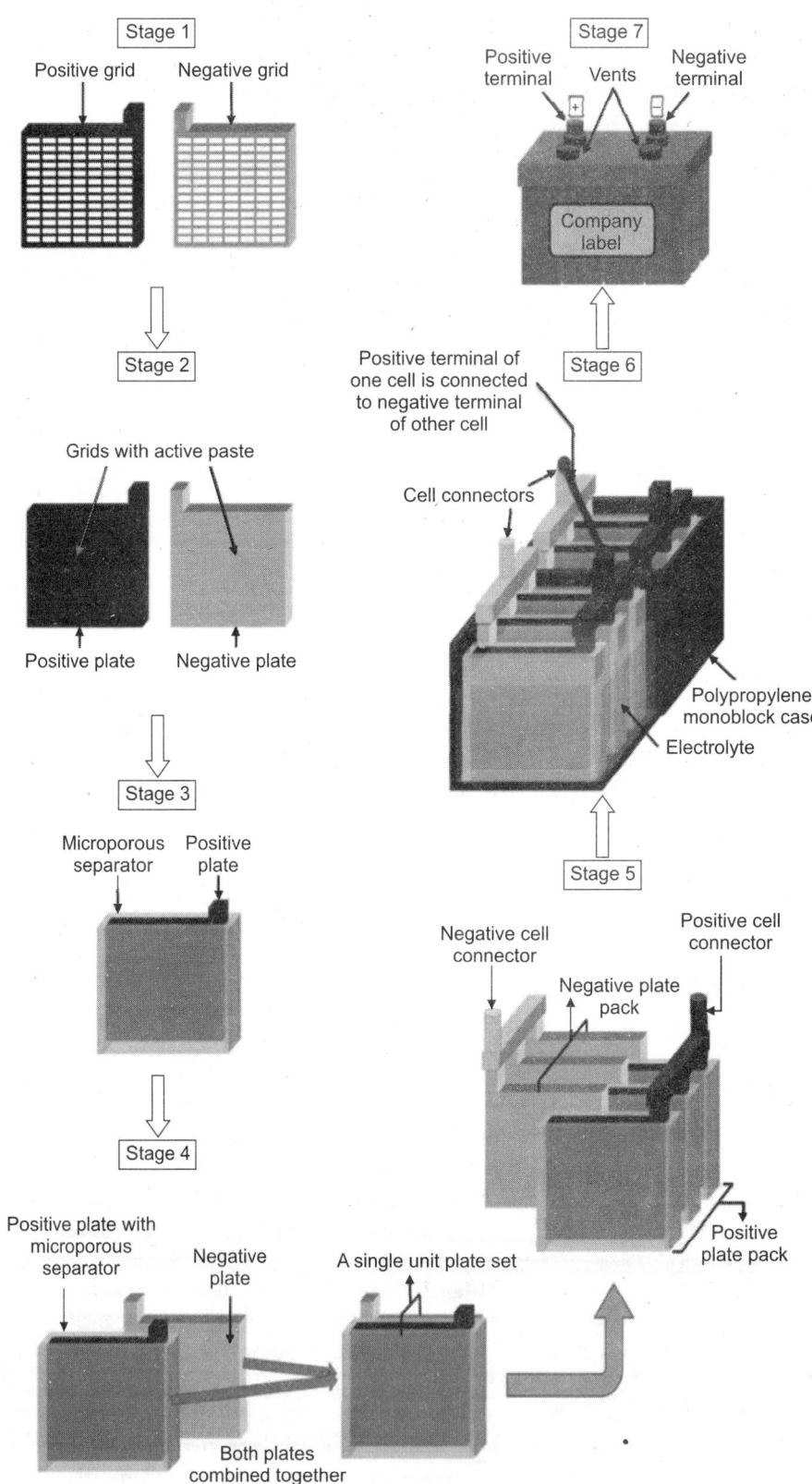

FIGURE 6.15

The schematic diagram of all the stages of battery design.

7

Applications of Batteries in Solar PV Systems

There are two types of solar PV systems; grid connected and standalone PV systems. The standalone system does not have any source of electricity when the sun is not shining. Therefore, in order to power the load in the dark hours, some medium for energy storage is required. Therefore, batteries are used to store energy in standalone solar PV systems. Depending on the power requirements and the battery parameters, the batteries in standalone PV systems can be connected in series, parallel and mixed type of connections. The combinations of these batteries used for electrical energy storage are known as battery array. The main parameters useful for practical applications are Voltage and ampere-hour. While showing a large number of batteries, a representative symbol of battery is used. The symbol of a battery is shown in Figure 7.1.

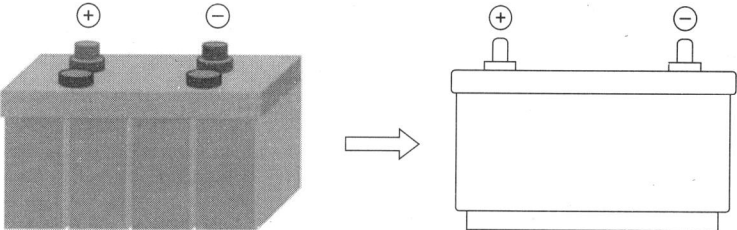

FIGURE 7.1
Schematic representation of a battery.

7.1

Why to Connect Batteries Together?

In order to meet the PV system demand of higher voltage or of higher current or both, batteries are connected together in series and parallel.

In many cases, in our solar PV systems, the requirement for current and voltage is higher than a single battery can supply. Therefore, in order to meet the PV system demand of higher voltage or of higher current or both, we need to connect several batteries together. The number of batteries to be connected together is decided by the magnitude of voltage and current desired in a PV system.

When batteries are connected together in series, the overall voltage increases but current remains the same. When the batteries are connected together in parallel, the overall current increases but the voltage remains the same. In all series or parallel connection of batteries, the total energy of the batteries always gets added irrespective of the batteries are connected in series or parallel.

In order to connect batteries in series and parallel, it is recommended that all the batteries that are to be connected together should be of the same ratings, i.e., same terminal voltage and same capacity. In order to understand the series and parallel connection of batteries, let us consider a standard lead-acid battery having

143

nominal voltage of 12 V and charge capacity of 150 Ah. This battery is shown in Figure 7.2.

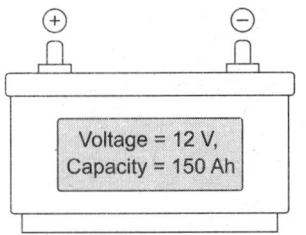

FIGURE 7.2

A single 12 V, 150 Ah sealed lead-acid battery.

Always remember the charge capacity (C) of battery is equal to the product of the current in ampere and time in hour (i.e., 1 ampere × 1 hour = 1 Ah).

EXAMPLE 7.1

Consider a 12 V battery with a charge capacity of 150 Ah. Find the amount of current given by battery if it is discharged in 5 hours.

Solution

$$\text{Current} = \frac{\text{Capacity (Ah)}}{\text{Discharge (h)}} = \frac{150 \text{ Ah}}{5 \text{ h}} = 30 \text{ A}$$

The battery connection can be configured into three types; series connection, parallel connection and mixed connection. A combination of series and parallel connected batteries can be called a battery array.

7.1.1
Series Connection of Batteries

For batteries connected in series, voltage is additive.

Batteries are connected together in series when the required PV system voltage is higher than the individual battery terminal voltage.

In a solar PV system, batteries are connected together in series when the required PV system voltage is higher than the individual battery terminal voltage. In series connection, the negative terminal of one battery is connected to the positive terminal of other battery. The positive terminal of the first battery in the series and the negative terminal of the last battery are used to obtain high voltage. In this type of connections, the voltage of each battery gets added. In this way, connecting the batteries in series increases the voltage. Series connection of batteries is shown in Figure 7.3.

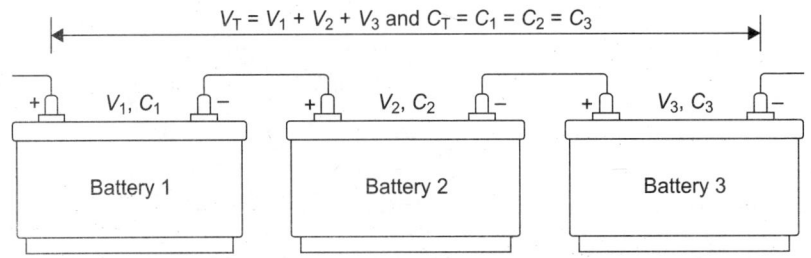

FIGURE 7.3

The schematic representation of series connection of batteries.

Let us say that three batteries of terminal voltage V_1, V_2 and V_3 are connected together in series. In series connection, the negative terminal of one battery is connected with the positive terminal of the other battery as shown in Figure 7.3. An example of the sum of voltage in series connected batteries is given in Table 7.1. Ideally, it is desired that the terminal voltage of all the series connected batteries is same. Note that, when the batteries are series connected, same current flow in all the batteries. So, the total current of series connected batteries remains same but the voltage increases.

TABLE 7.1 An Example of Summation of Voltages of Series Connected Three Batteries

Terminal voltage of battery 1	V_1	= 12.2 V
Terminal voltage of battery 1	V_2	= 12.0 V
Terminal voltage of battery 1	V_3	= 12.1 V
Total terminal voltage of series connected batteries	V_{total}	$V_1 + V_2 + V_3$ = 12.2 + ___ + ___ = ___ V

Charge capacity of batteries in series

We know from Chapter 6, the capacity of a battery expressed in terms of ampere-hour (Ah) is the product of current (A) and discharge rate (h). Since, the batteries are connected in series, the current that can flow in series connected batteries remains the same as that of a single battery. Due to this, the charge capacity of series connected batteries is as same as the charge capacity of a single battery.

7.2

Estimating Number of Batteries Required in Series

The number of batteries required in a series connection to give a particular voltage, higher than the single battery voltage, can be estimated. Consider a battery of voltage 12 V and capacity 150 Ah, then the number of batteries required to get voltage of 24 V will be equal to the required voltage divided by the voltage of a single battery, that is, 2 batteries are required as shown in Table 7.2. Figure 7.4 shows two batteries connected in series to get 24 V.

TABLE 7.2 Estimation of Number of Batteries Required in Series Connection for a Given Output Voltage

Parameter	Symbol	Value	Unit
Required battery array voltage	V_{series}	24	volt
Terminal voltage of a single battery (assuming all battery in series are identical)	V	12	volt
Ah capacity of single battery	Ah	150	ampere-hour
Number of batteries to be connected in series (N_s)	$N_s = V_{series}/V$	24/12 = 2	number
Ah capacity of series connected batteries	$Ah_{series} = Ah$	150	ampere-hour

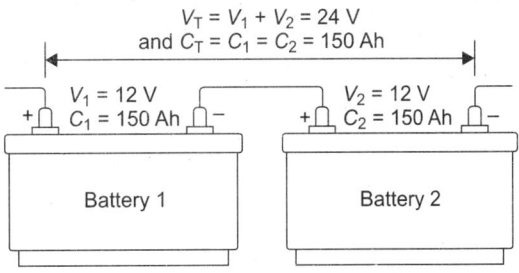

$$V_T = V_1 + V_2 = 24 \text{ V}$$
$$\text{and } C_T = C_1 = C_2 = 150 \text{ Ah}$$

$V_1 = 12 \text{ V}$
$C_1 = 150 \text{ Ah}$

$V_2 = 12 \text{ V}$
$C_2 = 150 \text{ Ah}$

Battery 1

Battery 2

FIGURE 7.4
Two batteries connected in series connection gives 24 V.

EXAMPLE 7.2

How can we obtain 36 V in a solar PV system by using 12 V lead-acid batteries?

Solution

Here, the capacity of the battery is not given. Let us assume that the capacity of each battery is equal to 150 Ah.

The capacity of each battery = 150 Ah

The voltage of each battery = 12 V

Output voltage required = 36 V

We know, by connecting the batteries in series, higher voltage is obtained. Also, the voltage of each battery in series is additive.

Therefore, we should divide the required voltage by the voltage of individual battery. In this way, number of batteries required = 36 V/12 V = 3 batteries.

Voltage across two batteries connected in series = 12 V + 12 V + 12 V = 36 V

For batteries connected in series, capacity remains the same which is equal to the capacity of a single battery. So, the capacity across two batteries connected in series will be 150 Ah.

The connection of three 12 V batteries in series to obtain 36 V voltage is shown in Figure 7.5.

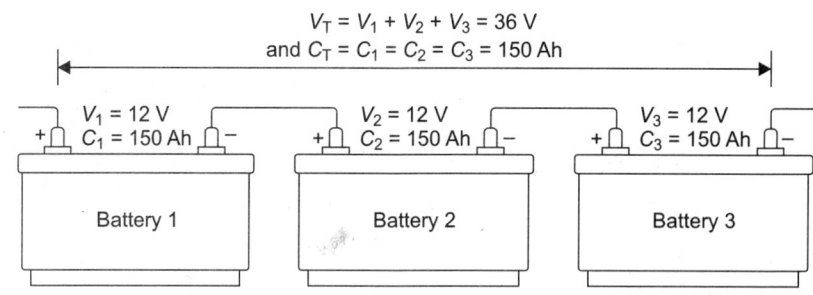

$$V_T = V_1 + V_2 + V_3 = 36 \text{ V}$$
$$\text{and } C_T = C_1 = C_2 = C_3 = 150 \text{ Ah}$$

FIGURE 7.5

Serial connection of three lead-acid 12V batteries.

ILLUSTRATION 7.1

Similar to Example 7.2, for getting the voltage of 48 V, four 12 V batteries of 150 Ah are connected in series combination (shown in Figure 7.6). By connecting the batteries in a string increases the voltage (i.e., 48 V), but the capacity (i.e., 150 Ah) remains the same.

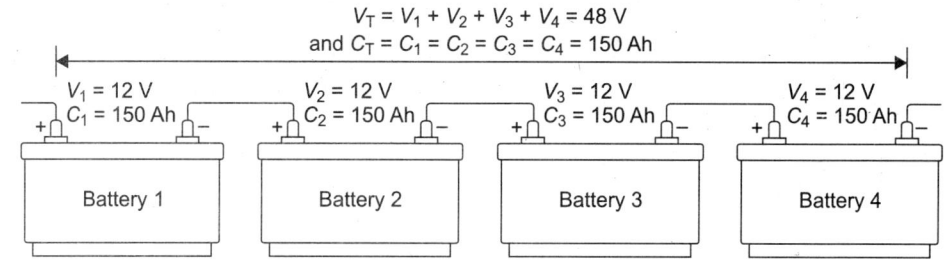

$$V_T = V_1 + V_2 + V_3 + V_4 = 48 \text{ V}$$
$$\text{and } C_T = C_1 = C_2 = C_3 = C_4 = 150 \text{ Ah}$$

FIGURE 7.6

Serial connection of four lead-acid 12 V batteries.

Above solved examples give an idea for doing calculation for batteries connected in series.

7.3

Estimating Total Energy Stored in Series Connected Battery Array

Generally, the electrical energy consumption is expressed in terms of kilowatt-hour (kWh). Hence, the estimation of energy stored in the battery array has to be calculated as follows to get an idea of the usage of electrical energy:

Let us consider, there are three batteries, each of 12 V, 150 Ah, connected in series, then the energy stored in a battery is given as

Energy = Product of the sum of voltages of three battery and capacity of a battery

Here, $\qquad\qquad C_T = C_1 = C_2 = C_3 = 150 \text{ Ah}$

and $\qquad\qquad V_1 = V_2 = V_3 = 12 \text{ V}$

So, the total voltage across battery connected in series

$$= V_T = V_1 + V_2 + V_3 = 12 + 12 + 12 = 36 \text{ V}$$

Therefore, energy stored in the battery array connected in series

$$= V_T \times C_T = 36 \times 150 = 5400 = 5.4 \text{ kWh}$$

The calculation of energy of a battery array can be done in simplified table form shown in Table 7.3.

TABLE 7.3 Calculation of Total Energy Stored in Series Connected Battery Array

No. of batteries in series connection N_S	Voltage of each battery $V_{battery}$ (V)	Capacity of each battery at h hours C_T (Ah)	Total Voltage V_T (V)	Total energy kilowatt-hour energy (kWh)
3	12	150	$N_S \times V_{battery} = 3 \times 12$ = 36	$V_T \times C_T = 36 \times 150 = 5400$ Wh = 5.4 kWh
4	24	500	$4 \times 24 = 96$ V	$96 \times 500 = 48000$ Wh = 48 kWh

7.4

Estimating Maximum Power from Series Connected Batteries

The power of the battery is calculated to determine the electrical power delivered to the electrical appliances connected to it. The estimation of power of an array of batteries connected in series is done in terms of watt or kilowatt as follows:

For calculation, consider a battery with specification given below:

Voltage of each battery = 12 V

Capacity of each battery at 10 hours = 150 Ah

Let us consider, the three batteries are connected in series.

Here, the current delivered by a battery ($I_{battery}$) = Capacity/Rating hour

$$= 150/10 = 15A$$

Now, Power of the array of 3 batteries connected in series

$$= \text{No. of batteries } (N_S) \times \text{Total voltage } (V_T)$$
$$\times \text{ Current delivered by a battery } (I_{battery})$$
$$= 3 \times 12 \times 15 = 540 \text{ W} = 0.54 \text{ kW}$$

The calculation can be done in easy table form as shown in Table 7.4:

TABLE 7.4 Estimation of Power of Array of Batteries for Series Connection

No. of batteries in series connection N_S	Voltage of each battery $V_{battery}$ (V)	Capacity of each battery at h hours C_T (Ah)	Rating hour (h)	Current of a battery for given rated hour $I_{battery}$ (A)	Total voltage V_T (V)	Total power kilowatt Power (kW)
3	12	150	10	C_T/h = 150/10 = 15	$N_S \times V_{battery}$ = 3 × 12 = 36	$V_T \times I_{battery}$ = 36 × 15 = 540 W = 0.5 kW
4	24	500	20	500/20 = 25	4 × 24 = 96	96 × 25 = 2400 W = 2.4 kW

Here, the calculated values for different number of batteries connected in series are shown in Table 7.5. The battery parameters are 12 V, 150 Ah at 10 h and the last row of each column is left blank which is to be filled by the students.

TABLE 7.5 Parameters of 2, 3, 6, 9 and 10 Batteries Connected in Series

N_S	V_T (V)	$I_{battery}$ (A)	Power (kW)	Energy (kWh)
2	24	15	0.36	3.6
3	36	15	0.54	5.4
6	72	15	___	10.8
9	108	15	1.62	16.2
10	___	___	___	___

7.5

Parallel Connection

For batteries connected in parallel, capacity is additive.

Batteries are connected together in parallel when the required PV system capacity is higher than the individual battery capacity.

Batteries are connected in parallel when high current is required. In parallel connection, the same type of terminals are connected together at one point. The positive terminals of all the batteries are connected together as one. Similarly, negative terminals of all the batteries are connected together as one. In this type of connection, the capacity of each battery is additive. So, connecting the batteries in a shunt (parallel) increases the capacity but the voltage remains the same which is equal to the voltage of a single battery. A parallel connection of batteries is shown in Figure 7.7.

Let us say that five batteries of capacities C_1, C_2, C_3, C_4 and C_5 are connected together in parallel. In parallel connection, the positive terminal of one battery is connected with the positive terminal of the other battery and negative terminal of one battery is connected with the negative terminal of the other battery as shown in Figure 7.7.

$$C_T = C_1 + C_2 + C_3 + C_4 + C_5$$
$$\text{and } V_T = V_1 = V_2 = V_3 = V_4 = V_5$$

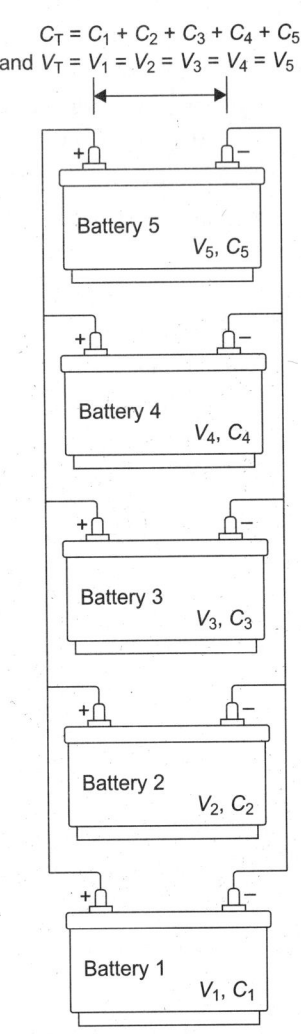

FIGURE 7.7

The schematic representation of parallel connection of batteries.

An example of the sum of capacity in parallel connected batteries is given in Table 7.6. Ideally, it is desired that the voltage of all batteries connected in parallel are same. Note that, when the batteries are connected in parallel, voltage is same for the batteries. So, the total voltage of parallel connected batteries remains the same but the capacity increases.

TABLE 7.6 An Example of the Summation of Capacities of Five Batteries Connected in Parallel

Capacity of battery 1	C_1	150 Ah
Capacity of battery 2	C_2	300 Ah
Capacity of battery 3	C_3	500 Ah
Capacity of battery 4	C_4	200 Ah
Capacity of battery 5	C_5	150 Ah
Total capacity of parallel connected batteries	C_{total}	$C_1 + C_2 + C_3 + C_4 + C_5 = 150 + \_\_\_ + \_\_\_ + \_\_\_ + \_\_\_ = \_\_\_$ Ah

Voltage of batteries in parallel: Since, the batteries are connected in parallel; the voltage drop across each battery connected in parallel remains the same as that of a single battery. Due to this, the voltage of parallel connected batteries is same as the voltage of single battery.

7.6

Estimating Number of Batteries Required in Parallel

The number of batteries required in a parallel connection to get a particular battery capacity higher than the capacity of a single battery can be estimated. Consider a battery of voltage 12 V and capacity 150 Ah rated at 10 hours, then the number of batteries required to get the capacity of 300 Ah will be equal to the required capacity divide by the capacity of a single battery, that is, 2 batteries are required as shown in Table 7.7. By connecting two batteries in parallel, we get an array of batteries of the capacity 300 Ah as shown in Figure 7.8.

TABLE 7.7 The Estimation of Number of Batteries Required in Parallel Connection for a Given Output Capacity

Parameters	Symbol	Value	Unit
Required battery array capacity	$Ah_{parallel}$	300	ampere-hour
Terminal voltage of a single battery (assuming all battery in parallel are identical)	V	12	volt
Ah capacity of single battery	Ah	150	ampere-hour
Number of batteries to be connected in parallel (N_P)	$N_P = Ah_{parallel}/Ah$	300/150 = 2	number
Ah capacity of parallel connected batteries	$Ah_{parallel} = N_P \times Ah$	300	ampere-hour

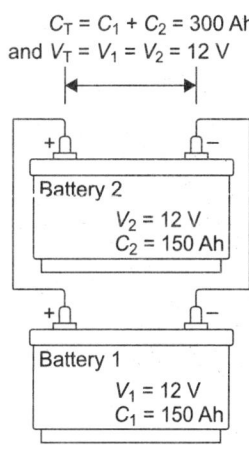

$$C_T = C_1 + C_2 = 300 \text{ Ah}$$
$$\text{and } V_T = V_1 = V_2 = 12 \text{ V}$$

Battery 2
$V_2 = 12$ V
$C_2 = 150$ Ah

Battery 1
$V_1 = 12$ V
$C_1 = 150$ Ah

FIGURE 7.8
Parallel connection of two lead-acid 150 Ah batteries.

EXAMPLE 7.3

Solution

How can we obtain 450 Ah capacity by using 12 V lead-acid batteries of 150 Ah?

The capacity of each battery = 150 Ah, the voltage of each battery = 12 V and output capacity required = 450 Ah

Always remember, Capacity (C) = 1 ampere × 1 hour (Ah)

We know by connecting the batteries in parallel, high current, in other words, high capacity is obtained. Also, the capacity of each battery in parallel is additive.

Now, the number of batteries needed

$$= \frac{\text{Total capacity required}}{\text{Capacity of one battery}} = \frac{450 \text{ Ah}}{150 \text{ Ah}} = 3 \text{ batteries}$$

Capacity across two batteries, connected in parallel = 150 Ah + 150 Ah + 150 Ah
$$= 450 \text{ Ah}$$

For batteries connected in parallel, voltage remains the same which is equal to the voltage of a single battery. So, the voltage across three batteries connected in parallel is

$$V_T = V_1 = V_2 = V_3 = 12 \text{ V}$$

Therefore, we connect three 12 V, 150 Ah batteries in parallel to obtain 12 V, 450 Ah high capacity as shown in Figure 7.9.

$$C_T = C_1 + C_2 + C_3 = 450 \text{ Ah}$$
$$\text{and } V_T = V_1 = V_2 = V_3 = 12 \text{ V}$$

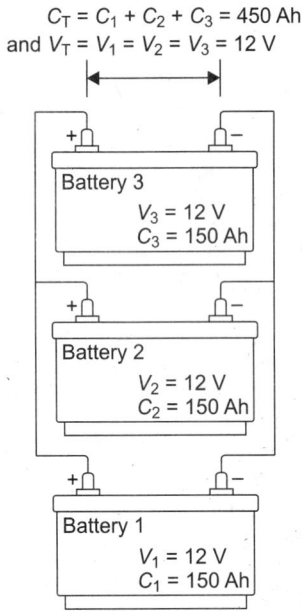

FIGURE 7.9

Parallel connection of three lead-acid 150 Ah batteries.

ILLUSTRATION 7.2 Similar to above example, when four 12 V battery of 150 Ah are connected in parallel, the voltage of 12 V and high capacity of 600 Ah is obtained as shown in Figure 7.10.

$$C_T = C_1 + C_2 + C_3 + C_4 = 600 \text{ Ah}$$
$$\text{and } V_T = V_1 = V_2 = V_3 = V_4 = 12 \text{ V}$$

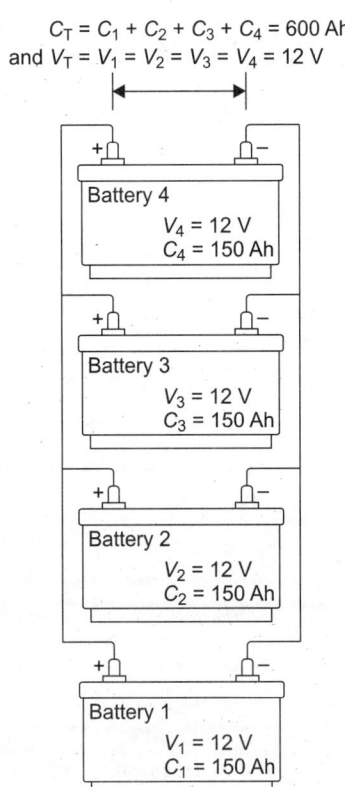

FIGURE 7.10

Parallel connection of four lead-acid 150 Ah batteries.

These solved examples give an idea for doing calculation for batteries connected in parallel.

7.7

Estimating Total Energy Stored in Array of Batteries Connected in Parallel

For batteries connected in parallel, the estimation of energy stored in the battery array is calculated as follows:

Let us consider, there are three batteries of 12 V, 150 Ah connected in parallel, then the energy stored in battery is calculated as

Energy = Product of the sum of capacities of three batteries and the capacity of a battery

Here, $C_1 = C_2 = C_3 = 150$ Ah

and $V_T = V_1 = V_2 = V_3 = 12$ V

So, the total capacity across batteries connected in parallel

$$= C_T = C_1 + C_2 + C_3 = 150 + 150 + 150 = 450 \text{ Ah}$$

Therefore, the energy stored in the battery array connected in parallel

$$= V_T \times C_T = 12 \times 450 = 5400 \text{ W} = 5.4 \text{ kWh}$$

The calculation of energy of a battery array can be done in simplified table form as shown in Table 7.8.

TABLE 7.8 Calculation of Total Energy Stored in Parallel Connected Battery Array

No. of batteries in parallel connection (N_P)	Voltage of each battery V_T (V)	Capacity of each battery at h hours (Ah)	Total capacity C_T (Ah)	Total energy kilowatt-hour energy (kWh)
3	12	150	$N_P \times C_T = 3 \times 150$ $= 450$	$V_T \times C_T = 36 \times 150 = 5400$ Wh $= 5.4$ kWh
4	24	500	– – – – – –	– – – – – –

7.8

Estimating Power for Parallel Connected Batteries

The estimation of power of an array of batteries connected in parallel is done in terms of watt or kilowatt as follows:

For calculation, let us consider a battery with specification given below:

Voltage of each battery = 12 V

Capacity of each battery at 10 hours = 150 Ah

Let us consider the three batteries are connected in series.

Here, the current delivered by a battery $(I_{battery}) = \dfrac{\text{Capacity}}{\text{Rating hour}} = \dfrac{150}{10} = 15$ A

Since, the current of battery is additive in parallel connection, therefore, the total current given by batteries connected in parallel (I_T)

= No. of batteries (N_P) × Current delivered by a single battery

= $3 \times 15 = 45$ A

Now, power of 3 batteries connected in parallel

= No. of batteries (N_P) × Voltage of single battery
 × Total current given by batteries connected in parallel (I_T)

= $3 \times 12 \times 15 = 540$ W = 0.54 kW

The calculation can be done in easy table form as shown in Table 7.9.

TABLE 7.9 The Estimation of Power of Array of Batteries for Parallel Connection

No. of batteries in parallel connection (N_P)	Voltage of each battery $V_{battery}$ (V)	Capacity of each battery at h hours (Ah)	Rating hour (h)	Current of a battery for given rated hour $I_{battery}$ (A)	Total current I_T (A)	Total power kilowatt Power (kW)
3	12	150	10	Ah/h = 150/10 = 15	$N_P \times I_{battery}$ = 3 × 15 = 45	$V_{battery} \times I_T$ = 12 × 45 = 540 W = 0.5 kW
4	24	500	20	– – – – – –	– – – – – –	– – – – – –

Here, the calculated values for different number of batteries connected in parallel is shown in Table 7.10. Here, the voltage of battery is 12 V and capacity at 10 hours is 150 Ah. The last row of each column is left blank which is to be filled by the students.

TABLE 7.10 Parameters of 2, 3, 6, 9 and 10 Batteries Connected in Parallel

N_P	V_T (V)	C_T (Ah)	I_T (A)	Power (kW)	Energy (kWh)
2	12	300	30	0.36	3.6
3	12	450	45	0.54	5.4
6	12	900	90	1.08	10.8
9	12	1350	135	1.62	16.2
10	12	– – –	– – –	– – –	– – –

7.9
Mixed Connection

In mixed type of connections, the total number of batteries used is equal to the product of number of batteries in series and number of batteries in parallel.

High voltage and high capacity is obtained by mixed type connection of batteries.

In mixed type of connections, both the combinations of series and parallel are used together. This type of connection is used when both voltage and current/capacity requirement increases the standard values of available batteries. Depending on the voltage requirement, the calculated numbers of batteries are connected in series and depending upon the current/capacity requirement, the numbers of such series combinations are connected in the parallel combination. The mixed connection of batteries is shown in Figure 7.11.

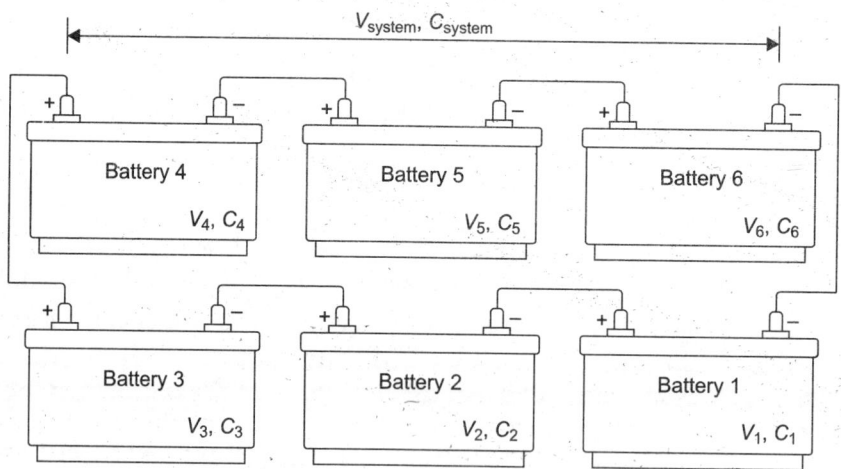

FIGURE 7.11
The schematic representation of mixed connection of batteries.

7.10
Estimating Number of Batteries to be Connected in Mixed Connection

For understanding the calculation for the estimation of a number of batteries connected in mixed connection, let us take the example of designing the battery system for the voltage requirement of 24 volts and capacity of 300 Ah. The specifications of batteries used here are

voltage = 12 V, capacity = 150 Ah and discharge rate = 10 hours

First, the values of the requirement are listed like,

Voltage required (V_{system}) = 24 V, and Capacity required (C_{system}) = 900 Ah

Now, list the standard values of the available battery given above.

Standard values are voltage (V_{battery}) = 12 V, and capacity (C_{battery}) = 150 Ah

We know in series combination, voltage is additive and in parallel combination, capacity is additive.

So, the number of batteries required for 24 V (N_S) = $\dfrac{V_{\text{system}}}{V_{\text{battery}}} = \dfrac{24\ \text{V}}{12\ \text{V}}$ = 2 batteries

Total voltage required (V_T)	Standard available battery (V_B)	Number of batteries required (N)	Round off the number (N_S)	Total voltage available (V_T)
24	12	24/12 = 2	2	2 × 12 = 24 V

Similarly, the number of batteries required for 300 Ah (N_P)

$$= \dfrac{C_{\text{system}}}{C_{\text{battery}}} = \dfrac{300\ \text{Ah}}{150\ \text{Ah}} = 2 \text{ batteries}$$

Total capacity required (C_s Ah)	Standard available battery (C_B Ah)	Number of batteries required (N)	Round off the number (N_P)	Total capacity available (C_s)
300	150	300/150 = 2	2	2 × 150 = 300 Ah

Therefore, the total number of batteries required in the mixed type of combination to make above battery system (N)

= (Number of batteries in series combination)

× (Number of batteries in parallel combination)

= $N_S \times N_P = 2 \times 2 = 4$ batteries

System voltage, V_s (volts)	Available battery voltage V_{battery} (volts)	Number of batteries in series ($N_s = V_s/V_{\text{battery}}$)	Number of batteries in parallel ($N_p = N/N_s$)
24	12	24/12 = 2	4/2 = 2

Now, the batteries are connected as shown in Figure 7.12.

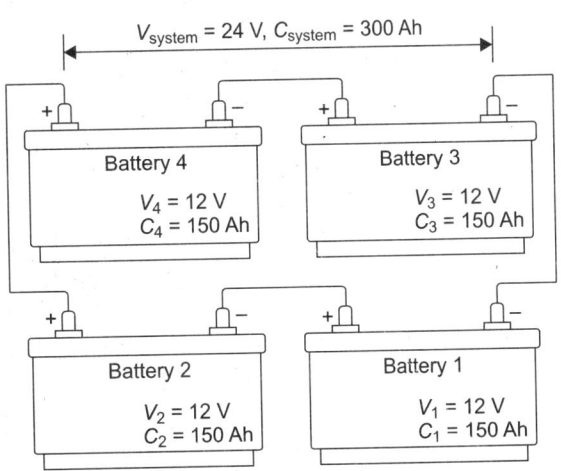

FIGURE 7.12

Mixed connection of four 12 V, 150 Ah sealed lead-acid battery to get voltage 24 V and capacity 300 Ah.

EXAMPLE 7.4

Design the battery system for the voltage requirement of 24 volts and capacity of 900 Ah. The specifications of available battery are: voltage 12 V and capacity (C) of 150 Ah.

Solution

First, list the values of the requirement:

Voltage required (V_{system}) = 24 V and Capacity required (C_{system}) = 900 Ah

Now, list the standard values of the available battery given above.

Standard values are

Voltage ($V_{battery}$) = 12 V and Capacity ($C_{battery}$) = 150 Ah

Here, we use $1C$ = 150 Ah

We know that in series combination voltage is additive and in parallel combination capacity is additive.

Therefore, the number of batteries required for 24 V (N_S)

$$= \frac{V_{system}}{V_{battery}} \frac{24\ V}{12\ V} = 2 \text{ batteries}$$

Total voltage required (V_s)	Standard available battery (V_B)	Number of batteries required (N)	Round off the number (N_S)	Total voltage available (V_s)
24	12	24/12 = 2	2	2 × 12 = 24 V

Similarly, the number of batteries required for 900 Ah (N_P)

$$= \frac{C_{system}}{C_{battery}} = \frac{900\ Ah}{150\ Ah} = 6 \text{ batteries}$$

Total capacity required (C_s Ah)	Standard available battery (C_B Ah)	Number of batteries required (N)	Round off the number (N)	Total capacity available (C_s)
900	150	900/150 = 6	6	6 × 150 = 900 Ah

Therefore, the total number of batteries required in the mixed type of combination to make above battery system

= (Number of batteries in series combination)

× (Number of batteries in parallel combination)

= $N_S \times N_P = 2 \times 6 = 12$ batteries

System voltage, V_s (volts)	Available battery voltage, $V_{battery}$ (volts)	Number of batteries in series ($N_s = V_s/V_{battery}$)	Number of batteries in parallel ($N_p = N/N_s$)
24	12	24/12 = 2	12/2 = 6

Now, the batteries are connected as shown in Figure 7.13.

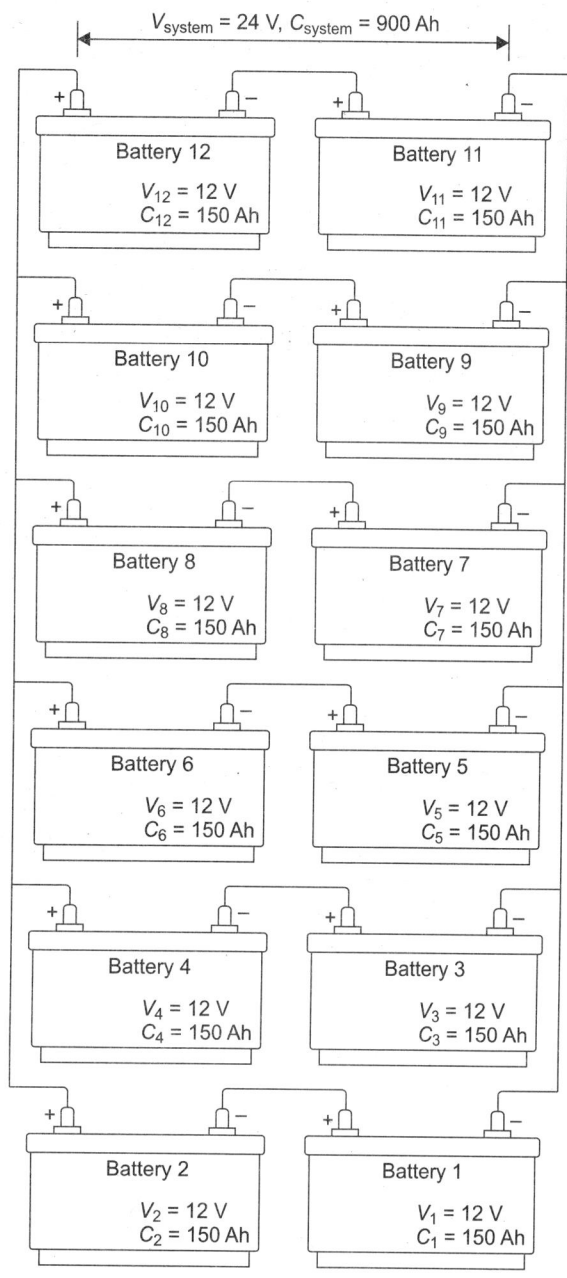

FIGURE 7.13

Mixed connection of twelve 12 V, 150 Ah sealed lead-acid battery to get voltage 24 V and capacity 900 Ah.

These solved examples give an idea for doing calculation for batteries connected in mixed type. In this part, the calculations are further simplified in the form of table shown in Table 7.11.

TABLE 7.11 Notations Used for Different Parameter Along with Expressions and Calculation for Energy and Power for Mixed Connection of Battery Arrays

	Notations	Formula	Given value	Calculated value	Units
No. of batteries connected in series	n		3		
No. of batteries connected in parallel	m		9		
Voltage or e.m.f. of each battery	$V_{battery}$		12		V
Capacity of each battery at h hours	$C_{battery}$		150		Ah
Discharge rate	h		10		h
Current produced by each battery as per capacity	$I_{battery}$	$C_{battery}/h$		15	A
Total number of batteries	N	$n \times m$		27	
Total voltage across connected batteries	V_{total}	$n \times V_{battery}$		36	V
Total capacity of batteries connected	C_{total}	$m \times C_{battery}$		1350	Ah
Total current produced as per capacity	I_{total}	$m \times I_{battery}$		135	A
Total power delivered as per capacity	Power	$V_{total} \times I_{total}$		4.86	kW
Total energy	Energy	$V_{total} \times C_{total}$		48.6	kWh

For calculation, we have consider a battery with specification given below:

Voltage or e.m.f. of each battery = 12 V

Capacity of each battery at 10 hours = 150 Ah

Here, the calculated values for different number of batteries connected in mixed type is shown in Table 7.12 and the last row of each column is left blank which is to be filled by the students.

TABLE 7.12 Parameters of 2, 3, 6, 9 and 10 Batteries Connected in the Mixed Type

Series	Parallel	Total number of batteries	V_{total} (V)	C_{total} (Ah)	I_{total} (A)	Power (kW)	Energy (kWh)
n	m						
2	10	20	24	1500	150	3.6	36
3	9	27	36	1350	135	4.86	48.6
6	6	36	72	900	90	6.48	64.8
9	3	27	108	450	45	4.86	48.6
10	2	___	___	___	___	___	___

 WORKSHEET 7.1: Design the battery system for the voltage requirement of 24 volts and capacity of 500 Ah. The specifications of available battery are; voltage 12 V and capacity (C) of 100 Ah.

First, list the values of the requirement:

Voltage required (V_{system}) = _____ V and Capacity required (C_{system}) = _____ Ah

Now, list the standard values of the available battery given above.

Standard values are voltage ($V_{battery}$) = _____ V and Capacity ($C_{battery}$) = _____ Ah

We know in series combination, voltage is additive and in parallel combination capacity is additive.

The number of batteries required for _____ V (N_S) = $\dfrac{V_{system}}{V_{battery}} = \dfrac{\_\_\_ \text{ V}}{\_\_\_ \text{ V}}$ = _____ No. of batteries.

Similarly,

The number of batteries required for _____ Ah (N_P) = $\dfrac{C_{system}}{C_{battery}} = \dfrac{\_\_\_ \text{ Ah}}{\_\_\_ \text{ Ah}}$ = _____ No. of batteries.

Total capacity required (C_T Ah)	Standard available battery (C_B Ah)	Number of batteries required (N)	Round off the number (N_S)	Total capacity available (C_T)
_____	_____	____ / ____ = ____	____	____ × ____ = ____ Ah

Therefore,

The total no. of batteries required in the mixed type of combination to make above battery system

= (Number of batteries in series combination) × (Number of batteries in parallel combination)

= $N_S \times N_P$ = _____ × _____ = _____ Number of batteries

Now, draw the batteries connection in space below.

System voltage, V_s (volts)	Available battery voltage, $V_{battery}$ (volts)	Number of batteries in series ($N_s = V_s/V_{battery}$)	Number of batteries in parallel ($N_p = N/N_s$)
_____	_____	____ / ____ = ____	____ / ____ = ____

7.11
Battery Bank Installation and Commissioning

Battery bank installation and commissioning is mainly of two types:

1. Replacing old battery bank by new batteries, and
2. Installation and commissioning of complete new battery bank.

For the first type, you must have total infrastructure ready, i.e., battery room, battery charger, battery stand and cabling from charger to battery and from battery to load, whereas in the second type, you will have to design/select all the above mentioned things as per battery bank capacity, that is, size of battery room, size and capacity of cables, battery stand, etc.

7.12
New Battery Bank Installation and Commissioning Work

In this section, we will discuss the replacement of old battery by new, including installation and commissioning of the same. In this case, the total infrastructure is ready and you have to replace the old batteries by new of same capacity. For carrying out this work, the following steps are involved:

1. As the battery is already connected to charger and load, you will have to shift the load to another available charger/battery in the system, such that battery should be isolated from load.
2. Switch off the charger connected to battery.
3. Remove all cables, inter-cell, inter-row connectors.
4. Drain the electrolyte and store it safely (note: while draining the electrolyte, proper care should be taken) and shift the old batteries to safe place.
5. Remove the old battery stand if damaged.
6. Assemble the new battery stand if necessary and arrange it in battery room so that new batteries can be kept on it.
7. Place the new batteries on stand. While placing batteries on stand, the polarity of batteries should be confirmed.
8. Fill the battery electrolyte of specific gravity 1185 up to filling level on the battery container.
9. Allow batteries to soak acid for minimum 8 hours.
10. Meanwhile, connect the inter cell connectors and charger to battery cables. Make battery bank ready for initial charging.

11. Continue the charging at starting rate till cell voltage reaches 2.35 V to 2.45 V.
12. Take hourly reading of cell voltage, specific gravity and temperature.
13. Once cell voltage reaches 2.35 V to 2.45 V, reduce charging current to finishing rate (finishing rate is 5% battery capacity) and continue the charging. Ensure that total Ah input remains the same.
14. In the process of charging, cell temperature should not exceed 50°C. If it exceeds, stop charging. Allow temperature to come down to 40°C and continue charging at finishing rate. Ensure that the total Ah input is maintained.
15. Cells are considered fully charged once the three consecutive hourly reading of cell voltage and electrolyte specific gravity is found to be constant, that is, above 1200.
16. Keep batteries idle for 4 hours.
17. Make the preparation for battery discharging. During discharging, isolate battery from charger.
18. Battery discharging can be done by means of water load or resistive load whichever is available/suitable.
19. Discharge batteries at C/10 or C/20 rate as per the battery specification.
20. Record specific gravity, cell voltage and temperature of all cells.
21. Note down the serial numbers of battery cells for which cell voltage has gone bellow 1.80 V (6 × 1.80 = 10.80 V for six cell battery).
22. Recharge the battery bank; follow steps 11 to 16, record specific gravity, cell voltages and temperature of all cells during recharging.
23. Follow steps 18 to 22 for the second discharge cycle.
24. If specific gravity of some of the cells is found below 1200 during the second discharging, the adjust the specific gravity by adding concentrated electrolyte.
25. For recharging, keep batteries on float charging the battery bank, i.e., final charging; follow steps 11 and 16. Record specific gravity and cell voltages of all cells during recharging.
26. After completion of procedure, keep batteries on float charging.

This process of new battery installation and commissioning takes about 6–7 days.

7.13
Inspection

Before testing the battery systems inspect the following components and conditions:

1. Battery: Verify that the battery is in good condition and fully charged.
2. Built-in hydrometer in the battery: The green eye must be showing in the hydrometer.
3. The voltage across the battery terminals with all loads OFF should be above 12 volts.
4. Verify that the battery connections are clean and tight.
5. Check all charging systems related to fuses and electrical connections for damage or looseness.

7.14
Battery Diagnosis

If the battery tests well but still fails to perform well, the following are some of the more common causes:

The electrical load has exceeded the maximum power transfer resistance.

The existing conditions in the charging system include the following possibilities:

1. An electrical short
2. A faulty voltage regulator
3. The battery has not been properly maintained, including the following situations:
   (a) A failure to keep the terminals tight
   (b) A failure to keep the terminals clean
   (c) A loose battery hold-down retainer
4. A power failure caused by an existing mechanical condition in the electrical system, such as a short or pinched wire.
5. Extended cranking periods due to a controller or human mistake problem.
6. Incorrect interpretation of the battery's built-in hydrometer.
7. There has been an insufficient ampere-hour charge rate for a discharged battery.
8. There is a continuous current drawn on the battery through excessive parasitic drain.
9. The battery is old.

Self-discharge is always occurring as a result of internal chemical reactions, even when the battery is not connected. In hot weather, this chemical reaction increases dramatically. This is why the number of discharged batteries will increase in very hot weather.

7.15
Battery Capacity Test

To carry out this test, use a high rate discharge tester, called Battery tester, in conjunction with Digital multimeter.

1. Turn the tester to the OFF position.
2. Turn the multimeter selector switch to the DV volt position.
3. Connect the tester and multimeter positive test leads to the positive battery post and both negative test leads to the negative battery post. The multimeter clips must contact the battery posts and not the tester clips. Unless this is done, the actual battery terminal voltage will not be indicated.
4. Turn the load control knob in a clockwise direction until the ammeter reads approximately half of the cold cranking ampere of the battery.
5. With the ammeter reading to the required load for 15 seconds, note the multimeter reading.
6. If the multimeter reading is 9.6 volts at 21 °C or more, the battery has a good output capacity and will readily accept a charge, if required.
7. If the voltage reading is below 9.6 volts at 21 °C and the battery is fully charged, the battery is damaged and a new battery must be installed. If you are unsure about the battery's state of charge, then charge the battery.
8. After the battery has been charged, repeat the Battery Capacity Test.
9. If the capacity test of battery, voltage is still less than 9.6 volts at 21 °C, then install a new battery.
10. If the voltage is 9.6 or more at 21 °C, the battery is satisfactory for service.
11. If the battery is found to be discharged only, check for a loose drive belt, loose electrical connection, charging system performance, and carry out the Battery Drain Testing.

    Caution: Avoid leaving the high discharge load on the battery for periods longer than 15 seconds.

7.16
Drain Testing with Ammeter In-Line

Check for current drains on the battery in excess of 50 milliamperes with all the electrical accessories off. Current drains can be tested with the following procedure:

Warning: *Do not attempt this test on a Lead-acid battery that recently been recharged. Explosive gases can cause personal injury.*

Caution: *To prevent damage to the meter, do not operate accessories that draw more than 10 A.*

Note:

- Many electronic devices like computers draw 10 mA or more continuously.
- Use an in-line ammeter or clamp meter between the battery positive or negative post and its respective cable.

1. Turn the switch to mA/A dc.
2. Disconnect the battery terminal and touch the probes.
3. Isolate the circuit causing the current drain by pulling out one fuse after another from the fuse junction panel while reading the display. The current reading will drop when the fuse on the bad circuit is pulled.
4. Reinstall the fuse and test the components (including connectors) of that circuit to find the defective component(s). Test conclusion. The current reading (current drain) should be less than 0.05 ampere. If current drain exceeds 0.05 ampere, a constant current drain is present (Components or devices which do not shut off properly are all possible sources of current drain).
5. If the drain is not caused by load, remove the fuses from the interior fuse junction panel one at a time, until the cause of the drain is located.
6. If the drain is still undetermined, remove the fuses one at a time at the power distribution box to find the problem circuit.

7.17
Battery Fault Detection

7.17.1
Electrical Fault Detection

In this section, we study various fault detections and the methods of detection.

The electrical faults can be detected with the help of multimeter. We can check voltage and current with the multimeter.

Caution: Do not measure current from battery directly with multimeter shown in Figure 7.14, as it may damage the battery and results into the sparks through battery, because when we measure the current through multimeter, it has zero resistance (means short circuit), so, it makes battery terminals short.

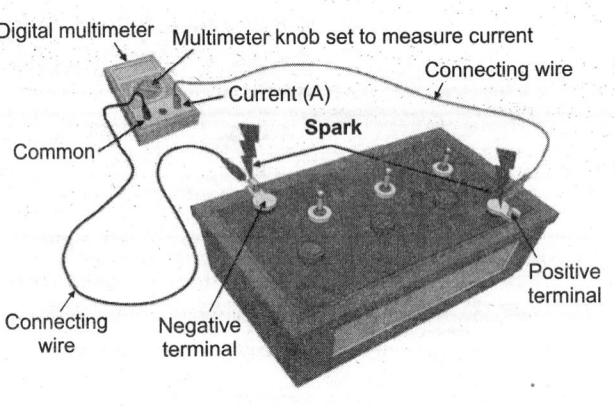

FIGURE 7.14

Shows the digital multimeter connected directly to battery and red colour cross at each terminal indicates the sparks generated.

A. Voltage

Voltage can be directly measured at battery terminals as shown in Figure 7.15.

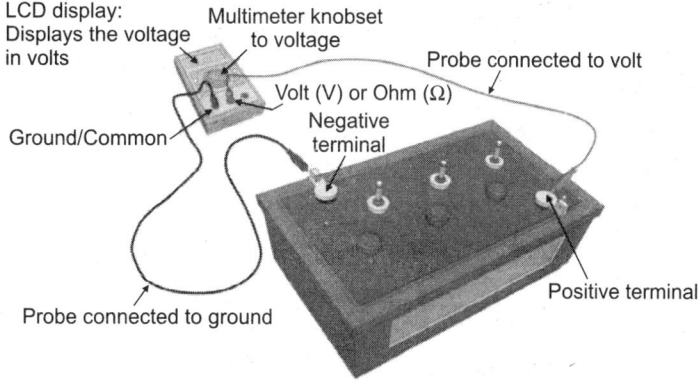

FIGURE 7.15
Multimeter measuring battery voltage.

The voltage range of the typical 12 V battery is 10.5 volts to 13.5 volts. If the voltage measured at terminal is out of this range, then battery is certainly faulty. If the measured value is below 10.5 V, then battery is over-discharged and if voltage measured is above 13.5 V, then battery is over-charged. Both the conditions are not good for the battery health. In order to avoid this situation, proper electronics devices should be fitted to cut-off the battery in any of the situations. Following is the table (Table 7.13) of some voltage stages with respective state of charge for particular 12 V batteries.

TABLE 7.13 Battery Voltages with State of Charge at that Voltage

S. No.	Voltage reading (volts)	State of charge (percentage)
1	13	100
2	12.5	70
3	11.5	45
4	10.5	20

B. Current

The current can only be measured when some load is connected to the battery. We can connect the multimeter/current meter in between the load and battery like in series combination or directly use clamp meter as shown in Figure 7.16.

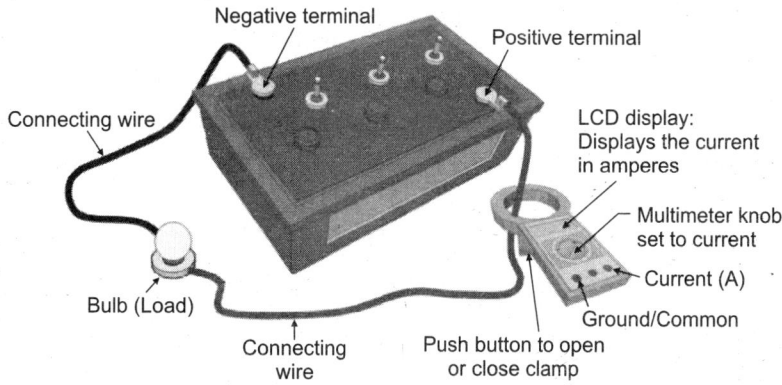

FIGURE 7.16
Current measurement using DC clamp meter.

If the multimeter/current meter shows any constant reading at fixed load, then battery is working fine. If the reading is fluctuating and load is also going on and off frequently, then there may be some loose contact or overloading. If both are not there, then there is some problem with battery.

C. Capacity

The capacity of the battery depends on the allowable depth of discharge, means, how much percentage of battery can be discharged. Normally, this capacity is given by the manufacturer. If the battery does not support much depth of discharge, means that the battery is faulty.

ILLUSTRATION 7.3

We purchased 100 Ah battery. Manufacturer says that its depth of discharge is 60%. We can use up to 60 Ah of the battery capacity. Now, we connect any load which takes 6 A current continuously on 12 V voltage. According to the depth of discharge (60%), this load should operate for at least 9–10 hours. If the battery can run this load for more than 9 hours, then battery is working fine and, if not, that means the battery is faulty.

7.17.2
Physical Faults Detection

The physical fault can be detected by observing the battery outside for any leakage of any loose contact of the battery terminals. Check for any crack or breakage on outside surface of battery from where there is leakage of electrolyte. If yes, then replace the external casing of battery. If the electrode contacts are physically disconnected from the internal connection, then get it soldered from the manufacturer.

7.17.3
Chemical Fault Detection

The chemical faults are generally related to the concentration of the electrolyte and amount of water in the electrolyte, also called specific gravity of the electrolyte. The typical range of specific gravity of a common battery should be between 1.1 to 1.4. By measuring the specific gravity, we can also measure state of charge of battery and according to the state of charge values, we can know about problem with the electrolyte.

For example, the readings of specific gravity for particular lead-acid battery were taken which is tabulated in Table 7.14.

TABLE 7.14 State of Charge and Specific Gravity for a Lead-acid Battery

S. No.	State of charge (%)	Specific gravity
1	100	1.380
2	75	1.300
3	50	1.230
4	25	1.190
5	0	1.100

7.17.4
Charging and Discharging Methods for Battery

There are various methods of charging and discharging the battery like constant current, constant voltage, first constant current and then constant voltage after some voltage level reached, and first constant voltage and then, after reaching some threshold level, constant current.

Charging methods

When the battery voltage drops down below some threshold level, then we have to charge that battery in a different method. When battery is reached at its cut-off point, then there is different method of charging to keep the voltage of the battery constant at its float value after charging. In all the methods, charging depends on the state of charge (SOC) of battery.

The battery is first charged with a constant current until its terminal voltage reaches the float potential value, $V_{battery}$ (float). After the battery is charged up to $V_{battery}$ (float), the current into the battery tapers off. As the current reaches a pre-defined threshold value, the voltage applied across the battery is slightly reduced so that small amount of charge keeps trickling into the battery (trickle charge phase). The highest voltage applied to a lead-acid battery is determined by the gassing voltage value.

ILLUSTRATION 7.4

The other battery is Li-ion battery which is used in the mobile phones. As we know, Li-ion battery has a high charging efficiency. It is charged at constant current up to the maximum specified voltage is reached. Subsequently, the battery voltage is held constant as the current reduces. The charging is stopped when current drops down to 5% of its rated current value. Trickle charge is usually not applied to Li-ion batteries.

The battery maintenance is very important. In order to make battery long lasting, we should properly maintain the battery. The battery maintenance depends on the type of battery used, but each and every battery requires a regular maintenance.

7.18
Physical Maintenance

The physical maintenance includes Cleaning of contact points regularly, regular checking of specific gravity, charging and discharging cycle observations. To any type of maintenance, the very first step we should do is to disconnect the battery from each and every electrical connections. The other step is that we should keep the neutralizing material according to battery chemistry. All these measurement should be done by disconnecting the battery from all electrical connections and allow the battery voltage to settle down at constant value.

7.18.1
Cleaning the Contacts Terminals

The battery contacts should be cleaned regularly every month because excess of copper sulphate which is light blue in colour gets deposited on the battery terminals. This excess of copper sulphate should be immediately removed with clean brush by removing the contact of nut bolts with spanner. For removing copper sulphate, the polish paper can also be used which should be used and thrown off. The frequency of cleaning contacts is generally a month but it depends on the usage of battery and the amount of copper sulphate that gets deposited. Figure 7.17 shows contact with copper sulphate deposited and contact after cleaning.

Contact with copper sulphate deposited   Contact after cleaning

FIGURE 7.17

Contact with copper sulphate deposited and contact after cleaning.

7.18.2
Specific Gravity Observation

The specific gravity can be observed in the tubular deep discharge vented liquid lead-acid batteries and not in sealed maintenance free batteries. To measure specific gravity, the instrument called Hydrometer is used. As the name suggests, it measures the specific gravity of acid with respect to water. The typical range of specific gravity for lead-acid battery is from 1.1 to 1.4 (Table 7.14). The measurement of specific gravity using battery hydrometer is shown in Figure 7.18.

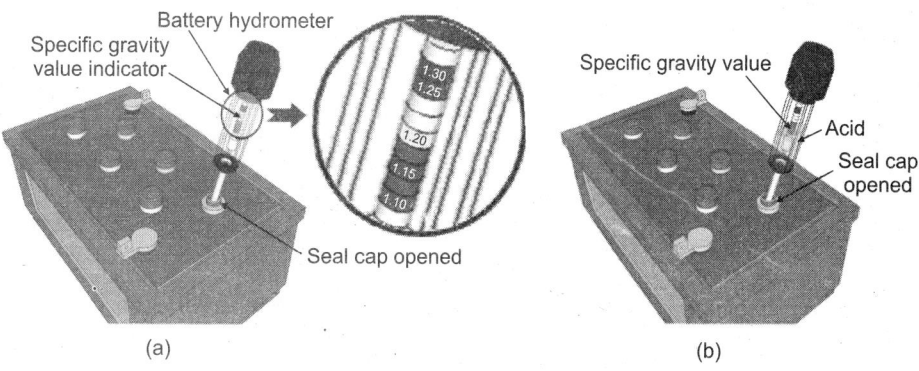

FIGURE 7.18

The measurement of specific gravity using battery hydrometer (a) before pressing rubber bulb and (b) after pressing rubber bulb.

(a)   (b)

7.18.3
Charging and Discharging Cycle

The observation of charging and discharging is very important for the battery life. The capacity of the battery is designed in such a way that the battery charging and its usage (discharging) should be almost equal. First, we should observe the discharging cycle, means the voltage at the time when discharge starts and at end when discharge is over and measure the duration of discharge and discharge current. After discharge cycle is over, start the charging and at end measure the time duration of charging, voltage at start and end and charging current. Current can be measured with non-contact multimeter called clamp meter (detail is explained in Section 7.19.4).

7.19
Instruments Used for Maintenance

There are various instruments used for maintenance and measurement of battery. The most commonly used instrument is multimeter to measure current, voltage and resistance and battery tester. The other instruments are; Hydrometer used to measure the specific gravity of the electrolyte concentration and Clamp meter to measure current while battery is in operating mode (charging and discharging).

7.19.1
Multimeter

A multimeter is an instrument used to measure voltage, current, resistance, etc. A multimeter should be used with utmost care. Generally, there are three contacts in the multimeter from which one is common terminal for ground or negative terminal, the one is used for voltage measurement and last one is used for current measurement as shown in Figure 7.19.

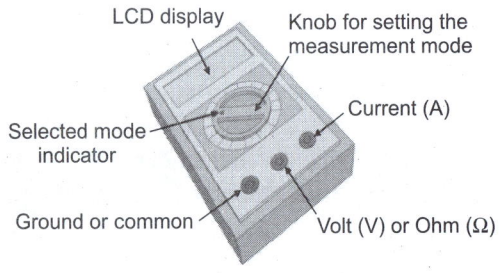

FIGURE 7.19
Digital multimeter with three contacts each with measurement notation.

When the multimeter contact points are configured to measure voltage, the internal resistance of multimeter is highest and when multimeter contacts are configured to measure current, the internal resistance of the multimeter is minimum. While measuring current, we should keep in mind that it should not get short circuited, otherwise it may damage the multimeter and/or fuses. This may damage the battery also. The multimeter for current measurement should always be connected in series between load and battery as shown in Figure 7.16.

7.19.2
Battery Tester

Repeated recharging of a secondary battery can lead to battery deterioration and increase its internal resistance. Problems can intensify when there is a short-circuit in the internal cell leading to voltage drop, overheating and complete battery malfunction. Worst of all, these problems can cause life-threatening fires and other accidents. The Hioki Battery HiTester, shown in Figure 7.20, gives a complete diagnosis of lead-acid batteries and is ideal for UPS back-up batteries.

FIGURE 7.20
Hioki Battery HiTester 3554.

7.19.3
Battery Hydrometer

Hydrometer is an instrument used for measuring specific gravity of the liquid. A hydrometer measures the amount of sulphuric acid in the electrolyte. The specific gravity of a liquid is the ratio of the density of the liquid to the density of water. The water is taken as a reference for the measurement of specific gravity. The specific gravity of water is considered as 1 (unity). The liquid lighter than water have specific gravity less than 1 (unity). The liquids heavier than water have specific gravity greater than 1. The markings on hydrometer are marked according to the liquids under measurement (specific gravity). If the liquids are lighter than the marking on hydrometer will be up to 1 and decreasing with some steps of 0.1 or less per step as shown in Figure 7.21.

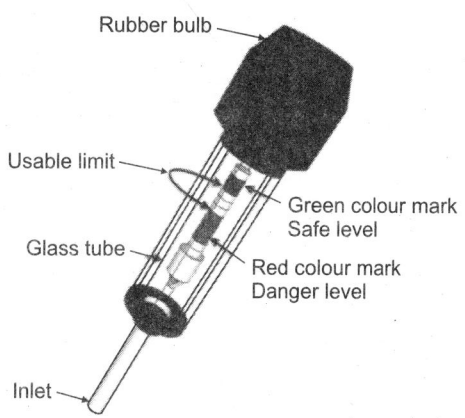

FIGURE 7.21
A typical battery hydrometer.

If the liquid under measurement have specific gravity greater than 1, the marking starts with 1 and increases with step of 0.1 or more per step according to the requirement as shown in Figure 7.18(a).

Battery hydrometer, shown in Figure 7.21, is one way of measuring SoC level of a Lead-acid battery. The SoC level can be determined from the density of the sulphuric acid solution used as electrolyte. A hydrometer calibrated is a standard tool to read specific gravity related to water at 25 °C for the maintenance of battery.

7.19.4
Clamp Meter

The clamp meter shown in Figure 7.22 is also called non-contact multimeter. It functions as multimeter only but the basic difference is that for measurement, the multimeter is to be physically connected to the equipment but for clamp meter, the meter has to be clamped from the wire connected. Clamping means there is one clamp which is opened first opened and passed through the wire from which current has to measured then it is closed and meter gives the reading of current passing through that wire as shown in Figure 7.16. Generally, the clamp meter is used to measure high current range (>10 A).

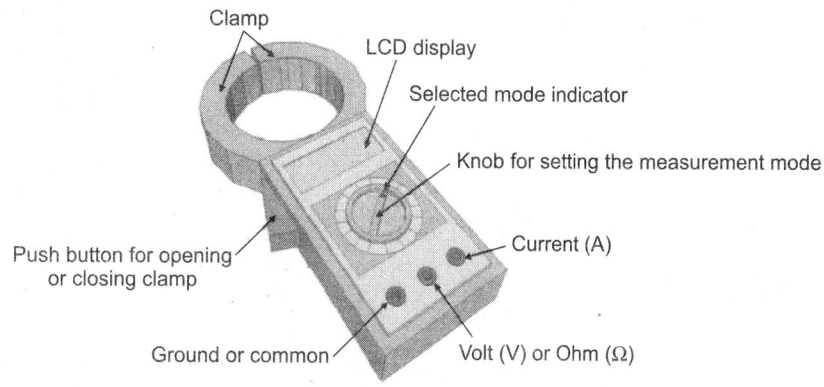

FIGURE 7.22
DC clamp meter with three contacts each with measurement notation.

Figure 7.23 shows flexible current probe which allows you to measure the current in several conductors at one time—a difficult undertaking using only the clamp jaws.

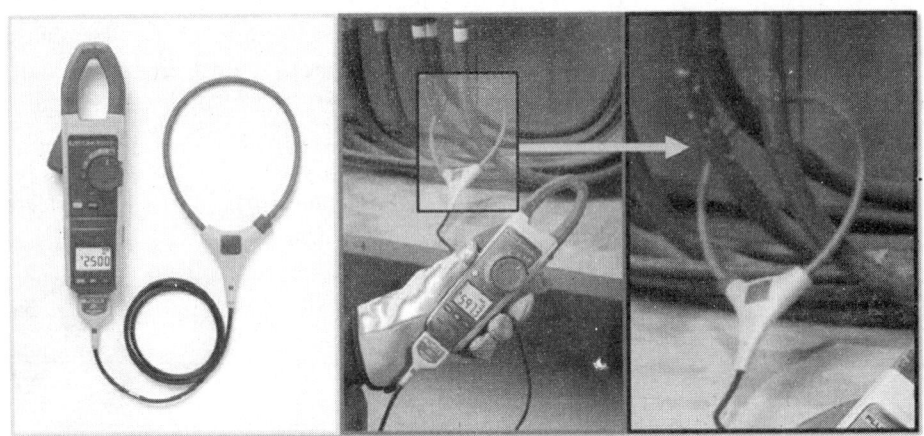

FIGURE 7.23
The Fluke True-rms AC/DC clamp meter with flexible current probe (iFlex).

7.20
Tools Required for Battery Maintenance

There are various tools used for the maintenance of battery. Here, we have listed some of the tools with their respective functions and physical appearance in Table 7.15.

TABLE 7.15 List of Tools used for Battery Maintenance

S. No.	Name of tools	Usage
1	Pliers	To open nuts and bolts, tie the wires, to hold the live wire, etc.
2	Wire cutter	To cut and strip the wire
3	Spanner (size 12″–13″)	To open nut bolt of contacts
4	Cleaning brush	To clean the battery contact terminals
5	Polish paper	To clean the rough contact surface

7.21
Safety Measures

There are certain safety measurement that should be taken while dealing with battery. They are as follows:

1. Connection diagram should be drawn before removing connections and should be kept for reconnections.
2. Polarity marking (+ or –) on the wires should be done before removing the connections.
3. Before doing anything with battery, it should be disconnected from electrical contacts.
4. Remove the metal items not of use in maintenance like jewellery, etc. and keep aside.
5. Keep the baking soda within the reach. In case the acid splits, then it should be immediately neutralized by baking soda.
6. Keep water also within the reach; in case the acid falls on the body, immediately wash it with water.
7. Wear the protective clothing like goggle for eyes and/or hand gloves, apron, etc.
8. Take the battery to open space for maintenance in case if any gas evaporates.

9. Use the tools with proper insulation to avoid the shock.
10. When operation of VRLA batteries is anticipated in an elevated temperature environment, the following recommendation should be followed to minimize the affects:
    (a) Use temperature compensated charging techniques.
    (b) Protect batteries from direct heat sources.
    (c) Install batteries with 1/2″ or greater spacing to allow for free air circulation.
    (d) Incorporate effective active or passive ventilation of the enclosure.
    (e) Increase the frequency of periodic maintenance and capacity testing activities.

7.22
Do's and Don'ts for Batteries

Do's	*Don'ts*
Keep batteries out of working, crowded, and living place.	Don't mix the battery types.
Always store charged batteries in a cool location.	Don't mix old batteries with new one's.
Keep safety instruments close to batteries (Like soda powder, hand glows, pliers, safety glass, etc.)	Never refill water before equalizing.
Maintain and update the record of watering and maintenance.	Never measure current across terminals.
Vent the battery in the open space.	Never bring flame, spark, ignite fire near battery.
Try to minimize the number of parallel connections.	Don't touch the terminals with bare hands.
Before first use, check the specific gravity of each cell.	
Clean the outside contacts to avoid corrosion.	
Always use different colour wires for different terminals.	
While working, avoid wearing metal ornaments and watches or any conductive material.	
For storage, strictly follow the guidelines given by the battery manufacturers because the mixture of materials used in the batteries can be explosives in nature under certain conditions which can cause explosion or burning.	

8
Charge Controller, MPPT and Inverters

A PV installation needs several components other than the PV panels. These components are jointly referred to as the Balance of System (BoS) and include batteries, battery charge controllers, DC to DC converters, Maximum power point tracking (MPPT), DC to AC converters (inverters) for AC loads and grid connected systems, supporting structures for mounting the PV panels, protection relays and so on. This chapter discusses Converters, Charge controllers and Inverters after introducing the basics of Direct current (DC) power and Alternating current (AC) power.

In the previous chapter, we have mainly studies solar PV modules and batteries. In the solar PV systems, there are several other components required to ensure the smooth and reliable operation of solar PV systems. In this chapter, the remaining solar PV system components, referred as Balance of System or BoS are discussed.

8.1
Need for BoS

In a solar PV system, there is a source which generates electricity and load that consumes electricity. For the reliable operation of solar PV systems, the power to the load should be made available whenever it is required by the user. In order to have reliable supply of the power from source to the load, there are several other components required in PV power systems. These components are referred as Balance of Systems (BoS).

The BoS components are mainly electronic components which are required to control the flow of power from source to load in controlled manner. For instance, in standalone solar PV system, where the batteries are used to store the electrical energy for night time applications, the protection of battery is required. The protection of battery is required to ensure that the batteries are not over-charged or over-discharge as both of these damage the batteries and reduces their lifetime. A device called charge controller is required in PV systems to protect the batteries. A device called maximum power point tracking (MPPT) is used to ensure that PV module is supplying maximum possible power to the systems. In the absence of MPPT, the PV module may work in sub-optimal condition and may not generate power to its potential. Since PV modules are expensive, it is important mainly for kilo-watt level system and above to ensure optimal performance of the PV modules and hence, a MPPT device will be required. Though charge controlling and MPPT are two different functions, many manufacturers club these functions into a single electronic device called MPPT charge controller (see Section 8.5 for more details).

One other component called inverter is an important part of BoS in PV systems. The PV module generates direct current power or DC power (see next Section) and the battery also stores energy which is available in the form of DC power. But most of the loads that we use work on the alternating current power or AC power. Therefore, before feeding the power from the PV module or the battery to the load, we need to convert DC power into AC power. The job of conversion of DC power into AC power is done by a device called inverter. In the absence of inverter, we will not be able to operate our AC loads using solar power.

From the above discussion, it is clear that in the solar PV power systems, several other components are required between the source of power (PV module) to the consumer of power (the load) for smooth and reliable operation of the system.

Normally, electrical power is generated as AC power in alternators or generators in remote locations and is transmitted to load centres in AC form. This is the major reason why we use AC loads rather than DC loads. We use AC power in our houses to power up AC loads like fan, light etc. We also use DC power to charge our cell phone batteries, laptop batteries etc.

As already explained, Solar PV panels generate electricty in DC form. We can power DC loads directly. To use AC loads we need to convert DC power generated by the Solar panel into AC power. This conversion from DC to AC is done by one of the power electronic converters namely Inverter.

| Other than PV modules and batteries, there are several other components required for ensuring the smooth and reliable operation of solar PV systems, and these components are referred as Balance of System (BoS). |

8.2

Power Converters and Their Efficiency

Many times in PV systems it is required to bring the current and voltage levels to the desired level. The desired current and voltage levels may be different than what the PV modules possibly can supply. Conversion can also be required from one type of power to other type; that is, the conversion of DC power to AC power or vice versa. The conversion of voltage level and current level or type of power can be obtained by using power converters. These power converters can be classified in the following ways:

- AC to DC converters (Rectifiers)
- DC to AC converters (Inverters)
- DC to DC converters

There are several examples of different types of power converters mentioned above. AC to DC type of power converter, also called rectifiers, is used in our computers. We supply AC power to computer but the components inside the computer need DC power. Therefore, rectifiers are used inside a computer to convert AC power into DC power. Batteries are used to store the energy in the form of DC. When we get power from battery, we get DC power output but many appliances likes fan, refrigerator, CFL lamp use AC power. Therefore, we need to convert DC power from battery to AC power using inverters in order to use power. This is an example of DC to AC conversion. We need to use devices like MPPT, charge controller, inverter in our PV systems. Within these devices, sometimes, we need to change voltage level or current level. The change in voltage level can be obtained using DC to DC converters.

| Some losses take place in power converters and, therefore, the efficiency of power converters is always less than 100%. |

A converter can be represented by a block diagram as shown in Figure 8.1. It can be considered a box which takes input power of some type and converts it to output power of desired type. When a power converter converts one type of power to other type, or when it changes value of current and voltage, some power is consumed in conversion process itself. Of the total input power, some power is lost in the converter as heat and the rest is transferred to output side. Therefore, we can write:

Output power = Input power – Losses

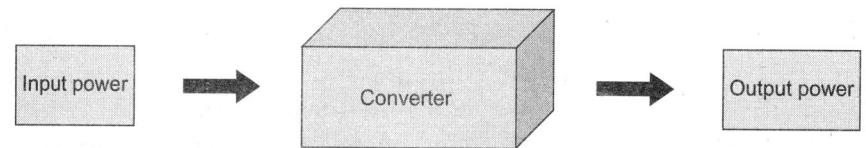

FIGURE 8.1

Converter which basically converts input power to output power.

In power conversion process, some amount of input power is always lost in the conversion process, therefore, the efficiency of converter is not 100%. Normally, about 5% to 25% power is lost within the power converters, and corresponding efficiency of the converters is in the range of 75% to 95%.

The efficiency of power converters can be given as:

$$\text{Efficiency of converter} = \left(\frac{\text{Output power}}{\text{Input power}}\right) \times 100$$

EXAMPLE 8.1

For a converter, 1000 watts of power is input and the output is 900 watts. What is the efficiency of the converter? Also, what is the power lost during conversion?

Solution

It is given that input power to the converter is 1000 watt and output power is 900 watt, therefore, efficiency is:

$$\text{Efficiency} = \frac{900}{1000} \times 100 = 90\%$$

In this case, the power conversion efficiency is 90%, which means that about 10% of power is lost within the power converter, i.e., 100 W is lost during conversion.

EXAMPLE 8.2

A power converter has specified input power of 300 watts and manufacturer specified efficiency is 88%. How much is power loss within the converter? What is the output power?

Solution

Following values are given:

Input power to inverter = 300 watt

Efficiency of power converter = 88%

The output power from the inverter can be calculated in the following manner:

$$\text{Efficiency of converter} = \left(\frac{\text{Output power}}{\text{Input power}}\right) \times 100$$

$$\text{Output power} = \frac{\text{Efficiency} \times \text{Input power}}{100} \text{ watt}$$

$$= \frac{88 \times 300}{100} = 264 \text{ watt}$$

In this way, we can see that though the input power to inverter is 300 watt, the output power is only 264 watt.

The amount of power lost within the power converter can be estimated in the following way:

$$\text{Output power} = \text{Input power} - \text{Losses}$$

or

$$\text{Losses} = \text{Input power} - \text{Output power}$$

$$= 300 - 264 = 36 \text{ watt}$$

Therefore, about 36 watts power will be lost within the power converter.

Problem 8.1: A DC TV operates at 24 V and consumes 120 watt power. Estimate the DC current required to run the TV?

Problem 8.2: For a converter, 2000 watts of power is input and the output power is 1700 watts. What is the efficiency of the converter? And what is the power lost during conversion?

Problem 8.3: For a power converter, specified input power is 500 watts and manufacturer specified efficiency is 87%. How much is power loss within the converter? What is the output power?

8.2.1
Importance of Efficiency of Power Converters

Higher efficiency power converter should be chosen in PV system, but higher efficiency converters are also more expensive.

It can be seen from Example 8.2 that the significant power can get lost within the power converters if the efficiency of the power converters in not high. The power lost in the power converters can make a significant impact on the cost of the solar PV systems, because solar PV modules are expensive and all the power generated by the PV modules should be utilized to run the load and not in power conversion. At the same time, it is also true that the efficient power converters are also expensive. Therefore, there is trade-off between the efficiency of power converter and the cost of the power converters. Appropriate judgement must be made on the selection of power converter keeping both cost and efficiency in mind.

 WORKSHEET 8.1 Complete Table 8.1 for a power converter.

TABLE 8.1 Power Conversion

Input power (watt)	Output power (watt)	Losses (watt)	Efficiency (%)
100	75	–	–
–	160	–	85
200	–	–	88
1000	–	120	–
–	250	50	–

8.3
AC to DC Converters

The AC to DC converters convert AC power into DC power. Sometimes, it is written as 'AC/DC' converters. The AC to DC converters are also referred as rectifiers. The function of a rectifier is shown in Figure 8.2. It can be noticed that the input current to the rectifier is an AC current while the output current from the rectifier is DC current. Such rectifiers are very commonly used in our daily life. For instance, many electronic gadgets we use in our houses require DC power. For instance, laptop, mobile phone, computer, etc. require DC power to operate. But in our homes, we get AC power supply, therefore, it is required to convert AC power into DC power for which we use rectifiers. Since the solar PV systems produce DC power and, therefore, rectifiers are not required in PV systems. Due to this reason, AC to DC converters are not discussed here in detail.

FIGURE 8.2

Rectifier or AC to DC converter which converts AC input to DC output.

AC input　　　Rectifier　　　DC output

We should write, when number of controllers are combined together, for instance, grid tied inverter have MPPT in-built, some MPPT may have charge controllers in-built.

8.4

DC to AC Converter (Inverters)

An inverter takes DC power as input and provides AC power as output.

Most of the appliances around us use AC power while the PV modules produce DC power. Therefore, the conversion of DC power to AC power is required before we can use it for running our appliances. Also, in standalone solar PV systems, the energy is stored in batteries, in the form of DC power. In this case also, when we want to make use of stored energy in batteries we need to convert the DC power stored in energy to AC power used by appliances. This conversion of DC power into AC power can be obtained using devices called DC to AC converters or DC/AC converters or inverters.

Input power: Inverter converts DC input power into AC output power as shown in Figure 8.3. Since input side is DC power side, therefore, the input power fed to the inverter can be given in terms of input DC current and input DC voltage.

$$\text{DC input power} = V_{dc} \times I_{dc}$$

Output power: The output of the inverter is AC power. The AC power can be given in terms of RMS value of current, RMS value of voltage and Power Factor (PF).

$$\text{AC output power} = V_{rms} \times I_{rms}$$

Efficiency of inverter: The efficiency of an inverter can be given in terms of output power and input power, and can be written in the following way:

$$\text{Efficiency of converter} = \left(\frac{\text{Output power}}{\text{Input power}} \right) \times 100$$

$$\text{Efficiency} = \frac{V_{rms} \times I_{rms} \times \text{PF}}{V_{dc} \times I_{dc}}$$

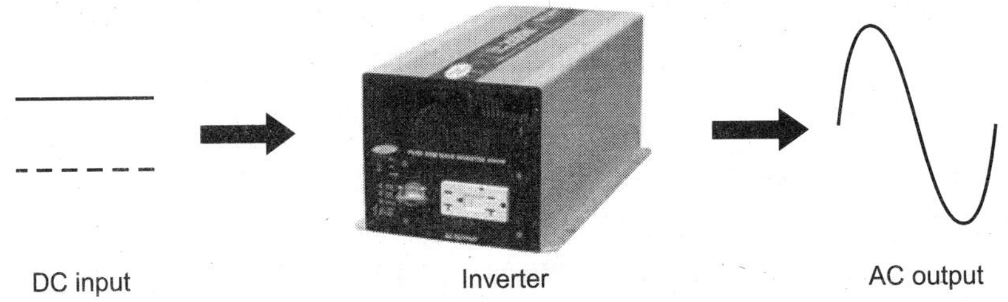

FIGURE 8.3
Block diagram of an inverter.

DC input   Inverter   AC output

EXAMPLE 8.3

Solution

Input DC power of an inverter is 300 W. Output AC power is 250 W. What is the efficiency of the inverter?

Following parameters are given for inverter:

Input power = 300 W

Output power = 250 W

Efficiency of inverter = $\dfrac{250}{300} \times 100$ = 83.3%

Problem 8.4: Input DC power of an inverter is 300 W. The efficiency of the inverter is given as 97%. What is the output of AC power?

Problem 8.5: Input DC power of an inverter is 500 W. The efficiency of the inverter is given as 92%. What is the output of AC power?

WORKSHEET 8.2   Complete Table 8.2.

TABLE 8.2   To Obtain Missing Quantities

Input power (W)	Output power (W)	Losses in inverter (W)	Efficiency (%)
300	260	–	–
–	400	–	85
400	–	–	84

8.4.1
Types of Inverters

The solar inverters are an important interface between the solar PV module and the load. Depending on whether battery is used in the PV system or not, the solar inverters can be classified in three broad categories:

Standalone inverters or Off-grid inverters

These inverters are not connected to grid. They are normally used in standalone PV power systems as shown in Figure 8.4. In standalone system, there is no back-up of power for energy storage, therefore, this type of inverters has battery back-up to supply the power to the load in case of non sunshine hours.

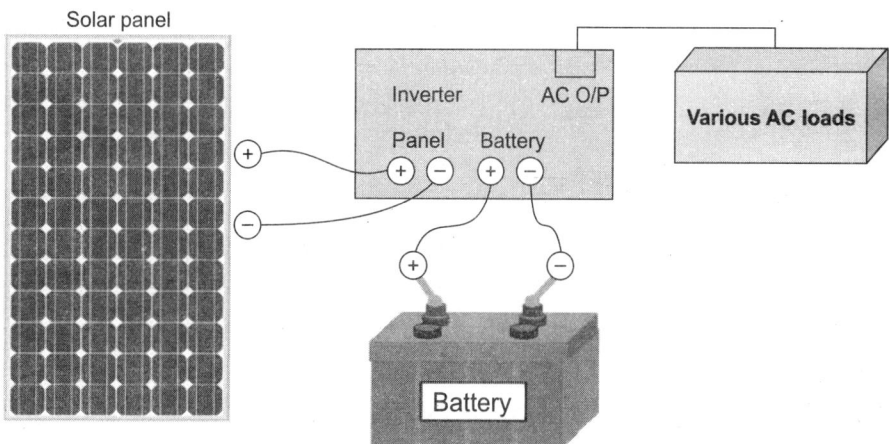

FIGURE 8.4

Inverter block diagram with DC battery input terminals and AC output terminals.

Grid-tie inverters or grid-interactive inverter

These inverters are connected to grid and do not have battery back-up. They have special circuitry to match inverter output voltage and frequency with that of grid. Grid is used as battery back-up when power generated by PV array is insufficient. These inverters also have in-built MPPT to extract maximum power from PV array.

When the sun is shining and PV array is generating more power than our usage, then the extra power after meeting our load is supplied to the grid. If PV array power is less than our load requirement then some power is drawn from the grid to make up the shortage power.

Battery back-up grid-tie inverters

These inverters are grid-tied but also have battery back-up like standalone inverters.

8.4.2
Inverter Specifications

Battery input

Battery voltage: Manufacturers specify the range of voltages, called DC input window that can be applied to the input of inverter.

DC current: It is the maximum DC current that the inverter can handle.

Solar panel input

Voltage range: Manufacturers specify the range of voltages, called DC input window that can be applied to the solar panel input of inverter.

Maximum short circuit current: It is the maximum current that the inverter can handle from the panel.

Output

Continuous output power (W): Inverter rated output power is the power level inverter which can maintain for a long period and so it is sometimes termed continuous output power. Generally, continuous output is specified at particular temperature. In practice, the available power output depends on temperature. Power output of a 500 watt (rated power) inverter as a function of temperature is shown in Figure 8.5 (For precise variation user's manuals can be referred). With increase in the temperature of the inverter than the rated temperature, its power output decreases because of increase in internal losses in inverter. This graph is only indicative to demonstrate that the power output of inverter decreases with increase in temperature. One must try to get the actual data sheet of inverter before purchasing, as the design and performance can vary from one manufacturer to other manufacturer.

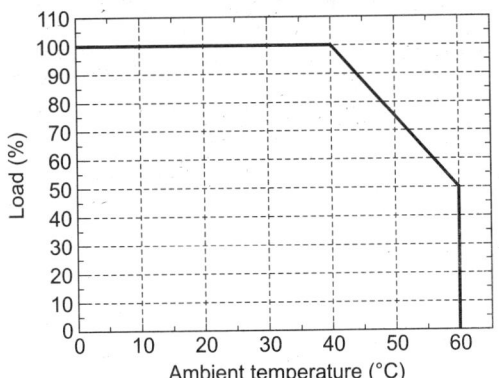

FIGURE 8.5

Dependence of continuous output power on temperature.

Output voltage: This is the AC output voltage that results at the output of inverter. It is either 230 V or 400 V since our loads also run at same voltage levels.

Frequency: Frequency is 50 Hz in India and 60 Hz in USA. Inverters are designed for specific frequency.

Efficiency: This is the ratio of output power to input power of a inverter. The efficiency of a inverter varies with the load connected to it at the output. Therefore, the rated efficiency is given for a particular load. Typical efficiency-vs-load curve of a inverter is presented in Figure 8.6 as a function of load. This graph is only indicative to demonstrate that the power output of inverter depends on the load. One must try to get the actual data sheet of inverter before purchasing, as the design and performance can vary from one manufacturer to other manufacturer.

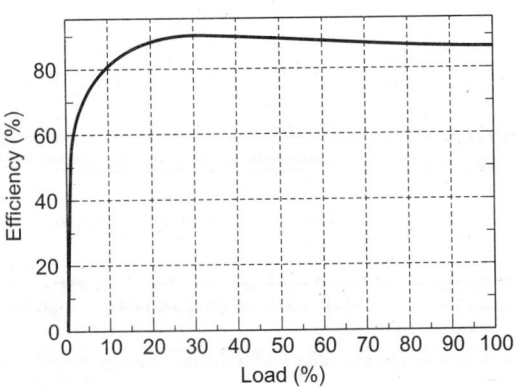

FIGURE 8.6

Inverter efficiency dependence on load (For precise variation user's manuals be referred).

Other specifications

No load power consumption: This is the power consumed by the inverter under no-load condition, i.e., the case when no load is working on an inverter. This no-load power consumption should be as small as possible to avoid power loss in inverter.

Surge power (W): Many inductive loads draw 5 to 6 times normal running power for few seconds during starting. This is called surge power. Inverter should be able to supply the surge power required by the inductive loads.

Output waveform: The inverters are supposed to convert a DC power into AC power output. A perfect AC power output should have sinusoidal behaviour, meaning the AC current and AC voltage should be pure sine wave. In practice, converting DC power into square wave AC power output is much simpler (and low cost) as compared to converting a DC power into perfect sine wave AC power output which is more expensive. On the other hand, the AC power with square wave is considered low quality AC power while the AC power with sine wave is considered high quality AC power. The quality of the AC power affects the performance and life of the appliances which use this AC power.

Commercially, inverters are available with the following types of output waveforms (also shown in Figure 8.7).

1. Square wave
2. Sinusoidal
3. Modified sinusoidal

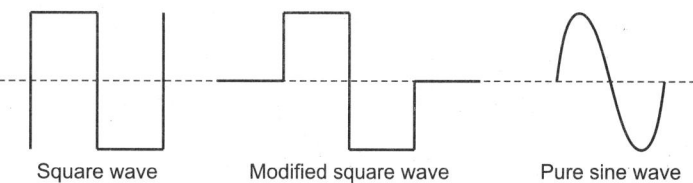

Square wave   Modified square wave   Pure sine wave

FIGURE 8.7

Different output waveforms of an inverter.

Quality of power in inverters: Pure sine wave is ideal for almost all AC loads and is considered as the best quality power. Any deviation from sinusoidal is said to introduce harmonics thereby degrading the quality of AC power. The extent of degradation of AC power or the quality of AC power is measured using the term Total Harmonic Distorsion (THD). In short, THD indicates the devation of waveform from pure sinusoid. The more the THD, the more the deviation from sinusoid and power is said to be of lower quality. From this discussion, we can say the following:

THD (sine wave) < THD (Modified sine wave) < THD (square wave)

The THD is specified by the inverter. It should be as low as possible. The THD value for good quality sine waver inverters is always less than 4%.

Typical inverter specifications of 500 W rated inverter are shown in Table 8.3.

Manufacturers provide charge controller features along with the inverter electronics. In such cases, the specifications of charge controllers become a subset of inverter specifications.

8.4.3 Typical Inverter Specifications

TABLE 8.3 Typical Inverter Specifications of 300 W Rated Inverter

OUTPUT	
Continuous power rating	500 W @ 25°C
AC output voltage (RMS)	220 V
AC output frequency	50 Hz
BATTERY INPUT	
Battery voltage	10 ~ 15 V
DC current	34 A
OFF mode current draw	< 1 mA
SOLAR PANEL INPUT	
Voltage range	25 ~ 42 V
Maximum short circuit current	16 A
CHARGER OUTPUT	
Maximum charging voltage	15 V
Maximum charging current	24 A

EXAMPLE 8.4

A house has the following AC loads rated at 230 V.

(i) Three 80 W lights

(ii) Two 100 W fans

(iii) A 60 W radio.

All the loads are powered simultaneously. A 12 V battery is available. Choose the appropriate inverter?

Solution

Output power estimation: Total AC load to be powered simultaneously is as follows:

Load	Wattage	Quantity	Total load
Light	80 W	3	240 W
Fan	100 W	2	200 W
Radio	60 W	1	60 W
			500 W

Input power estimation: Assume, inverter efficiency is 90%. Then

$$\text{Inverter input power} = \frac{\text{Output power}}{\text{Efficiency}} = \frac{500 \ W}{0.9} = 556 \text{ W}$$

Maximum input current estimation:

$$\text{Input current} = \frac{\text{Input power}}{\text{Voltage}} = \frac{556 \text{ W}}{12 \text{ V}} = 46.33 \text{ A}$$

The inverter should be able to supply this current, the wire should be chosen to withstand this amount of current.

Output voltage and frequency of inverter: These values should match with load rating values. So, 230 V and 50 Hz are to be chosen.

Surge capability of inverter: For accurate surge estimation, we need to know the surge of all individual loads. Normally, 3 to 4 times of output power is sufficient to meet the surge of loads. So, inverter should be capable of providing 500 × 4 = 2000 W surge power.

EXAMPLE 8.5

A house has the following AC loads rated at 230 V.

(i) Three 60 W lights

(ii) Two 90 W fans

(iii) A 60 W radio.

All the loads are powered simultaneously. A 12 V battery is available. Choose the appropriate inverter? Assume that inverter efficiency is 90%.

Solution

Output power estimation: Total AC load to be powered simultaneously is as follows:

Load	Wattage	Quantity	Total load
Light	60 W	3	180 W
Fan	90 W	2	180 W
Radio	60 W	1	60 W
			420 W

Input power estimation: Assume inverter efficiency is 90%. Then

$$\text{Inverter input power} = \frac{\text{Output power}}{\text{Efficiency}} = \frac{420 \text{ W}}{0.9} = 466.7 \text{ W}$$

Maximum input current estimation:

$$\text{Input current} = \frac{\text{Input power}}{\text{Voltage}} = \frac{466.7 \text{ W}}{12 \text{ V}} = 38.9 \text{ A}$$

The inverter should be able to supply this current, the wire should be chosen to withstand this amount of current.

Output voltage and frequency of inverter: These values should match with load rating values. So, 230 V and 50 Hz are to be chosen.

Surge capability of inverter: For accurate surge estimation, we need to know the surge of all individual loads. Normally, 3 to 4 times of output power is sufficient to meet the surge of loads. So, inverter should be capable of providing 466.7 × 4 = 1867 W surge power.

Problem 8.6 A house has the following AC loads rated at 230 V.

(i) Five 40 W lights
(ii) Three 60 W fans
(iii) A 40 W radio.

All the loads are powered simultaneously. A 24 V battery is available. Choose the appropriate inverter? Assume that inverter efficiency is 85%.

8.4.4
Troubleshooting

Troubleshooting is discussed in Table 8.4.

TABLE 8.4 Troubleshooting

Failure status	Probable reasons	Solutions recommended
No AC output volatge	Abnormal input voltage	Make sure that battery voltage is not either too low or too high
	Over temperature protection	Make sure that the ambient temperature is not too high and ventilation is not blocked. Lower ambient temperature or derate load usage.
	Short circuit protection	Make sure that the output is not short circuited or overloaded
	Over load protection	Make sure that the surge current is not too high or output volatge does not exceed the rated value.
Discharge period for battery is very short	Battery aged or broken	Replace the batteries
	Battery capacity too small	Consider the battery of larger capacity

8.5
DC to DC Power Converters

DC to DC converters are used for converting one level of DC voltage (usually raw, unregulated or un-controlled voltage level) to another level of DC voltage (regulated or controlled voltage level) as shown in Figure 8.8. Sometimes, DC to DC converter is also written as 'DC/DC' converters. Other than converting unregulated voltage level to regulated voltage level, the DC to DC converters are also used for converting one level of voltage to other level (higher or lower level). For instance, a PV system may be designed to give 24 volt but when we want to convert the DC power to AC power with output voltage of 230 V (device is called inverter), then the input voltage requirement to the inverter is high. In this case, a DC to DC converter is used which becomes a part of the inverter itself. These converters play a vital role in PV systems where they are used as charge controllers, maximum power point trackers and for interfacing the PV source with different types of loads. The DC to DC circuits are also used for noise isolation, power bus regulation and current boosting.

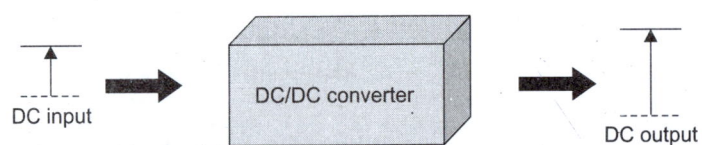

FIGURE 8.8
DC/DC converter which converts DC input to DC output.

In DC to DC converter, both input side and output side work on DC power, i.e., DC current flows at input side and DC current flows at output side. If we know the current and voltage at the input side we can find out the DC power feed at input side. Similarly, if we know the current and voltage at the output side, we can

In DC to DC power converters, both input side and output side carry DC power.

calculate the DC power at the output side. Once we know the DC power at the input side and DC power at the output side, we can calculate the efficiency of the DC to DC converters. Remember that power is the product of current and voltage.

EXAMPLE 8.6

For a DC to DC converter as shown in Figure 8.9, a battery of 25 V is connected and the input current is 4 A. At the output side, a voltmeter shows 50 V across the load and the output current is 1.8 A. Find

(i) Power input to the converter
(ii) Power output by the converter or absorbed by load
(iii) Power lost in the converter due to losses
(iv) Efficiency of the converter.

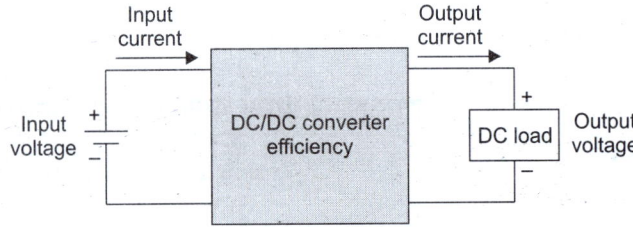

FIGURE 8.9
A typical DC/DC converter with input voltage, input current, output voltage, and output current.

Solution

Following parameters are given for the DC to DC converter:

Input side voltage = 25 V

Input side current = 4 A

Output side voltage = 50 V

Output side current = 1.8 A

The input power to the converter is the product of input current and input voltage.

Input power = input current × input voltage = 25 × 4 = 100 watt

The output power of the converter is the product of output current and output voltage.

Output power = output current × output voltage = 50 × 1.8 = 90 watt

Power loss inside the converter = Input power − Output power = 100 − 90 = 10 watt

$$\text{Efficiency of converter} = \left(\frac{\text{Output power}}{\text{Input power}} \right) \times 100$$

$$\text{Efficiency of converter} = \frac{90}{100} \times 100 = 90\%$$

Problem 8.7: For a DC to DC converter as shown in Figure 8.9, a battery of 30 V is connected and the input current is 5 A. At the output side, voltmeter shows 60 V across the load and the output current is 2 A. Find

(i) Power input to the converter

(ii) Power output by the converter or absorbed by load

(iii) Power lost in the converter due to losses

(iv) Efficiency of the converter.

 WORKSHEET 8.3: Complete Table 8.5 for a DC/DC converter.

TABLE 8.5 To Obtain Missing Quantities

Input voltage (V)	Input current (V)	Input power (W)	Output voltage (V)	Output current (A)	Output power (W)	Power loss (W)	Efficiency (%)
50	3	–	40	3	–	–	–
–	3	300	–	3	230	–	–

8.6

Charge Controllers

8.6.1
Function of a Charge Controller

In this section, we study a charge controller, its function, working, features etc.

Charge controllers, as the name implies, control the flow of charge from the battery and to the battery. They protect the battery by preventing over-charge or deep discharge of batteries to preserve their life and performance. When the battery gets overcharged by solar PV module, a charge controller will cut it off from the circuit so that no more charging is possible. Similarly, if a battery goes into deep discharge (or overdischarge) due to excessive use of batteries by the load, a charge controller detects and disconnects the battery from the circuit so that no current can be drawn from the battery. In this way, a charge controller protects the battery. Note that both overcharge and deep discharge conditions damage batteries. Both the situations result in decrease in the life of batteries. The block diagram of a standalone PV system with battery back-up and a charge controller is shown in Figure 8.10.

> Charge controllers protect the batteries by disconnecting it from the circuit in case of over charge or over discharge (deep discharge).

8.6.2
Working of Charge Controller

The status of over-charge and deep discharge is detected by measuring the voltage level of batteries. In overcharge condition, the battery voltage increases beyond a certain level and in deep discharge condition, the battery voltage decreases below a certain level. In overcharge and deep discharge voltage conditions, the charge controller disconnects the battery. Also, when the battery voltage level reaches within the normal operating level, the battery gets connected to the circuit. In case of over-charge, battery gets cut-off due to high voltage of battery. After high voltage cut-off, if the battery is used by load which means some discharge of battery, then its terminal voltage will fall. The charge controller will detect this and connect the battery again for charging.

Similarly, in the case of deep discharge, the battery gets cut-off due to low voltage of battery. Now, if the battery is under charging condition, its terminal voltage will increase after sometime due to charging. The charge controller will detect the increase in voltage and when voltage increases above the low voltage cut-off level, the charge controller will connect the battery to the circuit so that power can be extracted from the battery by the load.

> High voltage cut-off (due to over-charge) and low voltage cut-off (due to overdischarge) levels are preset in charge controllers.

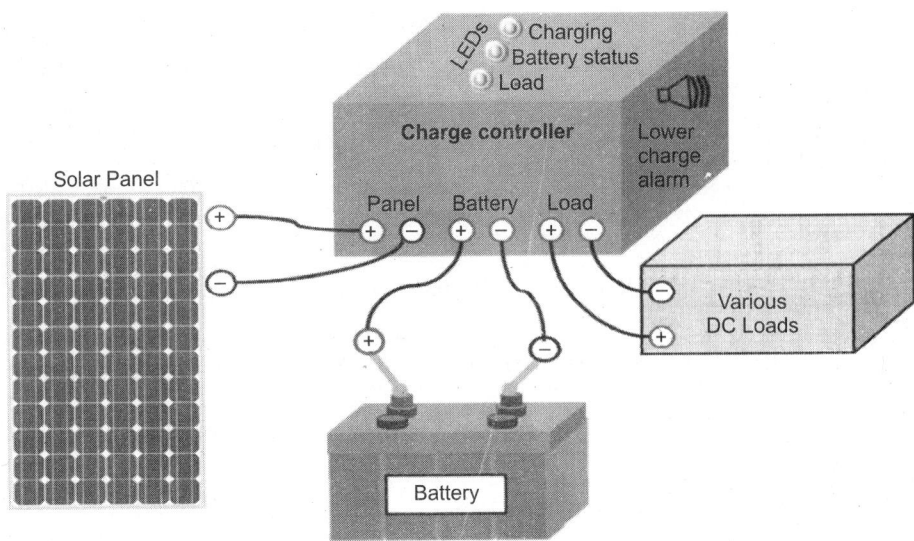

FIGURE 8.10

Basic block diagram of a standalone PV system with battery back-up and charge controller.

8.6.3
Types of Charge Controllers

The following two types of charge controllers are mostly used nowadays:

1. Pulse Width Modulation (PWM) charge controller or standard charge controller
2. Maximum Power Point Tracking (MPPT) charge controller.

PWM charge controllers have same nominal voltage across battery bank and PV array. MPPT charge controllers can have different voltages across battery bank and PV array and operate at the maximum power point tracking (MPPT) of the PV panel. MPPT charge controller allows us to have a solar panel array with a much higher voltage than your battery bank voltage.

For the same power flow, when voltage is high, current that will flow in the wires is small. Power is equal to current multiplied by voltage. Normally, it is desired to keep the current flow to small level. Therefore, a big advantage of having a higher voltage solar panel array is that we can use smaller gauge wiring to the charge controller, and the use of small gauge wire reduces the wiring cost. MPPT concept is further discussed in the next section.

> In solar PV system it is desired to keep high DC voltage to keep the low current for the same power flow. It saves cost.

8.6.4
Features of Charge Controller

For the operation of charge controllers, various voltage and current levels are defined. These levels are as follows:

Nominal system voltage: This is the voltage at which battery and charge controller operate in a PV system.

Nominal load current: This is the maximum load current that charge controller should be able to handle.

Nominal PV array current: This is the maximum PV array current that charge controller should be able to handle. This is nothing but the Array short circuit current. A safety factor of 1.25 is used to account for variation in Short circuit current at non STC.

Charge regulator set points: Charge controllers regulate the charging and discharging of a battery. Charge controller senses the voltage of the battery (or 'state of charge', SoC) and decides either to disconnect it from the source (PV array in this case) to prevent it from overcharging or to disconnect the load (from the battery output) to prevent deep discharging. Such controllers are mainly used where loads are unpredictable and the batteries are optimized or undersized to minimize the initial cost. The charge control algorithm has set points (threshold values) depending upon which it takes decisions. The commonly used set points are briefly described below and are shown in Figure 8.11.

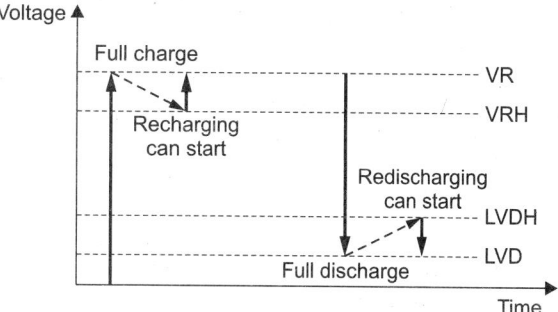

FIGURE 8.11

Commonly used set points and their behaviour in charge controllers.

Voltage regulation set point (VR): It is the maximum voltage up to which a battery can be charged (without getting overcharged). If this threshold is reached, the controller either disconnects the battery from the source or starts regulating the current delivered to the battery.

Voltage regulation hysteresis (VRH): It is the difference between VR and the voltage at which the controller reconnects the battery to the PV source and starts charging. If VRH is too small, it will result in tighter voltage regulation but the control will be oscillatory and may deteriorate the battery life. At the same time, a large value of VRH may lead to 'slight' overcharging of the battery during every cycle. So, in practice, there is a trade-off. VRH also determines how effectively the controller can charge the battery.

Low voltage disconnect (LVD): It is the minimum voltage up to which the battery can be allowed to discharge, without getting deep discharged. It is also defined as the maximum depth of discharge (DoD) of the battery. The charge controller disconnects the load from the battery terminals as soon as the battery voltage touches LVD, to prevent it from overdischarging.

Low voltage disconnect hysteresis (LVDH): It is the difference between LVD value and the battery voltage at which the load can be reconnected to the battery terminals. LVDH is not kept too small, or else the load will be switched on and off more frequently which can adversely affect the battery and the load.

8.6.5
Typical Specifications of PWM Charge Controller

Charge controllers are available for various ratings of Nominal system voltage and PV array current. Typical ratings of 12 V, 6 A rated PWM charge controller are shown in Table 8.6.

TABLE 8.6 Typical Ratings of 12 V, 6 A Rated PWM Charge Controller

Nominal system voltage	12 V
Nominal PV array current	6 A
Nominal load current	6 A
Regulation voltage	14 volts
Low voltage disconnect	11 volts
Low voltage reconnect	13 volts
Type of charging	Series PWM
Temperature	−20°C to 55°C
Self-consumption	10 mA maximum

An example datasheet 4.5 A, 12 V rated charge controller from morning Star Corporation is shown in Figure 8.12.

Electrical Specifications

Rated solar input	4.5 A
Maximum input (5 min.)	5.5 A
System voltage	12 V
Maximum solar voltage	30 V
Regulation voltage	14.1 V
Accuracy	60 mV
Self-consumption	6 mA
Temperature compensation	−28 mV/°C
Reverse current leakage	<10 µA
Operating temperature	−40°C to 85°C

FIGURE 8.12

Example datasheet of 4.5 A, 12 V rated PWM charge controller.

EXAMPLE 8.7

A house has the following DC loads rated at 12 V.

   (i) Three 40 W lights

   (ii) A 50 W fan

All the loads are to be powered simultaneously using two parallel connected modules. Each module has a peak current of 2.5 A and Short circuit current of 3.5 A. Choose the appropriate charge controller?

Solution

Total DC Load estimation:

Load	Wattage	Quantity	Total load
Light	40 W	3	120 W
Fan	50 W	1	50 W
			170 W

Nominal system voltage of charge controller: Same as rated voltage of load and PV array, i.e. 12 V.

Nominal PV array current: Nominal PV array current = 2 × 3.5 A = 7 A

Therefore, at the input side, the charge controller should be able to handle 7 A current.

Nominal load current:

$$\text{Nominal load current} = \frac{\text{Total DC load}}{\text{Nominal system voltage}} = \frac{170\ \text{W}}{12\ \text{V}} = 14.17\ \text{A}$$

Therefore, the output side, the charge controller should be able to handle about 14.17 A current.

Problem 8.8: A house has the following DC loads rated at 12 V.

   1. Four 30 W lights

   2. A 40 W fan

All the loads are to be powered simultaneously using two parallel connected modules. Each module has a peak current of 3.5 A and Short circuit current of 4 A. Choose the appropriate charge controller?

WORKSHEET 8.4: Complete Table 8.7 choosing PWM charge controller ratings for given load and PV array.

TABLE 8.7 To Obtain Missing Quantities

Load (W)	Load voltage rating (V)	Module	Nominal system voltage	Nominal PV array current	Rating of charge controller
Two 10 W lights = ____ W A 30 W fan = ____ W Total load = ____	12	Three modules of short circuit current of 3.5 A each.			
Four 15 W lights = ____ W Two 25 W fans = ____ W Total load = ____	12	Two modules of short circuit current of 3.5 A each.			

8.7

Maximum Power Point Tracking (MPPT)

Power delivered by a module depends on the load connected to the module. Consider a module whose *I-V* characteristics and the corresponding power drawn are shown in Figure 8.13. At short circuit conditions ($V = 0$), current delivered by the module is maximum and is 5.1 A. As voltage across the load is increased (by varying load) up to 17.3 V, power delivered to the load increases to 84 W (17.3 V × 4.86 A). Beyond this point, though the voltage is increased, power delivered decreases as the current decreases very sharply. So, the power delivered by the module has a point on *I-V* characteristics corresponding to maximum power and is called Maximum Power Point (MPP).

In order to extract the maximum power from PV modules, the load connected to the modules should work at maximum power point or the operating point of PV module-load combination should be at maximum power point. The operating point is the point of intersection of *I-V* characteristics of a source (PV modules) to a load (a fan, a TV, a resister, etc).

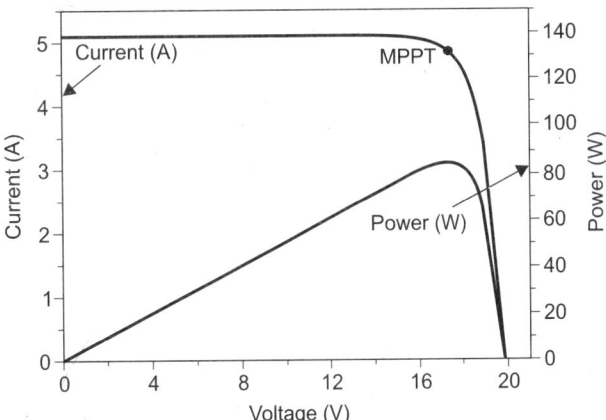

FIGURE 8.13

Definition of maximum power point (MPP).

There is only point in the *I-V* characteristics of PV module at which the power delivered by the module is maximum, called maximum power point.

8.7.1

Power Output from a PV Module

Solar PV modules are rated for peak power output. The output power of PV modules not only depends on input solar radiation but also on operating point (combination of current and voltage). For instance even under very bright sun light condition also, if PV module is operating in open circuit mode or short circuit mode the power output will be zero. There is one operating point of a PV module at which the power output is maximum (maximum power point) and this operating point changes with change in intensity of solar radiation falling on PV modules. There are electronic devices which ensure that at all light conditions, solar PV modules operate at maximum power point. This concept of maximum power point tracking is discussed in the following paragraphs.

8.7.2
Need for Maximum Power Point Tracking?

In practice, because of the changing ambient solar radiation, the *I-V* characteristics of PV modules change throughout the day. Therefore, it is not possible to choose a load such that the operating point is always at maximum power point or close to maximum power point.

Intensity of solar radiation varies throughout the day. On a typical day, radiation is less intense at 9 a.m. and increases till noon. As the intensity changes, the *I-V* characteristics of the module also change as shown in Figure 8.14. As a result, for a given load characteristics, the operating point also changes.

As an example, the operating point of a PV module and a resistive load for 1 p.m., 11 a.m. and 9 a.m. is schematically shown in Figure 8.14 and is denoted by *Z*, *Y* and *X* respectively. But for 1 p.m., 11 a.m. and 9 a.m., the maximum power point is *Z'*, *Y'* and *X'* respectively. In order to deliver maximum power, the actual operating points *X*, *Y* and *Z* should be made as close as possible to *X'*, *Y'* and *Z'*.

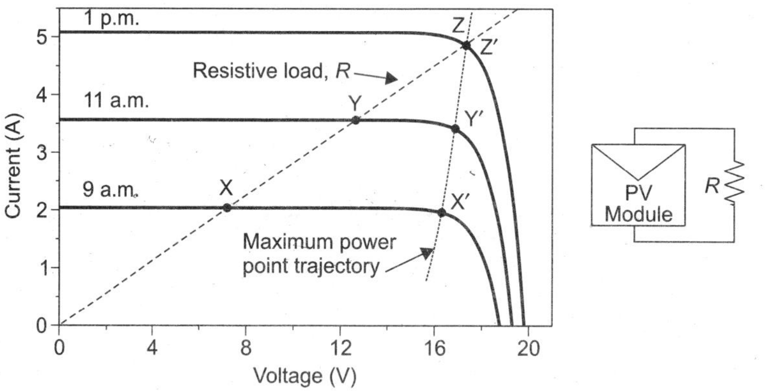

FIGURE 8.14

Operating points (*X*, *Y*, and *Z*) of a solar PV module under various daylight conditions when connected to a resistive load. The *X'*, *Y'* and *Z'* must be the operating point for maximum power transfer.

The MPPT device

PV module *I-V* curve changes throughout the day as the sunlight intensity changes, hence the maximum point also changes throughout the day.

There is a device whose function is to bring the operating point of a load close to the maximum power point under different operating conditions. This device is called maximum power point tracking or MPPT. In this way, the function of MPPT is to extract maximum available power from PV modules under any given condition (less radiation, more radiation, high temperature, etc.)

The maximum power tracking mechanism makes use of an algorithm and an electronic circuitry. The mechanism is based on the principle of impedance matching between load and PV module which is necessary for maximum power transfer. Thus, in theory, whenever the impedance of load is matches with the impedance of source, maximum power transfer takes place between source and load. In this way, the presence of MPPT between the source (PV Module) and load, ensures that maximum available power is extracted from PV modules.

8.7.3
MPPT Charge Controller

Many manufacturers combine the function of charge controller and MPPT in one single device which is called MPPT charge controller and is shown in Figure 8.15.

The function of MPPT device is to bring the operating point of a load close to the maximum power point of PV module under different operating conditions in order to extract maximum power.

Though MPPT and charge controller are two independent functions, many manufacturers provide these two functions in a single electronic circuitry and are called MPPT charge controllers.

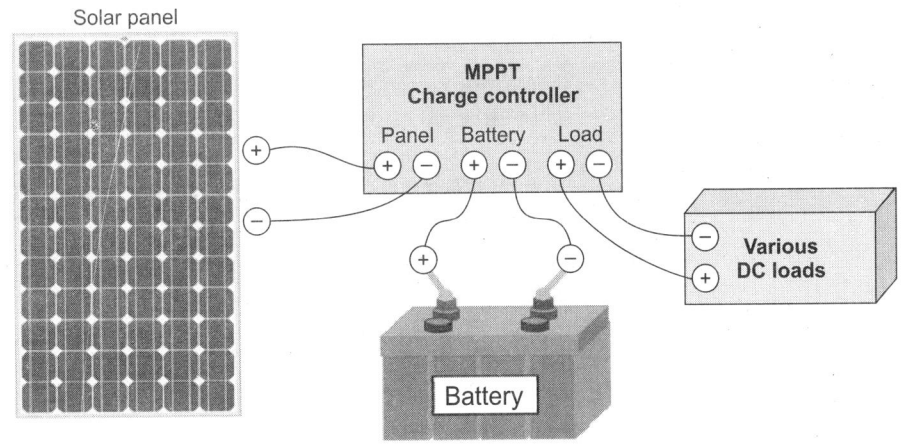

FIGURE 8.15
MPPT charge controller along with other system components.

MPPT and Sun-tracking for more power

MPPT is electronic tracking and Sun-tracking is mechanical tracking, both having the objective of generating more power using solar PV modules.

Though MPPT and charge controller are two independent functions, many manufacturers provide these two functions in a single electronic circuitry and are called MPPT charge controllers.

8.7.4
Specifications of MPPT Charge Controller

PV input

DC output to battery

MPPT device is used to extract maximum power possible from a PV module in all operating conditions. The sun-tracking is referred as mechanical tracking of a solar PV module in such a way that it is always perpendicular to the sunlight. In this way, the module should face eastward in the morning, southward in the noon time and westward in the evening to directly see the sun. When the PV modules are directly facing the sun all the time, they receive more solar radiation and, therefore, they generate more power.

Here it should be noted that the MPPT is not the same as the Sun-tracking of solar PV modules. In Sun-tracking, PV modules are rotated mechanically so that the radiation absorbed by a module is maximum, while in the case of MPPT, electronic circuitry is used to ensure that maximum amount of generated power is transferred to the load.

Maximum input power: This is the maximum power that the charge controller can handle from a PV array.

Maximum open circuit voltage: This is the maximum open circuit voltage that the charge controller can handle.

MPPT tracking voltage range: These are the voltage levels that the charge controller can handle.

Nominal battery voltage: This is the voltage at which battery operates in a system.

Voltage regulation set point (VR): It is the maximum voltage up to which a battery can be charged (without getting overcharged). If this threshold is reached, the controller either disconnects the battery from the source or starts regulating the current delivered to the battery.

Low voltage disconnect (LVD): It is the minimum voltage up to which the battery can be allowed to discharge without getting deep discharged. It is also defined as the maximum depth of discharge (DoD) of the battery. The charge controller disconnects the load from the battery terminals as soon as the battery voltage touches LVD, to prevent it from overdischarging.

Nominal PV array current or maximum charging current: This is the maximum PV array current that a charge controller should be able to handle. This is nothing but the array short circuit current. A safety factor of 1.25 is used to account for variation in Short circuit current at non STC.

DC load control

Nominal voltage: This is the maximum load voltage that a charge controller should be able to handle.

Maximum current: This is the maximum load current that a charge controller should be able to handle.

MPPT charge controller is rated by the output current that they can handle and not by the input current from the solar panel array as it is done in standard charge controllers. Typical specifications of 12 V, 6 A MPPT charge controller are shown in Table 8.8.

TABLE 8.8 Typical Specifications of 12 V, 6 A MPPT Charge Controller

PV input	
Maximum input power	80 W
Maximum open circuit voltage	95 V
MPPT tracking voltage range	26 ~ 75 V
DC output to battery	
Nominal battery voltage	12 V
Voltage regulation set point (VR)	12.6 ± 0.2
Low voltage disconnect (LVD)	10.5 ± 0.2
Maximum charging current	6 A
DC load control	
Nominal voltage	12 V
Maximum current	10 A

EXAMPLE 8.8

Consider a 1000 watt solar panel array that operates at 48 volts DC and battery bank at 24 volts DC. Choose the MPPT charge controller ratings for this system?

Solution

Following parameters are given for MPPT:

Wattage of solar PV modules = 1000 W

PV array operating voltage = 48 V

Battery bank operating voltage = 24 V

Wattage input by solar panel to MPPT charge controller is 1000 W. In this case, the solar PV modules are connected to the input side of MPPT and the battery is connected to the output side. Therefore, load for the MPPT is the battery. The specification for the MPPT is given in terms of the output voltage and output current it can handle. Therefore, we should calculate the current requirement of the MPPT for its load.

The input power to the MPPT is 1000 watt (PV modules), and assuming 100% efficiency, power at battery bank terminals would also be 1000 W. As battery bank is at 24 V, current to the battery bank can be found in following way:

$$\text{Power} = \text{Voltage} \times \text{Current}$$

or
$$\text{Current} = \frac{\text{Power}}{\text{Voltage}} = \frac{1000}{24} = 41.67 \text{ A}$$

Thus a 24 V, 41.6 A MPPT would work well in this case. As a precaution, we may increase the estimated current value by 25% to take into account special conditions that could occur causing the solar panel array to produce more power than it is normally rated for. This gives current as 51 A. So, 24 V, 51 A MPPT charge controller suits well for this system.

However, the chosen MPPT charge controller should be able to handle the array V_{oc} and V_{mp}.

Problem 8.9 Consider a 3000 watt solar panel array that operates at 36 volts DC and battery bank at 36 volts DC. Choose the MPPT charge controller ratings for this system?

 WORKSHEET 8.5: Complete Table 8.9.

TABLE 8.9 To Obtain Missing Quantities

Solar panel wattage (W)	Solar planes operating voltage (V)	Battery bank voltage (V)	Battery bank current (A)	Battery bank current (A) +25%	MPPT ratings
1000	24	24	41.67	51	24 V, 51 A
3000	36	36	–	–	–
4800	48	36	–	–	–

EXAMPLE 8.9

Consider using the following PV module and battery for designing 150 watt peak solar home system. Choose the MPPT charge controller ratings for this system?

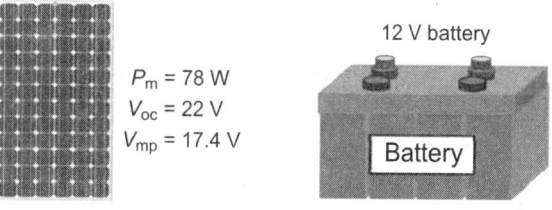

P_m = 78 W
V_{oc} = 22 V
V_{mp} = 17.4 V

12 V battery

Battery

Solution

Let the PV modules be connected in series:

V_{oc} (system) = 2 × 22 = 44 V

V_{mp} (system) = 2 × 17.4 = 34.8 V

P_m (system) = 78 × 2 = 156 W

The input power to the MPPT is 156 watt (PV modules), and assuming 100% efficiency, power at battery bank terminals would also be 156 W. As battery bank is at 12 V, the current to the battery bank can be found in the following way:

$$\text{Power} = \text{Voltage} \times \text{Current}$$

$$\text{Current} = \frac{\text{Power}}{\text{Voltage}} = \frac{156}{12} = 13 \text{ A}$$

Thus, a 12 V, 13 A MPPT would work well in this case. As a precaution, we may increase the estimated current value by 25% to take into account special conditions that could occur causing the solar panel array to produce more power than it is normally rated for. This gives the amperage as 16.25 A. So 24 V, 16.25 A MPPT charge controller suits well for this system.

However the chosen MPPT charge controller should be able to handle the array V_{oc} and V_{mp} accordingly.

9

Wires

In any electrical system, wires are needed to connect power supply and load together. The choice of wires which includes choice of materials for wires, diameter of wires, etc. plays an important role. In the case of solar PV applications, the appropriate choice of wires is even more important because a part of system may be working on DC current and another part of the system may be working on AC current. An appropriate choice of wires will reduce the electrical losses in wires and since solar PV power is expensive, it is important to minimize the power losses in wires as much as possible. Also, we should make appropriate choice of wires to avoid shock hazards and fire hazards in PV systems.

9.1
Introduction

Wire is a single, usually cylindrical, flexible string/rod of metal. Wires are generally used to bear mechanical loads and to carry electricity. Here the wire means electrical wire (wire to conduct electricity). Electrical wires are made up of metals because metals are the most electrically conductive materials, of which, silver is the most conductive element. But due to higher cost of silver, copper is used to make wires because it's cheaper and highly conductive after silver. Aluminium is also an important metal as a wire after copper, but for solar PV applications, as energy loss being an important consideration, copper wire is commonly used. Also, the durability of aluminium wire is less than the copper wire especially for thinner wires. So, it is not preferred for interior/home applications because it may break or may be weakened during installation.

Generally, wires are coated with any insulating material like polyvinyl chloride (PVC), nylon, polyester, etc., to prevent shock hazards and energy loss through unwanted current conduction and avoid short circuit between two wires running together. The choice of insulating material depends on quality and needs. Sometimes, the word 'cables' is used instead of wires. When bunch of wires run side by side wherein the wires may be bonded, twisted or braided together, then it is referred as 'cables' or 'wire cable'. A picture of wire and wire cable is given in Figure 9.1.

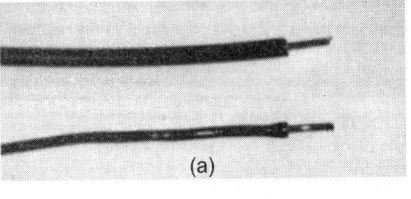
(a)

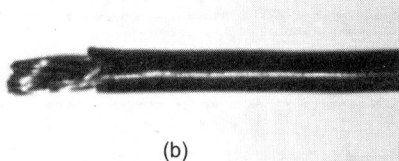
(b)

FIGURE 9.1
Commonly used electrical wires.

9.1.1
Why Appropriate Choice of Wires is Important?

Wires are a medium to transfer energy between the circuit components. As per the type and design of a PV system, wires would be required to connect solar PV modules to battery, connect a battery to inverter, loads to the inverter, an inverter to grid, etc. If you choose all the components in your PV system very efficiently but do not use appropriate wire, your system may not perform as per the expectations. An inappropriate choice of wires may become weak link in the PV system. For example, if large current is flowing in a certain part of your PV system and wire that you have chosen is very thin, then there may be lot of power loss in the thin wire, it may heat up and even burn. There may be fire in the system and whole PV system will stop working and in worst case, the entire PV system may get destroyed. So, it doesn't matter how much our system components are efficient, it is impossible to get the best performance with our PV system without making proper choice of wires. Performance sacrifice is not the only concern but there are some additional risks/hazards associated with improper use of wires like shock hazards, fire hazards, reliability, etc. That is why it is important to understand more about the wires so that appropriate choice can be made while designing a solar PV system.

> Appropriate choice of wires is important not only from the perspective of better system performance but also for avoiding shock hazards, fire hazards and improving reliability of PV systems.

9.2
Basics of Current Conduction

In order to make appropriate choice of wires for a given application, first we need to understand the flow of current and how wires behave when current flows through them. Electric current is the flow of charges or the flow of electrons under the presence of voltage. Current in a wire flows when there is a voltage applied across it and current flows from high voltage point to low voltage point. When current or electrons flow through a wire, the electrons collide with the atoms of materials from which wire is made. The collision results in slowing down of their speed, the voltage present across wire pushes electrons again, and electrons gain speed. This process of slowing down the speed of electrons and gaining speed by electrons continuously happens in wires. We can say that the collision of electrons is some kind of hindrance to electron flow through the wires. Scientifically, this hindrance is known as 'electrical resistance' or 'Resistance'. Ideally, we would like to have as less hindrance to electron flow in wires as possible or as less resistance of wires as possible. But, every wire possesses some resistance to current, even the best current conducting material will also have some resistance. It is impossible to have a wire that puts zero resistance to current flowing through it. Normally, the materials which offer less resistance in current flow are chosen as connecting wires and cables between system components. Aluminium (Al) and Copper (Cu) are the two commonly used materials used for making current conducting wires.

> Ideally, we would like to have as less hindrance to electron flow in wires as possible or as less resistance of wires as possible.

9.2.1
Resistance and Resistivity

Resistance is the property of a wire to resist the flow of current through it. Some material puts less resistance and some material puts more resistance to current flow through them. There are two terms related to resistance in the flow of current; one is resistivity and other is resistance. The resistivity is the intrinsic property of a material and it does not change with the dimensions of material. For example, an aluminium wire of a smaller diameter and a larger diameter will have same resistivity, i.e., resistivity is independent of physical dimensions of wires. It is to be noted that different materials have different resistivities. On the other hand, the resistance of the wire not only depends on the resistivity (which means type of the material) but also depends on physical dimensions like the length of conductor and cross-sectional area of a conductor. So, by just knowing the material of the conductor, we can't estimate the actual resistance in the circuit, and therefore, we have to know the dimensions of wire as well.

Electrical resistivity is a measure of how strongly a material opposes the electric current. A low resistivity of a material indicates that it allows the movement of electric charge more easily. The unit of electrical resistivity is the ohm metre (Ω-m) and commonly represented by the Greek letter ρ (rho) (Figure 9.2). Resistivity is property of material and it also depends on ambient conditions like temperature, humidity, etc.

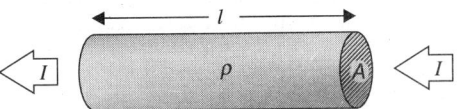

FIGURE 9.2

Current conduction through a piece of a conductor along its length.

The length of a conductor 'l' is in metres (m) and the cross-section area of the conductor 'A' is given in terms of square metres (m²). Cross-section area of a wire is related to its diameter (d). A wire with large diameter will have large cross-section area and wire with small diameter will have small cross-section area. There is a relationship between diameter and cross-section area, which is demonstrated in Figure 9.3. 'A' is the area of the circle whose diameter is d.

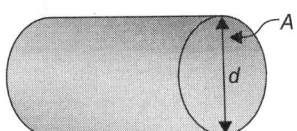

FIGURE 9.3

Schematic showing diameter (d) and cross-section area (A) of a wire.

The mathematical relationship between d and A is given by the following equation:

$$\text{Cross-section area (A)} = 0.785 \times d \times d$$

In the above equation, if the unit of diameter is 'mm', then the unit of cross-section area would be mm², and, if the unit of diameter is m, then the unit of cross-section area would be m². Normally, for the diameter, 'mm' is commonly used. The value of diameter of wires in 'mm' and corresponding cross-area in 'mm²' is given in Table 9.1 for ready reference. From this Table if you know the diameter of wire you can look-up the cross-section area of the wire or alternatively if you know the cross-section area of the wire you can look-up the diameter of the wire. This Table will be useful while calculating the size of wires for a given PV system.

TABLE 9.1 Value of Diameter and Corresponding Cross-section Area

Diameter (mm)	Area (mm²)	Diameter (mm)	Area (mm²)
0.5	0.20	5.5	23.75
1	0.79	6	28.26
1.5	1.77	6.5	33.17
2	3.14	7	38.47
2.5	4.91	7.5	44.16
3	7.07	8	50.24
3.5	9.62	8.5	56.72
4	12.56	9	63.59
4.5	15.90	9.5	70.85
5	19.63	10	78.50

After discussing the resistivity, let us now discuss the 'Resistance'. The symbol of electrical resistance is 'R' and it is measured in units of ohms (Ω). The resistance of a wire depends on resistivity (ρ) of the material from which it is made, length (l) and cross-section area (A) of the wire. The flow of current is depicted in Figure 9.2, and an expression of resistance is given as:

$$R = \rho \frac{l}{A} \tag{9.1}$$

From the previous expression [Eq. (9.1)] for the resistance, the following can be observed:

1. A wire with longer length will have higher resistance (see Figure 9.4). It indicates that the resistance of a wire increases with its length.

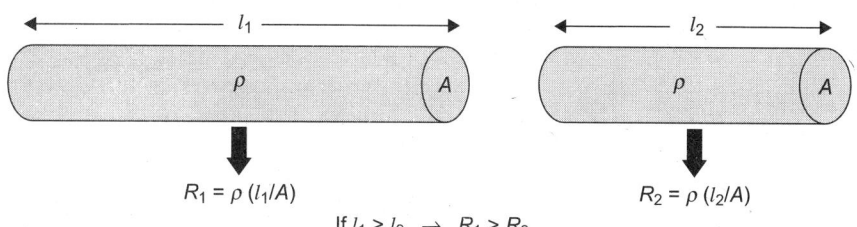

$$R_1 = \rho\,(l_1/A) \qquad R_2 = \rho\,(l_2/A)$$
$$\text{If } l_1 > l_2 \;\rightarrow\; R_1 > R_2$$

FIGURE 9.4

Dependence of resistance of a wire on its length. A wire with longer length will have higher resistance.

2. A wire with larger cross-section area or larger diameter will have lower resistance (see Figure 9.5). It indicates that the resistance of wire decreases with increase in its diameter.

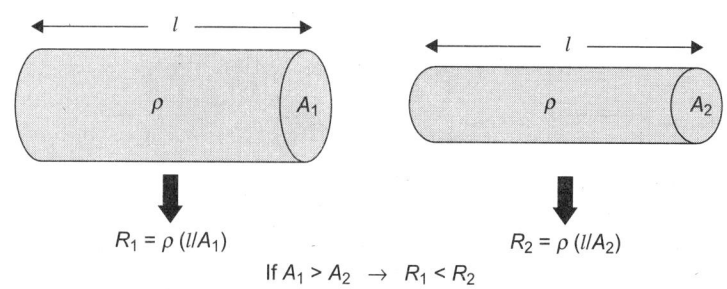

$$R_1 = \rho\,(l/A_1) \qquad R_2 = \rho\,(l/A_2)$$
$$\text{If } A_1 > A_2 \;\rightarrow\; R_1 < R_2$$

FIGURE 9.5

Dependence of resistance of a wire on its cross-section area or diameter. A wire with higher diameter or higher cross-sectional area will have lower resistance.

3. A wire with higher resistivity will have higher resistance (see Figure 9.6). Copper and aluminum have very low resistivity (in the range of 1×10^{-8} Ω-m) as compared to plastics, glass or wood (resistivity more than 1×10^{5} Ω-m). That is why copper and aluminum is chosen to make current conducting wires.

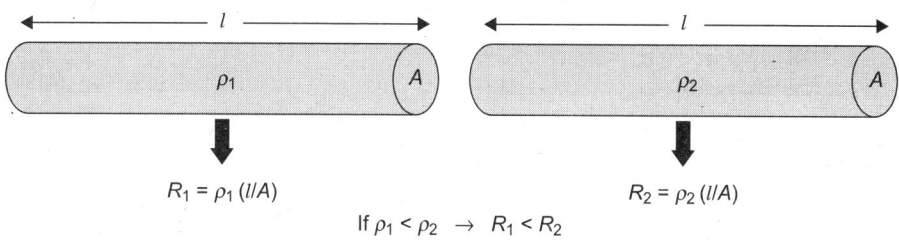

$$R_1 = \rho_1\,(l/A) \qquad R_2 = \rho_2\,(l/A)$$
$$\text{If } \rho_1 < \rho_2 \;\rightarrow\; R_1 < R_2$$

FIGURE 9.6

Dependence of resistance of a wire on its resistivity (ρ). A wire with lower resistivity will have lower resistance.

The resistance of wires and cables depends on their material, their length and their diameter.

Problem 9.1: There are two wires of copper and aluminum, each having same length and same diameter. Which wire will have higher resistance?

9.2.2
Voltage Drop in Wire When Current Flows:
Ohm's Law

It has been written earlier that the resistance of a wire causes some power losses in it. Other than power loss, the resistance of wire also results in some voltage drop in it. We do not want voltage drop to occur in wires, ideally, the voltage drop should be as small as possible. The drop in voltage in the wires depends on the resistance of the wire and current flowing through it. This relationship between voltage, current and resistance was given by the scientist named Georg Simon Ohm. Therefore, this law or rule is called Ohm's law.

Ohm's law states that "voltage drop (V) across a conductor is the product of resistance (R) of the conductor and current (I) flowing through it". This is depicted in Figure 9.7 and represented in Eq. (9.2).

FIGURE 9.7
Potential drop in a piece of current carrying conductor along its length.

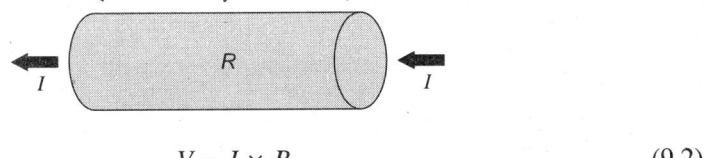

$$V = I \times R \tag{9.2}$$

From Eq. (9.2), it can be seen that for same value of resistance, higher current flow in the wire will result in higher voltage drop.

Voltage drop in DC circuits is higher

In solar PV system, some part of the system carries DC current and some part carries AC current. The voltage levels in the DC side of the system is lower, and therefore, for the same power, the current level in DC side of the system is higher. Remember that

Power = Voltage × Current (or $P = V \times I$)

For instance, PV modules output voltage is in the range of 15 V and 30 V and batteries terminal voltage is typically 12 V. Even if, several PV modules and batteries are connected in series, the typical voltage levels in DC side of standalone PV systems is 24 V, 36 V, 48 V, 72 V etc. Same is true for the terminal voltage of a battery bank. On the other hand, on the AC side, the output voltage of inverter is 230 V. Higher output voltage at AC side indicates that for the same power the lower current will flow in the wires.

Since the voltages are low at DC side of the system, higher current flows at DC side. Due to this reason, for the same power, there is larger voltage drop at DC side ($V = I \times R$) and hence it is important to choose appropriate conductor with low resistance to minimize voltage loss in the DC wires and cables in PV systems. When we choose wires with low resistance, it means that we should choose wires with low resistivity and large diameter. But large diameter wires also means more material, which means large diameter wires are more expensive than small diameter wires of same material. There is trade-off between cost and resistance of wires. Therefore, some cost optimization of wire with respect to their resistance is required.

In PV systems the drop in voltage in wires should be as low as possible, especially where DC current is flowing.

9.3
Type of Wires

Mainly the wires can be divided into the following four categories depending on their structures and applications:

1. Single-stranded
2. Multi-stranded
3. Single-core
4. Multi-core

9.3.1
Single-stranded and Multi-stranded Wire

Single-strand wire is also called solid-core wire. It is simply a solid wire consisting of one piece of metal wire. An example of single-stranded wire is shown in Figure 9.1(a). On the other hand, multi-stranded wire is composed of a bundle of wires or group of wires or strands of wire that are put together to make a large diameter conductor. An example of multi-stranded copper wire is shown in Figure 9.8.

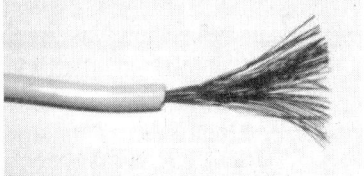

FIGURE 9.8
Multi-stranded wire.

The choice of wire, i.e., to choose single-stranded or multi-stranded depends on several parameters. These parameters include number of strands (number of small wires), flexibility of wire, strength of wire, break-resistance, etc. These parameters are important for better performance of the system especially for bigger systems with higher current levels with higher wire thickness.

Both the types of wires have some advantages and disadvantages. The comparison is made in the following paragraphs:

Cost: Stranded wires cost more because solid wire is cheaper to manufacture than multi-stranded wire.

Flexibility: Stranded wires are more flexible as compared to multi-stranded wires. The multi-stranded wires become useful where there is a need for flexibility in the wire like connections between circuit boards in multi-printed-circuit-board devices, where the rigidity of solid wire may produce too much stress as a result of movement during assembly or servicing.

Resistance: For the same cross-section area or diameter, a multi-stranded wire will have higher resistance than a single-stranded. This is due to the fact that the cross-section of the multi-stranded wire is not completely conducting metal as there will be air gaps between strands.

> For the same cross-section area the resistance of a multi-stranded wire is higher than the single-stranded wire.

9.3.2
Single-core and Multi-core Wire

Single core wire or cable is simply an insulated solid cylindrical wire similar to single-strand wire, while a multi-core wire has multiple cores. The term 'multi-core' is normally used in reference to a cable that has more cores.

There are two conventions for multi-core wires; one in which more than one insulated solid or stranded cores are bound together in a final insulating covering, and other in which one solid core is mounted by the insulating and conducting layers one after other depending on the number of cores like co-axial cylinders one over other separated by an insulator. The second type is also known as co-axial cables. The example of multi-core cables is given in Figure 9.9.

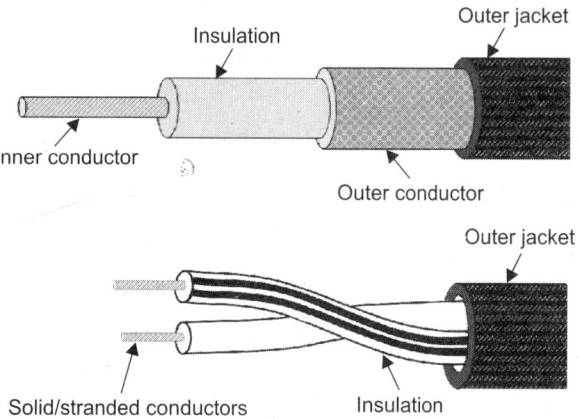

FIGURE 9.9
Schematic of two-core cables.

The advantages of multi-core cables are the reduced space requirement due to thin cable diameter, reduced ambient effects, increased UV protection due to reduced outer surface area (outer sheath), looking neat etc. Disadvantages are the higher cost, higher resistance compared to same size/diameter solid core conductor due to the involvement of insulating material between the individual cores.

9.4

Measurement of Wire Dimensions

It has been discussed so far that in solar PV systems, it is desired to have a low resistance wire so that the voltage drop in the wires is lower. Also, we have discussed that for a given material of wire, the resistance of wire depends on its diameter and length. Normally, it is easy to measure the length of the wire, we can use a scale or measuring tape to measure wire length. But measuring diameter of the wires accurately is not easy because of small dimension. In order to measure the diameter of wire some specific tools are developed which are discussed in this section.

9.4.1

Measuring Length of a Wire

Length of a wire can be measured by using measuring tape or ruler. The measuring tape may have marking in terms of inch and foot or cm and metre. The wire length between the system components should be as small as possible because extra wire length results in excessive voltage drop. But at the same time one should take about 2-3 feet extra length in order to avoid shortage situations during repairing works when required.

9.4.2

Measuring Diameter of a Wire

It is important to measure the diameter of wire to calculate the resistance of wire or possible voltage drop in the wire and thus to estimate whether a particular wire is suitable in a PV system or not. When we buy the wire from a market we may not get correct information about the wire diameter from the shopkeeper as he may not be well familiar with diameter rating of wires. And wire diameter may not be same as told by the shopkeeper. Hence as a PV system designer and installer, one should have the skills of measuring wire diameter.

Accuracy in measuring diameter of wires is required because a small variation in wire diameter may have large impact on voltage drop in the system.

Normally, wires that are used in solar PV systems have diameters in 'mm'. The measuring tape or scale is not the right tool to measure wire diameter. So, a measuring instrument with better accuracy level is needed. Accuracy in measuring diameter is required because a small variation in wire diameter may have large impact on voltage drop in the system.

Micrometer screw gauge

Micrometer screw gauge is a good low-cost option for measuring wire diameter with reasonable accuracy. It works on the 'screw' principle and normally, can measure diameters accurately from very low to 25 mm with an accuracy limit of 0.01 mm. Nowadays, digital micrometer screw gauges are also available in the market with even better resolution (accuracy level) of 0.001 mm. The images of manual and digital screw gauge are given in Figure 9.10.

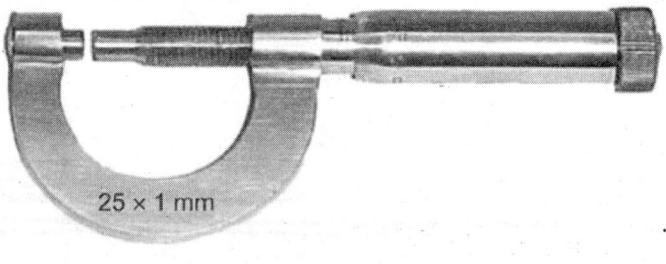

FIGURE 9.10
Micrometer screw gauge (manual and digital).

Standard wire gauge (SWG) Generally, wires are manufactured in some standard diameters according to some predefined standards. The term 'gauge' refers to the thickness of a thin sheet or diameter of wires. The Standard Wire Gauge is a tool to measure the predefined wire diameter which is represented in terms of wire gauge or gauge number. The wire with a particular gauge number will be of particular cross sectional area or diameter. In this way, by simply knowing the gauge number one can have the approximate idea of wire diameter or cross-sectional area. Once we know the cross-sectional area we can find out the resistance of wire, possible voltage drop in it under certain condition, and current carrying capacity of wire.

Standard Wire Gauge (SWG) is a well known metric standard tool for measuring wire diameters. It is an internationally accepted standardized wire gauge system which is followed in India also. An image of SWG is given in Figure 9.11 and wire size can be determined by simply using this wire gauge tool. This type of gauge measures wires ranging in size from number 0 to number 36. The wire to be measured is inserted in the smallest slot that will just accommodate the bare wire. The gauge number corresponding to that slot indicates the wire size. The slot has parallel sides and should not be confused with the semicircular opening at the end of the slot. The semicircular opening simply permits the free movement of the wire all the way through the slot.

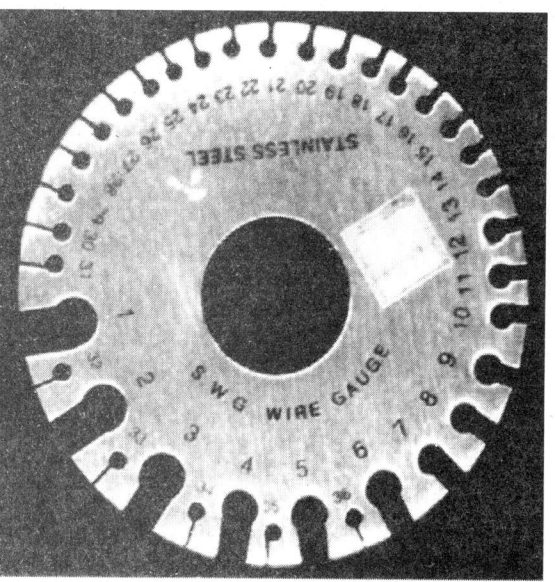

FIGURE 9.11
SWG measuring tool.

Reading of SWG

It can be seen from the image of SWG tool in Figure 9.11, that as the diameter or size of wire increases from small to large, the corresponding gauge number decreases from large to small. This can be little bit confusing as small wire gauge number represents large wire diameter. But it is simply a convention. Gauge numbers are useful in comparing the diameter of solid core wires, but not all types of wire or cable can be accurately measured with a gauge. Large wires are usually stranded to increase their flexibility. In such cases, the total cross-sectional area can be determined by multiplying the area of one strand by the number of strands in the wire or cable. Note that once we know the diameter of wire, we can calculate the cross-section area of the wire. As per the marking in SWG, the wire gauge numbers and corresponding diameters and cross sectional areas are given in Table 9.2. The wire dimension also changes with the temperature. As a standard, the relationship between gauge number and wire diameter is given for ambient temperature of 20 °C.

Wires are manufactured in pre-defined diameter as per the standards. Using SWG pre-defined wire diameters can be measured easily.

TABLE 9.2 Standard Wire Gauge (SWG) Dimensions

	Conductor diameter @20°C		Conductor cross-sectional area @20°C
SWG ↓	(inches)	(mm)	(mm^2)
4/0*	0.400	10.160	81.0731
3/0*	0.372	9.449	70.1231
2/0*	0.348	8.839	61.3615
1/0*	0.324	8.230	53.1973
1	0.300	7.620	45.6036
2	0.276	7.010	38.5945
3	0.252	6.401	32.1799
4	0.232	5.893	27.2749
5	0.212	5.385	22.7751
6	0.192	4.877	18.6808
7	0.176	4.470	15.6929
8	0.160	4.064	12.9717
9	0.144	3.658	10.5094
10	0.128	3.251	8.3009
11	0.116	**2.946**	6.8164
12	0.104	2.642	5.4822
13	0.092	2.337	4.2895
14	0.080	2.032	3.2429
15	0.072	1.829	2.6273
16	0.064	1.626	2.0765
17	0.056	1.422	1.5881
18	0.048	1.219	1.1671
19	0.040	1.016	0.8107
20	0.036	0.914	0.6561
21	0.032	0.813	0.5191
22	0.028	0.711	0.3970
23	0.024	0.610	0.2922
24	0.022	0.599	0.2818
25	0.020	0.5080	0.2027
26	0.018	0.4572	0.1642
27	0.0164	0.4166	0.1363
28	0.0148	0.3759	0.1110
29	0.0136	0.3454	0.0937
30	0.0124	0.3150	0.0779
31	0.0116	0.2946	0.0682
32	0.0108	0.2743	0.0591
33	0.0100	0.2540	0.0507
34	0.0092	0.2337	0.0429
35	0.0084	0.2134	0.0358
36	0.0076	0.1930	0.0293
37	0.0068	0.1727	0.0234
38	0.0060	0.1524	0.0182
39	0.0052	0.1321	0.0137
40	0.0048	0.1219	0.0117

*SWG (4/0 or 0000, 3/0 or 000, 2/0 or 00, 1/0 or 0)

9.5
Wire Sizing

While making electrical connection between any two components of a PV system, we need to select an appropriate wire/cable to minimize the voltage drop and power loss in the wire or cable. An inappropriate size of wire for a given application may result in severe damage to wire and PV system as well. Therefore, first we should be able to determine wire specifications or ratings (material, diameter, length, current carrying capacity, single-strand or multi-strand, etc.) according to current and voltage in the system. Once we determine the ratings of required wire then we can ask from the supplier to supply wire with particular ratings.

Following are the specifications that we need to identify for a wire:

- Wire material
- Length of wire
- Operating current
- Operating voltage
- Allowed potential drop
- Wire operating temperature (insulation rating)
- Wire size (thickness or SWG)
- Other specific requirements (like: fireproofing, UV-resistant, sunlight resistant etc.)

> Appropriate choice of wire should be made as per the system voltage and current requirements.

9.5.1
Type of Wire

A brief discussion about the wire material and their resistivity has been already given in the earlier Section 9.2.1. Normally, copper and aluminium wires are used. For solar PV system applications, copper wires are commonly used. But the selection of a particular wire is the matter of personal choice and depends on the type of application and budget too.

9.5.2
Length of Wire

As already discussed, for deciding the length of wire, the distance from one system component to the other system component is measured using a measuring tape along the favourable path. The system components may be far from each other or they may be very close to each other. For instance, normally PV modules are installed on the rooftop and batteries are installed inside the room. In such cases, the distance between the PV module and battery may be large. Similarly, in the case of large power plants, a PV module (which needs to be connected with inverter) may be installed far from inverter and in this case the required wire length may be long.

In case of single-core wire, the actual length of wire required is double the length of the path where wire needs to be laid down because we need two wires to complete the circuit. In the case of cables or multi-core wires, the one way length is the actual wire length.

9.5.3
Operating Current

In small and medium scale PV systems, the operating current levels are normally in the range of 1 A to 20 A. As the system size (power or load) increases, it is advised to increase the operating voltage rather operating current in a PV system. Remember that power is the product of voltage and current. Thus, same power level in the circuit can be obtained by either high current and low voltage or high voltage and low current.

In a PV system, it is desired to keep the current to a low level. This is done to keep the resistive losses to a low level. The resistive losses depend on the current (I) and resistance (R) of wire. But dependence on the current is very strong. A two time increase in current results in four times increase in losses. The resistive power losses are given as I^2R. So, the operational current levels remain at lower values than the rated ones.

As it's already discussed that the current in the wire depends on the applied potential and the load resistance ($V = I \times R$). So, it can be directly calculated by Ohm's law (see Eq. 9.2) for passive systems (e.g. battery and load). But in the case of PV (active) systems, e.g. PV module and battery, PV module and load, where the operating current is not constant and it varies during the whole day and whole year as well because of variation in solar insolation. In this way, the current in the wire depends on solar insolation and load profile too. Hence one should cautious about deciding the operating current level and the wire should be chosen to enough current carrying capacity under the consideration of this seasonal and daily variation. For these active systems, the current carrying capacity of the wire should be decided based on maximum possible current that can flow in the system. In solar PV systems, the current level at the DC side is normally higher than AC side. In this case the highest possible current in the PV system would be the short circuit current of the PV module array I_{sc} (which is the maximum possible current that can be produced by PV modules).

In order to be on the safe side, for the selection of wires, the maximum current in the system is multiplied by a factor of 1.25. It means the current is increased by 25% of the maximum value and then wires are chosen to carry this particular current. Current in the PV system can also be higher due to higher solar insolation than the Standard Test Condition (STC), or additional reflection on the module. For this as well, a factor of 1.25 is taken. So, overall, the I_{sc} is multiplied by $1.25 \times 1.25 = 1.56$ (or increased by 56%) and the wire is selected based on this final current. But remember that this additional 25% should be taken only when there is chance to have solar radiation higher than STC condition in the area where solar PV system is to be installed.

> While determining the operating current of a PV system, a safety factor of 50% is considered to be on the safe side.

EXAMPLE 9.1

For any particular section of the circuitry in two similar DC systems operating at 48 V, one person uses copper wire and another person uses aluminium wire. If length and diameter of wires used are same for both types of wires and are equal to 5 metres and 2 mm respectively. Find out the electrical resistance imposed by both types of wires. Which wire will cause the higher potential drop?

Given: Resistivity of copper wire = 1.72×10^{-8} Ω-m = 0.000 000 0172 Ω-m

Resistivity of aluminium wire = 2.82×10^{-8} Ω-m = 0.000 000 0282 Ω-m

Solution

First we calculate the resistances for both types of wires. Using formula

$$R = \rho \frac{l}{A}$$

where wire's cross-sectional area

$$A = \frac{\pi d^2}{4} = \frac{3.14 \times (2 \text{ mm})^2}{4}$$

$$= \frac{3.14 \times (0.002 \text{ m})^2}{4} = \frac{3.14 \times 0.002 \times 0.002}{4} \text{ m}^2$$

$$= \frac{3.14 \times 0.000004}{4} \text{ m}^2 = 3.14 \times 0.000001 \text{ m}^2$$

$$= 0.00000314 \text{ m}^2$$

For copper wire,

$$R = \frac{\rho \cdot l}{A} = \frac{(0.0000000172 \ \Omega\text{-m}) \cdot (5 \text{ m})}{(0.00000314 \text{ m}^2)}$$

$$= \frac{(0.0000000172 \times 5) \ \Omega\text{-m}^2}{(0.00000314 \text{ m}^2)} = \frac{0.000000086}{0.00000314} \ \Omega$$

$$= 0.0274 \ \Omega = 27.4 \text{ m}\Omega$$

For aluminium wire,

$$R = \frac{\rho \cdot l}{A} = \frac{(0.0000000282 \ \Omega\text{-m}) \cdot (5 \text{ m})}{(0.00000314 \text{ m}^2)}$$

$$= \frac{(0.0000000282 \times 5) \ \Omega\text{-m}^2}{(0.00000314 \text{ m}^2)} = \frac{0.000000141}{0.00000314} \ \Omega$$

$$= 0.0449 \ \Omega = 44.9 \text{ m}\Omega$$

> Thus, in spite of having very little difference between resistivities of both the wires, the implied resistance is significantly higher (almost double) for aluminium wire compared to copper wire.

Now, we calculate the voltage drop due to both types of wires, using formula

$$\Delta V = I_L \cdot R$$

Suppose, load current (I_L) = 1 A for the system for any wire type (copper/aluminium)

> Hence, aluminium wire is having higher potential drop that's why higher energy loss.

For copper wire, $\quad \Delta V = 1 \text{ A} \times 0.0274 \ \Omega = 0.0274 \text{ V} = 27.4 \text{ mV}$

For aluminium wire, $\Delta V = 1 \text{ A} \times 0.0449 \ \Omega = 0.0449 \text{ V} = 44.9 \text{ mV}$

Problem 9.2: Find a voltage drop in a copper wire of 10 metres length having a diameter of 0.5 mm. Assume that 5 A current is flowing in the wire.

Problem 9.3: Find a voltage drop in an aluminium wire of 10 metres length having a diameter of 0.5 mm. Assume that 5 A current is flowing in the wire.

Ampacity of wire

The current rating or current carrying capacity is popularly known as ampacity of wire and it is defined as 'the maximum amount of electrical current that a conductor or device can carry without any immediate or progressive degradation'. When electrical current flows through wire it causes potential drop and dissipates power in the form of heat. The generated heat results in increase in temperature of wire and its insulation. Commonly used wires (copper or aluminium) can conduct a large amount of current before melting but much before conductor's melting point, their insulation would be damaged by this generated heat. It is observed that the insulation (PVC) starts melting around 80 °C. Therefore, current carrying capacity of wire does not depend on the material itself but it depends on its insulation as well. While choosing a wire, one has to ensure that the maximum operating current that will in the wire is well within its ampacity rating.

> Ampacity is the maximum current carrying capacity of wire without causing any damage to it.

9.5.4
Operating Voltage

Normally, small and medium sized PV systems are designed at a voltage level of 12 V, 24 V, 48 V, 72 V etc. at DC side and for operating voltage of ~230 V at AC side if we are using inverter to run AC appliances. These operational values are much lower than the rated voltage levels of wires. Therefore, one needs not to worry about voltage ratings.

9.5.5
Allowed Potential Drop

It is a very important parameter, especially for solar PV systems. It is discussed earlier that every wire has a resistance due to which whenever any current flows through it, a certain voltage drop occurs in wires. Therefore, we always try to choose an appropriate wire to reduce the voltage drop. The voltage drop in wires depends on mainly four parameters:

1. Type of wire (copper or aluminium)
2. Current flowing through wire
3. Diameter of the wire
4. Length of wire.

To some extent, the temperature of the wire also has impact on the voltage drop in wires. As the operating temperature of wire increases, the voltage drop increases.

Usually, for the solar PV system wiring, the permitted voltage drop is 2% to 3% between two circuit nodes (from one equipment to other equipment). If we restrict the voltage drop to 2% to 3%, which means restricting the current (remember $V = I \times R$), the heat generated in wires is very small. Thus, by considering the voltage limit, the upper temperature limit is automatically taken care of. Also, this condition of lower potential drop means lower power losses that makes PV system energy efficient and longer life.

> In a solar PV system, the allowed voltage drop in wires is 2% to 3% of the source voltage.

Measurement of current and voltage drop

From the above discussion, we know that we need to select wire with limitation on current flow and limitation on voltage drop. We can use multimeter to measure the current flowing in a wire and voltage drop occurring across it. An arrangement to measure the current in circuit is shown in Figure 9.12. A multimeter is connected in series to measure current. Remember the value of the measured current should be less than the ampacity rating of the wires.

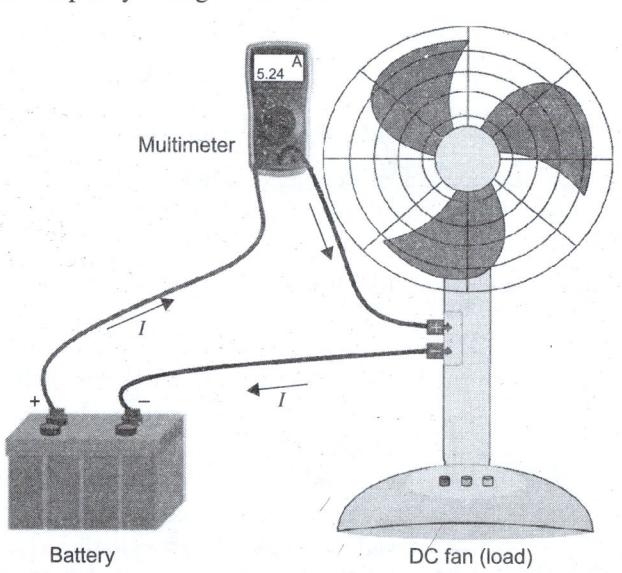

Multimeter

5.24 A

Battery

DC fan (load)

FIGURE 9.12

Current measurement in a simple DC system.

An arrangement for finding out voltage drop between two points in a system is shown in Figure 9.13. The voltage drop is nothing but the difference in the voltages between two points. Remember, we want to find out the voltage drop in a wire connecting two system components. Therefore, the two points between which we want to measure the voltage drop should be two ends of the wire. For voltage drop measurement between any two points of the circuit, the voltage is measured at these two distinct positions of the circuit and then the difference in voltages measured at these positions gives the voltage drop between them.

In graphical example (see Figure 9.13), the voltage at battery end of the wire is shown to be 11.82 V and the voltage at the fan end (load end) of the wire is shown to be 11.34 with reference to the negative terminal of the battery. Therefore, the voltage drop in the wire due to current flow is the difference of two voltages which is 11.82 V – 11.34 V = 0.48 V.

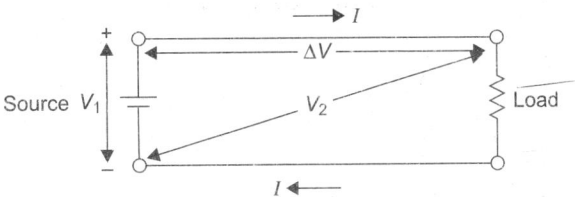

Voltage drop across one way wire from source to load

$$\Delta V = V_1 - V_2$$

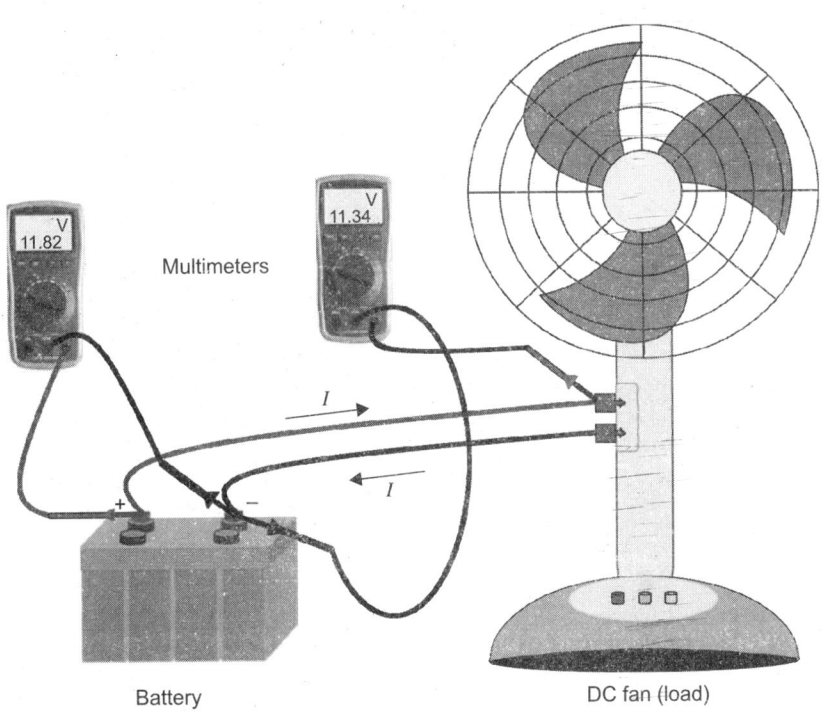

FIGURE 9.13

Voltage drop measurement in a simple DC system.

Multimeters

Battery

DC fan (load)

Problem 9.4: In a situation shown in Figure 9.13, if the voltage measured at the battery side is 12.2 V and voltage measure at the load side is 11.9. What is the voltage drop occurring in the wires?

9.5.6
Effect of Temperature on Wire Selection

The temperature has an impact on the resistance of wires and its current carrying capacity. As temperature increases, the resistance of wires also increases and when temperature reduces, the resistance of the wire decreases. The wire temperature could increase due to high ambient temperature (and exposure to direct sunlight) or it could also increase due to high current flowing through wires. The effect of temperature on the resistance of wire should be accounted in the design. Increase in temperature will also result in increase in the voltage drop in the wires. Therefore, while selecting the wires, the effect of temperature should be accounted in the design. Normally, the ambient temperature of the hottest period of the year of a particular location should be taken for wire sizing. Current carrying capacity of wire decreases with increasement in the temperature of wire.

The resistance variation of copper wire with temperature can be understood with the graph given in Figure 9.14. The graph is plotted to show the variation in the resistance as function of temperature. A ratio of resistance at temperature $T°C$ (wire temperature) to the resistance at $0°C$ (i.e. $R_{T°C}/R_{0°C}$) is plotted against the temperature of the wire. In this way, using the graph, we can obtain the $R_{T°C}/R_{0°C}$ at any temperature. Also, if we know the value of resistance of wire at 0°C, i.e., $R_{0°C}$, we can find out the value of resistance of wire at certain $T°C$.

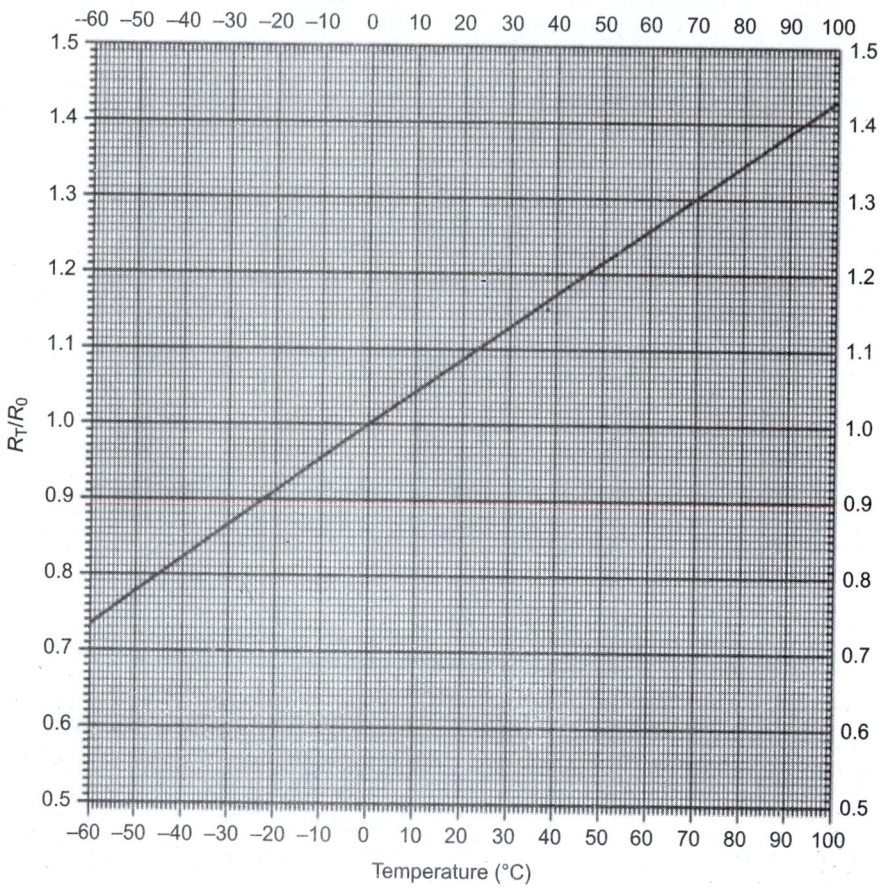

FIGURE 9.14

Copper wire resistance at temperature T°C (R_T) with respect to resistance at 0°C (R_0) or R_T/R_0 versus temperature of wire (°C).

EXAMPLE 9.2

A wire made of some conducting material has a resistance of 1.2 Ω at 0°C. The value of $R_{T°C}/R_{0°C}$ for 40°C is 1.12. Find the value of resistance at 40°C.

Solution

It is given that

$$R_{0°C} = 1.2 \ \Omega$$

$$\frac{R_{T°C}}{R_{0°C}} \ \text{at} \ 40°C = 1.12$$

$$\frac{R_{40°C}}{R_{0°C}} = 1.12 \quad \Rightarrow \quad R_{40°C} = 1.12 \times R_{0°C}$$

Putting the value of $R_{0°C}$, we can calculate the value of $R_{40°C}$.

$$R_{40°C} = 1.12 \times R_{0°C} = 1.12 \times 1.2 = 1.34 \ \Omega$$

EXAMPLE 9.3

Calculate the resistance of a copper wire at 60°C of particular length and cross-sectional area. The resistance of the same wire at 25°C is 2 Ω.

Solution

Given, the resistance of copper wire at 25°C ($R_{25°C}$) = 2 Ω

It is required to find out the resistance at 60°C ($R_{60°C}$) = ?

Using the graph (Figure 9.14), we can note that

$$\left(\frac{R_t}{R_0}\right)_{\text{at } 25°C} = \left(\frac{R_{25°C}}{R_{0°C}}\right) = 1.11$$

and

$$\left(\frac{R_t}{R_0}\right)_{\text{at } 60°C} = \left(\frac{R_{60°C}}{R_{0°C}}\right) = 1.26$$

We can take the ratio of above two equations

$$\frac{R_{60°C}/R_{0°C}}{R_{25°C}/R_{0°C}} = \frac{1.26}{1.11} = 1.135$$

$$\frac{R_{60°C}}{R_{0°C}} = 1.135 \times \left(\frac{R_{25°C}}{R_{0°C}}\right)$$

$$\Rightarrow \qquad R_{60°C} = 1.135 \times (R_{25°C}) = 1.135 \times 2 = 2.27 \ \Omega$$

Thus, the resistance of the copper wire will increase from 2 Ω (at 20°C) to 2.27 Ω (at 60°C).

Problem 9.5: A wire made of some conducting material has a resistance of 1.5 Ω at 0°C, and value of $R_{T°C}/R_{0°C}$ for 60°C is 1.25. Find the value of resistance at 60°C.

9.5.7
Wire Operating Temperature (Insulation Rating)

Operating temperature of wires needs to be identified very carefully. The wire material can withstand much higher temperature but the insulating material of the wires cannot withstand very high temperatures. Therefore, while selecting a wire, we must look at the temperature that the wire insulation can withstand. The insulation temperature rating should always be greater than or equal to the maximum operating temperature that can go during the hottest period of time.

Commonly available insulation temperature ratings with maximum allowable temperatures at the surface of the conductor are 60, 75, and 90°C depending on the type of insulating material. In hot climate, during the summer, the wire operating temperature can go up to 75°C. Therefore, to be safe, wire with high temperature ratings should be selected.

9.5.8
Wire Colour Codes

As you might have noticed, the wires (actually insulation material) come in different colours. The colours of insulating material of wires are chosen according to some standards. These colour standards or codes are applied to simply differentiate the wires in a circuit used for specific purpose. This is also one part of insulation ratings. The colour codes used in different countries are given in Table 9.3.

TABLE 9.3 Standard Wire Colour Codes

Region or country	Phases	Neutral	Protective earth/ground
India	red	black	green
European Union (EU)	brown, black, grey	blue	green/yellow
United States	black, red, blue (120/208/240 V); brown, orange, yellow (277/480 V)	white (120/208/240 V), grey (277/480 V)	green/yellow

9.5.9
Required Wire Size Calculations

Wire size, including the wire diameter and length of the wire, is one of the key parameters that determines the drop in voltage and power loss in PV systems. Therefore, after learning about the wire parameters like resistance, ampacity, voltage limit, their insulator, etc., let us now learn about how to determine the size of a wire for a given PV system. The objective here is to determine the size of the wire such that the 'voltage drop' in the wire is within the permitted limits.

For example, if a wire is connecting a battery to a television, and if the distance between battery and television is 5 metres along a favourable path, then total wire requirement is 5 + 5 = 10 metres (as two parallel wires are required to complete the circuit). Also, for deciding the wire size (diameter), two-way length (i.e. 5 + 5 = 10 metres) should be considered. This is demonstrated in Figure 9.15.

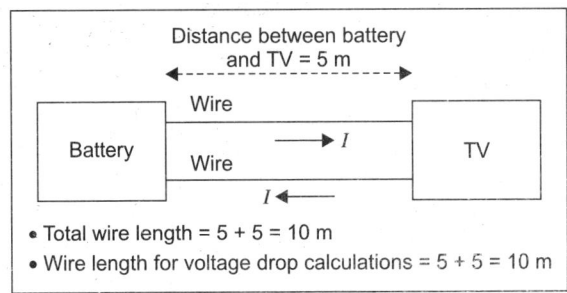

FIGURE 9.15

Actual wire length and wire length considered for voltage drop calculations.

There are three methods by which one can estimate the required wire size for a given application. Basically all these methods are same and the difference between them is in terms of approach and simplicity. These methods are discussed in the following paragraphs and they are:

1. Manual calculation of wire sizes
2. Wire size calculation using standard graphs
3. Wire size calculation using VDI (voltage drop index) method.

Note here that in 1st method, complete (two way, i.e., double the one way) wire length is taken into calculations independent of wires type (single core or multi-cores).

In 2nd and 3rd methods, 'one way' wire length is used as a parameter only but actually the two way wire length is considered for voltage drop calculations resulted in tables or graphs as in the case of 1st method.

In the case of single-core two ways, the wire size is the diameter of single core of any one wire. In the case of multi-core (two-core) wires, the wire size is the diameter of inner core (in case of co-axial cables) or the diameter of any one of the wires (in case of normal multi-core cables).

Finally, to decide total wire length required for making electrical connections, it is doubled for using single core wires or taken as it is (one way length) while using two-core wires depending on the choice.

Problem 9.6: Distance between DC power source and DC load is 7 m. In this situation, what distance should be taken in the calculation of voltage drop?

Manual calculation of wire sizes

The required size or the diameter of the wire in a PV system depends on resistance, length, current flowing, voltage levels and power levels in the wires. Depending on the parameters given, the calculation of wire sizes can be done in the following steps:

Step 1 Write down what is the allowable voltage drop (V_{drop}):   Normally, the permissible voltage drop is 2% to 3% of the PV system voltage V_{dc} (mainly we do this for DC side). In some cases, voltage drop as much as 5% is also allowed.

Allowable voltage drop

$$V_{\text{drop}} = \ldots\ldots \% \times V_{\text{dc}} = (\ldots\ldots/100) \times V_{\text{dc}} \text{ volts}$$

Step 2 Find out total wire length for connecting two points: This is the actual distance between two devices to be connected by wires along a favourable path, but note that the actual length of the wire is double than the actual distance, because in order to make a complete circuit, parallel connection or pair of wires are required (refer to Figure 9.15; actual wire length and wire length considered for voltage drop calculations).

$$\text{Total length of wire, } l = 2 \times \text{actual distance between two points}$$
$$= 2 \times \ldots\ldots = \ldots\ldots \text{ metre}$$

Step 3 Find out the current, voltage and power levels in the circuit: The current (I), voltage (V) and power (P) in a circuit are related to each other by the following relationship:

$$P = V \times I \qquad \text{(in DC circuit)}$$
$$P = V \times I \times \text{PF} \text{ (in AC circuit)}$$

Here PF is the power factor (refer to very basic Chapter 1 of this manual)

Thus, if any two quantities are known, we can estimate the third quantity. Normally, we need to find out the current flowing in the circuit to estimate voltage drop. From the above equation the current can be calculated as follows:

$$I = \frac{P}{V} \qquad \text{(in DC circuit)}$$
$$I = \frac{P}{V \times \text{PF}} \quad \text{(in AC circuit)}$$
$$\text{Current} = \ldots\ldots \text{ ampere}$$

Normally, as discussed in Section 9.5.3, about 25% more current than the calculated value is taken for wire size calculations as safety margin, i.e., we need to multiply the above current value by 1.25.

With the safety margin, the Current = ……. × 1.25 = ………. amperes

Note: If there is chance to have solar radiation more than STC condition, then multiplying factor should be 1.25 × 1.25 = 1.56.

Step 4 Find out the diameter of wire: If all the parameters mentioned in step 1 to step 4 are available, then it is possible to calculate the wire diameter. From our earlier discussion we know that the drop in voltage is related to current flow and resistance of the wire. Let us write voltage drop as V_{drop}. Then the expression for V_{drop} can be written as:

$$V_{\text{drop}} = I \times R$$

or

$$R = \frac{V_{\text{drop}}}{I}$$
$$R = \ldots\ldots \; \Omega \text{ (ohm)}$$
$$L = \ldots\ldots \text{ metre}$$

Since we would know the value of V_{drop} and I, therefore, from the above expression we can find out the value of R. Once the value of R is known, by looking up the ready to use tables (see Tables 9.4 and 9.5), we can find out the required diameter of the wire. In these tables, the resistance of wire is calculated for a given material, and for a given value of diameter and length.

These tables (Tables 9.4 and 9.5) are the look up tables for the resistance of the copper wire and aluminium wire respectively. In these tables, the operating temperature of 75°C is considered for wires to be on the safe side. The look up tables are made for a particular length of wire. From the calculated parameter you would know the value of R for a particular length of wire (as noted in Step 2), from the Tables you can read the value of diameter in mm and cross-section area in mm^2.

TABLE 9.4 Look Up Table Correlating Diameter, Cross-sectional Area and Resistance of the Wire for Various Lengths (for copper wire)

Diameter, d (mm)	Area, A (mm²)	Resistance of Wire, R (Ω) (for Copper wire) Total (two way) wire length, l (m)										
		1	2	4	6	8	10	12	15	20	25	30
0.5	0.20	0.1090	0.2180	0.4362	0.6543	0.8724	1.0904	1.3085	1.6357	2.1809	2.7261	3.2713
1	0.79	0.0273	0.0545	0.1090	0.1636	0.2181	0.2726	0.3271	0.4089	0.5452	0.6815	0.8178
1.5	1.77	0.0121	0.0242	0.0485	0.0727	0.0969	0.1212	0.1454	0.1817	0.2423	0.3029	0.3635
2	3.14	0.0068	0.0136	0.0273	0.0409	0.0545	0.0682	0.0818	0.1022	0.1363	0.1704	0.2045
2.5	4.91	0.0044	0.0087	0.0174	0.0262	0.0349	0.0436	0.0523	0.0654	0.0872	0.1090	0.1309
3	7.07	0.0030	0.0061	0.0121	0.0182	0.0242	0.0303	0.0363	0.0454	0.0606	0.0757	0.0909
3.5	9.62	0.0022	0.0044	0.0089	0.0134	0.0178	0.0223	0.0267	0.0334	0.0445	0.0556	0.0668
4	12.56	0.0017	0.0034	0.0068	0.0102	0.0136	0.0170	0.0204	0.0256	0.0341	0.0426	0.0511
4.5	15.90	0.0013	0.0027	0.0054	0.0081	0.0108	0.0135	0.0162	0.0202	0.0269	0.0337	0.0404
5	19.63	0.0011	0.0022	0.0044	0.0065	0.0087	0.0109	0.0131	0.0164	0.0218	0.0273	0.0327
5.5	23.75	0.0009	0.0018	0.0036	0.0054	0.0072	0.0090	0.0108	0.0135	0.0180	0.0225	0.0270
6	28.26	0.0008	0.0015	0.0030	0.0045	0.0061	0.0076	0.0091	0.0114	0.0151	0.0189	0.0227
6.5	33.17	0.0006	0.0013	0.0026	0.0039	0.0052	0.0065	0.0077	0.0097	0.0129	0.0161	0.0194
7	38.47	0.0006	0.0011	0.0022	0.0033	0.0045	0.0056	0.0067	0.0083	0.0111	0.0139	0.0167
7.5	44.16	0.0005	0.0010	0.0019	0.0029	0.0039	0.0048	0.0058	0.0073	0.0097	0.0121	0.0145
8	50.24	0.0004	0.0009	0.0017	0.0026	0.0034	0.0043	0.0051	0.0064	0.0085	0.0106	0.0128
8.5	56.72	0.0004	0.0008	0.0015	0.0023	0.0030	0.0038	0.0045	0.0057	0.0075	0.0094	0.0113
9	63.59	0.0003	0.0007	0.0013	0.0020	0.0027	0.0034	0.0040	0.0050	0.0067	0.0084	0.0101
9.5	70.85	0.0003	0.0006	0.0012	0.0018	0.0024	0.0030	0.0036	0.0045	0.0060	0.0076	0.0091
10	78.50	0.0003	0.0005	0.0011	0.0016	0.0022	0.0027	0.0033	0.0041	0.0055	0.0068	0.0082

For example, if the length of the wire is 10 m and the calculated value of resistance is 0.03 ohm (Ω) and if you are using copper wire, then from Table 9.4 for copper wire, the value of required diameter is 3 mm and cross-section area is 7.07 mm^2. These values are highlighted in Table 9.4.

Now you need to find out the wire in the market of this particular size (i.e. 3 mm diameter copper wire). As mentioned earlier that the wires of some standard diameter are manufactured. Now; you should look up Table 9.2 (Table of standard wire gauge dimensions), to find out the wire gauge that matches best for you and available in the market. If, you look at this table (see Table 9.2) carefully you will find that SWG 11 wire has diameter of 2.946 mm, very close to 3 mm. Therefore, you should choose or buy SWG 11 copper wire. These values are highlighted in Table 9.2.

TABLE 9.5 Look Up Table Correlating Diameter, Cross-sectional Area and Resistance of the Wire for Various Lengths (for aluminium wire)

Diameter, d (mm)	Area, A (mm²)	Resistance of Wire, R (Ω) (for Aluminium wire) Total (two way) wire length, I (m)										
		1	2	4	6	8	10	12	15	20	25	30
0.5	0.20	0.1773	0.3546	0.7093	1.0639	1.4186	1.7732	2.1279	2.6599	3.5465	4.4331	5.3197
1	0.79	0.0443	0.0887	0.1773	0.2660	0.3546	0.4433	0.5320	0.6650	0.8866	1.1083	1.3299
1.5	1.77	0.0197	0.0394	0.0788	0.1182	0.1576	0.1970	0.2364	0.2955	0.3941	0.4926	0.5911
2	3.14	0.0111	0.0222	0.0443	0.0665	0.0887	0.1108	0.1330	0.1662	0.2217	0.2771	0.3325
2.5	4.91	0.0071	0.0142	0.0284	0.0426	0.0567	0.0709	0.0851	0.1064	0.1419	0.1773	0.2128
3	7.07	0.0049	0.0099	0.0197	0.0296	0.0394	0.0493	0.0591	0.0739	0.0985	0.1231	0.1478
3.5	9.62	0.0036	0.0072	0.0145	0.0217	0.0290	0.0362	0.0434	0.0543	0.0724	0.0905	0.1086
4	12.56	0.0028	0.0055	0.0111	0.0166	0.0222	0.0277	0.0332	0.0416	0.0554	0.0693	0.0831
4.5	15.90	0.0022	0.0044	0.0088	0.0131	0.0175	0.0219	0.0263	0.0328	0.0438	0.0547	0.0657
5	19.63	0.0018	0.0035	0.0071	0.0106	0.0142	0.0177	0.0213	0.0266	0.0355	0.0443	0.0532
5.5	23.75	0.0015	0.0029	0.0059	0.0088	0.0117	0.0147	0.0176	0.0220	0.0293	0.0366	0.0440
6	28.26	0.0012	0.0025	0.0049	0.0074	0.0099	0.0123	0.0148	0.0185	0.0246	0.0308	0.0369
6.5	33.17	0.0010	0.0021	0.0042	0.0063	0.0084	0.0105	0.0126	0.0157	0.0210	0.0262	0.0315
7	38.47	0.0009	0.0018	0.0036	0.0054	0.0072	0.0090	0.0109	0.0136	0.0181	0.0226	0.0271
7.5	44.16	0.0008	0.0016	0.0032	0.0047	0.0063	0.0079	0.0095	0.0118	0.0158	0.0197	0.0236
8	50.24	0.0007	0.0014	0.0028	0.0042	0.0055	0.0069	0.0083	0.0104	0.0139	0.0173	0.0208
8.5	56.72	0.0006	0.0012	0.0025	0.0037	0.0049	0.0061	0.0074	0.0092	0.0123	0.0153	0.0184
9	63.59	0.0005	0.0011	0.0022	0.0033	0.0044	0.0055	0.0066	0.0082	0.0109	0.0137	0.0164
9.5	70.85	0.0005	0.0010	0.0020	0.0029	0.0039	0.0049	0.0059	0.0074	0.0098	0.0123	0.0147
10	78.50	0.0004	0.0009	0.0018	0.0027	0.0035	0.0044	0.0053	0.0066	0.0089	0.0111	0.0133

> Separate calculation for wire diameter estimation is required for connecting different points in the circuit if the voltage and current level in between points is not the same.

Note: The method described in above paragraphs is for estimating the size of the wire for connecting two points or two components in the system. This could be for connecting PV panel to the battery or connecting battery to the inverter, etc. Note that a separate calculation is required for finding out the size of each connection if the voltage and current level in different parts of the system is not the same.

Finding out voltage drop if diameter of wire is given

So far we were trying to calculate the wire diameter to suit a particular application in solar PV system where the permissible percentage drop in the voltage is mentioned. In some situation, your diameter of wire may be fixed, or only wire of certain diameter is available. In that case, it should be possible to estimate the drop in voltage, and then we can see if the estimated voltage drop is acceptable or not.

If wire diameter and length of the wire are given, then we can find out the resistance of the wire from the look up tables (Tables 9.4 and 9.5). Once we know the resistance of wire, then using the following expression, we can estimate the drop in the voltage in this particular wire:

$$V_{drop} = I \times R$$

EXAMPLE 9.4

Suppose a DC system is operating at 12 V and 10 A of voltage and current levels respectively. Wire size (diameter) and distance between power source and the load (one way wire length) are 2 mm and 6 metres respectively. If wire is made up of copper, what is the percentage voltage drop?

Solution

First we find the copper wire resistance for 2 mm diameter and 6 metres wire length using look up Table 9.4.

The resistance, $R = 0.0409 \ \Omega$

Thus, voltage drop in this particular wire is

$$V_{drop} = I \times R$$

$$V_{drop} = 10 \text{ A} \times 0.0409 \text{ } \Omega = 0.409 \text{ V}$$

$$\%V_{drop} = \frac{V_{drop}}{V} \times 100 = \frac{0.409 \text{ V}}{12 \text{ V}} \times 100 = 3.4 \text{ \%}$$

Problem 9.7: Suppose a DC system is operating at 12 V and 5 A of voltage and current levels respectively. Wire size (diameter) and distance between power source and the load (one way wire length) are 1 mm and 12 metres respectively. If wire is made up of aluminium, what is the percentage voltage drop?

EXAMPLE 9.5

In a particular section of PV system, there are 6 PV modules of similar ratings interconnected (3 parallel combinations in a series of 2) and the final output of the panel is connected to charge a compatible battery. The module ratings at STC are as given in Table 9.6:

TABLE 9.6 Table for Example 9.5

Parameters	Ratings
Rated power (P_{max})	40 W
Nominal voltage (V)	12 V
Module efficiency	11.50%
Current at rated power (I_{mp})	2.32 A
Voltage at rated power (V_{mp})	17.2 V
Short circuit current (I_{sc})	2.52 A
Open circuit voltage (V_{oc})	21.6 V

Find out the current in the circuit from panel to battery for which wire sizing should be performed. Take appropriate assumptions wherever it is required and also specify them.

Solution

This is an active system and different from the simple source connected to load. Here the current is always varying, so, we size the wire for the maximum current that may happen in the circuit depending on acquired safety level. For deciding operating current for wire sizing, we follow the stepwise procedure (see Section 9.5.9) as follows:

Step 1 Compute the resultant PV panel short-circuit current (I_{sc}): Short-circuit current (I_{sc}) of each module = 2.52 A (as given). Since two modules are connected in series (voltage will be doubled but current will be same) and there are 3 such combinations connected in parallel (voltage will be same but current will be tripled).

So, short-circuit current (I_{sc}) of the panel = 3 × 2.52 A = 7.56 A

Step 2 Enhance the wire's current carrying capacity:

(i) To handle full current:

It is done by increasing I_{sc} by 25%.

Current level = I_{sc} + 25% of I_{sc} = $I_{sc} \times 1.25$ = 7.56 A × 1.25 = 9.45 A

(ii) To handle excessive currents caused by higher (more than STC) insolation due to cloud/snow reflection:

It is done by again increasing the current by 25%, i.e., directly increasing I_{sc} by 56% ($I_{sc} \times 1.25 \times 1.25 = I_{sc} \times 1.56 = 7.56$ A $\times 1.56 = 11.8$ A).

Thus, wire sizing should be done at the current level of 11.8 A or at least 9.45 A depending on safety and conservativeness.

EXAMPLE 9.6

Calculate the wire size needed for a 24 V DC PV system for connecting a battery to a DC load such that the voltage drop between battery and DC load does not exceed 2% of system voltage. The distance between battery and DC load (i.e. one way wire length) is 12 feet. The total load connected in the system is of 500 W. Use copper wire for the system.

Solution

In order to calculate the wire size or wire diameter, we can use stepwise method described in Section 9.5.9.

Step 1 Write down what is allowable voltage drop (V_{drop}): In this case allowable voltage drop = 2% of system voltage

System voltage = 24 V

Therefore, the voltage drop, $V_{drop} = 2\% \times V_{dc} = (2/100) \times 24 = 0.48$ V

Step 2 Find out total wire length for connecting two points: In this case, the distance between battery and DC load = 12 feet. One way wire length = 12 feet = 12×0.3048 m = 3.6576 m (1 foot = 0.3048 metre).

But total wire length is double of the one way wire length. Therefore, total (two way) wire length

$$l = 2 \times 12 \text{ feet} = 24 \text{ feet} = 7.3152 \text{ metres}$$

Step 3 Find out the current, voltage and power levels in the circuit: In this case, total load connected or power = 500 watt

The system voltage, V = 24 V

Therefore, the current in the system can be calculated as:

$$I = \frac{P}{V} = \frac{500}{24} = 20.83 \text{ A}$$

This is the current that the wire must be able to carry between two points for which this calculations are being done. Normally, we should take safety margin of 25% for current carrying capacity of wire. Therefore, the desired current carrying capacity of wires = $I \times 125\% = I \times 1.25$.

I (for wire size calculation) = $I \times 1.25 = 20.83 \times 1.25 = 26.04$ A

Step 4 Find out the diameter of wire: First we calculate the resistance using the formula

$$V_{drop} = I \times R$$

or

$$R = \frac{V_{drop}}{I}$$

$$R = \frac{V_{drop}}{I} = \frac{0.48 \text{ V}}{26.04 \text{ A}} = 0.0184 \ \Omega$$

Now, we use the look up Table 9.4 and will find out the wire diameter for calculated resistance of wire (R) = 0.0184 Ω, and for total wire length (l) = 7.3152 m.

When we look into Table 9.4, there is no value matching 7.3152 metres length, therefore, we should take the closest length to this, which is 8 metres. Similarly, when we look the column for 8 metres length, there is no value of resistance that matches 0.0184 Ω and we should try to look at the closest possible match. In the Table, the closest possible match for the value of resistance is 0.0178.

So, we will find the wire size corresponding to wire length l = 8 m and resistance R = 0.0178 Ω. Now, looking up in Table 9.4, corresponding to these values we find that the diameter of wire, d = 3.5 mm and the corresponding cross-sectional area, A = 9.62 mm^2. Now, for the wire diameter (d) of 3.5 mm (using Table 9.2), the wire gauge is SWG # 9, i.e., the gauge number is 9.

So, wire size is 3.5 mm (diameter) or 9.62 mm^2 (cross-sectional area) or SWG # 9 (wire gauge number).

Problem 9.8: Calculate the wire size needed for a 96 V DC PV system for connecting a battery to a DC load such that the voltage drop between battery and DC load does not exceed 2% of system voltage. The distance between battery and DC load (i.e. one way wire length) is 5 metres. The total load connected the system is of 5000 W. Use copper wire for the system.

Wire size calculation using standard graphs

In this section, we have used the method of manual calculation to estimate the wire sizes for a particular situation in solar PV system. Wire sizes can also be estimated using standard graphs in a quicker way. The method of using standard graphs is presented here. Idea here is the same, that for a given permissible voltage drop and the required length of wire, we need to calculate the resistance of the wires, and from these values we can estimate the required diameter of the wires. The same thing is presented in the form of graphs and hence it is easier to read or find out the wire diameters using graphical method.

The voltage drop graphs are created using resistance values at 75 °C of operating temperature. These graphs provide the idea about length of wire (in feet) for 12 V, 24 V and 48 V at 2% voltage drop and for 24 V and 48 V at 3% voltage drop with respect to current in the wire and its diameter. Normally, DC systems operate at either of these voltage levels and allowed potential drops are also in the range of 2–3% and copper wire is used to reduce energy loss. So, the following graphs provide easier way to estimate the appropriate wire diameter.

Note: While using the following graphs, the length of wire should be taken only one way (i.e., the distance between the system components along desired wiring path). This is only to calculate wire size (diameter/cross-sectional area/SWG) but in actual we have to purchase the full (i.e., two ways) length of the wire.

All five graphs for different operating voltage, different percentage of voltage drops and copper wire are provided as follows.

How to read the graphs?

The graphs are plotted to find out the diameter of the wire for a given wire length and current flowing through it for different voltage level, allowable voltage drop and for a given material like copper (see the standard graphs). In this way, all the parameters that affect the wire diameter are accounted for.

The Y-axis of the graph is wire length in the units of feet and the X-axis of the graph is current in the units of ampere (A). In each standard graph, several curves are plotted corresponding to different diameters or gauge number of wires.

In order to find out the appropriate wire gauge for a particular solar PV application, choose an appropriate graph corresponding to system voltage and allowable percentage voltage drop (for example, see the captions of Figures 9.16 to 9.20).

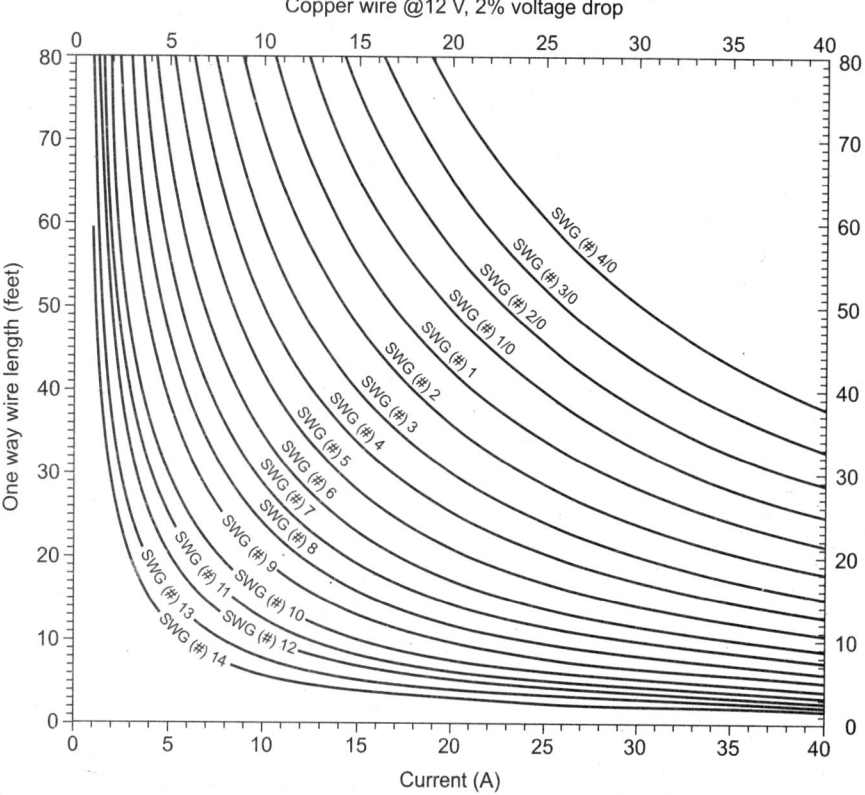

FIGURE 9.16

Wire length (in feet) for various current levels in a 12 V (DC side) PV system in which allowable voltage drop is 2% (for copper wire).

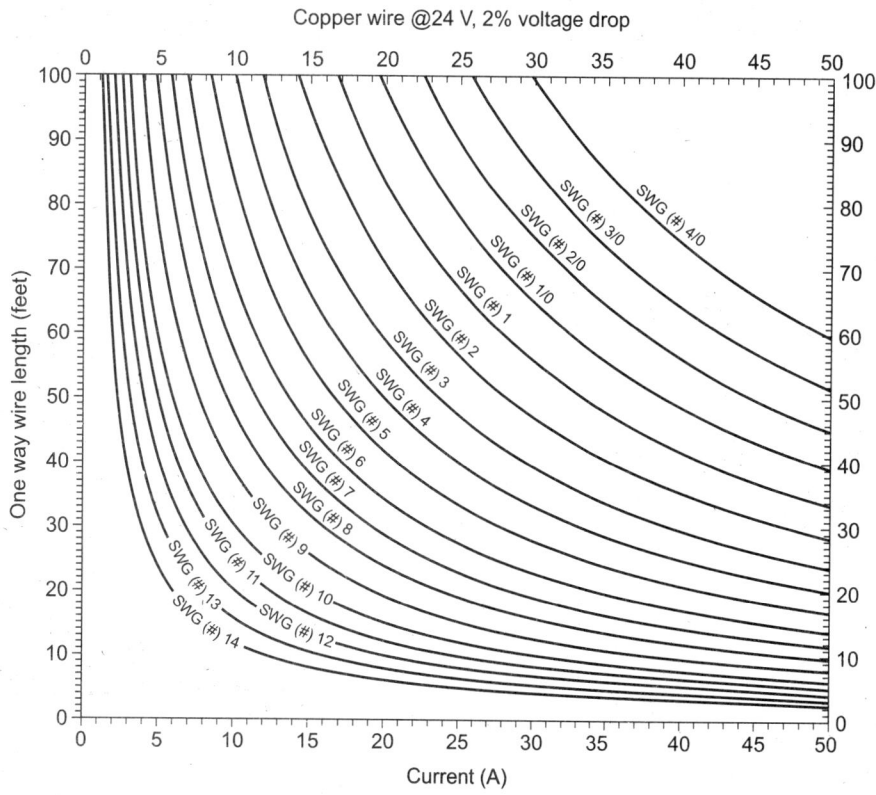

FIGURE 9.17

Wire length (in feet) for various current levels in a 24 V (DC side) PV system in which allowable voltage drop is 2% (for copper wire).

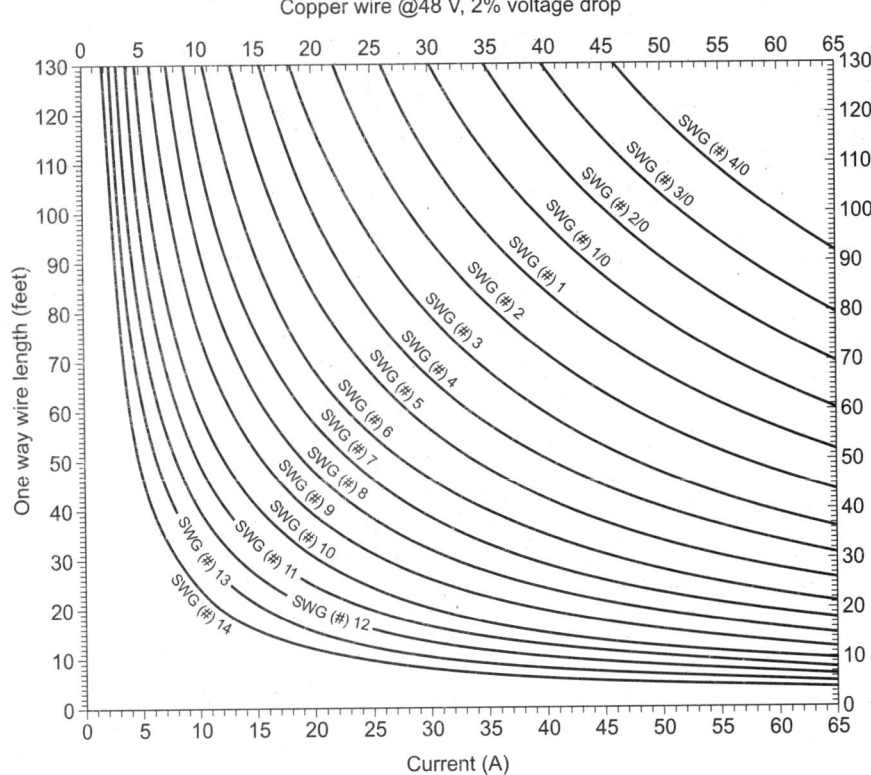

FIGURE 9.18

Wire length (in feet) for various current levels in a 48 V (DC side) PV system in which allowable voltage drop is 2% (for copper wire).

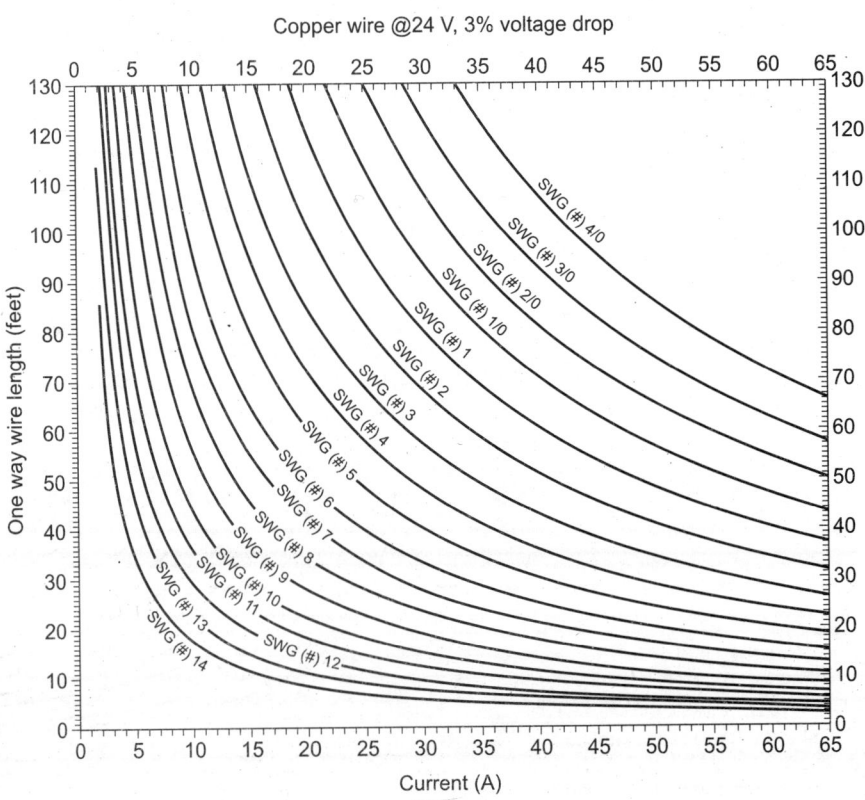

FIGURE 9.19

Wire length (in feet) for various current levels in a 24 V (DC side) PV system in which allowable voltage drop is 3% (for copper wire).

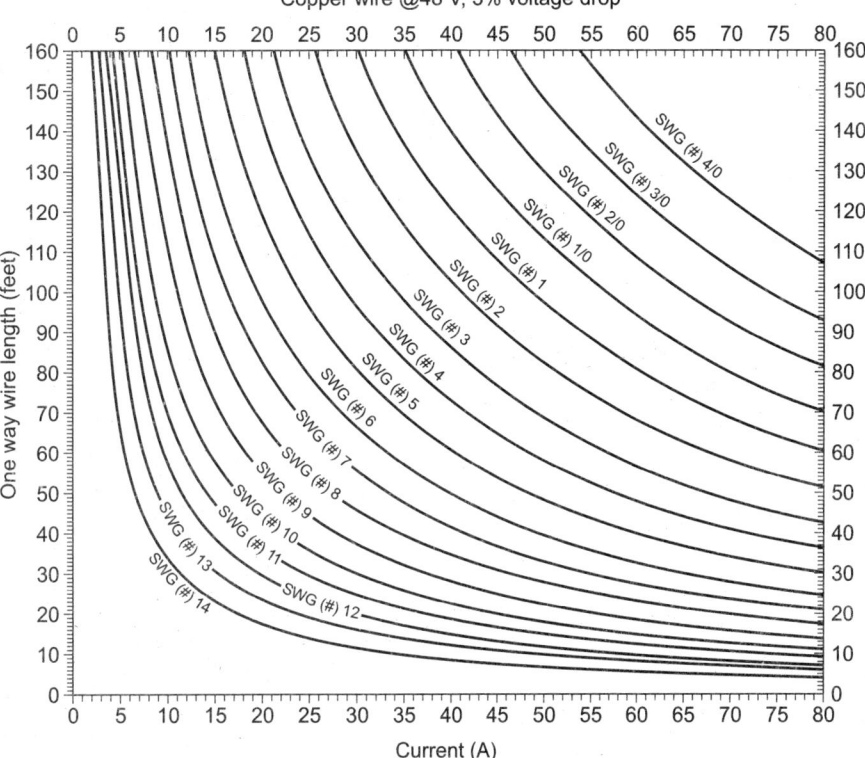

FIGURE 9.20

Wire length (in feet) for various current levels in a 48 V (DC side) PV system in which allowable voltage drop is 3% (for copper wire).

For wire sizing using the standard graphs sequential approach is to be followed as given below:

Step 1: For proper standard graph selection, first note down the current value in particular part of PV system for which wire sizing is to be done. Also note down the estimated length of the wire (one way) connecting two points in PV system along favourable path, note down the allowed % potential drop, DC system operating voltage and off course wire material (copper).

Step 2: Now select the appropriate graph corresponding to the values of different parameters in previous step. After selecting the appropriate standard graph, draw a vertical line on X-axis for the noted current value and draw a horizontal line on Y-axis for noted value of wire length. Instead of drawing perpendicular lines, one can use two scales to locate the intersection point for finding standard wire gauge number.

For example, these vertical and horizontal lines are drawn in Figure 9.16 for current value of 20 A and wire length of 50 feet (Please note that Figure 9.16 is for 12 V system voltages where allowable voltage drop is 2%) as shown in Figure 9.21.

The intersection point of vertical line for current and horizontal line for length of wire is very near to curve for the wire having SWG of 1/0. Thus, for this application (example), the standard wire gauge number is 1/0. Now you can look at Table 9.2 of standard wire gauge dimension. The SWG # 1/0 is corresponding to wire diameter of 8.23 mm.

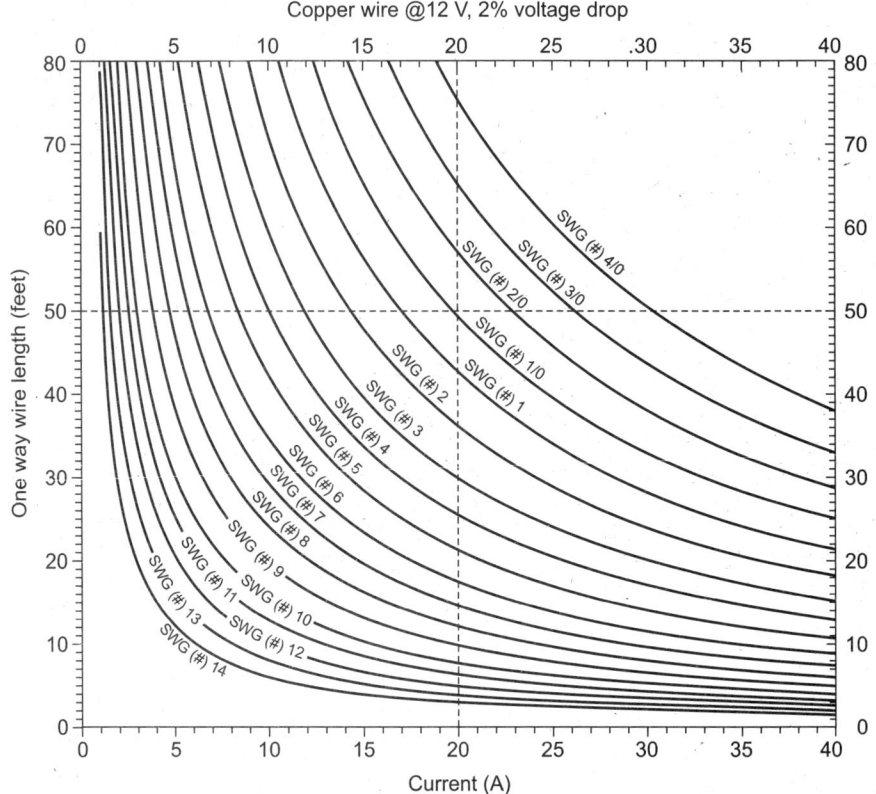

Copper wire @12 V, 2% voltage drop

FIGURE 9.21

Wire length (in feet) for various current levels in a 12 V (DC side) PV system in which allowable voltage drop is 2% (for copper wire).

The method for finding diameter of wire presented in paragraphs (how to read graphs) can be used for any other situation as well. But one thing is to be carefully considered, if the intersection of these two horizontal and vertical lines corresponding to wire length and current levels is in between two lines of standard graphs, then always higher diameter (means lower SWG #) wire should be selected between these two wires. This is for being more cautious to meet the specified voltage drop level/condition.

In this way, for this particular application, one need to choose a wire of 8.32 mm diameter. This is very large size for wire. One way to reduce the diameter of a wire is to increase the voltage level of the system, which will result in reduction in current, means lower voltage drop, which means that wires of smaller diameter can be used.

EXAMPLE 9.7

Calculate the wire size needed for a 24 V DC PV system for connecting a battery to a DC load such that the voltage drop between battery and DC load does not exceed 2% of system voltage. The distance between battery and DC load (i.e. one way wire length) is 12 feet. The total load connected the system is of 500 W. Use copper wire for the system.

Solution

Step 1 Note the values of parameters to find wire size using standard graphs:

$$\text{Current in the circuit, } I_L = \frac{P}{V} = \frac{500 \text{ W}}{24 \text{ V}} = 20.83 \text{ A}$$

For enhancing the current carrying capacity, wire is designed for

$$I_L \times 125\% = I_L \times 1.25 = 20.83 \times 1.25 = 26.04 \text{ A}$$

The one way wire length = 12 feet (given)
Allowed voltage drop = 2%
System operating DC voltage = 24 V
Using the copper wire

Step 2 See the appropriate standard graph to calculate the wire size: See Figure 9.17, (copper wire @ 24 V, 2% voltage drop).

So, put the two straight lines corresponding to one way wire length (12 feet) and current level (26A) as shown in Figure 9.22 and see the location of the intersection point.

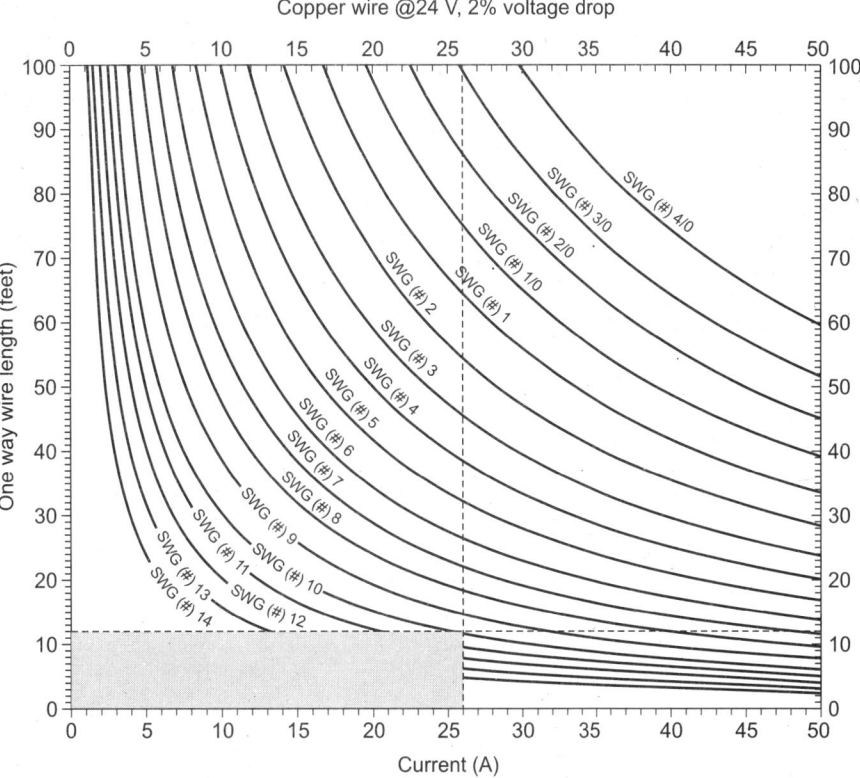

Copper wire @24 V, 2% voltage drop

FIGURE 9.22
Figure of Example 9.7.

We can see that the point of intersection is between SWG #10 and SWG #9 graphs. It is just above the AWG #10, so, it can also be used with slight performance relaxation. But to be in the safe side as it is strictly given in the problem that the voltage drop should not exceed the 2% level, we use the SWG #9 wire. So, up to SWG #10 (#14, #13, #12, #11 and #10) are not applicable as shown in the dark region. Thicker wire (i.e. SWG #9), is found adequate to the given circuit up to 2% voltage drop.

The actual required length of wire = 12 feet (2-core cable with each wire of size SWG # 9)

or   12 × 2 = 24 feet (single-core wire of size SWG #9).

Problem 9.9: Solve this problem using a graph method. Calculate the wire size needed for a 24 V DC PV system for connecting a battery to a DC load such that the voltage drop between battery and DC load does not exceed 3% of system voltage. The distance between battery and DC load (i.e. one way wire length) is 12 feet. The total load connected in the system is of 500 W. Use copper wire for the system.

VDI (Voltage Drop Index) method of wire sizing

It is another way to calculate wire sizing for a PV system and there is an equation to calculate VDI. It is an easy, fast and flexible way to calculate the approximate wire size (SWG #). After calculating VDI, the wire size can be determined using the voltage drop index chart for copper wire as given in Table 9.7. Here the wire size can be calculated for any voltage drop and any nominal system voltage. So, it is even more flexible than the previous methods.

$$VDI = \frac{Ampere \times Feet}{\% \, Voltage \, drop \times Voltage}$$

Where; Ampere shows maximum current (in amperes) through circuit, Feet shows one way wire distance (i.e. the distance between the system components along favourable wiring path), % voltage drop means the desired percentage of voltage drop (suppose it is 2%, then put 2 in the formula), and voltage shows nominal system voltage.

TABLE 9.7 Voltage Drop Index (VDI) Chart for Copper Wire

Wire size (SWG #)	VDI	Ampacity (ampere)
4/0	60	195
3/0	52	179
2/0	45	165
0	39	150
1	34	136
2	29	123
3	24	111
4	20	101
5	17	91
6	14	81
7	12	73
8	10	64
9	8	55
10	6	46
11	5	39
12	4	33
13	3	27
14	2	21

Here one way wire length is used as a parameter to calculate wire size only. Actually, we have to purchase the full (i.e. two ways) wire length.

EXAMPLE 9.8

Calculate the wire size needed for a 24 V DC PV system for connecting a battery to a DC load such that the voltage drop between battery and DC load does not exceed 2% of system voltage. The distance between battery and DC load (i.e. one way wire length) is 12 feet. The total load connected in the system is of 500 W. Use copper wire for the system.

Solution

Step 1 Note down the values of parameters to calculate VDI:

(i) Current in the wire for which wire is to be sized:

$$\text{Current in the circuit, } I_L = \frac{P}{V} = \frac{500 \text{ W}}{24 \text{ V}} = 20.83 \text{ A}$$

For enhancing the current carrying capacity, wire is designed for

$$I_L \times 125\% = I_L \times 1.25 = 20.83 \times 1.25 = 26.04 \text{ A}$$

(ii) The one way wire length = 12 feet (given)

(iii) Allowed voltage drop = 2%

(iv) System operating DC voltage = 24 V

(v) Using copper wire.

Step 2 Calculate VDI for the given values of parameters:

$$\text{VDI} = \frac{\text{Ampere} \times \text{Feet}}{\% \text{ Voltage drop} \times \text{Voltage}}$$

$$\text{VDI} = \frac{26.04 \times 12}{2 \times 24}$$

$$\text{VDI} = 6.5$$

Step 3 Using VDI table, we calculate the wire size as follows:

Wire size (SWG #)	VDI
9	8
10	6

Here calculated VDI (6.5) is greater than 6 and between 6 and 8, means the wire size should be between SWG#10 and SWG#9. Since the calculated value is close to SWG#10 (VDI = 6) and it can be used, but according to the strict potential drop condition which is not exceeding the 2% value; thicker wire (SWG #9) is found to be adequate in the given example. Now, one can find out the wire diameter and its cross-sectional area corresponding to SWG #9 (using the Table 9.2) and this is 3.65 mm (diameter) or 10.51 mm^2 (cross-sectional area).

Problem 9.10: Solve this problem using VDI method. Calculate the wire size needed for a 24 V DC PV system for connecting a battery to a DC load such that the voltage drop between battery and DC load does not exceed 3% of system voltage. The distance between battery and DC load (i.e. one way wire length) is 12 feet. The total load connected in the system is of 500 W. Use copper wire for the system.

9.5.10
Other Specific Requirements

9.6
Junction Box

If someone is willing to pay more for further performance enhancement and cable life, one can purchase cables with some extra features like flame retardant, UV-resistant, sunlight resistant, etc.

It is a smaller but the important part of the system. Junction boxes are devices that contain the electrical wiring junctions or interconnections that facilitates the home wiring network to interface with the main power supply (see Figure 9.23). Junction boxes are generally considered more pleasant compared to exposed electrical wire junctions.

It is usually constructed of metal or hard plastic. Generally, junction boxes are either of a square or rectangular shapes consisting of a door on the front of the box allowing access to the interior of the box. The entire cover may swing upward or downward to allow access to the junctions within the device.

There are various types of junction boxes available in the market and right kind of junction box can be easily found serving the specified purpose. Ratings (current, voltage, operating temperature, insulation, protection level etc.) should be carefully checked and in the case of wire selection, it is better to choose the oversized junction box to avoid heating and energy loss.

FIGURE 9.23
A typical solar PV junction box.

The basic purpose of a junction box is to conceal the electrical junctions from sight. The internal configuration varies a little bit depending on the junction box design and features incorporated but serving the basic common purpose.

The advantages of junction boxes into an electrical circuit are:

1. Provides neater means of concealing electrical junctions.
2. Give protection for the wiring interface at various junction points.
3. Helps to deal with sparks due to junction overloading for some reason, and thus limits the amount of damage that is caused.
4. Allows the connections made within the box to be shut down in an emergency situation, iff provided with a safety switch.
5. Allows to accommodate additional electrical junctions or larger electrical cables, iff purchased with a higher capacity and extra junction points.
6. Helps to avoid wire shortage situations due to repairing works.
7. Gives an opportunity to make the system energy efficient by maintaining tight connections and using lesser spare wire.
8. A typical junction box life time is comparable to the lifetime of solar PV panel.
9. Ease to identify faults and check system performance.
10. Allows to incorporate additional features into the system without cutting or disturbing previous wiring.
11. Provides protection against shock hazards.

9.7
Checklist

1. Wirings are of correct rating and with required special features, if any.
2. The cable clamps are properly installed to support the wiring.
3. Grounded conductors are properly indicated.
4. All junction boxes are easily accessible.
5. The wire thickness was measured after removing insulation present on it.
6. Some 1-2 feet extra wire length has been kept to overcome wire shortage situations during repairing work.
7. The conductor rating of the PV circuit is at least 156% of the rated short circuit current.
8. The components used are certified components, such as ISO (International Organization for Standardization), BIS (Bureau of Indian Standards) IEC (International Electrotechnical Commission).
9. Sometimes, in AC cables, 3 wires are given in a multi-core cables. Then there is one extra wire is to prevent electrical shocks and grounding in case of short circuit conditions.
10. Some companies make wires/cables specially dedicated to solar applications. The system components like this can be purchased from them.

10

Solar PV System Design and Integration

A system is defined as the set of things working together as parts of a mechanism or an interconnecting network to perform a specific talk. A solar PV system is a system whose function is to generate electricity using sunlight and supply electricity to the load when required. In order to achieve this objective, many components are connected together in solar PV system, other than PV modules. For example, a solar PV module can converts sunlight into electricity. This electricity is available when sunlight is there. But the load may need electricity supply during non-sunshine hours. Therefore, in order to make the use of electricity generated by PV modules by the load as per desire, there is need to store energy for nighttime applications. For energy storage application, batteries are required. The battery stores energy in the form of DC, sometime, loads can use only AC power, therefore, the conversion of DC power into AC power is required. This power conversion is done by a device called inverter. The load may require constant power supply, which may not be possible to provide by the PV modules or batteries in the system. Therefore, some kind of power conditioning may be required. In this way, in order to supply a reliable power to the load using PV module, other than PV modules, several other components are required. The combination of all the components is referred as solar PV system. In previous Chapters, we have discussed in details about the components of PV systems. In this chapter, we will discuss the PV system as a whole and design of a solar PV system.

In PV systems, several components are connected together to provide reliable power to the load.

10.1
Types of Solar PV Systems

There are many ways in which PV modules and loads can be connected together in PV systems. The type of connection depends on the type of load, the availability of grid and other power generator, etc. The solar PV (SPV) systems can broadly be divided in three categories, as given below:

1. Standalone SPV system
2. Grid-connected SPV system
3. Hybrid SPV system.

In this section, we will discuss the system configuration of three types of systems mentioned above.

10.1.1
Standalone SPV System

There are many locations in India where electricity grid is not available. In this case, if we need to design a power system, solar PV modules will be only source of the power supply. This type of SPV systems are known as standalone PV systems. They do not depend on grid or any other electric power supply. That is why they are also called off-grid PV systems. In the standalone PV systems, if the load needs to be operated in the nighttime, there has to be some means of energy storage. Therefore, batteries are an important part of standalone systems. But, if the load needs to be operated during the daytime only, like solar water pumping, then the use of battery can be avoided.

The standalone solar PV systems are suitable for small electrical loads located at the remote places where Grid supply is not present. Some of the examples of standalone PV systems are solar lanterns, solar home lighting systems, solar water pumping systems, etc.

Standalone solar PV systems are one where the only source of power is solar PV modules.

Even in the standalone PV system, there are different ways to configure the systems depending on the type of load and control circuitry. Based on these, the standalone solar PV system can be categorized in the following ways:

- SPV system with only DC load
- SPV system with DC load and Electronics control circuitry
- SPV system with DC load, Electronics control circuitry and Battery
- SPV system with AC/DC load, Electronics control circuitry and Battery.

SPV system with only DC load

This type of PV system configuration is the simplest of all SPV system configurations. This type of system configuration is used when the load is operated during the daytime only. In this system, there are only two components; first is SPV modules or array of modules and the second component is the load itself. This type of system is shown in Figure 10.1. Since the load is DC and PV modules also generate DC power, in this configuration, the load is directly connected to the SPV modules or array of modules. This system is designed for operating during sunshine hours only. As the sunshine varies throughout the day, the electricity generated will also vary. Therefore, this type of system configuration is chosen when the precise operation of the load is not required. For example, the use of solar water pumps to lift water for drinking application or irrigation. In this case of solar water pumping, it is not required to pump fix amount of water every hour. Variation in pumped water per hour due to variation in solar radiation intensity is acceptable. Another example is running of DC fan directly using solar PV modules; this will be acceptable solution when the operation of DC only daytime is required and the constant speed of the fan throughout the day is not required.

In this system configuration, there is no control circuitry for optimal utilization of the power generated by SPV module/array, therefore, this system is also called unregulated system. This system is mostly suited for operating direct DC loads in which the rate of generation of electricity is not so critical.

A DC load directly connected to solar PV modules is simplest possible PV system.

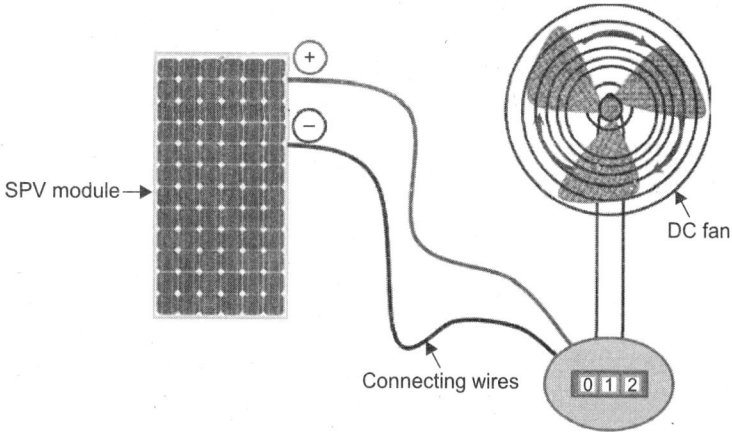

FIGURE 10.1

Simple SPV system with DC load only.

SPV system with DC load and electronics control circuitry

This type of SPV system configuration is similar to the previous system configuration but the only difference is the use of control circuitry is added to improve the utilization of the power generated by SPV module/array. This control circuitry can be electronic solar charge controller (SCC) (voltage or current regulator) or a maximum power point tracker (MPPT), etc. A charge controller (between solar PV modules and DC load) may regulate the voltage or current supplied from the PV module to the DC load and hence it can regulate the function of the load. The MPPT circuit is used to extract maximum power from the PV modules under all conditions. Thus, the use of MPPT in this system configuration will ensure the best utilization of PV modules. As shown in Figure 10.2, the control circuit is added between the PV modules and the DC load.

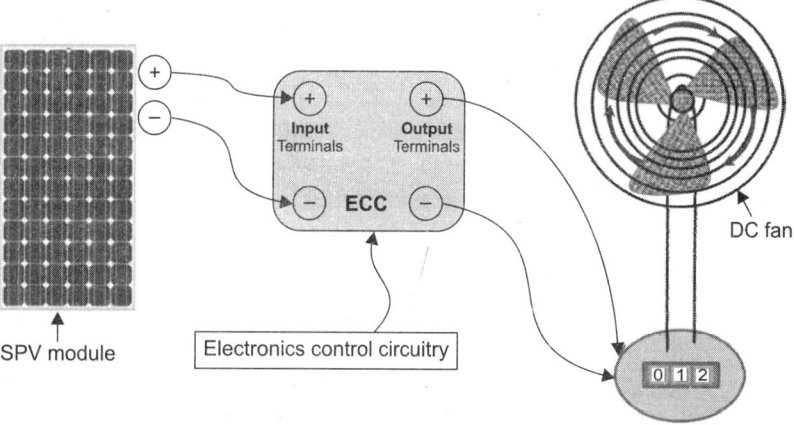

FIGURE 10.2

SPV system with DC load and control circuitry.

The control circuit is inserted for smooth operation of the load and/or to ensure the maximum utilization of the PV panel. In this configuration, the PV system cost will be higher due to extra cost of the additional component but the extra cost should be balanced with the increase in the system performance. This type of system configuration is suitable for operating a daytime DC load where the precise function of the load is not required like DC fan or DC pump, etc. as shown in Figure 10.2.

SPV system with DC load, electronics control circuitry and battery

In most situations, we need to run the load during the non-sunshine hours. Therefore, in the PV system configuration, a battery is added to store the energy for the night applications. This SPV system has four main components which includes; SPV module/array, electronics control circuitry, battery/batteries and DC load as shown in Figure 10.3.

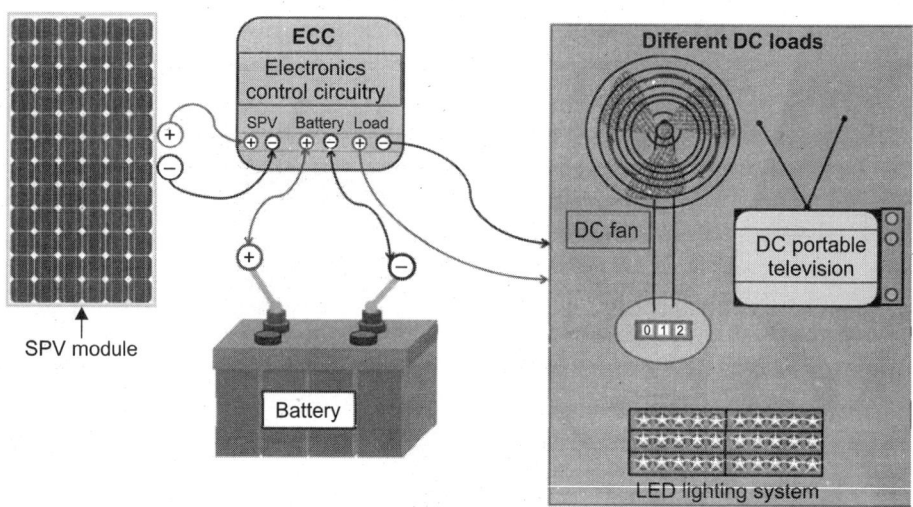

FIGURE 10.3

SPV system with DC load, electronic control circuitry and battery.

In this type of PV system configurations, batteries store the energy during the daytime. The energy generated by the PV modules is used to charge the batteries. The energy stored in the batteries is used to drive the load during the daytime as well as during the night-time. The control circuit controls the flow of charges into the battery and out of the battery. The control circuit protects the battery from overcharging and overdischarging.

This system can be used for operating direct DC loads like DC television, LED lighting system (e.g. home lighting, street lights), etc. The LED lamps work on the DC power. The LED lamps for lighting of offices and homes are now becoming common applications. Moreover, the LED based solar lanterns are also been used widely and available in various shapes, sizes and cost.

SPV system with AC/DC load, electronics control circuitry and battery

The solar PV modules generate power in the DC form and the batteries store the energy in the DC form, therefore, it is easy to operate DC loads in the solar PV systems. But most of the loads around us use AC power. Therefore, we need to make a PV system configuration which can supply power to AC loads as well. In order to do this, an additional system component which converts DC power into AC power is added in the PV system configuration. This component is called inverter. Also, the batteries are used for energy storage device which provides output in DC form. Therefore, in this type of PV system configuration, both AC and DC loads can be operated. The various components, used in this SPV system are; SPV module/arrays, electronics control circuitry, battery/batteries, inverter, AC and DC loads as shown in Figure 10.4. In many cases, DC load may not be connected in the system.

Inverter in the PV system is used to convert DC power into AC power. Most of the loads around us use AC power for their operation.

This system is a universal system in which any type of AC or DC load can be operated. This type of PV system configuration is the most commonly used as standalone PV system. All kinds of load like fan, computer, TV, tubelights, CFL, LED lamps etc. can be operated using this type of system configuration. This system can be suitable for remote locations where there is no grid connectivity. This system configuration is also useful in areas where grid electricity is available only for shorttime. In this case, the solar PV system will be an additional source of electricity.

A standalone SPV system with battery storage and capacity to operate both AC and DC loads is most commonly used PV system.

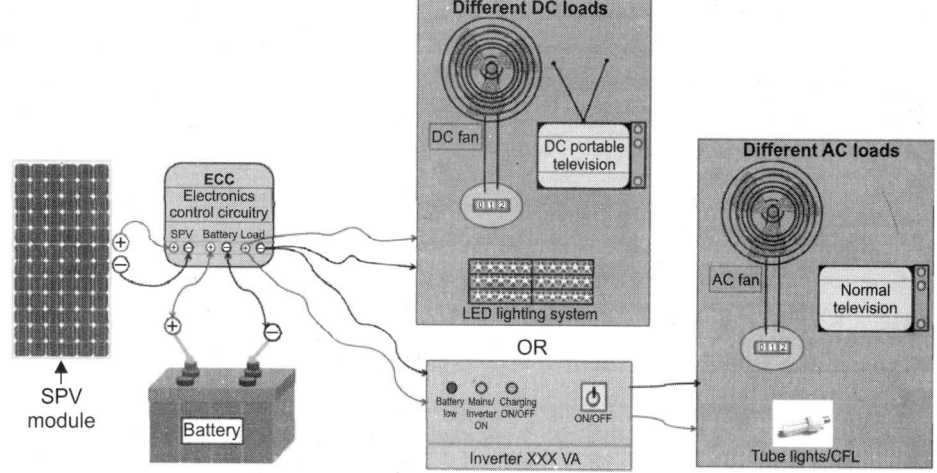

FIGURE 10.4

SPV system with electronics control circuitry, battery, inverter, AC/DC loads.

10.1.2
Grid-connected SPV System

One may be seeing electricity grid everyday. Grid is a network of the transmission lines or wires from various power plants to our homes and industries. The function of these wires is to transfer electricity from power plants to our homes. The whole country is connected with the grid. Using the grid, the power generated at one place can be transferred to any other places and can be used. For example, if power is generated in Gujrat, then using the grid, it can be transferred to Madhya Pradesh and can be utilized in Madhya Pradesh. The network of the grid in the form of wires is hundreds of kilometre long.

The existing electricity grid can also be used for transferring the power generated by a large solar PV power plants. The solar PV plants are normally of more than 1 MW capacity. In the grid connected solar PV systems, the power generated by the solar PV modules is feed into the existing electricity grid and that is why they are called grid connected SPV systems. The function of large solar PV power plants is to generate electricity and supply it to the grid whenever there is sunlight. The solar PV power plants do not consume power and they do not need power during the night hours. Therefore, in the grid connected solar PV plants, the storage of energy in the form of battery is not required. However, in many countries, the small capacity (1 to 5 kW) solar PV systems installed for household usage can also be connected with the grid. When the PV systems at houses are connected with the grid, the systems use grid as energy storage medium. When more electricity than required by the household is generated, the extra electricity is transferred to the grid, and when load needs more electricity than the electricity produced by the PV modules, the electricity is taken from the grid. In this type of grid-connected household PV system, no battery storage is required. In very rare grid-connected PV systems, people use battery for storing energy.

The configuration of grid connected SPV system is different from the off-grid or standalone solar PV system. There are two main components in the grid connected PV system, a solar PV module and a solar inverter. Among these, the solar inverter is the most important component which converts DC power generated by PV modules into AC power and feeds into the grid at desired voltage and frequency.

Based on the use of battery or no battery in the grid-connected systems, they can be divided in two categories:

1. Grid-connected SPV system without battery storage
2. Grid-connected SPV system with battery storage.

Grid connected SPV system without battery storage

Grid connected SPV system contains only three components; SPV array, Grid tied inverter, and the grid in which this system is connected as shown in Figure 10.5. This type of system configuration is used for large capacity solar PV plants. The electricity generated by the PV system is needed to be feed to the grid. Therefore, the voltage and frequency of the PV system generated electricity should be same as that of the grid voltage and frequency. Normally, Indian grid works on 50 Hz frequency, therefore, the output of the grid connected solar inverter should also be 50 Hz. The voltage level of the grid can be different, depending on the point where the electricity is being fed to the grid. The voltage level could be 230 V, 440 V, 11 kV, 33 kV etc.

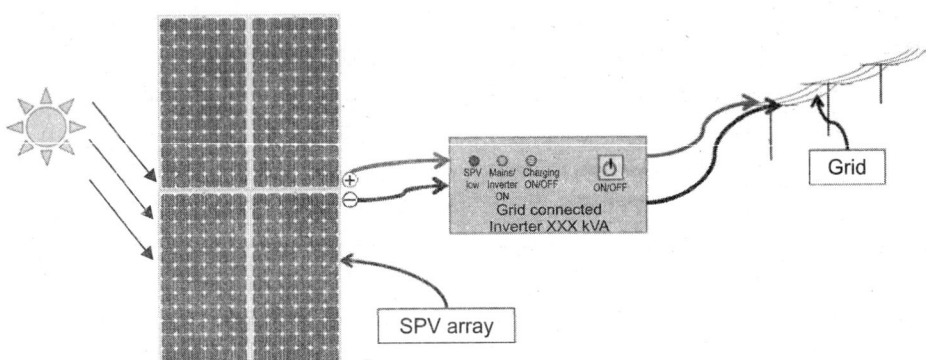

FIGURE 10.5

Grid connected SPV system without battery.

The grid connected inverter also has electronic control circuitry which regulates the generated electricity with the help of solar charge controller (SCC), Maximum Power Point Tracking (MPPT), etc. (as studied in previous chapters). The function of the electronic control circuit is to maintain the voltage and frequency as desired. In this type of PV systems configuration, no energy storage is used because the main function of such systems is to generate power when the sun shines. The PV plants themselves do not consume power and, therefore, no energy storage for non-sunshine hours is required.

PV system configuration of a grid connected system is used for large PV power plants. Using the grid, the power can be transferred to long distances.

Grid connected SPV system with battery storage

In this type of PV system configuration, an energy storage component is added in the systems. An example of such system is shown in Figure 10.6.

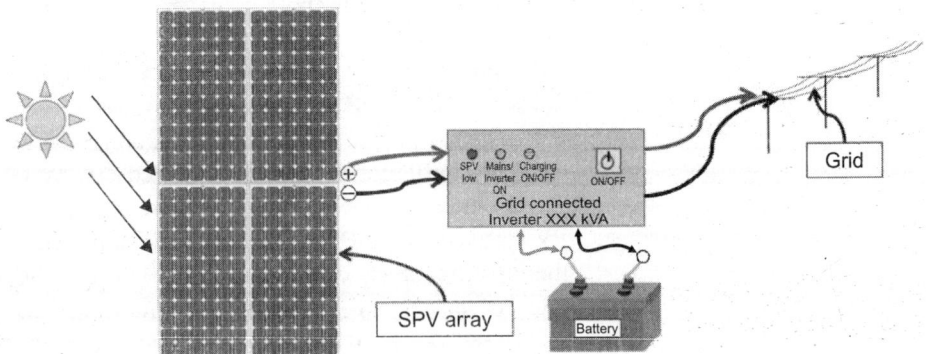

FIGURE 10.6

Grid connected SPV system with battery.

The addition of energy storage elements depends on the operation of the load, whether it has to be operated only during the day or even at night-time or 24 hours. This type of PV system configuration is used in telecom towers or hospitals where the running of load for 24 hours is critical. The energy is stored in the battery to supply the electricity when grid electricity is not available.

10.1.3
Hybrid SPV System

The PV modules generate power when sunlight is falling on it. The solar PV system can generate power during the daytime only. During the night, since the sun does not shine, the SPV system cannot generate power. In order to fulfill the load requirement during night, one option is to use battery bank for energy storage. The use of battery bank not only increases the cost of system significantly, but it also reduces the reliability because the battery bank requires maintenance. Another option is to supply power to the load during non-sunshine hours to use another power generating unit. The other power generating unit could be diesel generator, wind mill, fuel cell, etc. In this way, a system will have two power generating units; one is solar PV modules and other could be any other power generating unit. There can be more than two power generating units connected to a system. For example, PV modules, wind turbine and diesel generator. These types of system configuration where multiple power generating units are connected in a system is called Hybrid SPV system. The use of multiple power generating unit ensures that the power is supplied to the load whenever it is demanded. In this way, the hybrid systems are basically used to increase the reliability of load operation.

SPV-diesel generator hybrid system

In this system, there are two power generating sources; one is SPV and other is a diesel generator as shown in Figure 10.7. The switching of power source is controlled with the help of Electronic Control Circuitry (ECC). In this case, a diesel generator generates the power in the AC waveform but it requires to be regulated in order to supply to load. The function of power regulation is done by ECC. When solar PV modules generate power, the ECC connects the load to SPV and in the absence of sunlight, the ECC connects the load to the diesel generator. In this system, both AC and DC loads can be operated.

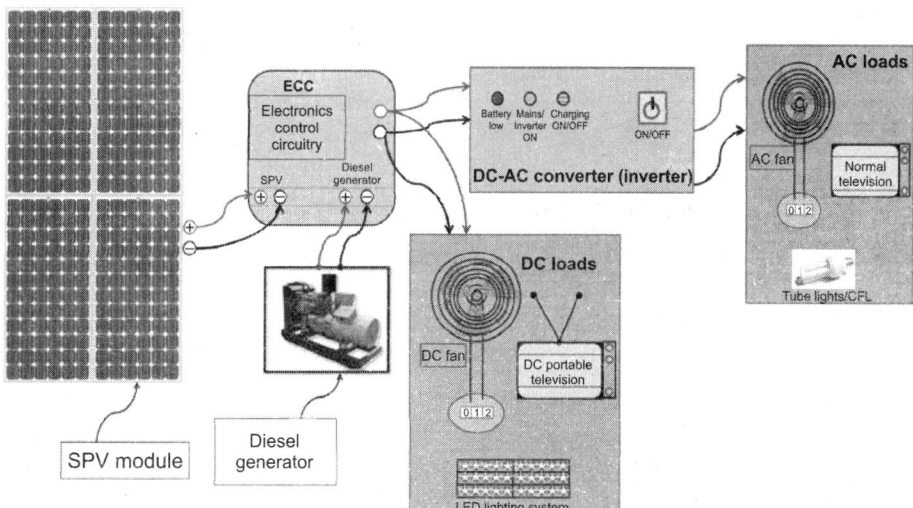

FIGURE 10.7
SPV-diesel generator hybrid system.

Solar PV-diesel hybrid system use two power generating units; PV module and diesel generator which increases the reliability of the system.

SPV-wind hybrid system

In this system, there are two power generating sources; one is SPV and other is a wind turbine as shown in Figure 10.8. The connection of power sources to the load is controlled by Electronic Control Circuitry (ECC). In this case, since both PV power and wind power is fluctuating in nature, some battery back-up may be used in this type of system configuration.

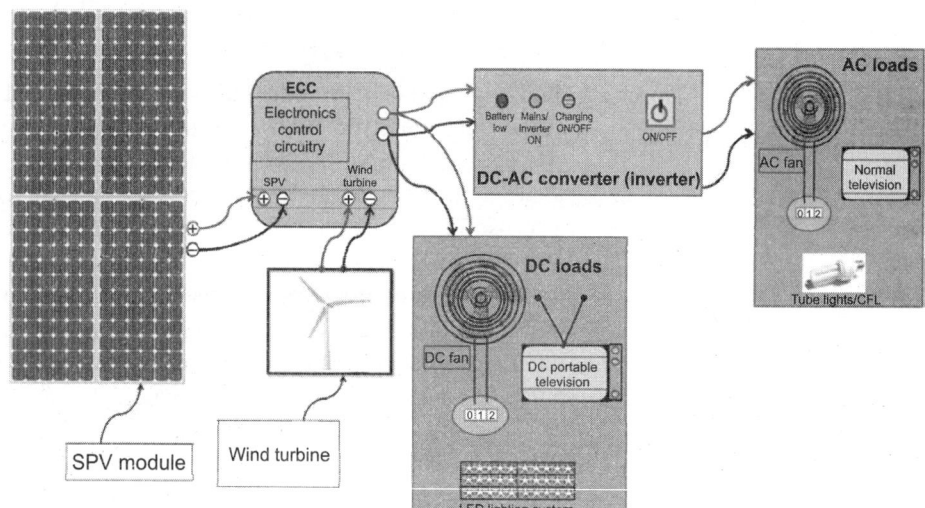

FIGURE 10.8
SPV-wind turbine hybrid system.

10.2

Design Methodology for SPV System

In this section, we will learn how to design a solar PV system to meet the requirement of a given household. Each household has different sets of equipments, so, the pattern of usage is different and, therefore, each house has different requirements of electricity. We, as a designer and installer of solar PV system should take care of varying requirements, should understand them well and then should try to design solar PV systems. In this way, each solar PV system is custom designed to meet the requirement of our customer. So far in the previous Chapter, we have learned enough about all the components that are used in solar PV system. Therefore, it should be easy for us to use appropriate component in solar PV systems to ensure that reliable electricity of required amount is supplied to the customer.

The design of a solar PV system is about determining the number and ratings of components used in solar PV system to supply reliable electricity to the load when required.

Let us now look at the design of a solar PV system. What is the meaning of PV system design? The design of a SPV system is calculated the values of different components required to make the complete PV system (like SPV modules, battery, charge controller, etc.) which is capable of supplying electricity to the connected load as required. The design first requires the estimation of the amount of electricity required by the load and then the design involves the determination of capacity and size of various components to be used in PV system. A solar PV system design requires a lot of information beforehand, before starting the design. The information include the location of installation, amount of sunlight available, number of loads to be connected, number of hours of usage for each load, available components in the market and their ratings, temperature of location, etc. Since many parameters come into play in the design of solar PV systems, most of the time it is acceptable to do which is called 'approximate design'. In this case, the designed system will not be 100% correct but it serves the purpose. The approximate design is useful when your system size is not too large, i.e., it is within few kW range or smaller. But if our system size is going to be in several 10s of kW or 100s of kW, then it is advisable to do more 'precise design'. In the precise design, all the parameters that affect the performance of the PV system are taken into account. The design of a solar PV system can be categorized in the following two ways:

1. Approximate design
2. Precise design

10.2.1
Approximate Design of Standalone System

For small PV systems, the approximate design methodology is commonly used. In approximate design, some simple assumptions are made due to which the numbers of parameters considered in the design are less and, therefore, design is simple and hence approximate. As compared to the precise design parameters, such as exact amount of solar radiation, temperature variation at location, the variation of loads according to season are not considered.

In this section, we will mainly focus on the design of a standalone PV system which consists of solar PV modules, batteries, inverter, charge controller and loads.

Most of the PV applications require the operation of the load during the non-sunshine hours and smooth operation of the load during sunshine hours irrespective of the variation in radiation intensity. This necessitates the use of battery in a standalone PV system. Whenever a battery is used, a charge controller is also used to ensure long battery life. Most of the loads are of AC types, which require an inverter to be used in the system to convert DC into AC. An MPPT circuit can also be used in the system to optimize the PV source utilization. A generic configuration of this type of system is shown in Figure 10.9(a). In the block diagram, shown in Figure 10.9 (a), MPPT control electronics, charge controller and the inverter circuit are put together in the same box, termed 'electronic control and power electronic circuit' and the battery is shown to interact with the PV panel and the load through this block.

In approximate design, assumption are made and some parameters like the effect of temperature and radiation is neglected to make PV system design simple.

Energy flow diagram and design flow

In the standalone PV system, energy is generated by solar PV modules. It is stored in batteries and then supplied to the load when required. Therefore, the flow of energy is from module to battery and then to load. The energy flow path of this configuration is shown in Figure 10.9 (b). The energy flow diagram is useful in designing the solar PV system. It is shown that during the sunshine hours energy flows from the PV source to the battery through electronic circuitry (mainly through the power converter units like MPPT and charge controller which is controlled by electronic circuits). When the load is operating, the energy flows from the battery to the load through the electronic circuitry (mainly charge controller, and through inverter in the case of AC loads). Overall energy flows from the PV panel to the load through the power converters and the battery.

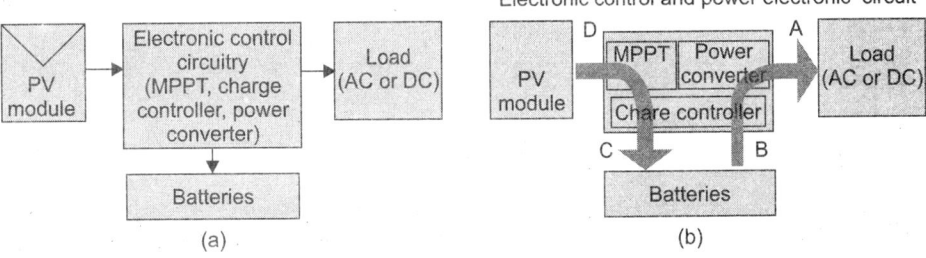

FIGURE 10.9

(a) Configuration of a PV system in which battery is used for energy storage together with required electronic control circuitry, (b) Energy flow diagram of a PV system used for system design.

The system design proceeds in the reverse direction than that of energy flow. Thus, first the loads and their requirements (power, hours of operation, energy requirement, etc.) are identified and then sizing is done. It is then followed by the battery sizing, power converter sizing, charge controller and MPPT circuit design followed by the PV panel sizing.

The design of a standalone PV system proceeds in the reverse direction of the energy flow.

The approximate design of solar PV systems can be done in the following design steps:

Step 1: Determine the connected load and their energy estimation (watts, and Wh).

Step 2: Determine the size and choice of electronics components (their power rating, voltage and current at input and output of the electronics).

Step 3: Determine the battery size (their number, capacity, voltage and Ah ratings).

Step 4: Determine the PV module size (their number, power rating, voltage and current ratings).

Step 5: Determine the size of wires (in mm), fuse (A), Junction box (V, A) sizing, etc.

Let us now begin learning the design of solar PV system by considering steps in the design one by one.

Step1: Load estimation

The load refers to any appliance that needs to be powered by the PV system. In this step, one needs to estimate how much energy is required for the operation of the load. Energy consumed by a load in a given day is obtained by simply multiplying its power rating by the number of hours of operation. Thus, the unit of energy would be watthour or watt-hr or simply Wh. If there are more loads of the same type, then total energy consumed by each type of load is obtained by multiplying **Wh** by the number of loads of given type. Normally, the tables are prepared for the estimating the energy requirement for each load. Tables are created for both AC and DC types of load. Normally, in our households, only AC types of loads are being used. But these days, with the increase in application of LED lamps (which is a DC load), DC loads are also being used.

 WORKSHEET 10.1: Example Table 10.1 to be filled for estimation of energy.

TABLE 10.1 Estimation of Energy

Column numbers						
1	2	3	4	5 = (3 × 4)	6	7 = (5 × 6)
S. No	Name of appliance	watts (W)	No. (#)	Total watts (W × No.) (W)	No. of hours (n)	Energy = (Total watts × No. of hours) (Wh)
1						
2						
3						
4						
				Total power =		Total energy =

How to fill energy estimation table?

A table has following 7 columns to fill:

- The first one is serial number.
- Second one is the name of appliance which should be filled with the name of appliances to be used, for example, Fan, TV, CFL, etc.
- Third column should be filled with the individual wattage of the appliance listed in column 2. The wattage of each appliance is written on the appliance or on its cover. Normally, the wattage rating will vary between 5 to 1000 watt.

- Fourth column is for listing the total number of same appliances of the same type. Thus, if a household is using 3 CFL of 12 watt each, then in front of power rating, you will put 3. Same has to be done with all type of appliances used in a particular case.

- Fifth column is for estimating total wattage of all components of the same type. So, if there are three CFL of 12 watt each, then the total power of CFL is 12 × 3 = 36 watt. You need to do this for all type of appliances. Total power of all the appliances connected in the household can be estimated by adding all the values of the column 5 at the bottom of the table.

- Sixth column is for total number of hours for which that appliance will be operating in a day. The number of hours of operation can be averaged if there are more appliances of same type operate for different hours per day.

- Seventh column is for estimating the energy required for the each appliance. Energy consumed by a load in a given day is obtained by simply multiplying its power rating (watt) by the number of hours (h) of operation, i.e., the number in column 5 has to be multiplied by the number in column 6. The product of multiplication that is the energy in Wh is to be noted in column 7. In order to find out the total energy consumed by the household, all the values of column 7 has to be added at the bottom of the table.

In the above calculation, the hours of usage in the table is given on per day basis, therefore, the energy consumed by the appliances is also on per day basis. Also, at the end of the table, the total energy consumed by all the appliances in the household is also on per day basis. The estimation of monthly energy estimation can be obtained by multiplying daily energy consumption by the number of days in that particular month.

An example of a household for the estimation of energy consumed by its AC loads is given in Table 10.2.

TABLE 10.2 Example of Estimation of Daily Energy Consumed by AC Loads of a Household

Column numbers						
1	2	3	4	5 = (3 × 4)	6	7 = (5 × 6)
S. No	Name of appliance	watts (W)	No. (#)	Total watts (W × No.) (W)	No. of hours (n)	Energy = (Total watts × No. of hours) (Wh)
1	Fan	100	1	100 (100 × 1)	6	600 (100 × 6)
2	Tubelight	50	2	100 (50 × 2)	8	800 (100 × 8)
3	CFL	18	5	90 (18 × 5)	5	450 (90 × 5)
4	LCD TV	80	1	80 (80 × 1)	5	400 (80 × 5)
				Total wattage = 370 W (100 + 100 + 90 + 80)		Total energy = 2250 Wh (600 + 800 + 450 + 400)

This table gives total wattage of the load connected in a given household and total daily energy consumed by all alliances in that household.

Similar to the energy estimation for the AC loads, daily energy estimation of the DC loads can be estimated. Same table can be filled for DC loads as well. In most cases, there are no DC loads in the houses. In that case, the total energy consumed by the DC loads will be zero. But in future, it is possible that DC loads may come in use and therefore, a separate table (Table 10.3) for DC loads is prepared.

TABLE 10.3 Example of Estimation of Daily Energy Consumed by DC Loads of a Household

				Column numbers		
1	2	3	4	5 = (3 × 4)	6	7 = (5 × 6)
S. No	Name of appliance	watts (W)	No. (#)	Total watts (W × No.) (W)	No. of hours (n)	Energy = (Total watts × No. of hours) (Wh)
1	DC fan	50	1	50 (50 × 1)	4	200 (50 × 4)
2	LED light	15	2	30 (15 × 2)	8	240 (30 × 8)
3	DC pump	1000	1	1000 (1000 × 1)	5	5000 (1000 × 5)
				Total wattage = 1080 W (50 + 30 + 1000)		Total energy = 5640 Wh (400 + 240 + 5000)

 WORKSHEET 10.2: Fill in Table 10.4 given for the estimation of daily energy consumption by all AC load connected in the household.

TABLE 10.4 Load Chart (AC)

				Column numbers		
1	2	3	4	5 = (3 × 4)	6	7 = (5 × 6)
S. No	Name of appliance	watts (W)	No. (#)	Total watts (W × No.) (W)	No. of hours (n)	Energy = (Total watts × No. of hours) (Wh)
1	Fan	60	1	___ × 1 = ___	4	___ × ___ = ___
2	Tubelight	35	–	35 × 2 = ___	8	___ × ___ = ___
3	Computer	400	1	400 × ___ = ___	5	___ × ___ = ___
				Total wattage = ___ W (___ + ___ + ___)		Total energy = ___ Wh (___ + ___ + ___)

Problem 10.1: . A household has 3 CFL lamp of 12 watt each used for 6 hours per day, and a fan of 50 watt used for 10 hours per day. Estimate the total daily energy consumed by the households. All the loads use AC power.

Problem 10.2: A household has only DC loads. There are 5 LED lamps of 5 watt each and two DC fans of 30 watt each. There is also a TV that works on DC power and consumes 80 watt. All loads are operated for two hours per day. Estimate the total energy consumed in a day by all the loads.

Step 2: Sizing and choice of electronics components (volts and amperes)

After estimating the energy requirement of the load, the next step is to choose appropriate electronics suitable for this PV system. The Electronic components include an Inverter (DC-AC converter), DC-DC converter (for higher or lower DC voltages) and MPPT/charge controllers (for optimal generation of electricity). The determination of capacity of these components depends on the total voltage and current of the loads. In the case of inverter, the capacity of inverter is given in terms of voltage × current or VA. The capacity of the inverter depends on the total wattage of the load and inverter efficiency. Inverter efficiency is output power capacity (watt) divided by input power capacity (watt).

Inverter selection: The inverter should be selected in such a way that it should supply the desired power to the load. The desired power for the load is the total power (see Table 10.2) of connected to the load. The total connected power of the load is equal to the desired output power of the inverter. In practice, it is good to choose an inverter having power capacity higher than the total connected load.

Once knowing the output power of the inverter we need to know what power must be supplied to the inverter. By considering the efficiency of the inverter, one can estimate the required input power to the inverter. Relationship between output power, input power and efficiency of inverter is shown in Figure 10.10.

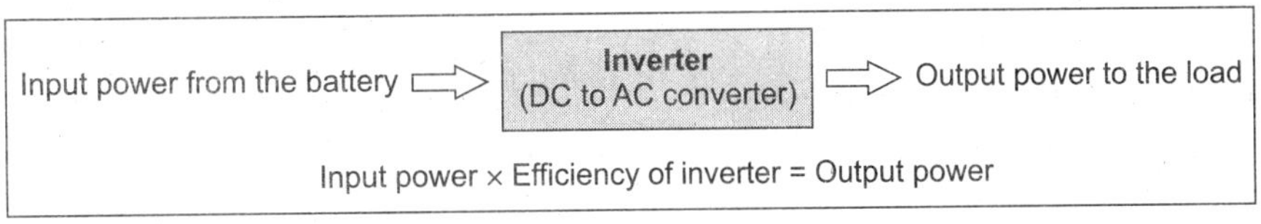

Input power from the battery ⇒	**Inverter** (DC to AC converter)	⇒ Output power to the load
	Input power × Efficiency of inverter = Output power	

FIGURE 10.10

Relationship between output power, input power and efficiency of inverter.

The desired output power of the inverter is equal to the total power of connected load. In practice, inverter of higher power capacity than the power of total connected load is chosen.

$$\text{Efficiency} = \frac{\text{Output power}}{\text{Input power}} \times 100$$

$$\text{Input power} = \frac{\text{Output power}}{\text{Efficiency}} \times 100$$

Here, three parameters are given. The only parameter to estimate here will be input power capacity of inverter.

Let us consider the example of the household given in Table 10.2 for which we need to determine the appropriate inverter now. The output power capacity of the inverter will be equal to the total wattage of the AC loads that needs to be powered (see Table 10.2). Consider a load and energy estimation chart for AC loads given in Table 10.2. In that table, the total wattage for all appliances is calculated as 370 watts. This value should be equal to output power capacity of the inverter. Consider, inverter efficiency equal to 93%. In this case, calculation will be as follows (Table 10.5):

TABLE 10.5 Estimation of Required Input Power to the Inverter for a Given Connected Load

Load	Inverter capacity		
	Inverter		
Total wattage of load (W)	Output (W)	Efficiency (%)	Input (VA) (output (W) × 100) ÷ Efficiency
370	370	93	(370 × 100) ÷ 93 = 37000 ÷ 93 = 397.84 VA ≈ 400 VA

We have done calculation of input power (Table 10.5) that must be fed into the inverter. Similarly, we can do the calculation of input energy that must be fed into the inverter to get sufficient energy output to meet the demand of the load. Both input power and input energy for the inverter are higher than the output power and energy due to efficiency losses of the inverter. An example of the estimation of required input energy at the inverter input is given in Table 10.6.

TABLE 10.6 Estimation of Required Input Energy to the Inverter for a Given Energy Consumption of All the Loads

Total energy (Wh)	Efficiency (%)	Total Energy (Wh)
2250	93	2250 × (100/93) ≈ 2420

Matching the calculated inverter capacity with the available in the market: An inverter takes DC input power and converts it into AC output power. Once we estimate the size or power capacity of the inverter we need to see what is available in the market. A choice of inverter is important as the available inverter will decide what input DC voltages it can take at input side. For example, if available inverter which matches the estimated power rating can take only 'X' volt as input voltage, then all our other system design should be done for 'X' volt.

For this example, our estimated power rating of inverter is 400 VA. The standard value of inverter available in market is 400 VA with 12 volts DC input and 230 V AC output. Because the inverter input can take only 12 V DC, therefore, we have to fix the rest of the system (battery and PV module) voltage to 12 V (For SPV system with inverter, the system voltage mainly depends on the DC input voltage of the inverter).

High DC voltage means less current: Normally, it is good to choose an inverter which can take high input DC voltage. High voltage will require less current in the system for the same power flow. Power is the product of current and voltage (power = voltage × current). Thus, for the same power flow, if voltage increases, current decreases. Lower current flow in the system has many advantages. Less current means less power loss and thinner wires, this also means less cost of the system.

In this example of standalone system design the estimated power rating of the inverter is 400 VA. For the same inverter power rating, there can be different DC input voltages and corresponding different current flow in the system. Consider three cases with system voltages of 12, 24, 48 volts (assuming inverter input can take these DC voltages) and corresponding estimated current flow in the system, as given in Table 10.7.

TABLE 10.7 Estimate of Current in the PV System for Different DC Voltages of the System (Power = Voltage × Current is Used in this Table)

Total system wattage (VA)	System voltage (V)	System current (A)
400	12	400 ÷ 12 ≈ 34 A
400	24	400 ÷ 24 ≈ 17 A
400	48	400 ÷ 48 ≈ 9 A

It can clearly be seen from Table 10.3 that as the system DC voltage or inverter input DC voltage increases the current flow in the system decreases. Also, the lower DC current in the system has many advantages, therefore, if it is possible we should try to choose higher system voltages. However, we see later that higher system voltage requires more number of batteries. This is one of the limitations.

It is good to choose an inverter with higher DC input voltage, for less current and less power losses in the circuit. If possible, we should choose higher system DC voltage.

 WORKSHEET 10.3: Estimate of current in the PV system for different DC voltages of the system. Use the power rating of system or inverter as 1000 VA. Fill in the blanks in Table 10.8.

TABLE 10.8 Estimate Current for Different DC Voltages

Total system wattage (VA)	System voltage (V)	System Current (A)
_____ W	12	_____ ÷ 12 = _____ A
_____ W	24	_____ ÷ 24 = _____ A
_____ W	48	_____ ÷ 48 = _____ A

WORKSHEET 10.4: A solar inverter needs to be selected to supply the AC power to total load of 500 watt. Fill in the blanks in Table 10.9.

TABLE 10.9 To Obtain Missing Quantities

Load	Inverter		
Total wattage of load (W)	Output power (W)	Efficiency (%)	Input (VA) = (output (W) × 100) ÷ Efficiency
_____ W	_____ W	90	(_____ × 100) ÷ 90 = _____ VA ≈ _____ VA

 WORKSHEET 10.5: A solar inverter is chosen to supply energy of 2000 Wh per day to the connected load in a household. How much energy must be supplied at the input side of the inverter? Fill in the blanks in Table 10.10.

TABLE 10.10 Estimation of Energy

Total energy (Wh)	Efficiency (%)	Total energy (Wh)
_____ W	90	_____ × 100 ÷ 90 = _____ W

DC-DC converter selection: If there are DC loads in the system, then we may require different voltage levels of DC voltage. This is because various DC load may requires different DC voltages for proper functioning. The function of converting one DC voltage level to other DC voltage level is obtained by using DC to DC converters. The choice of the DC to DC converter depends on the connected DC loads, particularly input voltage range of the DC appliances. For the design, first we need to list down the input voltages for each of the DC appliance that is planned to be connected to the system. An example is shown in Table 10.11.

TABLE 10.11 DC Voltage Range of Various Loads

S. No.	Name of the DC load	Input voltage (volts)
1	Fan	12
2	LED light	12
3	DC pump	24

When several different DC loads are connected in PV system, a DC to DC converter may be required to supply required DC voltage to different loads.

Now, as seen from Table 10.11, the operating voltage of the motor (pump) is 24 V and that for the fan and LED lighting is 12 V. So, choose a DC to DC converter with multiple outputs with 12 V and 24 V output. The input voltage to DC-DC converter will be the system voltage which can be 12 V or 24 V or 48 V or any other value. The high voltage is more preferable because as the system voltage increases, the current flowing in the system will decrease, hence the thickness of wire decreases ultimately the cost and wear and tear.

Solar charge controller (SCC) or MPPT selection: The solar charge controller or MPPT should be chosen as per the required input and output voltage and current of load and battery. The chosen charge controller or MPPT should be able to handle the currents and voltages that are likely to be flowing in the system. For the SPV system considered in this example, the SCC or MPPT should be chosen with output voltage and current handling capacity approximate to 12 Volts and 34 A respectively (Table 10.12). A detailed discussion about the MPPT and SCC charge controller is given in Chapter 8.

TABLE 10.12 System Specification

Energy (Wh)	Wattage (VA)	Voltage (V)	Maximum current (A)
2420	400	12	34

Step 3: Determining the batteries size (their number, capacity, voltage and Ah ratings)

The battery sizing should be done after the inverter (DC-AC) sizing for AC and DC loads after the selection of DC-DC converter. As discussed earlier, the design of PV systems proceeds in the opposite direction of energy flow. The inverter and DC to DC converters will have some losses because they will have less than 100% efficiency. Therefore, we have to choose batteries in such a way that they should not only supply the power and energy required by the load, but also be able to supply the loss of energy in inverter and/or DC to DC converters, i.e., the loss occurring at converter has to be compensated by the battery.

Please remember that in this example, the energy that needs to be supplied to the load is 2250 Wh and energy that needs to be supplied at the input of inverter is 2420 Wh. In order to supply this much energy how many batteries of what capacity are required? In order to size battery, we have to consider several other parameters of batteries as well. These parameters are as follows:

- System voltage ampere-hour (Ah) capacity of the battery
- Depth of discharge (DoD) of battery
- Number of days of autonomy

Consider system voltage and estimate Ah capacity: In this example, we need to supply 2420 Wh energy to the input of the inverter and system voltage chosen is 12 V. Therefore, in order to find out Ah capacity to be supplied, we need to divide energy by voltage as:

$$\text{Energy} = W \times h = V \times I \times H$$

Therefore,

$$Ah = \frac{Wh}{V} = \frac{V \times I \times h}{V} = Ah$$

For this example, the Ah capacity to be supplied to the inverter is estimated in Table 10.13.

TABLE 10.13 Estimation of Ah Capacity

Energy (Wh)	System voltage (V)	Ah capacity to be supplied
2420	12	2420 ÷ 12 = 201.66 Ah

WORKSHEET 10.6: Fill in the blanks in Table 10.14 for estimating Ah that needs to be supplied to the inverter input. Total energy supplied to the inverter and system voltage is given in Table 10.14.

TABLE 10.14 To Obtain Ah Capacity

Energy (Wh)	System voltage (V)	Ah capacity to be supplied
5640	24	____ ÷ ____ = ____ Ah

Considering the DoD of batteries: The DoD of batteries indicates how much of the total charge of the battery can be used. If the DoD is 50%, means only 50% of the total charge stored in the battery can be used. In solar PV, normally the deep discharge batteries are used with DoD in the range of 50% to 60%. Due to this fact, that is, DoD is not 100%, the actual battery Ah capacity required to supply the required energy to the inverter will be higher as compared to estimated 201.66 Ah. The estimation of the Ah capacity is given in Table 10.15.

TABLE 10.15 An Example of Estimating the Usable Charge or Ah Capacity of Battery if the DoD of Battery is Given

Required capacity (Ah)	DoD (%)	Actual capacity (Ah)
2420 ÷ 12 = 201.66 Ah	50	201.66 ÷ 0.5 = 403.32

Consider number of days of autonomy: The batteries in standalone PV systems store energy to supply the power to the load during non-sunshine hours. In situations like rainy season, it is possible that the sunlight is not available for several days. In this case, during the cloudy days, if we still want to supply the power to the load, we should store more energy in the batteries. The number of cloudy days for which we want to store the energy is referred as 'number of days of autonomy'. This means that whatever estimation we have after considering the DoD, we need to increase the capacity of the batteries to store extra energy for the number of days of autonomy. Therefore, if we want to store energy for one extra day, then our battery capacity should be double (one capacity for today and one for extra day), and if we want to store the energy for two extra days then our battery capacity should be three times (one capacity for today two times capacity for two extra days). An estimation of battery Ah capacity after considering two days autonomy is given in Table 10.16.

TABLE 10.16 Estimation of Battery Ah Capacity

Actual Ah capacity after DoD (Ah)	Number of days of autonomy	Final required battery capacity (Ah)
403.3	2	403.3 × 2 = 806.6

From Table 10.16, we can see that the total Ah capacity of the battery required is 806.6 Ah for supplying 2420 Wh energy to the input of inverter everyday. These calculations considered 12 V as system voltage, 50% DoD of batteries and 2 days of autonomy.

One line calculation for estimating battery capacity: We have seen from above discussion that DoD of battery, system voltage and the number of days of autonomy affects the estimation of Ah capacity of the battery. All the three parameters can be put together in one simple equation for the estimation of total Ah capacity of batteries required for a given standalone PV system. The equation is presented below:

$$\text{Total Ah capacity of battery} = \frac{\text{Energy input to inverter} \times \text{No. of days of autonomy}}{\text{DoD} \times \text{System voltage}}$$

In Table 10.13, the daily energy that needs to be supplied at the inverter input is 2420 Wh. We have chosen 12 V as system voltage, 50% DoD of batteries and two days of autonomy. Using these parameters and using above equation, we can do the calculations of total Ah capacity of battery required:

$$\text{Total Ah capacity of battery} = \frac{2420 \times 2}{0.50 \times 12} = 806.6 \text{ Ah}$$

This estimated total Ah capacity of batteries after considering DoD, system voltage and the number of days of autonomy is same as we estimated in step 3 (Section 10.2.1). Please note here that the capacity of the battery is dependent of system voltage. In this case we have chosen 12 V, but we can also choose 24 V depending on the availability of inverter.

Number of batteries: From the above estimation, for the example of standalone PV system considered in this case, we need to provide 806.6 Ah of batteries with terminal voltage of 12 V. Now, we have to choose appropriate batteries available in the market. Let us consider that batteries of 12 V, 150 Ah capacity. Batteries of other capacities, such as 100 Ah, 50 Ah, 200 Ah, etc. can also be considered. We are assuming that these batteries have 50% DoD.

Now, our total Ah capacity of the battery to be provided is 806.6 Ah and the battery that we are considering is 150 Ah. Therefore, the total number of batteries required are:

$$\text{Total number of batteries} = \frac{\text{Total Ah capacity required}}{\text{Ah capacity of one battery}}$$

$$\text{Total number of batteries} = \frac{806.6}{150} = 5.37 \cong 6 \text{ batteries}$$

Calculations suggest that we need to use 5.37 batteries. We can convert this in round figure that is 6. Therefore, we need to take 6 batteries of 150 Ah capacity, 12 V in this system.

Note: Here that we have taken 12 V batteries and the input voltage to the inverter is also 12 V. This means that we need to connect all the batteries in parallel. The connection of batteries is shown in Figure 10.11. In case if our chosen system voltage is 24 volt, then we need to connect two batteries together in series to get 24 volt. Also remember that it has been discussed earlier that higher system voltage is normally chosen in design to reduce the current flow in the circuit.

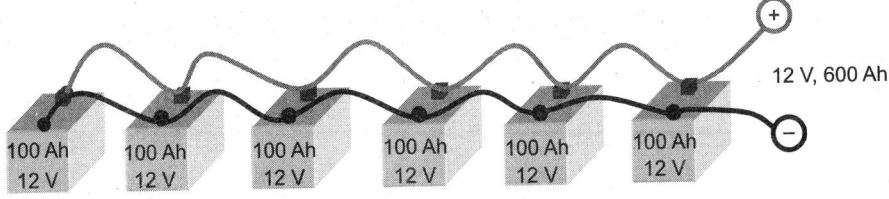

FIGURE 10.11

Six batteries connected in parallel configuration.

Step 4: Determine the PV modules size (their number, power rating, voltage and current ratings)

The SPV module must supply enough energy to the battery, so that battery can supply enough energy to the inverter, in order to supply enough energy to the load as per the need. In Table 10.13, the input energy to be supplied at the input of inverter is 2420 Wh. This energy is supplied by the Battery bank. Now, since the battery efficiency is not 100%, more energy needs to be supplied to the battery input (see Figure 10.12). The relationship between the input and output energy of the battery with its efficiency can be presented by the equation below:

$$\text{Battery efficiency} = \frac{\text{Output energy}}{\text{Input energy}} \times 100$$

$$\text{Input energy} = \frac{\text{Output energy}}{\text{Battery efficiency}} \times 100$$

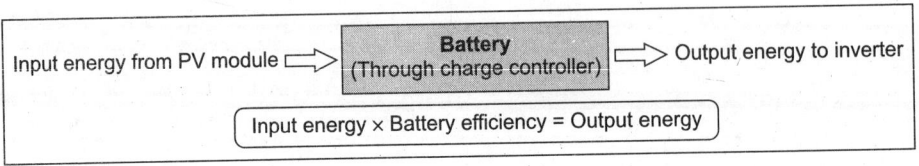

FIGURE 10.12

Relationship between input energy and output energy of the battery.

From the above expression, if we know the energy supplied by the battery to the inverter and efficiency of the battery, then we can estimate the input energy that must be supplied to the battery bank (see Figure 10.12). This input energy must be produced by PV modules on daily basis. Typically, the efficiency of the batteries is 80% to 90%. Table 10.17 shows an example calculation for the estimation of energy to be generated by PV module considering the efficiency of the batteries.

TABLE 10.17 To Estimate Daily Energy That Need to be Supplied by the PV Module

Total energy (Wh)	Battery efficiency (%)	Energy from SPV module (Wh)
2420	95	2420 ÷ 0.90 = 2688.9 ≈ 2689 Wh

From Table 10.17, we can see that for the loads considered in this example, the solar PV module should supply 2689 Wh of energy everyday. Now, we need to find out how many modules of what power rating we should connect in the system to supply the required energy everyday.

Daily solar radiation in terms of equivalent sunshine hours: At this point, in order to estimate the number of PV modules requirement, we need to know the amount of solar radiation availability at the location where PV system is being installed. The solar radiation data is available in the form of Table for several cities of India. If the solar radiation data of the given location is not available, then solar radiation data of nearby station should be considered.

Solar radiation data are given on daily basis, monthly basis or yearly basis. In this example, since we are working with daily energies, we need to consider daily solar radiation. The daily solar radiation is given in terms of $kWh/m^2/day$. Typical daily solar radiation in India varies between $4–7$ $kWh/m^2/day$. Suppose, at the location for which we are designing this system, the daily solar radiation is 5 $kWh/m^2/day$. The solar PV modules are rated for solar radiation intensity of 1000 W/m^2 or 1 kW/m^2 (Standard Test Condition or STC). Therefore, this solar radiation of 5 $kWh/m^2/day$ can be written in the following way;

$$\text{Daily solar radiation} = 5 \ kWh/m^2 \ day = 5 \ kW \times h/m^2 \times day$$

$$= 5 \ h/day \times 1 \ kW/m^2$$

$$= \text{STC power density} \times \text{Equivalent daily sunshine hours}$$

In this way, we can say that for 5 $kWh/m^2/day$, the solar radiations is equal to 5 hours of 1 kW/m^2 or the equivalent daily sunshine hours is 5.

 WORKSHEET 10.7: Fill in Table 10.18 to estimate the equivalent sunshine hours for daily solar radiation:

TABLE 10.18 Equivalent Sunshine Hours for Daily Solar Radiation

Name of location	Daily solar radiation ($kWh/m^2/day$)	Standard Test Condition (STC) power density (kW/m^2)	Equivalent daily sunshine hours (hours/day or hr/day or h/day)	Daily solar radiation = STC power density × Daily sunshine hours ($kWh/m^2/day$)
Indore	5.5	1	5.5	1 × 5.5 = 5.5
Chennai	4.5	1	–	–
Gandhinagar	7	–	7	–

Now, in this example, we are considering that the daily solar radiation of the location is 5 $kWh/m^2/day$. From the above discussion, we can estimate that the daily equivalent sunshine hours is 5 h/day.

PV module sizing: For this example, we need to supply daily energy of 2689 Wh/day. So, the unit of the term daily energy includes hour/day term. The daily energy can be written in the following way:

$$\text{Daily energy} = 2689 \, \frac{W \times h}{day} = 2689 \, \frac{W}{h \times day}$$

From the daily solar radiation, we know that for the location, the daily solar radiation is 5 h/day. Therefore, if we divide the daily energy that needs to be supplied by the PV module by the daily solar radiation, we will get the answer in watt, which is power term. This power is nothing but the required power of PV modules. The estimation of PV module power is given in Table 10.19.

TABLE 10.19 Estimation of PV Module Power Using Equivalent Daily Sunshine Hours

Daily energy to be supplied by SPV module (Wh)	Equivalent daily sunshine hours (h)	SPV module wattage (W)/Wp
2689	5.0	2689 ÷ 5.0 = 537.8 ≈ 540 watts or watt peak

Thus, from Table 10.19, we can see that the total of 540 watt peak of PV modules will be required to supply the required energy. Now, the next step is to find out what PV modules are available in the market and how many modules we do need to use and how do we need to connect them.

 WORKSHEET 10.8: Daily energy that needs to be produced by PV module at a given location is given. Fill in Table 10.20 for the estimation of solar PV module power using equivalent daily sunshine hours.

TABLE 10.20 Estimation of SPV Module Power

Daily energy to be supplied by SPV module (Wh)	Equivalent daily sunshine hours (h)	SPV module wattage (W)
_____ Wh	6.0	_____ ÷ _____ = _____ watts
5940	4.5	_____ ÷ 4.5 = _____ ≈ _____ watts

Selection of PV modules: The total PV module power required is 540 watt peak (or W_p). The PV modules of many ratings are available in the market. The PV modules rating can be 40 W_p, 60 W_p, 75 W_p, 100 W_p, 120 W_p, 200 W_p, etc. Now, let us choose a PV module of 75 W_p for this purpose. This module sizes are commonly available. In order to find out the number of PV modules we need to divide the total PV module power required by the single PV module power available in the market:

$$\text{Total number of PV modules} = \frac{\text{Total estimated module power}}{\text{Power of single module}}$$

$$\text{Total number of PV modules} = \frac{540}{75} = 7.2 \approx 8 \text{ PV modules}$$

The number of modules estimated to 7.2, which is rounded to next higher number of 8. Thus, we can see that we need total of 8 PV modules of 75 W_p power rating. The 75 W_p module will have voltage at maximum power point of about 15 V. In this example, we have chosen 12 V as system voltage, which is matching the module voltage. It means that we need to series connection of PV modules to increase the voltage; therefore, all the 8 PV modules must be connected in parallel to supply the power. Figure 10.13 shows the connection of PV modules, and Figure 10.14 shows the complete system.

FIGURE 10.13

Connection of PV modules for the example considered here.

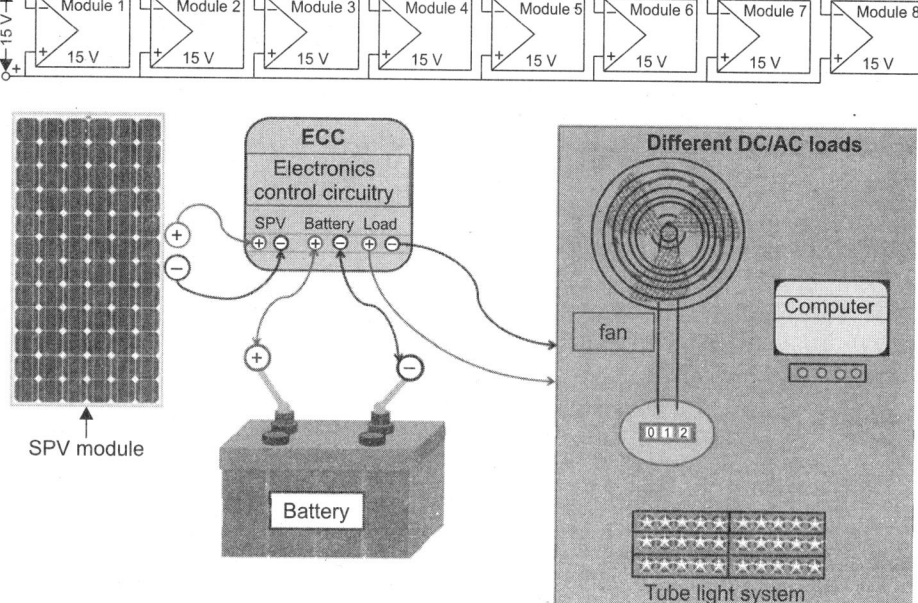

FIGURE 10.14

Overall designed standalone PV system for the load considered in the above example.

Step 5: Fuse, wire and junction box selection

Fuses, wires and junction boxes should be chosen for the maximum possible currents and voltages that are likely to occur in the system. Mainly, the parameter used for choosing these products is current. Normally, a standalone system will have DC side as well as AC side. Therefore, we need to look at the maximum voltage and current for DC and AC sides. This estimation of maximum current is useful in deciding the appropriate components, fuses, junction boxes and wires. Note that, the maximum value of current and voltages depends on the power level in the circuit. Here, various tables (Tables 10.21–10.24) are made to estimate the maximum values of voltages and current in the system based on the power level.

Calculating maximum DC system parameters like voltage and current:

TABLE 10.21 Maximum Direct Current (DC) and Voltage

System	Max DC wattage (W)	System DC voltage (V)	Max DC current (A)
1	570	12	570 ÷ 12 ≈ 48
2	___ W	___ V	___ ÷ ___ = ___
3	1320	24	1320 ÷ 24 ≈ 55

Calculating maximum AC system parameters like voltage and current:

TABLE 10.22 Maximum Alternating Current (AC) and Voltage

System	Max AC wattage (W)	System AC voltage (V)	Max AC current (A)
1	370 W	230	370 ÷ 230 = 1.61 ≈ 2
2	___ W	230	___ ÷ 230 = ___

Calculation for various electric components like switch fuse, standard wire gauge (SWG) for DC connections:

TABLE 10.23 DC Wiring, Fuse and Junction Box Selection

System	Max DC voltage (V) and current (A)	SWG	Fuse	Switch/Junction box
1	12 V, 48 A			
2	____ V, ____ A			
3	24 V, 55 A			

Calculation for various electric components like switch, fuse, standard wire gauge (SWG) for AC connections:

TABLE 10.24 AC Wiring, Fuse and Junction Box Selection

System	Max AC voltage (V) and current (A)	SWG (wire)	Fuse	Switch/Junction box
1	230 V, 2 A			
2	230 V, ____ A			

This completes the design of a complete standalone solar PV system. From the description that is presented by step by step manner, it looks a long process. But once you are in practice, the solar PV system design can be done in very short time.

EXAMPLE 10.1

Design a Solar PV system for a house which contains 3 fans of 70 watts each running for 4 hours a day, 3 tubelights of 35 watts each running for 8 hours a day and a refrigerator of 250 watts running for 6 hours a day (consider battery autonomy zero days).

Solution

Step 1 Prepare AC load chart:

S. No.	Name of appliances	watts (W)	No. (#)	Total watts (W × No.) (W)	No. of hours (n)	Energy (Total watts × No. of hours) (Wh)
1	Fans	70	3	210 (70 × 3)	4	840 (210 × 4)
2	Tubelight	35	3	105 (35 × 3)	8	840 (105 × 8)
3	Refrigerator	250	1	250 (250 × 1)	6	1500 (250 × 6)
				Total wattage = 565 W (210 + 105 + 250)		Total energy = 3180 Wh (840 + 840 + 1500)

Step 2 Electronics component selection:

(a) Inverter capacity selection

Load		Inverter		
Total wattage of load (W)	Efficiency (%)	Output (W)	Input (VA) (output (W) × 100) ÷ Efficiency	
565	93	565	(565 × 100) ÷ 93 = 56500 ÷ 93 = 607.52 VA ≈ 610 VA	

Total energy (Wh)	Efficiency (%)	Total energy (Wh)
3180	93	3180 × 100 ÷ 93 ≈ 3420

(b) Solar charge controller selection

Energy (Wh)	Wattage (W)	Voltage (V)	Maximum current (A)
3420	565	12	48

Here the system voltage is 12 volts.

Step 3 Battery sizing:

(a) Battery capacity

Energy (Wh)	System voltage (V)	Battery capacity (Ah)	DoD (%)	Actual battery capacity (Ah)
3420	12	3420 ÷ 12 ≈ 285 Ah	50	285 ÷ 0.5 = 570 Ah

Step 4 SPV sizing:

(a) Energy calculation

Total energy (Wh)	Battery efficiency (%)	Energy from SPV module (Wh)
3420	95	3420 ÷ 0.95 = 3600 Wh

(b) SPV module wattage estimation

Energy from SPV module (W)	Number of sunshine hours (h)	SPV module wattage (W)
3600	4.5	3600 ÷ 4.5 = 800 watts

Step 5 Wiring, fuse and junction box selection:

(a) Maximum direct current (DC) and voltage

System	Max DC wattage (W)	System DC voltage (V)	Max DC current (A)
1	4 × 160 = 640	12	640 ÷ 12 = 53.33 ≈ 55 A

(b) DC wiring, fuse and junction box selection

System	Max DC voltage (V) and current (A)	SWG	Fuse	Switch/Junction box
1	12 V, 45 A			

(c) Maximum alternating current (AC) and voltage

System	Max AC wattage (W)	System AC voltage (V)	Max AC current (A)
1	600 W	230	600 ÷ 230 = 2.6 ≈ 3 A

(d) AC wiring, fuse and junction box selection

System	Max DC voltage (V) and current (A)	SWG (wire)	Fuse	Switch/Junction box
1	230 V, 3 A			

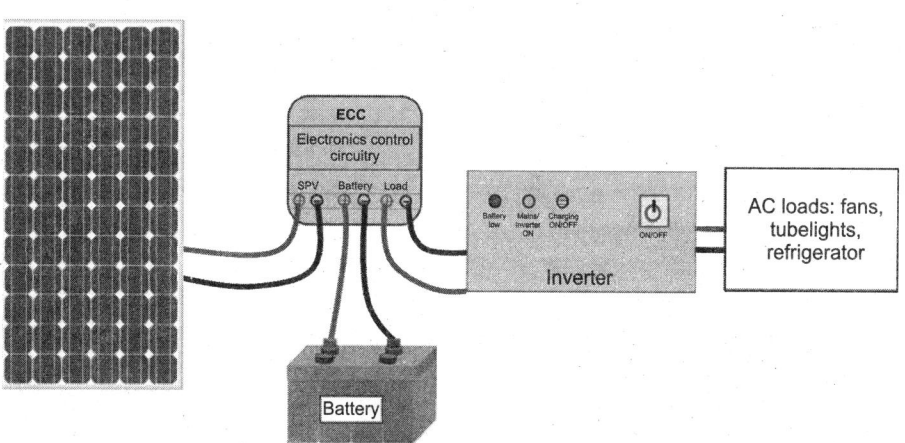

FIGURE 10.15
Overall PV system.

EXAMPLE 10.2

Design a SPV system for a factory which contains 1 hp motor (1 hp = 747 W) operating for 4 hours a day, 8 tubelights, each of 50 watts operating for 7 hours a day. Consider a 1 day autonomy for battery.

Solution

Step 1 Prepare AC load chart:

S. No.	Name of appliances	watts (W)	No. (#)	Total watts (W × No.) (W)	No. of hours (n)	Energy (Total watts × No. of hours) (Wh)
1	Motor	747	1	747 (747 × 1)	4	2988 (747 × 4)
2	Tubelight	50	8	400 (50 × 8)	7	2800 (400 × 7)
				Total wattage = 1147 W (747 + 400)		Total energy = 5788 Wh (2988 + 2800)

Step 2 Electronics component selection:

(a) Inverter capacity selection

Load	Inverter		
Total wattage of load (W)	Efficiency (%)	Output (W)	Input (VA) (Output (W) × 100) ÷ Efficiency
1147	93	1147	(1147 × 100) ÷ 93 = 114700 ÷ 93 = 1233.33 VA ≈ 1235 VA

Total energy (Wh)	Efficiency (%)	Total energy (Wh)
5788	93	5788 × 100 ÷ 93 ≈ 6225 Wh

(b) Solar charge controller selection

Energy (Wh)	Wattage (W)	Voltage (V)	Maximum current (A)
6225	1147	24	48

Here, the system voltage is 24 volts.

Step 3 Battery sizing:

(a) Battery capacity

Since one day autonomy has to be considered, so, the energy to be stored into battery will be double.

Energy (Wh)	System voltage (V)	Battery capacity (Ah)	DoD (%)	Actual battery capacity (Ah)
6225 × 2 = 12450	24	12450 ÷ 24 ≈ 520 Ah	50	520 ÷ 0.5 = 1040 Ah

Step 4 SPV sizing:

(a) Energy calculation

Total energy (Wh)	Battery efficiency (%)	Energy from SPV module (Wh)
6225*	95	6225 ÷ 0.95 = 6552.6 ≈ 6555 Wh

* The total energy to be store in battery is 12450, but the energy from module for daily charging will be 6225 Wh only.

(b) SPV module wattage estimation

Energy from SPV module (W)	Number of sunshine hours (h)	SPV module wattage (W)
6555	4.5	6555 ÷ 4.5 = 1456.6 ≈ 1460 watts

Step 5 Wiring, fuse and junction box selection:

(a) Maximum direct current (DC) and voltage

System	Max DC wattage (W)	DC system voltage (V)	Max DC current (A)
1	1460	24	1460 ÷ 24 = 60.88 ≈ 62 A

(b) DC wiring, fuse and junction box selection

System	Max DC voltage (V) and current (A)	SWG	Fuse	Switch/Junction box
1	24 V, 60 A			

(c) Maximum alternating current (AC) and voltage

System	Max AC wattage (W)	System AC voltage (V)	Max AC current (A)
1	1147 W	230	1147 ÷ 230 = 4.98 ≈ 5 A

(d) AC wiring, fuse and junction box selection

System	Max DC voltage (V) and current (A)	SWG (wire)	Fuse	Switch/junction box
1	230 V, 5 A			

EXAMPLE 10.3

Design a solar PV system for a house which contains 3 fans of 70 watts each running for 4 hours a day, 3 tubelights of 35 watts each running for 8 hours a day and a refrigerator of 250 watts running for 6 hours a day.

Solution

Step 1 Prepare AC load chart:

S. No.	Name of appliances	watts (W)	No. (#)	Total watts (W × No.) (W)	No. of hours (n)	Energy (Total watts × No. of hours) (Wh)
1	Fans	70	3	210 (70 × 3)	4	840 (210 × 4)
2	Tubelights	35	3	105 (35 × 3)	8	240 (30 × 8)
3	Refrigerator	250	1	250 (250 × 1)	6	1500 (250 × 6)
				Total wattage = 565 W (210 + 105 + 250)		Total Energy = 2580 Wh (= 210 + 240 + 1500)

Step 2 Electronics component selection:

(a) Inverter capacity selection

Load	Inverter		
Total wattage of load (W)	Efficiency (%)	Output (W)	Input (VA) (Output (W) × 100) ÷ Efficiency
565	93	565	(565 × 100) ÷ 93 = 56500 ÷ 93 = 607.52 VA ≈ 610 VA

The nearest inverter capacity available to 610 VA is 650 VA, so, the inverter capacity installed will be of 12 V, 650 VA (input side).

(b) Solar charge controller selection

Energy (Wh)	Wattage (W)	Voltage (V)	Maximum current (A)
2580	565	12	48

Here, the system voltage is 12 volts.

Step 3 Battery sizing:

(a) Battery capacity

Energy (Wh)	System voltage (V)	Battery capacity (Ah)	DoD (%)	Actual battery capacity (Ah)
2580	12	2580 ÷ 12 = 215 Ah	50	215 ÷ 0.5 = 430 Ah

(b) Standard battery capacity available

Actual battery capacity (Ah)	Standard battery capacity (Ah)	Total number of batteries (#)
430	150	430 ÷ 150 = 2.86 ≈ 3

(c) Number of connections in series and/or parallel

Number of batteries (#)	System voltage (V)	Standard battery voltage (V)	Series connections	Parallel connection
3	12	12	12 ÷ 12 = 1	3 ÷ 1 = 3

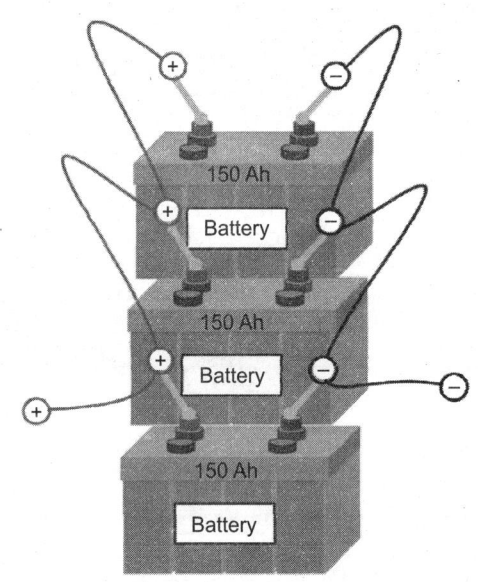

FIGURE 10.16
Three batteries in parallel connection.

Total battery capacity will be

$$3 \times 150 \text{ Ah} = 450 \text{ Ah}$$

Step 4 SPV sizing:

(a) Energy calculation

Total energy (Wh)	Battery efficiency (%)	Energy from SPV module (Wh)
2580	95	2580 ÷ 0.95 = 2716 ≈ 2720 Wh

(b) SPV module wattage estimation

Energy from SPV module (W)	Number of sunshine hours (h)	SPV module wattage (W)
2720	4.5	2720 ÷ 4.5 = 604.5 ≈ 605 watts

(c) Standard SPV module capacity

Actual SPV module capacity (W)	Standard SPV module capacity (W)	Total Number of SPV modules (#)
605	90 or 160	605 ÷ 90 = 6.72 ≈ 7 or 605 ÷ 160 = 3.78 ≈ 4

(d) Number of modules in series or parallel

Number of SPV modules (#)	System voltage (V)	Standard SPV module voltage (V)	Series connections	Parallel connection
4	12	12	12 ÷ 12 = 1	4 ÷ 1 = 4

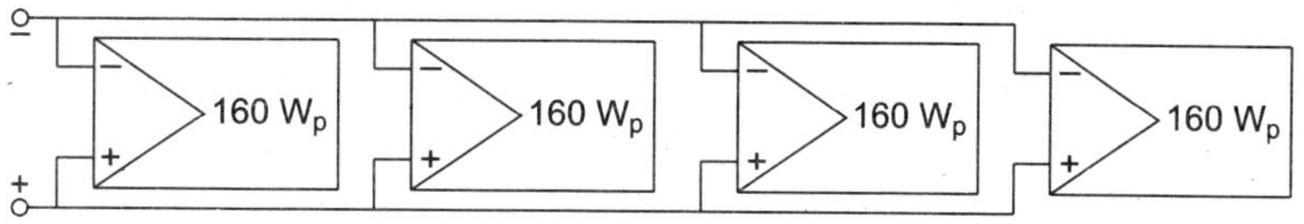

FIGURE 10.17
Modules in parallel.

Step 5 Wiring, fuse and junction box selection:

(a) Maximum direct current (DC) and voltage

System	Max DC wattage (W)	System DC voltage (V)	Max DC current (A)
1	4 × 160 = 640	12	640 ÷ 12 = 53.33 ≈ 55 A

(b) DC wiring, fuse and junction box selection

System	Max DC voltage (V) and current (A)	SWG	Fuse	Switch/junction box
1	12 V, 45 A			

(c) Maximum alternating current (AC) and voltage

System	Max AC wattage (W)	System AC voltage (V)	Max AC current (A)
1	600 W	230	600 ÷ 230 = 2.6 ≈ 3 A

(d) AC wiring, fuse and junction box selection

System	Max AC voltage (V) and current (A)	SWG (wire)	Fuse	Switch/Junction box
1	230 V, 3 A			

10.2.2
Solar PV System Design Chart

Design of a solar PV system is done in four steps which includes; estimation of daily energy consumption, inverter calculations, battery calculations and finally, solar PV module calculations. The step by step approach is presented in the form of design chart. A PV system designer can fill various tables (Tables 10.25 to 10.28) given in the chart and can come up with the design of PV system for a given application. This chart can be printed and kept with the designer, so that whenever he/she meets new clients, the design chart can be filled up. With the system, design and approximate cost can also be communicated to clients.

TABLE 10.25 Solar PV System Design Chart

Design Chart 1: Daily Load Energy Estimation

Input parameters					Calculated parameters	
A_1	A_2	A_3	A_4	A_5	$A_6 = (A_3 \times A_5)$	$A_7 = (A_5 \times A_6)$
S. No.	Name of appliances	Watts (W)	No. (#)	No. of hours (n)	Total watts (W × No.) (W)	Energy (Total watts × No. of hours) (Wh)
1						
2						
3						
4						
5						
6						

Total wattage (add all the values above) = _____ W

Total energy (add all the values above) = _____ Wh

TABLE 10.26 Inverter Calculations

Design Chart 2: Inverter Calculations

Input parameters				Calculated parameters		
B_1	B_2	B_3	B_4	$B_5 = (B_4 \times B_1)$	$B_6 = (B_3 \times B_1)$	$B_7 = (B_4 \div B_2)$
Efficiency	Input voltage (DC)	Total load energy (Wh) = A_7	Total load (W) = A_6	Inverter capacity or input power (watts)	Input energy to inverter (Wh)	Input DC current to inverter (A)

TABLE 10.27 Battery Calculations

Design Chart 3: Battery Calculations

Input parameters							Calculated parameters			
C_1	C_2	C_3	C_4	C_5	C_6	C_7	C_8	C_9 $= C_7 \div C_2$	C_{10} $= C_8 \div C_3$	C_{11} $= C_9 \times C_{10}$
Efficiency (%)	Voltage of single battery (V)	Capacity of single battery (Ah)	Total output energy = B_6 (Wh)	DoD (%)	Days of autonomy (#)	Input DC voltage to inverter (V)	Total capacity of battery (Ah)	No. of batteries in series (#)	No. of batteries in parallel (#)	Total number of batteries (#)

TABLE 10.28 PV Module Calucations

Design Chart 4: PV module calculations

Input parameters								Calculated parameters					
D_1	D_2	D_3	D_4	D_5	D_6	D_7	D_9	$D_{10} = D_9/D_1$	$D_{11} = D_{10}/D_7$	D_{12}	$D_{13} = D_{11}/(D_2 \times D_{12})$	$D_{14} = D_{11}/D_2$
Battery efficiency = C_1	Wattage of PV module P_m (W)	Peak current of module, I_m (A)	Peak voltage of module, V_m (V)	Name of location	Average daily solar radiation (kWh/m²-day)	Average daily 1000 W/m² equivalent solar radiation hours (hours)	Daily energy input to inverter = A_6	Total daily energy input to the battery = output from PV module	Total solar PV module wattage	No. of PV modules in series = same as number of batteries in series	No. of PV modules in parallel	Total number of PV modules

10.2.3
Look Up Table for PV System Design

PV systems are designed for grid-connected or off-grid applications. In this chapter, PV system design, mainly for the off-grid system, is considered. When we look at the off-grid PV systems for households, we will find that there is some pattern of usage in terms of loads. The amount of electricity used depends on the economic status of a given household. A small household will normally need one or two lights, a little bigger household would need fan, and even little bigger household would need TV and computer and so on. As the income of a household increases, its requirement for electricity also increases. Based on this information, i.e., the income level, we can see some defined pattern of loads and their electricity consumption. In this section, certain loads like CFL, fan, TV, etc. is assumed and the total daily energy consumption is estimated. In different scenario, different number of loads are assumed. In this way, depending on the load and their number connected in a household, a table (see Table 10.29) is prepared for totally daily energy consumption.

Table 10.29 can be used as a quick reference for finding out daily energy consumption depending on the amount of loads connected. Once we know the daily energy consumption, next thing we want is the sizes of inverter, battery and PV module which can supply the total daily energy required by the load. Another look up table (Table 10.30) is prepared which provides the sizing of the PV system components based on daily energy consumption. In this way, by using Table 10.29 and Table 10.30, one can find out the PV system components sizes to fulfill given energy requirement.

TABLE 10.29 Look Up Table for the Estimation of Daily Energy Based on Different Loads and Their Numbers

S. No.	CFL			Fan	Fridge	TV	Computer	Music System	Total power (W)	Total energy (Wh)
	5 W	14 W	20 W	50 W	200 W	100 W	250 W	150 W		
1	3	0	0	0	0	0	0	0	15	75
2	3	1	0	0	0	0	0	0	29	145
3	3	2	1	0	0	0	0	0	63	315
4	3	2	1	1	0	0	0	0	113	715
5	2	2	2	2	0	0	0	0	178	1190
6	2	3	1	2	0	0	0	0	172	1160
7	3	4	2	4	1	0	0	0	511	2755
8	3	3	2	3	1	1	0	0	547	2585
9	3	4	2	4	1	1	1	0	861	3805
10	4	3	3	4	1	1	1	1	1022	4010
11	4	3	4	4	2	1	1	1	1242	4710
12	5	4	3	5	2	2	1	1	1391	5405
13	3	5	2	5	2	2	2	1	1625	6075
14	2	6	3	6	2	1	2	2	1754	6470
15	4	5	4	6	2	2	2	2	1870	6850

Note: In this Table, it is assumed that CFL is used 5 hours per day, fan is used 8 hours per day, TV is used 3 hours per day, computer is used 3 hours per day, music system is used 1 hour per day. It is always recommended to do actual calculations of total daily energy based on the clients input.

TABLE 10.30 PV System Component Sizes to Fulfill a Given Daily Requirement of Energy

S. No.	Energy (Wh)	Load wattage (W)	SPV capacity (W$_p$)	Total battery capacity (Ah)	Inverter rating (VA)	1 battery capacity (Ah)	System voltage (V)	No of batteries in			Battery bank voltage (V)	I_m (A)	V_m (V)
								Series	Parallel	Total			
1	75	15	30	18	100	18	12	1	0	1	12	2	15
2	145	29	60	35	100	35	12	1	0	1	12	4	15
3	315	63	120	70	100	70	12	1	0	1	12	8	15
4	715	113	270	165	200	165	12	1	0	1	12	18	15
5	1190	178	450	270	200	135	12	2	1	2	12	30	15
6	1160	172	450	270	200	135	12	2	1	2	12	30	15
7	2755	511	1000	600	600	150	12	4	1	4	12	70	15
8	2585	547	1000	600	600	150	12	4	1	4	12	70	15
9	3805	861	1400	900	1000	150	12	2	3	6	24	50	30
10	4010	1022	1500	950	1400	165	12	2	3	6	24	50	30
11	4710	1242	1800	1200	1400	150	12	2	4	8	24	60	30
12	5405	1391	2000	1200	1500	150	12	2	4	4	24	70	30
13	6075	1625	2200	1440	2000	180	12	4	2	8	48	40	60
14	6470	1754	2400	1440	2000	180	12	4	2	8	48	40	60
15	6850	1870	2500	1600	2000	200	12	4	2	8	48	45	60

Grid-connected Solar PV Power Systems

Solar PV systems can broadly be divided in two categories; one is standalone PV system (which use battery for energy storage) and other is grid-connected systems which may or may not use any battery and interact with the grid. This chapter is mainly devoted to grid-connected PV systems.

11.1

Introduction to Grid-connected PV Systems

Small capacity grid connected PV systems are normally used for household applications and large capacity systems are used for power plant applications.

11.1.1

Grid-connected PV Systems for Small Power Applications

Grid connected system can also be broadly divided in two categories:

1. Grid-connected PV systems for small power applications, e.g. in households.
2. Grid-connected PV systems for large power applications, e.g. in solar power plants.

Main components of a grid-connected solar PV systems are (a) solar PV modules, (b) a power conditioning unit or inverter and (c) load or grid. An electric grid can be considered as a large sink of energy wherein energy generated by solar PV can be supplied or taken from the grid when required. The idea of the connecting PV system to the grid is to use the grid as energy storage medium so that the use of battery can be avoided as much as possible.

Grid-connected system for small power applications and for large power applications are little different from each other. These differences are discussed in the following paragraphs.

The main purpose of the grid-connected systems that are used for small power household applications is to generate energy and consume it within the household itself. Typically, the power rating of this type of PV system can be in the range of 1 kW to several 10s of kWs. The role of grid connectivity in case of small power household system is to supply excess generated energy to the grid (if more energy is generated by PV system then required by the load) or take energy from the grid if there is any shortage. However, in many cases, some batteries are added to ensure that loads always get the energy, even if grid power is not available. It is possible in many parts of the world that due to the shortage of power, there is load shedding and grid power may not be available. This situation can easily be imagined in India. But, in Germany, there are millions of solar PV systems installed on the rooftops and connected to the grid but they do not use any battery back-up because the grid power availability is very good. An example of a grid-connected system for small power applications is shown in Figure 11.1. The power conditioning unit (PCU) or inverter plays a very important role in the small grid-connected PV power systems. Since the system can take power from the grid or can feed power to the grid, the PCU should have facility to flow the power in both directions from PV system to grid and vice versa. It is also possible that some PCUs are only one directional, i.e., they are designed to control the power flow in one direction only, mainly from grid to PV system. In this case, the grid becomes an additional source of power for PV system but excess power generated by PV system cannot be supplied to the grid. The inverter systems (with PV modules) used in India is an example of these types of systems. It is to be noted that the bidirectional PCUs are more expensive then a single directional PCUs.

Under Jawaharlal Nehru National Solar Mission, it is planned that there will be about 2000 MW of such PV systems to be installed in India by year 2022.

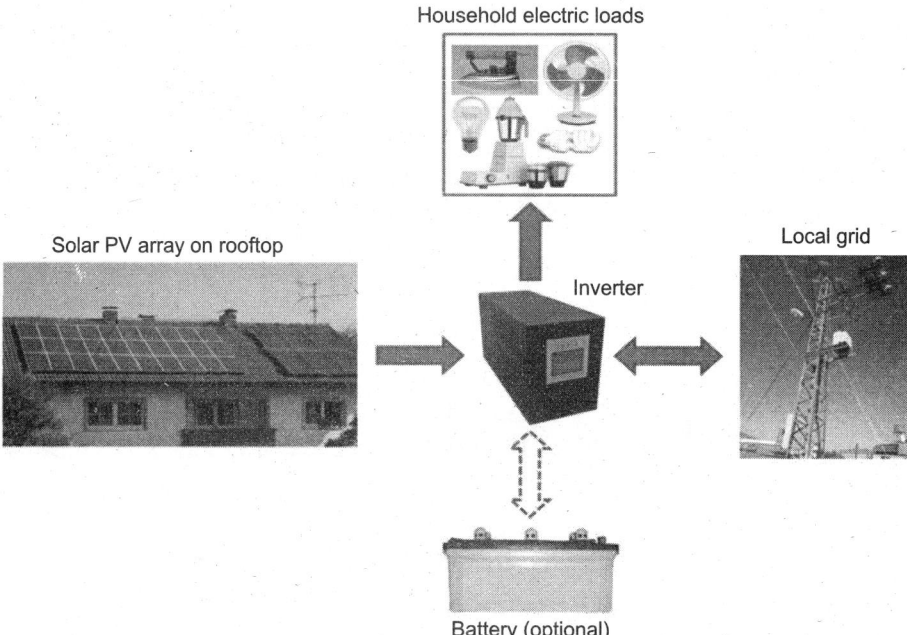

FIGURE 11.1
Grid-connected PV system with small power applications.

11.1.2
Grid-connected PV Systems for Large Power Applications

The grid-connected PV systems for large power applications are mainly designed to act as power plants and the main purpose of these power plants is to generate power and supply it to the grid. In this way, they are equivalent to coal power plant or hydro plants. Since the main purpose of this type of grid-connected PV system is to supply the power to the grid, their power ratings are normally in the range of 1 MW to several 10s of MW. It is assumed that a grid is a big sink of energy and a large amount of energy generated by PV plants can be feed into the grid and no battery storage is planned in such plants. Battery storage for such large power would also be very expensive. An example of a grid-connected PV power plant is shown in Figure 11.2.

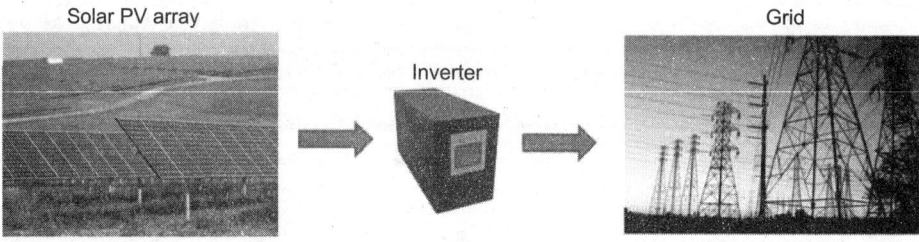

FIGURE 11.2
Grid-connected PV system for large power applications.

Under Jawaharlal Nehru National Solar Mission it is planned that about 18000 MW of solar power plants, including solar PV as well as solar thermal, will be installed in India by year 2022.

Grid connected plant sizes and their applications

The grid connected PV systems for small power applications (1 kW–100 kW) are used to supplement distributed AC power supply in domestic, commercial and industrial applications. These systems supply power to the captive daytime loads connected to the AC grid power supply. The surplus power generated is automatically transmitted to the remote loads connected onto the grid power supply.

The grid connected PV systems for large power applications are of two types, the systems connected to distribution grid and the systems connected to transmission or generation grid.

Medium to large size (100 kW–1 MW) grid-connected solar PV power plants are used to feed power to the local power distribution grid. The distribution grid is employed to supply power to a small village or a cluster of villages or to a large industry or an industrial complex.

Power capacity of grid-connected PV system range from 1 kW to several MW. Different capacity PV systems are suitable for different applications.

Large to very large size (1 MW–100 MW) grid-connected solar PV power plants are used to feed power to the main AC transmission or generation grid.

Problem 11.1: What is the difference between standalone system and a grid-connected solar PV system?

Basic operation of grid-connected PV system

The basic operation of a grid-connected PV system for small or large power applications is very similar. The output of the grid-connected PV system is tied to the grid (electrical power supply). Worldwide, the grid carries AC power. Due to the shortage of power generation in India, the grid is not powered all the time. Due to this reason, the operation of this type of system depends on the availability of the grid. When the grid is not available or when the grid is not powered, the output of PV system cannot be fed to the grid.

The system mainly consists of solar PV array and DC to AC inverter. The DC output of solar PV array is converted to AC by the inverter. The inverter has a built-in controller which extracts maximum power output from the solar PV array. The voltage level, phase and frequency of the inverter to feed AC output are matched with that of grid. The inverter feeds AC current into the grid and is made available to the load connected to it via grid.

An example of grid-connected PV system

Power systems can be characterized by voltage and current levels. When we design a solar PV system, we have to design for the given voltage and current. When we choose an inverter we choose it for certain input current and input voltage, as well as certain output current and output voltage. Remember here that the power level at the input and output depends on the current level and voltage level.

For example, a 2.4 kW PV modules may be connected in such a way that the arrangement will provide you 24 V voltage level and 100 A current level (and the product of the current and voltage = 24 × 100 = 2.4 kW). We should remember that the PV modules will produce DC power. In this way, we can write that 2.4 kW PV system is 24V/100 A DC output. In a grid-connected system, the output of solar PV modules will be fed to input of an inverter. So, an inverter would receive 24 V/100 A DC at its input. The output of an inverter will be AC power. The voltage output of inverter will always be equal to the voltage level of the grid to which it is connected. The voltage level of a single phase line is normally 240 V. Therefore, the output voltage level of an inverter would be 240 V AC. On the other hand, if the inverter is feeding to high tension three phases grid, then the output of the inverter could be 415 V, 11,000 V or 11 kV or even 33 kV. The current level at the output of an inverter will depend on input power.

In an inverter, output power is always lower than the input power due to losses in inverter. The amount of losses is measured by the efficiency of the inverter. The relationship between inverter efficiency, its input power and output power is given in Figure 11.3.

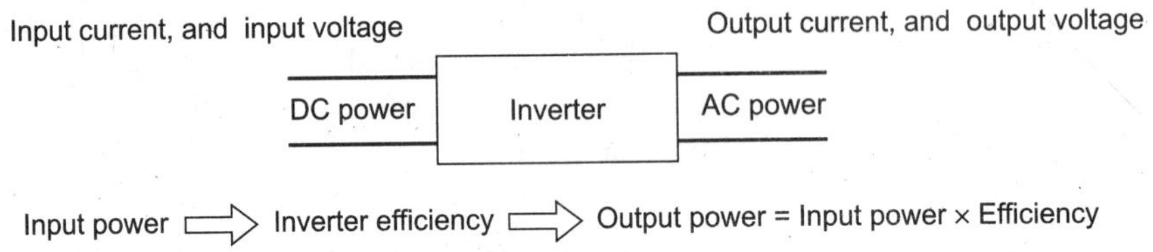

FIGURE 11.3
Indication of input and output voltage, current and power on a grid-connected inverter.

During DC power to AC power conversion in a grid-connected inverter, some power is lost in inverter.

The efficiency of a grid-connected inverter is very high and inverters are available with as high efficiency as 98%.

Normally, the efficiency of grid-connected inverters is quite good. The inverters are available with as high efficiency as 98%. Though the efficiencies are high, still some power loss occurs in the DC power to AC power conversion. Based on the above discussion, the following equation can be written:

Power output = Power input × Inverter efficiency

Power loss in inverter = Output power − Input power

Estimation of AC current fed into the grid

Consider an example system with 2.4 kW DC PV array rated for 24 V/100 A DC output. In an ideal system with no losses (100% efficiency), the output of inverter would be 240 V/10 A AC and would generate 2.4 kW of AC power when connected to 240 V AC grid. In a real system, the actual AC power generated would be typically 2 kW as a result of power lost in converting DC power to AC power. In order to calculate AC power and current fed into grid, use the following two steps:

Step 1 AC power fed into grid:

AC power fed into grid = DC power produced by PV array
                        − Power lost in converting DC power to AC power.

Step 2 AC current fed into grid:

AC current fed into grid = AC power fed into grid/AC voltage

EXAMPLE 11.1

A solar PV array is rated at 100 V/50 A DC. System power losses are 20%. What is the AC power fed into the grid? If the grid voltage is 240 V AC, what is the AC current fed into the grid?

Solution

Here,

DC power = 100 V × 50 A = 5000 W = 5 kW

Power lost = $5000 \times \dfrac{20}{100}$ = 1000 W = 1 kW

AC power fed into grid = DC Power − Power loss = 5 kW − 1 kW = 4 kW = 4000 W

AC current fed into grid = $\dfrac{\text{AC power}}{\text{AC voltage}} = \dfrac{4000}{240}$ = 16.67A

Problem 11.2: A solar PV array is rated at 96 V/150 A DC. System power losses are 22%. What is the AC power fed into the grid? If the grid voltage is 240 V AC, what is the AC current fed into the grid?

11.2
Configuration of Grid-connected Solar PV Systems

Based on their function, the grid-connected solar PV power systems for small power applications are classified into mainly two types, with and without battery back-up. The grid-connected PV systems for small power applications can also be classified into two types based on their end-use or application.

1. Captive power systems
2. Grid support power systems

The grid connected PV systems for a large power applications have only one application to supplement grid power, such systems do not have battery back-up.

11.2.1
Grid-connected PV Systems without Battery Back-up

The systems without battery back-up are more common and consists of two main components, solar PV array and grid tied inverter. The controller to extract maximum DC power from PV array is in-built in an inverter. This type of system is easy to install, efficient and cost-effective, however, it has no means of supplying AC power when the grid is not available.

In small power applications, as long as the solar array produces more power than the local load demands, the surplus power is fed into the utility distribution grid. The surplus power is supplied to remote loads via the distribution grid. During morning and evening, when the local load demands more power than what the solar array can produce, the deficit power is taken from the grid. The grid supplies power during night as well. Figure 11.4 shows schematic of grid connected PV system without battery backup.

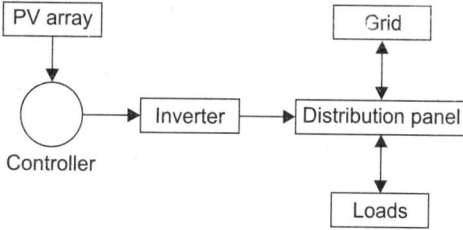

FIGURE 11.4
Grid-connected solar PV power system without battery back-up.

Grid-connected PV system without battery back-up cannot supply power to the load when grid is not available.

In large power applications, power generated by the system is fed to the transmission or generation grid at all times. The combined conventional grid power and PV generated power is supplied to loads by distribution transformers via distribution grid.

11.2.2
Grid-connected PV Systems with Battery Back-up

The grid-connected PV systems with battery back-up are used in small power applications.

Other than solar PV array and inverter, systems with battery back-up consist of two additional components, battery bank and charge controller. The DC output of a solar PV array is used to charge battery bank. The charge controller controls the battery bank charging voltage and current to ensure that the battery bank is neither overcharged nor overdischarged. The surplus DC energy generated by array is converted to AC by the inverter and is supplied to the load via grid. This type of system can supply AC power even when grid is not available. This type of system is however difficult to install due to more components. It is also less efficient and expensive due to additional battery back-up.

When grid is available, the system operation is identical to the system without battery back-up. The energy stored in the battery bank is not cycled when grid is available. A solar PV array maintains the battery bank in the float charge condition. When grid fails, battery back-up is used to supply DC input to the inverter in addition to the solar PV array. The inverter output is isolated from the grid and supplies power to the back-up loads.

Grid-connected PV system with battery back-up can supply power to the load even when grid is not available.

Figure 11.5 shows a schematic of grid connected solar PV system with battery back up.

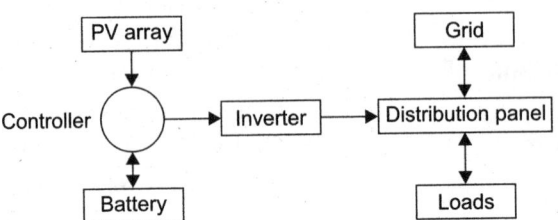

FIGURE 11.5
Grid connected solar PV system with battery back-up.

11.2.3
Grid-connected Solar PV Captive Power System

The grid-connected PV captive power systems are used in small and medium power applications. The term captive means that the power generated by solar PV array is used by the local load connected to the utility grid. In this system, the amount of power generated by a solar PV array is less than the power consumed by the local load. The AC power output of the inverter is connected to the local load via the utility grid. The excess power required by the load is drawn from the grid. For example, if a grid-connected solar PV system is capable of producing 5 kW power during a day, and the load consumption is 8 kW, then 3 kW of power is drawn from the grid.

The amount of power generated by a solar PV array can be more than the power consumed by the local load in this type of system, and used in an industry, particularly on weekends. The surplus PV power is fed to the grid and supplied to remote loads via the grid. For example, if grid connected solar PV system is produces 5 kW power during a day, and the load consumption is 3 kW, then surplus 2 kW of power is supplied to remote load via the grid. Figure 11.6 shows a schematic of grid-connected solar PV captive power system.

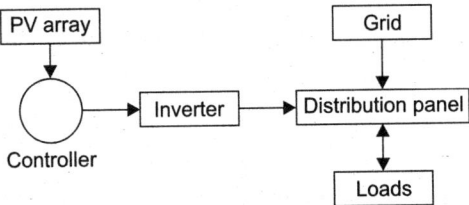

FIGURE 11.6
Grid-connected solar PV captive power system.

11.2.4
Grid Support Solar PV Power System

The grid support solar PV power systems are used in small power applications. The grid support solar PV power systems are designed to supply power to the load when grid is not available. When grid is available, load draws power from the grid and solar generated power is used to charge battery bank. If surplus solar power is available, it is supplied to load. Any additional solar power is fed back into the grid.

In this configuration, when grid fails, a battery bank supplies power to the load and solar array charges the battery bank. If surplus solar power is available, it is supplied directly to the load, and when solar PV power is not available, for example on cloudy days or at night, the grid can be used to charge the battery if required. The solar PV power is given the first priority for use, second priority is given to the battery and the grid is given the last priority. Figure 11.7 shows a schematic of grid support solar PV power system.

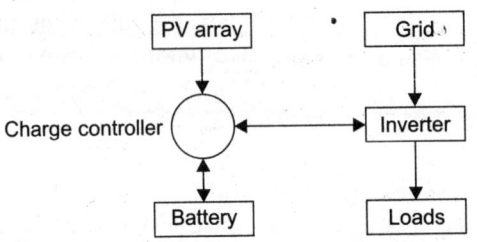

FIGURE 11.7
Grid support solar PV power system.

11.3

Components of Grid-connected Solar PV Systems

A grid-connected solar PV system typically consists of the following components:

1. Solar PV array
2. Array combiner box
3. DC cabling
4. DC distribution box
5. Inverter
6. AC cabling
7. AC distribution box.

The interconnection of these components in a grid-connected solar PV system is shown in Figure 11.8. In the following sections, each of these components are discussed in detail.

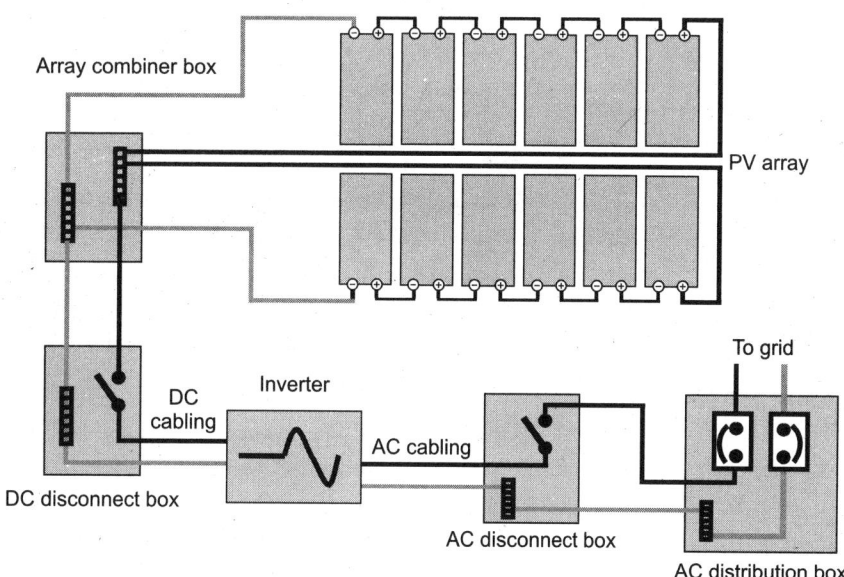

FIGURE 11.8
Grid-connected solar PV system components interconnection diagram.

11.3.1
Solar PV Array

A solar PV array is used to covert solar energy into DC electrical energy. The array consists of a number of solar PV modules connected in series and/or parallel combinations. The series connection is used to increase voltage output while a parallel connection is used to increase current output. A number of modules are connected in series in a series string and a number of series strings are connected in parallel to make a series-parallel connected solar PV array. A number of modules can also be connected in a parallel string.

Series-connected solar PV string: *Increasing DC voltage*

A number of solar PV modules are connected in series in a series-connected solar PV string as shown in Figure 11.9. The series connection is used to increase DC voltage output of the string. The DC current output of a string is not increased by series connection. Typical voltage output of a series connected string is in the range of 100–1000 V DC and typical current output is in the range of 5–10 A DC. The solar string is made to operate at maximum power point when connected to inverter. For more details about the series connection of PV modules, refer to Chapter 5 and Chapter 6.

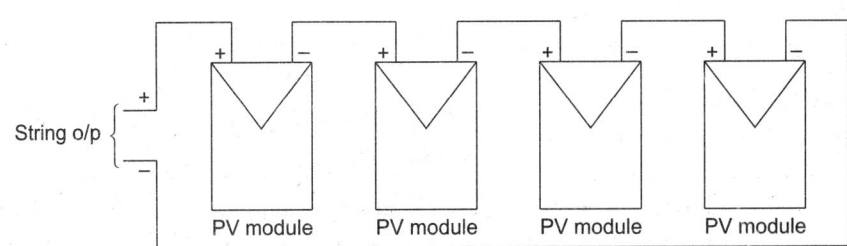

FIGURE 11.9

Series connected solar PV string.

In a PV module string, a number of solar PV modules are connected in series to increase the voltage output.

DC voltage and current of series-connected PV module string: DC voltage of a number of PV modules connected in string can be estimated in the following steps:

Step 1 DC voltage of series-connected solar PV string: The total voltage of series connected solar PV string can simply be calculated by multiplying the DC voltage of individual PV module by the number of PV modules to be connected in series.

DC voltage of series connected solar PV string = DC voltage of individual solar PV module × number of modules connected in series

From this, if we know the desired string voltage and the voltage of individual module, then dividing the desired string voltage by individual module voltage will give us the number of modules to be connected in series.

Step 2 DC current of series connected solar PV string: DC current of series connected solar PV string = DC current of individual solar PV module.

Step 3 DC power output of series connected solar PV string: DC power output of series connected solar PV string = DC voltage of series connected solar PV string × DC current of series connected solar PV string.

EXAMPLE 11.2

A solar PV module is rated for V_{oc} = 40 V, V_{mp} = 32 V, I_{sc} = 8.5 A and I_{mp} = 8 A. Design a solar PV string to produce DC voltage output of 384 V. What will be the DC current output of the string? What will be the DC power output of series-connected string?

Solution

Since while delivering power, the PV modules are supposed to operate at maximum power points, therefore, current and voltage at maximum power point, i.e. V_{mp} and I_{mp} are considered in calculations.

Step 1: DC voltage of series-connected solar PV string = DC voltage of individual solar PV module × Number of modules connected in series.

Therefore, the number of modules in series = $\dfrac{\text{String voltage}}{\text{Module voltage}} = \dfrac{384}{32} = 12$.

Thus, 12 PV modules need to be connected to get string voltage of 384 V.

Step 2: DC current of series-connected solar PV string = DC current of individual solar PV module.

Therefore, DC current of string = 8 A

Step 3: DC power output of series connected solar PV string = DC voltage of series connected solar PV string × DC current of series connected solar PV string = 384 V × 8 A = 4608 W or 4.6 kW.

Problem 11.3: A solar PV module is rated for V_{oc} = 36 V, V_{mp} = 30 V, I_{sc} = 8.5 A and I_{mp} = 7.9 A. Design a solar PV string to produce DC voltage output of 120 V. What will be the DC current output of the string? What will be the DC power output of series-connected string?

Parallel-connected solar PV strings: *Increasing current*

A number of solar PV modules are connected in parallel in a parallel-connected solar PV string as shown in Figure 11.10. The parallel connection is used to increase DC current output of the string. The DC voltage output of a string remains same in parallel connection. Typical voltage output of a parallel-connected string is in the range of 20–30 V DC and typical current output is in the range of 50–200 A DC. The solar string is made to operate at maximum power point when connected to inverter. For more details of parallel connection of PV modules, refer to Chapter 5 and Chapter 6.

FIGURE 11.10

Parallel connected solar PV string.

In parallel connection, several PV modules or PV module strings are connected in parallel to increase the current output.

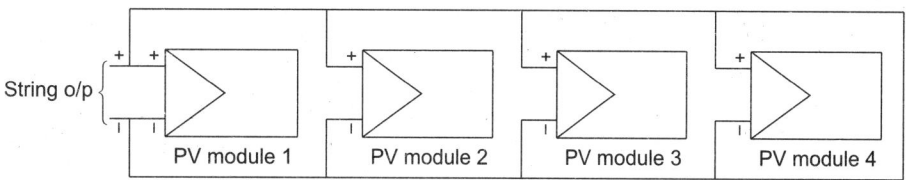

DC voltage and current of parallel-connected PV module string: DC voltage of a number of PV modules connected in string can be estimated in the following three steps:

Step 1 DC current of parallel connected solar PV string: Total current of parallel-connected PV modules can be estimated simply by multiplying the DC current of individual PV module and the number of modules in parallel string.

DC current of parallel connected solar PV string = DC current of individual solar PV module × Number of modules connected in parallel.

On the other hand, if we know the desired current from a parallel-connected solar PV string and current of an individual PV module, we can divide the desired current of string by individual module current to calculate the required number of PV modules in string.

Step 2 DC voltage of parallel-connected solar PV string: DC voltage of parallel-connected solar PV string = DC voltage of individual solar PV module.

Step 3 DC power output of parallel-connected solar PV string: DC power output of parallel-connected solar PV string = DC voltage of parallel-connected solar PV string × DC current of parallel-connected solar PV string.

EXAMPLE 11.3

A solar PV module is rated for $V_{oc} = 40$ V, $V_{mp} = 32$ V, $I_{sc} = 5.5$ A and $I_{mp} = 5$ A. Design a solar PV string to produce DC current output of 200 A. What will be the DC voltage output of the string? What will be the DC power output of parallel-connected string?

Solution

While delivering power, the PV modules are supposed to operate at maximum power points, therefore, current and voltage at maximum power point, i.e., V_{mp} and I_{mp} are considered in calculations.

Step 1: DC current of parallel-connected solar PV string = DC current of individual solar PV module × Number of modules connected in parallel.

Therefore, the number of modules in parallel $= \dfrac{\text{String current}}{\text{Module current}} = \dfrac{200}{5} = 40$.

Step 2: DC voltage of parallel-connected solar PV string = DC voltage of individual solar PV module.

Therefore, DC voltage of string = 32 V

Step 3: DC power output of parallel-connected solar PV string = DC voltage of parallel-connected solar PV string × DC current of parallel-connected solar PV string = 32 V × 200 A = 6400 W or 6.4 kW.

Series-parallel connected solar PV array

When there is need to increase both current and voltage, PV module strings are connected in series-parallel combination. In such configurations, a number of series PV module strings are connected in parallel as shown in Figure 11.11. In such cases, the voltage output of array is identical to the voltage output of a PV string and current output of PV strings increases in multiple of number of parallel connected strings. Typical voltage output of a series-parallel connected solar PV array is in the range of 100–1000 V DC and typical current output is in the range of 50–200 A DC. The solar array is made to operate at maximum power point when connected to inverter. For more details of series-parallel connection of PV modules, refer to Chapter 6.

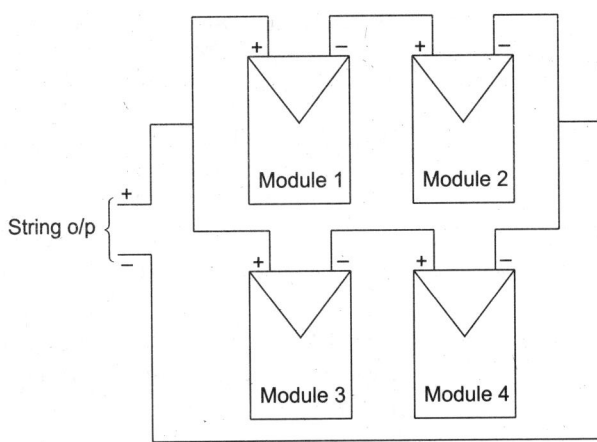

FIGURE 11.11

Series-parallel connected solar PV array (mark strings, array).

When there is need to increase both current and voltage, several PV module strings (which provides high voltage) are connected in parallel combination.

DC voltage and current of series-parallel connected PV module array: In such configuration, several PV strings are connected together in parallel. Since the PV module strings themselves have many modules connected in series, and therefore, strings have high DC voltage. When we connect several PV modules strings in parallel currents of all the strings get added and in this way, we get high current as well. Thus, both high voltage and high current can be achieved in series-parallel configurations.

Step 1 DC voltage of series-parallel connected solar PV array: DC voltage of series-parallel connected solar PV array = DC voltage of series-connected string.

Step 2 DC current of series-parallel connected solar PV array: Total current of series-parallel connected PV modules can be estimate simply by multiplying the DC current of individual PV module string with number of strings to be connected in parallel.

DC current of series-parallel connected solar PV array = DC current of individual series connected string × Number of strings connected in parallel.

On the other hand, if we know the desired current from a series-parallel connected solar PV array, and current of an individual PV module string, we can divide the desired current of array by individual module string current to calculate the required number of PV module strings to be connected in parallel.

Step 3 DC power output of series-parallel connected solar PV array: DC power output of series-parallel connected solar PV array = DC voltage of series-parallel connected solar PV array × DC current of series-parallel connected solar PV array.

EXAMPLE 11.4

A solar PV string is rated for V_{mp} = 400 V and I_{mp} = 8 A. Design a series-parallel connected solar PV array to generate 16 kW DC power. What will be the DC output voltage and current of the array?

Solution

While delivering power, the PV modules are supposed to operate at maximum power points, therefore, current and voltage at maximum power point, i.e., V_{mp} and I_{mp} are considered in calculations.

Step 1: DC voltage of series-parallel connected solar PV array = DC voltage of series connected string.
   Therefore, DC voltage of array = 400 V.

Step 2: DC power output of series-parallel connected solar PV array = DC voltage of series-parallel connected solar PV array × DC current of series-parallel connected solar PV array.

   Therefore, DC current of array = $\dfrac{\text{DC power of array}}{\text{DC voltage of array}} = \dfrac{16{,}000}{400} = 40$ A.

Step 3: DC current of series-parallel connected solar PV array = DC current of individual series-connected string × Number of strings connected in parallel.
   Therefore, the number of strings in parallel = $\dfrac{\text{DC array current}}{\text{DC string current}} = \dfrac{40}{8} = 5$.

Problem 11.4: A solar PV string is rated for V_{mp} = 460 V and I_{mp} = 100 A. Design a series-parallel connected solar PV array to generate 46 kW DC power. What will be the DC output voltage and current of the array?

11.3.2
Array Combiner Box

An array combiner box is used to electrically interconnect solar PV strings to make an array. The combiner box also houses DC voltage and current protections used in a solar PV array. A schematic of array combiner box is shown in Figure 11.12.

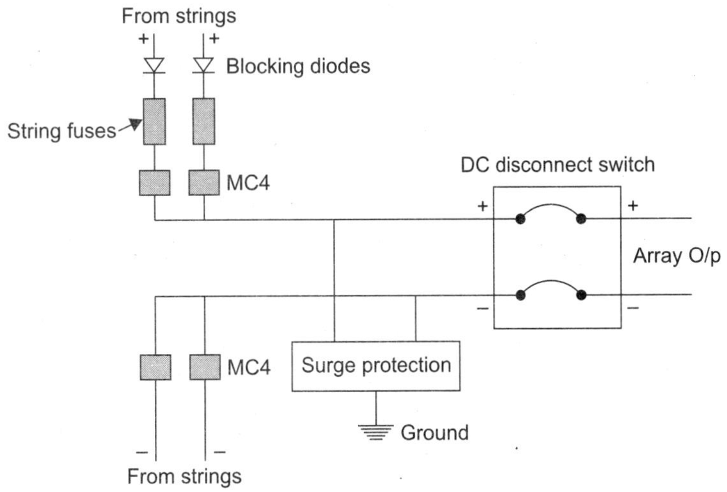

FIGURE 11.12
Array combiner box arrangement.

The DC cables from the string are connected to the box using MC4 connectors. The positive and negative string connections are separately terminated and combined inside the box using shorted terminal strips. The positive and negative output cables from the array combiner box are secured to the box using sealed cable glands. The DC surge protection devices are housed inside the box. The optional string fuses and blocking diodes can also be housed inside the combiner box. An optional 2 pole DC disconnect switch is also mounted inside combiner box.

The combiner box is rated for Protection Class II (double insulation) for protection against electric shock from high DC voltage output of array. The Ground Fault Detector Interrupter (GFDI) is used for grounded PV arrays. The box also needs to be rated for ingress protection rating of IP65 (Digit 6 stands for total protection against dust and digit 5 stands for limited protection against low pressure water jets from any direction).

> An array combiner box is used to electrically interconnect solar PV strings to make an array.

11.3.3
DC Cabling

The PV modules used in a string are connected in series using DC cables. The DC cables are also used to interconnect strings to make an array and connect PV array output to Inverter DC input. The string cables are rated for a minimum of 1.25 times the string short circuit current at each location (refer to Chapter 9 for more details), string fuses are optional. But, the string DC cables are typically rated for 1.5 times string short circuit current to be on the safer side. The string blocking diodes are not required for small systems using typically less than four strings.

11.3.4
DC Distribution Box

DC distribution box is used to distribute DC cables to inverter. Two-pole DC disconnect switch is used to isolate PV array from inverter. The DC surge protection devices can be incorporated with DC distribution box. The output of this box is connected to Inverter DC input as shown in Figure 11.13.

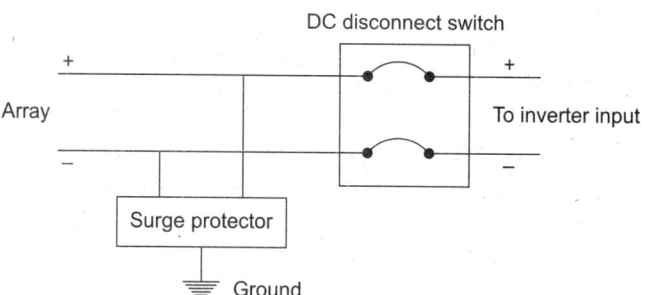

FIGURE 11.13
DC distribution box diagram.

11.3.5
Grid-connected Inverter

The grid-connected inverter is used to convert PV array DC output to AC voltage and current. The output of grid-connected inverter is tied to mains AC grid. The AC voltage, frequency and phase of the inverter output are matched with mains AC grid voltage, frequency and phase. The inverter injects AC current into the mains AC grid at mains AC voltage and supplements mains AC power supply to the load. The presence of mains AC grid voltage (which means grid should be 'on' or powered) is essential for the operation of grid connected inverter.

The grid-connected inverter has Maximum Power Point Tracker (MPPT) controller input stage used to extract maximum DC power from solar PV array at all times. The inverter MPP tracking voltage range needs to match MPP voltage range of the array. The MPP voltage of the array varies with solar radiation, operating temperature and other environmental factors (refer to Chapter 8 for details).

The grid-connected inverter has built-in DC and AC voltage and current protections. The DC and AC disconnect switches are also integrated with the inverter. Islanding protection is mandatory for grid-connected inverter. Islanding is used to isolate inverter output from grid in the event of grid failure. Islanding protection is used to protect operators working on the mains AC grid from electrical shock or electrocution when the grid power is not available.

Grid-connected inverters are available with and without transformer isolation at the output. An external transformer is used at the output of inverter before connecting the inverter output to the mains AC grid. The external transformer is also used to step up Inverter AC output voltage to the mains AC grid voltage.

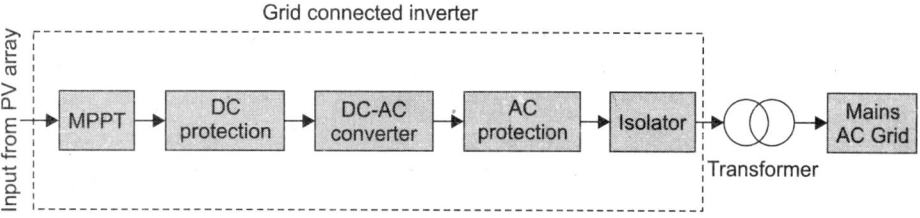

FIGURE 11.14
Grid connected inverter diagram.

Before connecting a output of a grid-connected inverter to the grid, an isolation transformer is required which is either in-built in inverter or connected externally.

Central inverter

There are 3 main types of grid-connected inverters; Central inverter, string inverter and module inverter. These inverter types are based on the way the solar modules are interconnected to form an array.

The central inverter is typically used in a solar PV grid-connected system for large power application. A number of series strings are connected in parallel combination to form a large array (see Figure 11.15). The central inverter can be used when all modules used in an array are identical type, make and power rating. The module MPP current needs to match in a series string connection and the string MPP voltage needs to match when a number of series strings are connected in parallel. The central inverter is not used when one or more strings are under partial or complete shading during the day.

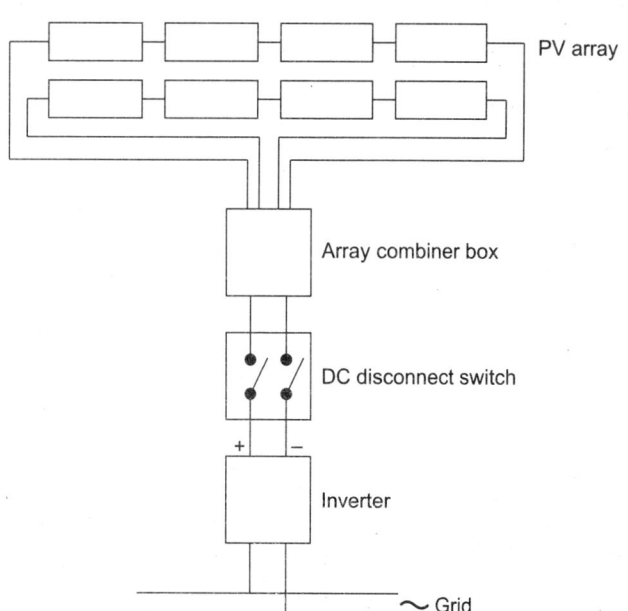

FIGURE 11.15
Central inverter diagram.

The central inverters are typically rated for 250 kW – 1 MW output power and 400 V – 1000 V DC array voltage. These inverters are typically used in large to very large size installations ranging from 1 MW – 100 MW. The use of central inverters in very large installations allows better management of AC cable routing. The central inverters are typically installed in controlled environment and are used in plants having hostile ambient temperature, humidity and dust conditions. The central inverter is suitable for use with array employing either crystalline silicon or thin film module technology.

Central inverters are used with large capacity power plants having capacity in the range of MW.

A number of central inverters are used in master-slave configuration in a large size (MW) power plant. For example, 4 of 250 kW rated central inverters may be used in a 1 MW power plant. The 1 MW array has four sections of 250 kW each and DC output of each section is connected to 250 kW rated inverter. Among these inverters, one will act as control inverter called master inverter, which controls other inverters called slave inverter. One master inverter and 3 slave inverters outputs are connected in parallel with the distribution grid. The master inverter is operational at all times and monitors the output of slave inverters and controls their operation based on the level of total available array power output. For example, if the plant generates 500 kW, then only one slave inverter is operational in addition to the master inverter. The master-slave arrangement is used to maximize the efficiency of DC to AC conversion process and the operating life of the inverters.

Series string inverter

The series string inverter is used when a number of PV modules are connected in series combination to form a string (see Figure 11.16). The number of inverters used depends on the number of strings. A set of series string inverters can be used with PV array when series strings use modules having non-identical type, make or power rating. The module MPP current needs to match with that of other modules connected in a series string connection, however, the string MPP voltage need not match MPP voltage of other strings as each string has its own inverter. The series string inverters are also used when one or more strings are under partial or complete shading during the day. The use of string inverter maximizes power output of individual series string. The series string inverters are normally not suitable for use with PV array employing thin film technology due to low string currents.

The series string inverters are typically rated for 10 kW–100 kW output power and 200–600 V DC string voltage. These inverters are typically used in medium to large size installations ranging from 100 kW to 1 MW. The AC cable sizing for string inverter configuration becomes unmanageable beyond 1 MW plant rating. The series string inverters are typically installed outdoors and are rated for IP54 or IP65 (Water and Dust Ingress Protection) for operation in hostile conditions.

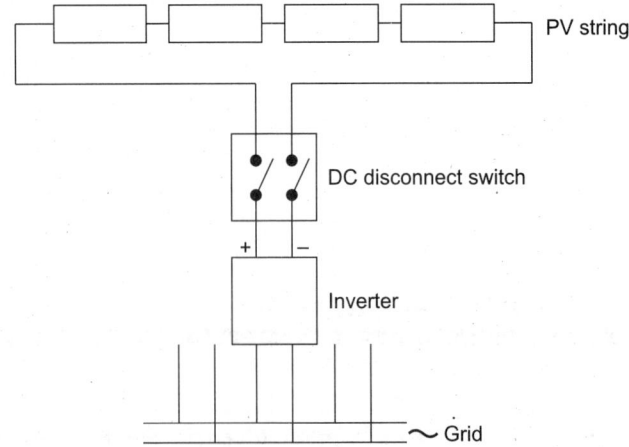

FIGURE 11.16

Series string inverter diagram, each string has its own string inverter.

The series string inverters are normally not suitable for use with PV array employing thin film technology due to low string currents.

Parallel string inverter

The parallel string inverter is used when a number of PV modules are connected in parallel combination to form a string (see Figure 11.17). A set of parallel string inverters can be used with PV array when two or more parallel strings use modules having non-identical type, make or power rating. The module MPP voltage needs to match with that of other modules connected in a parallel string connection, however, the string MPP current need not match MPP current of other strings as each string has its own inverter. The parallel string inverters are used when one or more strings are under partial or complete shading during the day. The use of parallel string inverter maximizes power output of individual string.

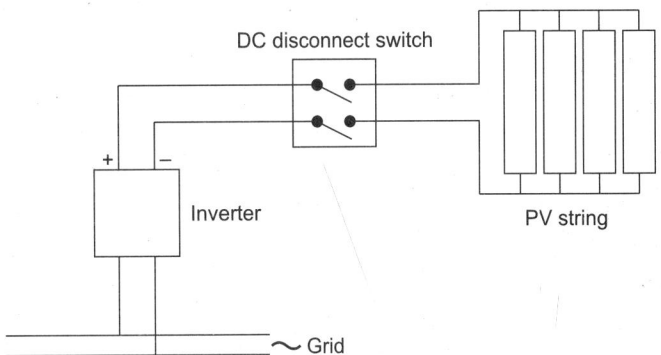

FIGURE 11.17
Parallel string inverter diagram.

The parallel string inverters can be used with thin film modules having large voltage output and small current output. The current output of the parallel string is the sum total of the individual module currents and the parallel string inverter input current rating can be selected to match this. The parallel string inverters are typically installed outdoors and are rated for IP54 or IP65 (Water and Dust Ingress Protection) for operation in hostile conditions.

The parallel string inverters are used with thin film modules having large voltage output and small current output.

Module inverter

The module inverter is used with each module when a number of dissimilar PV modules (non-identical type, make or power rating) are used in an array or when the modules can be shaded differently due to non-uniform shading pattern (see Figure 11.18). A set of module inverters can be connected to grid in parallel and they operate independent of each other. Neither the module MPP voltage nor the MPP current needs to match these parameters with other modules as each module has its own inverter. The use of module inverters maximizes power output of individual modules and, in turn, delivers maximum power output from the array. The voltage and current input rating of the module inverter is selected to match the range of voltage and current output ratings of the modules.

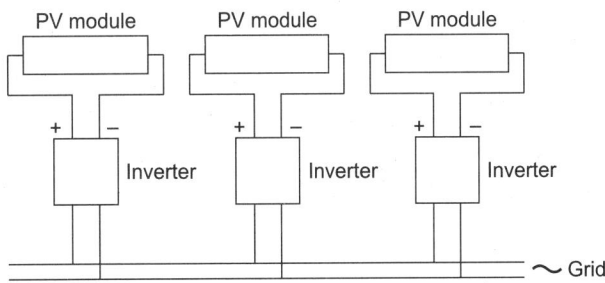

FIGURE 11.18
Module inverter diagram.

When module inverter is integrated with the PV module, it is called piggy-back inverter and the module is termed AC module as it delivers AC output directly compatible with mains AC grid voltage. AC modules are directly interfaced with the mains AC grid.

The module inverters are installed outdoors and are rated for IP65 (Water and Dust Ingress Protection) for operation in hostile conditions.

11.3.6
AC Cabling

The outputs of inverters used with the solar array are connected to AC distribution box using AC cables. The cables are rated for a minimum of 1.25 times the AC circuit breaker current rating. The AC cables are rated for indoor environment when the inverter is located indoors, for example, a central inverter. The AC cables are rated for outdoor environment when the inverter is located outdoors, for example, string or module inverter.

11.3.7
AC Distribution Box

AC distribution box is used to distribute AC cables to transformer or load. A two-pole AC circuit breaker is used to isolate inverter from transformer or load. The AC circuit breaker current rating is typically 1.2 times the maximum load current. The AC line fuses and surge protection devices can be incorporated with AC distribution box. The output of AC distribution box is connected to transformer or load via AC energy meter used to monitor PV generated energy as shown in Figure 11.19.

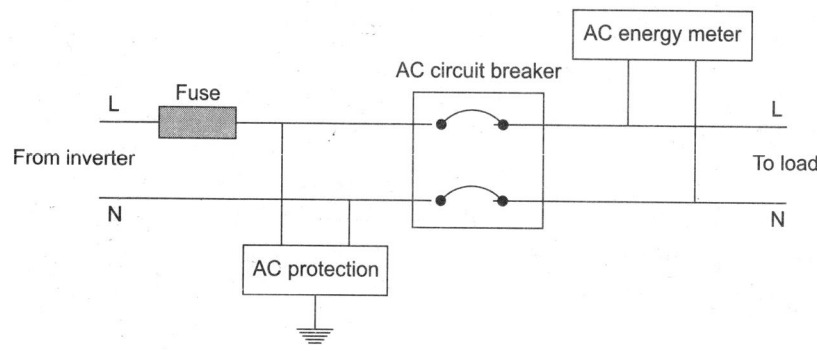

FIGURE 11.19
AC distribution box diagram.

The low voltage transformer can be incorporated with the inverter. An external transformer is required for AC load circuit isolation when transformerless inverter is employed. A three-phase low to medium voltage step-up transformer is used when the output of inverter is connected to medium voltage grid at the distribution level (11 kV–33 kV).

AC energy metering and net metering

AC energy metering is required to determine the amount of energy produced by solar PV system. The metering configuration used depends on the application. The PV energy meter connected in series with the inverter output is used to monitor PV generated energy. The load energy meter connected in series with the load is used to monitor energy consumed by load. The net energy meter is used to monitor net energy import from or export to the grid.

The PV and load energy meters are uni-directional and register the flow of energy in forward direction. The net energy meter is bi-directional and registers the flow of energy in both forward and reverse directions. It is shown in Figure 11.20 that three energy meters; (a) PV meter, (b) Load meter and (c) Net meter can be used in a PV system. Minimum two energy meters are required to determine overall energy flow (see Figure 11.20).

> Load energy meters are uni-directional and register the flow of energy in forward direction. The net energy meter is bi-directional and registers the flow of energy in both forward and reverse directions.

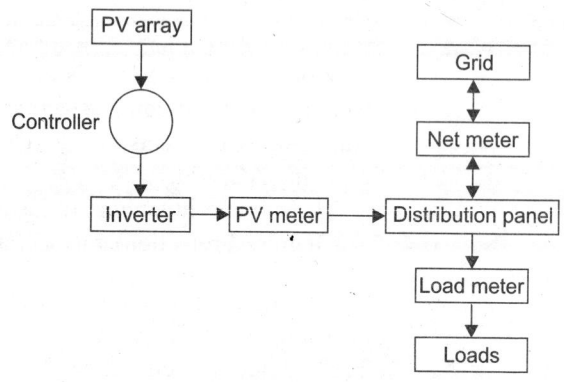

FIGURE 11.20
AC energy metering in a grid connected system.

When the PV energy generated is less the energy consumed by the load, the net energy meter runs in forward direction (positive reading). If PV generated energy is greater than energy consumed by load, then energy is exported to grid. In this case, the net meter runs in reverse direction (negative reading). Thus, net meter can run in forward as well as reverse direction. During certain period if the more energy is consumed by the load (than produced by PV), then the net meter reading will be positive and if more energy is produced by the PV modules than consumed by the load, then net meter reading will be negative. Negative net meter reading implies that energy is fed to grid.

Positive net meter reading: If PV generated energy is less than energy consumed by load, energy is imported from grid. The energy flow in the Net meter is in the forward direction.

Energy consumed by load = PV generated energy + Energy drawn from grid

Net meter reading is positive when energy is drawn from grid.

Negative net meter reading: If PV generated energy is greater than energy consumed by load, energy is exported to grid. The energy flow in the Net meter is in the reverse direction.

PV generated energy = Energy consumed by load + Energy fed to grid

Net meter reading is negative when energy is fed to grid.

Net meter reading is positive when energy is drawn from grid and net meter reading is negative when energy is fed to grid.

EXAMPLE 11.5

If PV meter reads 10 kWh and Load meter reads 8 kWh, what will be the Net energy meter reading?

Solution

PV meter reading = 10 kWh

Load meter reading = 8 kWh

Since PV generated energy is greater than energy consumed by load, it indicates that energy is fed to the grid.

PV generated energy = Energy consumed by load + Energy fed to grid

Energy fed to grid = PV generated energy – Energy consumed by load
= 10 kWh – 8 kWh = 2 kWh

Net energy flow is 2 kWh into the grid and hence the net energy meter would read – 2 units. The negative sign indicates the energy is fed to the grid.

EXAMPLE 11.6

If net energy meter reads +4 kWh and load meter reads 10 kWh, what is the PV generated energy?

Solution

From the definition, net energy meter reading is positive, indicating that more energy is consumed by the load than produced by PV.

Net energy meter reading: +4 kWh

Load meter reading: 10 kWh

Energy consumed by load = PV generated energy + Energy drawn from grid

PV generated energy = Energy consumed by load – Energy drawn from grid
= 10 kWh – 4 kWh = 6 kWh

Therefore, PV generated energy is 6 kWh.

Problem 11.5: In a PV system wherein net metering is done, if PV meter reads 20 kWh and load meter reads 10 kWh, what will be the net energy meter reading?

11.4

Grid-connected PV System Design for Small Power Applications

Some basic principles to be followed when designing a quality grid-connected PV power plant for small power applications are as follows:

1. Select a packaged system that meets the owner's needs. Customer criteria for a system may include meeting annual energy requirements, reduction in monthly electricity bill, environmental benefits, desire for back-up power, initial budget constraints, etc.

2. Size and orient the PV array to provide the expected electrical power and energy.

3. Ensure the roof area or other installation site is capable of handling the desired system size.

4. Locate the array to minimize shading and interference with obstructions.

5. Ensure that suitable cable ducts are available to lay DC cables from array to the inverter.

6. Ensure control room is available indoors to house inverter as well as DC and AC distribution boxes.

7. Specify sunlight and weather resistant materials for all outdoor equipment.

8. Design the system with a minimum of electrical losses due to wiring, fuses, switches, and inverters.

9. Design the system in compliance with all applicable building and electrical codes.

10. Ensure the design meets local utility interconnection requirements.

10.4.1

Steps of System Design

The energy flow happens from PV array to the load and the PV system design should proceed in the reverse direction of energy flow.

We need to design the system to meet annual energy consumption requirements. The energy flow happens from PV array to the load and the PV system design should proceed in the reverse direction of energy flow, i.e., from load to PV array. In the reverse path, we should account for all losses in PV system. In the grid-connected PV system, since power capacity is normally large as compared small standalone system, and hence power losses in DC as well as AC cables must also be considered.

A simple block diagram of grid-connected PV system is shown in Figure 11.21. In this case, the PV system is assumed to be connected with the grid. The PV design analysis is presented assuming that all the power required by the load is to be supplied by the PV array alone. However, since the grid is connected to the PV system, any additional power generated by the PV array (than required by the load) will be supplied to the grid, and any deficit of power required by the load will be drawn from the grid. In principle, a grid-connected PV system can also be design to take some percentage of power from the PV array and some percentage of power from the PV array, or a grid connected PV system can be considering the rooftop area available for the installation of PV module as limiting factor. If the whole rooftop area is covered by PV modules, the power generated may be surplus or in shortage, depending on the case power can either be fed to the grid or power can be drawn from the grid. In this way, there are a number of possibilities of a grid-connected PV system design, and design depends on the constraint which may come from load side, grid side or physical infrastructure side.

There are a number of possibilities of a grid-connected PV system design, and design depends on the constraint which may come from load side, grid side or physical infrastructure side.

Step 1 Estimate annual energy usage: In this step, the estimation of energy consumption by the load is done. The process is explained in detail in Chapter 2. As an example, let us assume that energy consumed by the load is 15 kWh or 15 units per day.

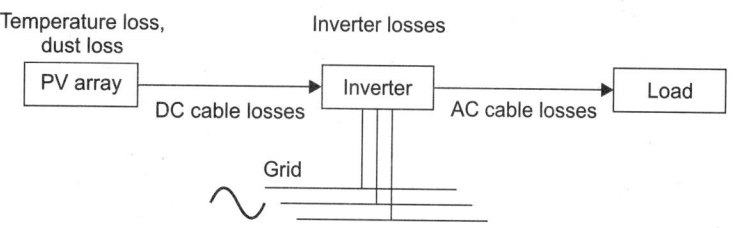

FIGURE 11.21

Block diagram of grid-connected PV system with indications of various losses in PV system.

We can consider any additional load or allowances in load in near future. For example, adding new fans or computers in future. Let us assume that another four kWh will be consumed by the future loads. Then the total estimated energy of the loads will be:

$$\text{Current load} + \text{Future load} = 15 + 5 = 20 \text{ kWh/day}$$

Based on the daily energy requirements, monthly and yearly energy requirements can also be estimated.

Step 2 Average daily solar radiation in terms of equivalent sunshine hours:
Average daily solar radiation for a given location, where solar PV plants is to be installed, is normally given in terms of kWh/m²/day. Normally in India, the daily solar radiation varies between 4 to 7 kWh/m²/day. Now, since the solar PV modules are rated for standard test condition (STC) which is equal to sunlight power density of 1000 W/m² or 1 kW/m² and temperature of 25 °C. It means that a 100 W_p PV module will provide output power of 100 W_p only when the condition corresponding to STC is matched.

Suppose at a given location average daily solar radiation is 5 kWh/m²/day, this can be written as 1 kW/m² × 5 hour/day (for detailed discussion, refer to Chapter 10). In this way, we can say that daily solar radiation of 5 kWh/m²/day is equal to solar power density of 1 kW/m² for 5 hours per day. Although the sunshines for longer hours in a day, and intensity changes from morning to evening. In this case, 5 hours/day is referred as equivalent sunshine hours. The equivalent sunshine hours is very useful concept because PV modules are rated for STC condition.

Step 3 Estimate the AC power supplied to the load: AC power output (in terms of kW) can be obtained by dividing the total energy supplied to the load (given in terms of kWh) by the equivalent daily hours of sunshine (given in terms of hours or 'h'). In this example, daily energy consumed is 18 kWh and h is taken as 5 hours.

$$\text{AC power to load (in kW)} = \frac{\text{Daily energy to load (in kWh)}}{\text{Equivalent daily sunshine hours (in h)}}$$
$$= \frac{20 \text{ kWh}}{5 \text{ h}} = 4 \text{ kW}$$

Step 4 Estimate the AC power output of inverter or PV plant output power:
The AC output power losses consist of transformer and AC cable losses. The AC output power losses are typically of the order of 2% to 5%. In this example, let us say this is 5%.

$$\text{AC power output of inverter (in kW)} = \frac{\text{Power fed to load (kW)}}{(1 - \text{AC power losses})}$$

Thus, inverter AC output power $= \dfrac{4}{1-(5/100)} = \dfrac{4}{1-0.05} = \dfrac{4}{0.95} = 4.21 \text{ kW}$

Step 5 Estimate the DC power input to inverter: The input to inverter will be DC power. The input DC power will be more than the inverter output AC power due to losses in the inverter. The inverter power losses consist of MPPT tracking and DC to AC conversion losses. The inverters are becoming very efficient and power losses in inverter are in the range of 2% to 5%. Let us assume that inverter losses are 3% in this example.

$$\text{Inverter DC power input (in kW)} = \frac{\text{Inverter AC power output (kW)}}{(1 - \text{Inverter power losses})}$$

Thus, inverter DC input power $= \dfrac{4.21}{1 - (3/100)} = \dfrac{4.21}{1 - 0.03} = \dfrac{4.21}{0.97} = 4.34$ kW.

Step 6 Estimate DC power output of PV array: Between the PV array and the inverter input, there are DC cables. The DC cables also have power losses. The DC cable losses depend on the cable thickness and length. Typical systems are designed for maximum DC cable losses of 3%. Due to the cable losses, the PV array will have to produce more power. Assuming DC cable losses of 3%:

$$\text{PV array DC power output (in kW)} = \frac{\text{Inverter DC power input (kW)}}{(1 - \text{DC cable losses})}$$

Thus, PV array DC output power $= \dfrac{4.34}{1 - (3/100)} = \dfrac{4.34}{1 - 0.03} = \dfrac{4.34}{0.97} = 4.47$ kW

In this way, the estimated size of PV array is 4.03 kW. Remember that this power rating of the PV modules is power rating under STC condition, which means it is peak power rating with subscript 'p', i.e., 4.47 kW_p or almost equal to 4.5 kW_p.

Step 7 Take operating losses in account: In practice, while PV modules operate in field, there are several losses that can occur. Some losses are small and some are large. The module or PV array output gets reduced by the following way:

1. Manufacturing tolerance/module mismatch loss
2. Module temperature loss
3. Module soiling loss

Module mismatch losses: The typical manufacturing tolerance of PV module output power is +/- 3%. The module mismatch loss is, therefore, 3%.

Module temperature losses: In order to determine module temperature losses, module average operating temperature needs to be determined. The Normal Operating Cell Temperature (NOCT) is defined as module cell temperature under STC of 25°C. Typical PV module NOCT is specified at 45°C. The average operating temperature of the module cell depends on the average ambient temperature conditions. For average ambient temperature of 30°C, the module average operating temperature is 50°C.

The temperature coefficient for output power of PV module is in the range of 0.25%/°C to 0.5%/°C. This power temperature coefficient gives an indication of loss of power for a given module for every degree centigrade rise in temperature. The crystalline silicon modules have power temperature co-efficient of about 0.45%/°C while thin film modules have lower temperature coefficient ranging from 0.2%/°C to 0.3%/°C. Normally, the power temperature coefficient of PV modules is given in the datasheet of manufactures. It mostly depends on material of PV modules but to some extent also depends on the manufacture as well. Note here that the temperature coefficient is given in terms of per degree centigrade. Thus, if PV module is characterized at STC condition of 25 °C and if average operating temperature is 50 °C, then the loss in power output of module or array due to increase in temperature is:

- The percentage power losses for crystalline silicon modules or PV array due to temperature:

$$\text{Module temperature loss} = 50\,°C - 25\,°C \times \frac{0.45\%}{0\,°C} = 11.25\%$$

- The percentage power losses for thin film PV modules due to temperature, assuming power temperature coefficient of 0.3%/°C:

$$\text{Module temperature loss} = 50\,°C - 25\,°C \times \frac{0.3\%}{0\,°C} = 7.5\%$$

This power temperature coefficient gives an indication of loss of power for a given module for every degree centigrade rise in temperature. This coefficient mostly depends on the material of PV module but to some extent also on the manufacturer.

Module soiling losses: The modules are typically soiled by dust, dirt, bird droppings etc. The periodic cleaning of modules is recommended to minimize soiling loss. Typical module soiling loss is estimated at 5%.

Thus, the total PV module losses while in operation include:

$$\text{Total module loss} = \text{Mismatch loss} + \text{Temperature loss} + \text{Soiling loss}$$
$$= 3\% + 11.25\% + 5\% = 19.25\%$$

Step 8 Estimate final required PV array capacity: The PV array must supply the DC power required as estimated in Step 6, but the array must also supply the operating losses estimated in Step 7. Considering this, the total PV array required would be:

$$\text{Final PV array power output (in kW)} = \frac{\text{PV array DC power output (kW)}}{1 - \text{operating losses}}$$
$$= \frac{4.5}{1 - (19.25/100)} = \frac{4.5}{1 - 0.192} = \frac{4.5}{0.808}$$
$$= 5.57\ kW_p$$

Thus, the final PV array capacity required is 5.57 kW$_p$. Remember the subscript 'p' is added in power, i.e., W$_p$ to indicate that this power rating is for STC condition.

Step 9 Estimate required number PV modules: For this purpose, one can choose the modules that are available in the market, their making and power rating. PV modules are available in the capacity of 30 W$_p$ to 300 W$_p$. Normally, for applications needing PV modules in several kW$_p$, we should choose modules of higher wattage rating. In higher wattage rating, crystalline Si PV modules of 230 W$_p$, 235 W$_p$ and 240 W$_p$ are easily available. For example, if one choose to use PV modules of 240 W$_p$, which is nowadays available, then the total number of PV modules required would be:

$$\frac{5.57\ kW}{240} = \frac{5570}{240} = 23.20$$

or taking the next integer value, we can say 24 PV module will be required.

The connection of these PV modules would depend on the inverter power rating and input DC voltage the inverter can take.

Step 10 Estimate inverter power rating: In Step 6, it is estimated that the DC power input to inverter is 4.34 kW, it means that an inverter should be able to process this much power. Normally, for the safety purpose little higher power rating is chosen. This is required because reflection from clouds or other objects may temporarily increase the sunlight falling on module, resulting in higher power generation. About 10% higher inverter capacity should be chosen. Also, we have considered about 3% mismatch losses, in case there is no mismatch in modules. This extra power would appear at inverter input, we should take safety for this purpose as well. Overall, our inverter capacity should be 10% to 15% higher than input power value estimated in Step 6.

$$\text{Inverter power rating (in kW)} = \frac{\text{DC input power to inverter (kW)}}{1 - \text{saftey factor}}$$

$$= \frac{4.34}{1 - (15/100)} = \frac{4.34}{1 - 0.15} = \frac{4.34}{0.85} = 5.11 \text{ kW}$$

Note that this is the input power rating of inverter. Due to losses within inverter, the output power rating of the inverter will be less.

Step 11 PV array configuration: The PV array configuration or the number of PV modules to be connected in series or in string, and the number of parallel strings depend on the inverter voltage ratings. The PV string V_{oc} and V_{mp} must be within allowable limits of inverter ratings. Maximum I_{sc} of the PV array should also be within acceptable limit to the inverter.

Final array configuration is selected based on inverter input DC voltage window of operation. Inverter manufacturer specifies a range of V_{mp} values for its MPPT operation. Based on module tolerance and its minimum and maximum temperature of operation, a range of module V_{mp} output is determined. For a number of modules, connected in a series string, a range of string V_{mp} values is calculated. The number of modules in a series string is determined such that its range of V_{mp} output falls well within the permitted range of V_{mp} values of the inverter. This is demonstrated in Figure 11.22.

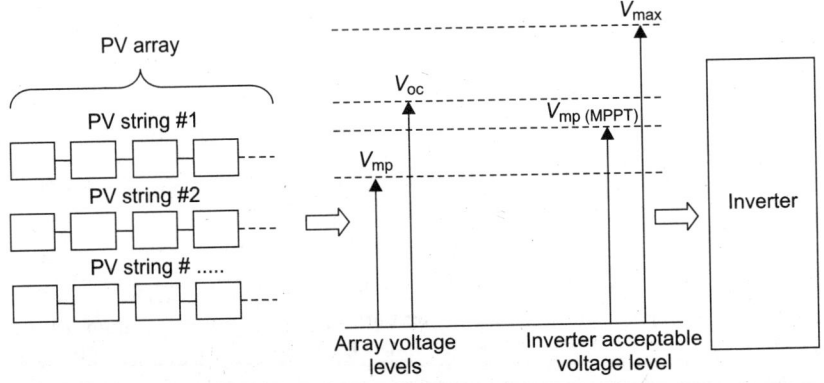

FIGURE 11.22
Array voltage level and voltage levels acceptable at the input of inverter.

Inverter manufacturer also specifies maximum input DC voltage rating. Based on module tolerance and its minimum temperature of operation, maximum module V_{oc} output is determined. For a number of modules connected in a series string, maximum string V_{oc} output is equal to the maximum module V_{oc} multiplied by the number of modules. The maximum array V_{oc} is equal to the maximum string V_{oc} for a number of strings connected in parallel to make an array. It is then verified that the maximum array V_{oc} is less than maximum input DC voltage rating of the inverter. This is demonstrated in Figure 11.22.

It is also verified that the maximum array I_{sc} is within the maximum input DC current rating of the inverter. The maximum module I_{sc} is determined based on

The PV array configuration or the number of PV modules to be connected in series (as string) and the number of parallel strings depends on the inverter voltage ratings.

module tolerance, maximum available solar radiation and maximum temperature of operation. The maximum string I_{sc} is equal to the maximum module I_{sc} for a series connected string, and the maximum array I_{sc} is maximum string I_{sc} multiplied by the number of strings in an array.

Determining the number of modules in string

Let us now go to find out the number of modules we should be connecting in a string. This is decided by considering the allowable V_{mp} and V_{max} at the input of inverter and V_{mp} and V_{oc} of the PV modules selected for installation.

Table 11.1 gives the list of commercially available PV modules with their parameters. These modules can be used for grid-connected PV system applications. Using these PV modules, the PV systems of capacity from few kW to MW level plants can be installed. Normally, for MW level plants, higher wattage rating PV modules are preferred. Table 11.2 gives the typical parameter of commercially available grid-connected inverter. The main parameters of these inverters are maximum DC input voltage, maximum power point tracking voltage range, maximum DC input current, efficiency of inverter and its AC power rating. Referring to Figure 11.21, and by using Table 11.1 and Table 11.2, we can estimate the number of panels that we can connect in a PV string and the number of such strings that will be required for given power applications.

TABLE 11.1 Typical Parameters of Commercial PV Modules

S. No.	Model X	P_m (W_p)	V_{oc} (V)	I_{sc} (A)	V_m (V)	I_m (A)
1	Module 1	125	22.1	7.9	18.2	6.9
2	Module 2	135	22.0	8.38	17.7	7.63
3	Module 3	145	22.4	8.5	18.35	7.9
4	Module 4	200	32.5	8.42	26.1	7.66
5	Module 5	210	41.59	7.13	33.81	6.21
6	Module 6	230	36.0	8.45	28.6	8.05
7	Module 7	240	37.38	8.45	30.60	7.85

TABLE 11.2 Typical Parameter of Commercially Available Grid-connected Inverters

AC power output (kVA)	Model	Maximum DC input voltage (V)	Maximum power point (MPP) voltage tracking range (V)	Maximum DC current (A)	Peak efficiency (%)
5	Inveter 1	600	80–120	50	97.0
10	Inveter 2	600	100–160	75	97.5
17	Inveter 3	600	400–800	35	98.2
250	Inveter 4	600	330–600	800	97.5
500	Inveter 5	600	330–600	1470	98.6
1000	Inveter 6	1000	460–875	2100	98.6

Number of PV modules required: In this example, total PV array capacity required is 5.57 or about 6 kW$_p$ (from Step 8). Suppose we choose Module 3 (from Table 11.1) for this installation. The rated power capacity of Module 3 is 145 W$_p$. Therefore, the number of Module 3 required for 6 kW$_p$ system would be:

$$\text{Total no. of modules required} = \frac{\text{Total PV plant capacity}}{\text{Rated power of one module}}$$

$$= \frac{6 \text{ kW}_p}{145 \text{ W}_p} = \frac{6000}{145} = 41.37$$

To round off, we need about 42 PV modules of 145 W$_p$ for this PV system.

Number of PV modules in a string: In order to determine the number of PV modules in the array, we should look at the acceptable voltage rating of inverter and try to match it with the voltage ratings of strings as per the presentation given in Figure 11.21. The V_{oc} of PV Module 3 is 22.4 V, V_{mp} is 18.35 V and I_m is 7.9 A. Now, from Step 10, the inverter power rating is 5.11 kVA. Let us say that there is a commercial inverter available in the market is 5 kVA (see Inverter 1 in Table 11.2). Its Maximum Power Point (MPP) voltage tracking range is 80 V–120 V and maximum input DC current is 50 A.

Since when we connect PV modules in series, the voltage gets added, therefore, we need to connect many Module 3 in series to get the required voltage in the range of Inverter 1. If we divide V_{mp} range of Inverter 1 with the V_{mp} of the Module 3, we will get number of PV modules to be connected in series to form one string is:

$$\text{No. of modules in string} = \frac{V_{mp} \text{ voltage of selected inverter}}{V_{mp} \text{ of selected PV module}}$$

Since the inverter V_{mp} tracking range is 80 V to 120 V, let us have an average of it, that is, 100 V. This 100 V will be the V_{mp} of the PV module string. Note that any other voltage level within the inverter tracking range can also be chosen. We have to only ensure that the array V_{mp} point should lay within the inverter V_{mp} range in all operating condition

$$\frac{100}{18.35} = 5.44$$

The above calculation shows that we will have to connect 5.44 PV modules in series, or to round it off, we get 6 modules. The V_{mp} of 6 module series will be

$$18.35 \times 6 = 111.9$$

It is still in the range of V_{mp} tracking of inverter and should be acceptable. Also, remember that if the temperature of cells in module is higher than 25 °C, the actual module V_{mp} in the field will be lower. It means that the V_{mp} of 6 PV modules in series are within acceptable limit.

Number of PV strings in parallel: In total, we need to connect 42 PV modules in this grid-connected PV system. One of the string of PV modules will have 6 PV modules. Therefore, the number of strings to be connected in parallel will be:

$$\text{No. of strings in parallel} = \frac{\text{Total no. of PV modules in system}}{\text{No. of modules in a string}}$$

$$= \frac{42}{6} = 7$$

Thus, we need to connect 7 strings of 6 modules in parallel. Note, that when we connect strings in parallel, the current of each string gets added. The total current of the parallel combination will be the sum of current of each string. We have to make sure that the total current of the strings is within the limit of the inverter. In this example, the maximum DC current limit of Inverter 1 is 50 A. In this case, the Module 3 I_{sc} is 8.5 A, and 7 strings are connected in parallel, therefore, the total current of all the strings will be:

$$\text{Total current of strings in parallel} = \text{Current of one string} \times \text{Total number of strings}$$

$$= 8.5 \times 7 = 59.5 \text{ A}$$

When inverter rating does not match with PV array rating, then, either we choose some other inverter to fit our PV array requirements or we change your PV system requirements to match with the inverter rating.

From this calculation, we can see that the current of 7 strings put together is higher than the maximum allowable DC current of the inverter. It suggests that the Inverter 1 is NOT suitable for this application. Therefore, in such cases, either we choose some other inverter to fit our PV array requirements or we change our PV system requirements to match with the inverter rating.

Step 12 Select Balance of System (BoS) components:

DC BoS components: Various Balance of Systems (BoS) components are required to integrate the system. PV array support structure, DC cables, string and array combiner boxes and DC distribution boxes are used on the DC system side.

PV array support structure is of three types; fixed, manual tracking and auto-tracking. The structure is usually custom designed to suit the type of modules used, string and array design and the type and the slope of terrain where the array is installed. The module mounting frames are typically fabricated using galvanized iron or aluminum sections and are designed to withstand outdoor temperature, humidity, wind and other environmental factors. The modules are either bolted onto the frames or held with clips. The frames are secured onto roof structure or on ground using suitable support members. The support members are typically fabricated using metal sections matching module frame sections or using treated wooden sections. The support structures are typically grouted into concrete blocks secured onto terrace or firm ground. The support structures can also be rammed into soft ground.

The string/array combiner box are typically double insulated and rated for IP65. The surge protection devices are typically rated for 600 V to 1000 V DC. The double pole DC disconnect switch is rated for minimum of 1.25 times PV array short circuit current. The DC disconnect switch inside array combiner box is used to isolate PV array from the DC cables in the building and the inverter. The Ground Fault Detector Interrupter (GFDI) device is typically designed to detect 5% of PV array maximum output current as ground fault current and interrupt DC input circuit.

The DC disconnect switch and surge protection devices are also housed in the DC distribution box located near the inverter. Alternatively, they are integrated with the inverter DC input circuit. The DC disconnect switch inside DC distribution box is used to isolate DC circuit inside building from the inverter.

If the DC cables are rated for a minimum of 1.25 times the string short circuit current at each location, string fuses are optional. The string blocking diodes are also optional for small size power plants using less than four strings. The DC cables are either rated for outdoor environment or are housed inside conduits which, in turn, are rated for outdoor use.

DC cable size is selected such that the total power loss over the entire length of DC cables is within 3% of the rated PV array output power.

The total length of string DC cables is two times (positive and negative cables) the distance between modules and the string combiner box. The total length of array DC cables (positive and negative cables) is two times the distance between array combiner box and inverter. The DC cable size is selected such that the total power loss over the entire length of DC cables is within 3% of the rated PV array output power.

AC BoS components: The BoS components on the AC system side are AC circuit breakers, AC overvoltage protection devices, AC output transformers, AC cables, AC distribution boxes and AC energy meters.

The AC circuit breakers and AC overvoltage protection devices are typically integrated with the inverter output AC circuit. Alternatively, they can be housed inside AC distribution box to facilitate the isolation of inverter output near AC output transformers or loads. The AC circuit breakers are typically rated for 1.2 times the maximum AC output current of the inverter.

The AC voltage protection devices are typically rated for 400 V AC for 230 V single phase circuits and 600 V AC for 415 V three phases circuits.

The AC output transformer is normally built within the inverter for LV circuits and is rated for 1.2 times the maximum AC output power of the inverter. For MV circuits, an external three phase step-up transformer is used to supply AC power to MV grid. The MV transformer is rated for 1.05 to 1.1 times the maximum AC output power of the inverter. The AC input and output circuit breakers and AC voltage protection devices are used with AC output transformer. The transformer losses are typically in the range of 2% to 5% of its rated output power.

The AC cables are typically rated for 1.2 times the maximum AC current carried. The AC cables from inverter output to transformer housed inside control room are rated for indoor environment. The AC cables from transformer output to load housed inside building are also rated for indoor specifications. The AC cables from transformer output to grid are rated for outdoor environment. The total length of LV AC cables is twice the distance between inverter and transformer or load. The total length of MV AC cables is twice the distance between transformer and grid distribution centre. The AC cable size is selected such that the total power loss over the entire length of AC cables is within 2% of the rated inverter AC output power.

> AC cable size is selected such that the total power loss over the entire length of AC cables is within 2% of the rated inverter AC output power.

Step 13 Select energy meter: The energy meters are used to monitor energy generated by PV power plant, energy consumed by load and energy supplied to grid by the plant.

In PV power plant for small power applications, net energy meter is used to monitor net energy drawn by load from grid or net energy supplied by inverter to grid. The net energy meter is rated for Low Tension (LT) grid voltage and PV power plant maximum output AC current or maximum load AC current whichever is higher. The PV generated AC energy and the AC energy consumed by the load can be monitored by separate energy meters. Alternatively, DC energy meter can be used at the output of PV array to monitor PV generated DC energy. In PV power plant for large power applications, three phases AC energy meters are used to monitor energy produced by PV power plant and supplied to MV grid. These energy meters are rated for MV AC voltage. Additionally, inverter also monitors AC energy produced by PV power plant.

Problem 11.6: Design a grid-connected PV system for fulfilling the load energy requirement of 12 kWh/day. Assume that grid is available full time and no battery storage is required. Give the details of all component selected for this plant. Take the average ambient temperature of 25 °C, and average solar radiation of 5.5 kWh/m²/day.

Problem 11.7: Design a grid-connected PV system for fulfilling the load energy requirement of 25 kWh/day. Assume that grid is available full time and no battery storage is required. Give the details of all component selected for this plant. The plant is to be installed in Chennai where average solar radiation is 5.7 kWh/m²/day.

11.5
Grid-connected PV System Design for Power Plants

The PV systems which are designed for power plant applications have primary function to feed power to the grid only, and not to any local load like in captive power plants. When we design a captive power plant, the basic criterion is to design PV system to meet energy demands of the local load. Here, the grid connectivity helps to supply the load if there is additional energy demand or excess generated energy is fed to the grid. On the other hand, when we design a solar PV system for power plants, the basic concept is to fix the size or capacity of power plant and then design the plant to get the best yield or best electricity generation from the plant. For instance, under Jawaharlal Nehru National Solar Mission, the government is awarding the contracts to install solar PV power plants in capacity of 5 MW_p. There are other schemes in which the PV plants can be installed in capacity of 1 MW_p. In such situation, the PV plant installer tries to design the plant in such a way that the losses in the plants are minimum and, therefore, energy generation is maximum. Mostly, the electricity generated in PV power plants is sold to the government at predefined rates. In the PV plant design, we can do the design in two parts:

1. Part 1: Estimation of energy output of PV plant
2. Part 2: Determining the configuration of PV plant (string size, inverter rating, etc.).

In small grid-connected PV plants or in standalone PV system design, the design or sizing of components is done in the reverse order of energy flow. But in PV power plants, the design or sizing of the components is done in the direction of energy flow. This is done because, as discussed, the PV plant capacity is fixed in advance. In this section, let us see how we can design MW scale power plants and how much energy can be generated from these plants.

> In PV power plants, the design or sizing of the components is done in the direction of energy flow.

11.5.1
Estimation of Energy Output of PV Plant

Step 1 Fixing the capacity of PV power plant: The first step is to fix the size or capacity of power plant. This is normally fixed by the government scheme under which the PV power plant is being installed as the main purpose of PV power plants is to generate electricity and sell it to the government. Typical power rating of these plants is 1 MW_p, 2 MW_p or 5 MW_p. Some governments are also installing PV power plants of very large capacities, ranging up to 500 MW_p. The capacity of the overall plant is normally in the multiple of 1 MW_p. In this case, let us design the power plant for 1 MW_p capacity. Figure 11.23 shows the arrangement of a large capacity PV power plant with associated losses.

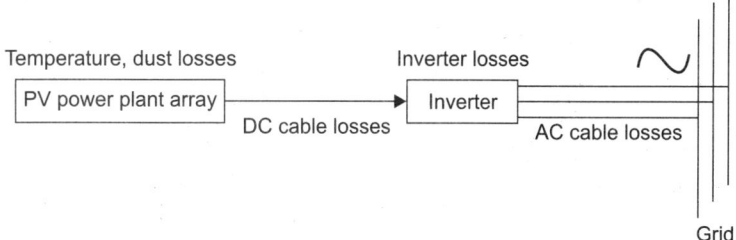

FIGURE 11.23

Arrangement of a large capacity PV power plants with associated losses.

Step 2 Average daily solar radiation and equivalent sunshine hours: As discussed in Section 11.4.1 (steps of system design), we should get daily solar radiation data of a location where PV plant is being installed. Using this data we can estimate the amount of electricity that can be generated using a power plant of given capacity. The solar radiation for a given location, where solar PV plants is to be installed, is normally given in terms of $kWh/m^2/day$. Normally, in India, the daily solar radiation varies between 4 to 7 $kWh/m^2/day$.

Since the solar intensities change on day to day and month to month basis. Therefore, average daily solar radiation falling on a given location also changes. If we want more accurate estimation of possible energy production from 1 MW plant, we should try to get monthly average data for the site, and therefore, we should estimate the possible electricity generation for each month. Also, note that solar radiation data are available on horizontal surface. In order to collect more solar radiation, solar PV modules are installed as tilted facing south. The tilt angle

Solar radiation data at the plane of array (not on horizontal surface) of solar PV modules should be considered in solar PV power plant design.

varies from one site to other site. Therefore, it is important that the solar radiation data is obtained for tilted plane or on the plane of array (PoA). Normally, the solar radiation data is always higher on PoA as compared to solar radiation data on horizontal surface. As an example for some site, these solar radiation data is given in Table 11.3.

TABLE 11.3 Solar Radiation Data of Some Location, Giving Average Daily and Monthly Solar Radiation Data (The Radiation Data Vary from One Site to Other Site)

Month	Radiation on horizontal radiation (kWh/m^2)	Radiation on plane of array (kWh/m^2)	Equivalent daily sunshine hours (Hours)	No. of days	Monthly radiation on plane of array (kWh/m^2)
January	4.95	5.50	5.50	31	171
February	5.50	6.12	6.12	28	171
March	5.8	6.45	6.45	31	200
April	5.9	6.66	6.66	30	200
May	5.93	6.59	6.59	31	204
June	5.58	6.20	6.20	30	186
July	5.49	6.10	6.10	31	189
August	4.63	5.15	5.15	31	160
September	4.68	5.20	5.20	30	156
October	4.70	5.23	5.23	31	162
November	4.84	5.38	5.38	30	161
December	4.87	5.42	5.42	31	168
			Annual solar radiation on plane of array (kWh/m^2)		2128

Solar radiation data vary from one site to other site, also for the same site solar radiation data on the plane of array of modules are different for different tilt of PV modules.

Let us assume that we need to design this 1 MW_p plant using solar radiation data given in Table 11.3. In this section, we will do the calculation for one month, and it is expected that the readers will do the calculation for other months on their own.

Equivalent sunshine hours

Let us take the month of January for the calculations. For the site under consideration, the average daily solar radiation on the plane of array for the month of January is 5.5 $kWh/m^2/day$ (see Table 11.3). The average daily solar radiation of 5.5 $kWh/m^2/day$ is equal to solar power density of 1 kW/m^2 for 5.5 hours per day (for details refer to Chapter 10.

Thus, in this case, equivalent sunshine hours are 5.5 hours per day and monthly equivalent sunshine hours is $5.5 \times 31 = 170.5$ or 170.5 hours per month (for the month of January). Note that these hours are for the radiation on the plane of array, i.e., for tilted surface.

Step 3 Estimating the energy production over a given period: In this example, we will do calculation for the month of January. For the month of January, the average daily solar radiation is 5.5 $kWh/m^2/day$ (see Table 11.3) and corresponding average daily sunshine hours is 5.5 hours. The estimation of possible energy from the plant can be obtained by simply multiplying the PV plant capacity with the daily solar radiation data on the plane of array or plane of modules. In this example, the PV plant capacity is 1 MW_p. Therefore, the maximum possible energy produced by the plant in the month of January is:

Monthly energy production

= PV plant capacity × Average sunshine hours × Number of day in month

= 1 MW_p × 5.5 hours × 31

= 1000,000 × 5.5 × 31 = 170500000 Wh

On dividing by 1000, we will get electricity in terms of kWh.

Therefore, $\dfrac{170500000}{1000}$ Wh = 170500 kWh

This is the electricity produced by the plant in the month of January. Similarly, we can also calculate the electricity produced by 1 MW$_p$ PV plant in other months as well. Calculation for each month is given in Table 11.4. We can see from this table that a total of 2.12 Million kWh electricity can be produced by this 1 MW$_p$ PV power plant.

TABLE 11.4 Monthly and Annual Electricity Production Potential of 1 MW$_p$ Solar PV Plant for a Location Under Consideration

Month	Power plant capacity	Monthly radiation on PoA (kWh/m²)	Equivalent monthly sunshine hours (hours)	Monthly energy production (kWh)
January	1 MW$_p$	171	171	170500
February	1 MW$_p$	171	171	171360
March	1 MW$_p$	200	200	199950
April	1 MW$_p$	200	200	199800
May	1 MW$_p$	204	204	204395
June	1 MW$_p$	186	186	186000
July	1 MW$_p$	189	189	189100
August	1 MW$_p$	160	160	159650
September	1 MW$_p$	156	156	156000
October	1 MW$_p$	162	162	162130
November	1 MW$_p$	161	161	161400
December	1 MW$_p$	168	168	168020
Total electricity production potential by 1 MW plant in one year without considering any losses (kWh)				2,128,305
				2.12 Million kWh

Note here that we have not taken any losses in the PV plant in account. In the following calculation, we need to consider all kind of losses to estimate the actual energy that can be delivered to the grid by this 1 MW PV plant.

Step 4 Consider losses at PV array level: We can see from Table 11.4 that the total electricity production potential for site under consideration (for which solar radiation data is taken), and for the month of January is 170500 kWh. This electricity production is for ideal condition given by standard test condition (STC) wherein PV module temperature (more precisely temperature of cells in modules) of 25 °C is considered. In practice, due to non-deal conditions, several losses occur at PV module level which reduces PV module output. These losses include:

1. Module temperature loss
2. Module soiling loss due to dust
3. Module mismatch loss
4. DC cable loss
5. Solar radiation loss

Module temperature losses: This is discussed in Section 11.4.1 where the design of grid connected plant for small power application is considered. The loss of power due to temperature is given by temperature coefficient of power. The crystalline silicon modules have power temperature coefficient of about 0.45%/°C while thin film modules have lower temperature coefficient ranging from 0.2%/°C to 0.3%/°C.

Also, it should be noted that the cells in PV modules are at $20\,°C$ to $25\,°C$ higher temperature than the ambient temperature, and, it is the cell temperature which results in power losses (refer to Chapter 3). Suppose, for the site for which this plant is designed will have $35\,°C$ ambient temperature in the month of January, and the cell temperature is $20\,°C$ higher than the ambient temperature, i.e., the cell temperature is $35 + 20 = 55\,°C$. Then, the percentage of power losses for crystalline silicon modules or PV array due to temperature is:

$$\text{Module temperature loss} = 55\,°C - 25\,°C \times \frac{0.45\%}{°C} = 13.5\%$$

Module soiling losses: This is the loss due to dust settlement on the PV module which hinders solar radiation entering inside and thus reduces power output. Normally, even after regular cleaning of PV modules, the losses are in 1% to 2% range. For this example, let us take it 1.5%.

Module mismatch losses: The typical manufacturing tolerance of PV module output power is +/– 3%. Let us take these losses to be about 1.5%.

DC cable loss: This is the resistive losses that happens in DC cables which connect modules. Typically, cable thickness is chosen to keep the losses within 2%. For this example, let us assume these losses to be about 1.2%.

Solar radiation loss: This is the loss due to the reflection of PV modules from the glass surface. This should be normally within 2% to 4%. Here, let us consider this as 2.5%.

In this way, the total PV module losses will be the sum of all the losses mentioned here. Among all losses, the loss of temperature is most dominant which depends on the selection of a site. Normally, the sites which have higher temperature also have higher solar radiation. The advantage of higher solar radiation is normally more than the loss of power due to higher temperature.

Thus, total module losses are = 13.5% + 1.5% + 1.5% + 1.2% + 2.5% = 20.2%.

Step 5 Energy generation potential after considering module losses: So far we have estimated the energy generation potential of 1 MW plant for a given site under ideal condition. In Step 4, the estimated losses at module level is about 20.2% for the month of January. Ideal energy generation for the month of January in the power plant is 170500 kWh. After considering the losses, the energy output of 1 MW_p PV plant would be:

Energy generated after considering module level losses

= Ideal energy generated without losses × (1 – PV module level losses)

$= 170500 \text{ kWh} \times \left(1 - \dfrac{20.2}{100}\right) = 170500 \text{ kWh} \times (1 - 0.202)$

$= 170500 \text{ kWh} \times (0.798)$

= 136059 kWh (in the month of January)

Similar to this, calculations can also be done for other months.

Step 6 Available energy at the output of inverter: Electricity gets generated by PV modules and then it flows at the input of inverter in the DC form. This DC power is converted to AC power by inverter. Other than converting DC power to AC power, the inverter also performs the function of maximum power point tracking (MPPT).

In this PV plant design, we are so far doing the calculations in terms of energy. At the inverter level, the energy output of the inverter will be less than the energy that gets into the inverter due to losses in inverter. The inverter power losses consist of MPPT tracking and DC to AC conversion losses. The high power inverters (range of several 100 kW to MW) are becoming very efficient and power losses in inverter are in the range of 1.5% to 3%. Let us assume that inverter losses are 2% in this example. The energy coming at the input of inverter in this example for the month of January is 136059 kWh. Then, the available energy at the output of inverter will be:

Energy at output of inverter (kWh)

$$= \text{Energy at input of inverter (kWh)} \times (1 - \text{losses at inverter})$$

$$= 136059 \text{ kWh} \times \left(1 - \frac{2}{100}\right) = 136059 \text{ kWh} \times (1 - 0.02)$$

$$= 136059 \text{ kWh} \times (1 - 0.98)$$

$$= 133337.8 \text{ kWh (in the month of January)}$$

Step 7 Energy fed to the grid: Inverter is connected to the grid through AC cables and isolation transformer, if it is already not a part of inverter. There are some losses that occur in AC cables too. This loss is normally very small and usually less than 1%. In this example, let us say this loss is about 0.5%. The energy available at the output of the inverter is 133337.8 kWh is eventually the energy fed to the grid will be:

Energy fed to the grid (kWh)

$$= \text{Energy at output of inverter (kWh)} \times (1 - \text{losses in AC cables})$$

$$= 133337.8 \text{ kWh} \times \left(1 - \frac{0.5}{100}\right) = 133337.8 \text{ kWh} \times (1 - 0.005)$$

$$= 133337.8 \text{ kWh} \times (0.995)$$

$$= 132671.1 \text{ kWh (in the month of January)}$$

Thus, the electricity fed to the grid after considering all the losses in the month of January (from 1 MW plant and for this particular location) is 132671.1 kWh.

Similar calculations can also be done for other months. The summary of calculation for each month is presented in Table 11.5.

TABLE 11.5 Monthly Electricity Generation that can be Fed to the Grid from 1 MW$_p$ Plant

Month	Power plant capacity	Equivalent monthly sunshine hours (hours)	Monthly energy production (without any losses) (kWh)	Monthly energy production (considering all losses) (kWh)
January	1 MW$_p$	171	170500	132666
February	1 MW$_p$	171	171360	133335
March	1 MW$_p$	200	199950	155581
April	1 MW$_p$	200	199800	155464
May	1 MW$_p$	204	204395	159040
June	1 MW$_p$	186	186000	144727
July	1 MW$_p$	189	189100	147139
August	1 MW$_p$	160	159650	124224
September	1 MW$_p$	156	156000	121384
October	1 MW$_p$	162	162130	126153
November	1 MW$_p$	161	161400	125585
December	1 MW$_p$	168	168020	130736
Total annual electricity production (kWh)			2128305	1656034
			2.12 Million kWh	1.65 Million kWh

PV plant performance ratio

A PV power plant performance ratio is the ratio of actual electricity fed to the grid to that of electricity that would be produced by given plant capacity in the absence of any losses. It can be given as:

$$PV \text{ plant performance ratio} = \frac{\text{Electricity fed to grid}}{\text{Electricity generated by plant in absence of any losses}}$$

Typically, the performance ratio of PV power plants varies between 70% to 80%, and these days, the performance ratio of at least 75% is expected from power plants.

In this case, the electricity generated by 1 MW$_p$ PV module in whole year is 2.12 Million kWh and after considering all the losses, the electricity that can be fed to the grid is 1.65 Million kWh. Therefore, the Performance Ratio of plant is:

$$\text{Performance ratio} = \frac{1.65}{2.12} = 0.778 \text{ or } 77.8\%.$$

Sankey diagram for overview of energy losses in PV power plants

It has been discussed that the loss of electricity occurs in many ways between the generation of electricity at the module level to feeding of the electricity to the grid. The losses due to temperature, dust, DC cable losses, AC cable losses, inverter losses, etc. can be presented in the form of Sankey diagram to get good overview of overall energy flow in PV power plants. An example of energy flow in PV plant of 1 MW with various losses occurring at different stages is shown in Figure 11.24.

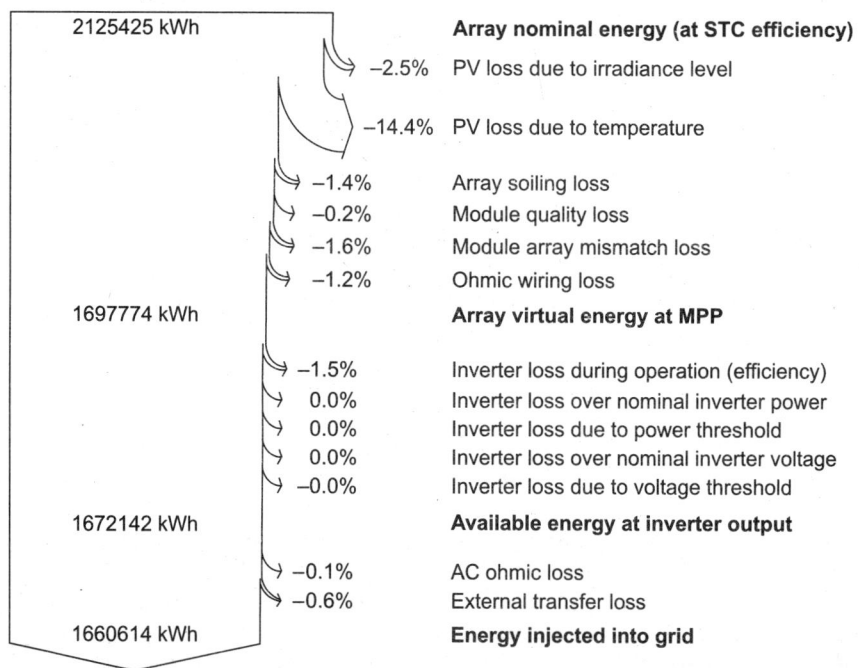

FIGURE 11.24
Sankey diagram of PV power plant showing various losses at different stage of conversion.

11.5.2
Determining Configuration of PV Plant

So far we have studied at the electricity generation in 1 MW$_p$ PV plant, we have considered various losses and estimated the electricity fed to the grid for the month of January. We have not considered the number of PV modules which will be required in 1 MW$_p$ PV plant. A detailed description of how to select a PV module and how to select an inverter is given in Section 11.4.1, Step 10 of this chapter to read that again. The details about how to size a wire for a given application is given in Chapter 9. The details about series and parallel connection of PV modules and corresponding addition of their currents and voltages are given in Chapter 5. Here, we will do the calculations without a detailed discussion. One is advised to read the Section 11.4.1 and Chapters 5 and 9 as mentioned above.

Total PV array capacity

In this case of PV power plant system, it is decided that we will have PV array capacity of 1 MW$_p$ for which we have done the loss calculations. Also, the efforts are made to generate as much energy as possible (remember in other small power applications, the plant capacity is decided based on the energy requirement of the load).

Inverter rating

Since this PV plant is being designed for 1 MW$_p$ PV array capacity, the inverter in the plant should also be able to process such power level. Therefore, the inverter should also be of 1 MW or 1000 kVA rating. Although, due to temperature losses and other losses, the power fed to the inverter would be lower than 1000 kVA, but when the losses are low, there may be chance that whole 1000 kVA power gets fed into the inverter.

Select PV module and inverter

Let us first make a choice of PV modules for use in this 1 MW$_p$ PV plant. Normally, for large scale power plants, PV modules of higher wattage ratings are chosen. Looking at the PV module parameters given in Table 11.1, let us choose a PV Module 7 having rated wattage of 240 W$_p$. The other parameters of PV Module 7 are as follows:

1. Rated power of Module 7 = 240 W$_p$
2. Open circuit voltage (V_{oc}) = 37.38 V
3. Voltage at maximum power point (V_{mp}) = 30.60 V
4. Short circuit current (I_{sc}) = 8.45 A
5. Current at maximum power point (I_{mp}) = 7.85 A

Now, let us select an inverter. After looking at Table 11.2, we can choose Inverter 6 whose power rating (1000 kVA) matches with the need. The other parameters of Inverter 6 are as follows:

1. AC power output = 1000 kVA
2. Max DC input voltage range = 1000 V
3. MPP tracking = 460 – 875 V
4. Max DC current = 2100 A DC
5. Peak efficiency = 98.6%

Using small capacity inverters

Note that, many times, one can also use small capacity inverters for large power applications. For instance, in order to design 1 MW$_p$ plant, instead of using one 1000 kVA inverter, one can also use two inverters of 500 kVA capacity. In the extreme case, one can use one inverter for each string or even one inverter for each module as well.

Number of PV modules required

In this example, total PV array capacity required is 1 MW$_p$ and we have chosen 240 W$_p$ PV module for installation. Therefore, the number of modules required for this plant would be:

$$\text{Total no. of modules required} = \frac{\text{Total PV plant capacity}}{\text{Rated power of one module}}$$

$$= \frac{1\,\text{MW}_p}{240\,\text{W}_p} = \frac{1000,000}{240} = 4166.6\ \text{modules}$$

To round off, we need about 4167 PV modules of 240 W$_p$ for this 1 MW$_p$ PV power plant.

Number of PV modules in a string

In order to determine the number of PV modules in the array, we should look at the acceptable voltage rating of inverter and try to match it with the voltage ratings of strings as per presentation given in Figure 11.21. The V_{oc} of PV Module 7 is 37.38 V, V_{mp} is 30.60 V and I_m is 7.85 A. Also, for Inverter 6 of 1000 kVA, its Maximum Power Point (MPP) voltage tracking range is 460 V–875 V and maximum input

DC current is 2100 A. While deciding the number of PV modules in a string, we have to ensure that V_{mp} of the string is within the V_{mp} range of inverter and V_{oc} of the string is less than the maximum DC voltage of Inverter.

Since when we connect PV modules in series the voltage gets added. Therefore, we need to connect many Module 7 in series to get the required voltage in the range of Inverter 6. If we divide V_{mp} range of Inverter 6 with the V_{mp} of the Module 7, we will get the number of PV modules to be connected in series to form one string as:

$$\text{No. of modules in string} = \frac{V_{mp} \text{ voltage of selected inverter}}{V_{mp} \text{ of selected PV module}}$$

Since the inverter V_{mp} tracking range is 460 V to 875 V, let us have an average of it, that is, about 667 V. This 667 V will be the V_{mp} of the PV module string. Note that any other voltage levels within the inverter tracking range can also be chosen. We have to only ensure that the array V_{mp} point should lay within the inverter V_{mp} range in all operating conditions.

$$\text{Number of 240 W}_p \text{ modules in strings} = \frac{V_{mp} \text{ of inverter}}{V_{mp} \text{ of module}} = \frac{667}{30.60} = 21.79$$

<table>
<tr><td>While designing the number of PV modules to be connected in series (as string) in PV power plant, we have to take care that V_{mp} of string should lay within V_{mp} tracking range of Inverter under all possible operating condition.</td><td>The above calculation shows that we will have to connect 21.79 PV modules in series, or to round it off, we get 22 modules. While designing the number of PV modules to be connected in series (as string), we have to take care that V_{mp} of string should lay within V_{mp} tracking range of Inverter under all possible operating conditions.</td></tr>
</table>

Number of PV strings in parallel

In total, we need to connect 4167 PV modules for this 1 MW$_p$ PV power plant. One of the string of PV modules will have 22 PV modules. Therefore, the number of strings to be connected in parallel will be as follows:

$$\text{No. of strings in parallel} = \frac{\text{Total no. of PV modules in system}}{\text{No. of modules in a string}}$$

$$= \frac{4167}{22} = 189.4 \text{ parallel strings}$$

To round off we will have to connect 190 parallel strings (each having 22 PV modules in series) in this 1 MW$_p$ power plant.

Note, that when we connect strings in parallel, the current of each string gets added. The total current of the parallel combination will be the sum of current of each string. We have to make sure that the total current of the strings is within the limit of the inverter. In this example, the maximum DC current limit of Inverter 1 is 2100 A, and I_{sc} of Module 7 is 8.45 A. The maximum current of a PV module will be the maximum current of a string. Therefore, the total current of 190 strings connected in parallel will be:

Total current of strings in parallel = Current of one string × Total number of strings
$$= 8.45 \times 190 = 1605.5 \text{ A}$$

From this calculation, we can see that the current of 190 strings put together is less than the maximum DC current limit of inverter (which is 2100 A). Therefore, this design is acceptable and can be implemented.

This completes the design of 1 MW$_p$ solar PV power plant. In summary, the details of 1 MW$_p$ plant is presented in Table 11.6. Due to rounding off that we have done in design, the PV plant parameters are slightly different from targeted value.

TABLE 11.6 Summary of Parameters of Designed 1 MW$_p$ PV Power Plant

Power rating of selected PV module	240 Wp
Number of PV modules in a string	22
Number of strings in parallel	190
Total number of modules used in plant	22 × 190 = 4180
Total rated peak power of plant	4180 × 240 = 1003200 W$_p$
V_{mp} voltage of PV array	22 × 30.60 = 673.2 V
I_{mp} current of PV array	190 × 7.85 = 1491.5 A
Expected annual energy generation of plant	1.65 million kWh

Determining Balance of System (BoS) components of PV power plant

Various Balance of Systems (BoS) components are required to integrate the system. PV array support structure, DC cables, string and array combiner boxes and DC distribution boxes are used on the DC system side. The design of BoS components should be done in same manner as discussed in previous section (refer to Section 11.4, Step 12). It is important to make appropriate choice of components, particularly cables. The DC cable size is selected such that the total power loss over the entire length of DC cables is within 2% of the rated PV array output power and this loss should be less than 1%. Normally, for large scale power plants, efforts are made to keep this less within limits.

Designing PV plants using software

At commercial level, the PV plants are designed in similar fashion. There are many software are available in the market which can be used to design a solar PV power plant. The PV plant design software have recorded the data of solar radiation for several location of the world, they will have temperature data, data of standard PV modules, etc. Once we specify a location, they take these data automatically or we can provide the data. The software then calculates the parameters (as given in Table 11.6) of required power plant. But they also provide much more detailed information. Software can provide daily generation of electricity, daily losses, and we can plot the charts of generation with losses for each month and lot more. An example of summary sheet of 1 MW$_p$ power plant is given in Figure 11.25.

PV module	Si-poly	Model	**STP 275-24/Vd**		
		Manufacturer	Suntech		
Number of PV modules		In series	18 modules	In parallel	205 strings
Total number of PV modules		Nb. modules	3690	Unit Nom. power	275 W$_p$
Array global power		Nominal (STC)	**1015 kW$_p$**	At operating cond.	851 kW$_p$ (60°C)
Array operating characteristics (50°C)		U mpp	546 V	I mpp	1559 A
Total area		Module area	7160 m^2		

Inverter		Model	**RPS TL1110**		
		Manufacturer	Bonfiglioli		
Characteristics		Operating voltage	460–875 V	Unit Nom. power	1000 kW Ac

PV array loss factors

Thermal loss factor	Uc (const)	28.8 W/m^{2}K	Uv (wind)	0.0 W/m^{2}K/m/s
⇒ Nominal Oper. Coll. Temp. (G = 800 W/m^2, Tamb = 20°C, Wind velocity = 1 m/s.)			NOCT	45°C
Wiring ohmic loss	Global array res.	6.3 m Ohm	Loss fraction	1.5% at STC

Array soiling losses	Jan.	Feb.	Mar.	Apr.	May	June	July	Aug.	Sep.	Oct.	Nov.	Dec.
	0.4%	0.5%	1.0%	3.3%	4.2%	3.9%	1.0%	0.2%	0.3%	0.2%	0.2%	0.3%

Module quality loss			Loss fraction	0.2%
Module mismatch losses			Loss fraction	1.5% at MPP
Incidence effect, ASHRAE parametrization	IAM = 1 – bo(1/cos i – 1)		bo Parameter	0.05

System loss factors

AC loss, transfer to injection	Grid voltage	33 kV		
	Wires	245618 m 3 x 5000 mm^2	Loss fraction	0.1% at STC
External transformer	Iron loss	1008 W	Loss fraction	0.1% at STC
	Resistive/Inductive losses	0.9 m Ohm	Loss fraction	0.1% at STC

FIGURE 11.25

An example summary sheet of a 1 MW$_p$ power plant.

Problem 11.8: Design a 500 kW$_p$ solar PV power plant to be installed in Pune. Estimate annual energy output of the plant. Use PV module and Inverter with following ratings:

PV module rating

- Rated power of Module = 240 W$_p$
- Open circuit voltage (V_{oc}) = 37.0 V
- Voltage at maximum power point (V_{mp}) = 30.5 V
- Short circuit current (I_{sc}) = 8.5 A
- Current at maximum power point (I_{mp}) = 7.8 A

Inverter rating

- AC power output = 500 kVA
- Max DC input voltage range = 1000 V
- MPP tracking = 460 – 875 V
- Max DC current = 1000 A DC
- Peak efficiency = 98.2%

Problem 11.9: A PV module of rating as mentioned in Problem 11.8 is used in a 1 MW$_p$ power plant. The plant is being set up at location where the average temperature reaches up to 45 °C. Estimate the module level losses that can occur in this power plant.

Problem 11.10: Design a 10 MW$_p$ solar PV power plant to be installed in Rajasthan. Estimate monthly energy generation as well as monthly energy losses in the plant. Use PV module and inverter specification as given in Problem 11.8. Make a table to provide the summary of all power plant parameters.

Problem 11.11: A location has solar radiation of 5.7 kWh/m^2/day. A 100 kW$_p$ PV plant is installed at this location. Consider an ambient temperature of 25 °C, what will be the estimated annual energy generation from the plant. Assume, there are no other losses in the plant.

12

Installation, Troubleshooting and Safety

As a technician of solar PV system, the most important thing, after identifying the needs of an user and designing an appropriate PV system, is to install it properly so that the system can work satisfactorily during the expected life of the system. Any mistakes in the installation of PV system would cause disruption in electricity supply to the load, dissatisfaction to the user and worst, disbelief for the PV technology that it cannot work and provide reliable electricity. All this has to be avoided as much as possible, especially as a technician, we would like to have long carrier in this field.

Once the design of PV system and installation is done properly, the chances of failure of PV system is very less. Even if it fails to supply electricity to the load due to some reason, as a technician we should be able to detect the fault and repair it as soon as possible. Our knowledge about each and every component will be useful in detecting the fault and repairing it. Each PV system component has a role to play, and they function in certain manner under a given condition, troubleshooting faults and repairing or removing them will be the key.

Above all, the personal safety of the person installing and troubleshooting is very important. All care must be taken to avoid any accidents or possible health hazards caused by the PV system. In this chapter, we will discuss the issues related to installation, troubleshooting and safety.

> For a solar technician most important thing is to install it properly so that the system can work satisfactorily during the expected life of the system.

12.1

Summary of PV System Components

There are various components needed to make a complete solar PV system depending on the requirements of the load. The load could be domestic like fans, TV, etc. It could be water pump, a grid-connected load or a solar power plant. In designing and installing all possible types of PV system, several components are used in PV system. The list of system components includes:

1. Solar PV module
2. Module mounting structures
3. Batteries
4. Electronics control circuitry (Charge controllers, Inverter or DC-DC converters)
5. Load (AC or DC type)
6. Junction boxes or combiner boxes

7. AC and DC cables

8. Energy meter

9. Circuit breakers

10. Power distribution box

Note that all the above components may not be there in all PV systems. Depending on the load and power rating, as well as user requirements, certain components may be added or removed. An example of a solar PV system with its possible components for domestic applications is shown in Figure 12.1.

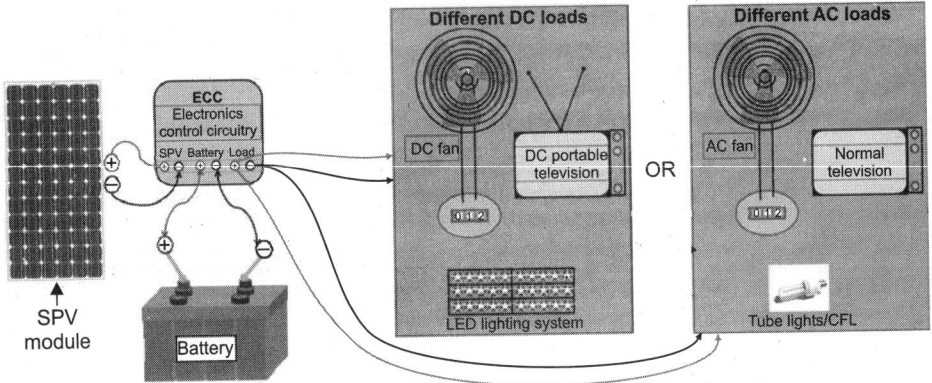

FIGURE 12.1

A simple solar photovoltaic system with its components.

12.2

Summary of Types of Solar PV Systems

There are three basic configuration of solar photovoltaic system. These include:

1. Standalone SPV system

2. Grid-connected or On-grid SPV system

3. Hybrid SPV system

All possible types of PV system configuration can be categorized under one of the above categories.

12.2.1

Standalone Solar PV System

The self-dependent or autonomous solar PV systems are known as standalone PV systems. They do not depend on grid or any other electric power supply, that is why they are also called off-grid PV systems. These systems are suitable for small electrical loads located at the remote places where grid supply is not present. The standalone PV systems are best suited for domestic applications. As shown in Figure 12.2, the standalone system can be with AC/DC load, electronic circuitry, battery, inverter, etc. (The details are given in Chapter 10).

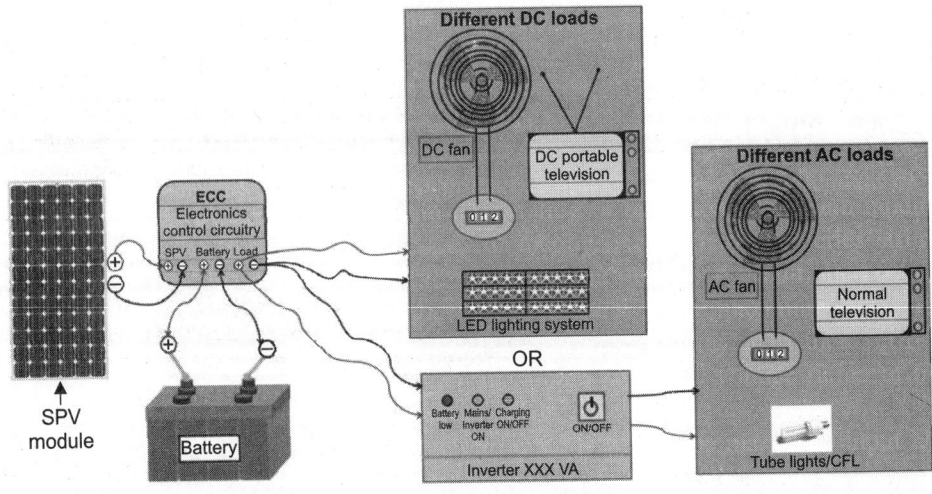

FIGURE 12.2

Standalone SPV system.

12.2.2
Grid-connected or On-grid SPV System

The grid-connected SPV system is a SPV system which supplies the power generated by the SPV system to the grid. The grid connected SPV system has different components depending on the requirement of the system. The main component of this system is grid-connected inverter which converts the DC into AC (see Figure 12.3). The battery may or may not be present in the grid-connected SPV system. This system is also called On-grid or Grid interactive system because this SPV system communicates with the grid power supply to match the phase and also to avoid the islanding situation. The grid connected system can have capacity ranging from as small as 10 kW to as large as several 10s of MWs. The details of the system can be found in Chapter 11.

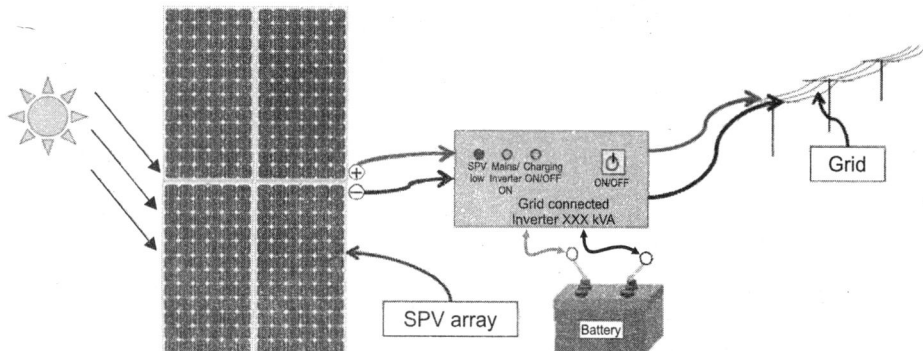

FIGURE 12.3

SPV grid-connected or grid-tied or on-grid SPV system.

12.2.3
Hybrid Solar PV System

These types of system have more than one power supply. One of the power supply is solar PV modules and other could be wind turbine, a diesel generator or a biomass system. The hybrid solar PV systems are not discussed here.

The standalone PV systems and grid-connected PV systems differs from each other in their power handling capacity. The standalone PV systems are normally small, few kW to 10 kW and does not have very high current and voltage levels. These are also normally roof mounted and in some cases ground mounted. The area covered by PV modules in standalone system is not very large. On the other hand, grid-connected PV systems can have very large capacities. The MW level solar PV plants can cover very large area up to 100s of acres, and therefore, the scale of installation is very different than the standalone solar PV systems. For this reason, the installation and troubleshooting of PV system is divided in two categories:

- Installation and troubleshooting of standalone solar PV systems
- Installation and troubleshooting of PV power plants

12.3

Installation and Troubleshooting of Standalone Solar PV Systems

Installation is a process in which the different components are connected in a systematic order to make a perfect working solar PV system to meet predefined demands. Different types and different number of components are used in PV system depending on the requirements. For example, in a simplest possible standalone solar PV system without a battery, a DC fan and solar PV module/s can be connected together in a simple manner as shown in Figure 12.4. In this case, the installation of PV system includes putting the required number of PV module, connecting them together in appropriate series and parallel combination (if required), connecting the output of PV panels to the input of fan, and installation gets completed. However, in a large power capacity PV system, there are many other components that are needed for proper functioning of solar PV system. For example, a grid-connected system with battery back-up. In that case, the installation would required interconnection of all the components properly to get desired delivery of energy to the load.

> Installation is a process in which the different components are connected in a systematic order to make a perfect working solar PV system to meet predefined demands.

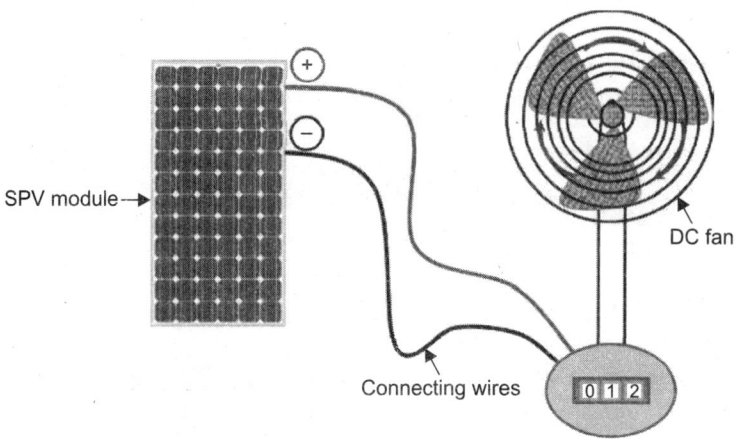

FIGURE 12.4
Simple standalone SPV system.

In this manner, the different SPV systems are connected in a different systematic order according to the requirement.

12.3.1
Installing PV System Components: BoS

The Balance of System components contains the electronics for the solar photovoltaic, including wires that are used to interconnect various components. The electronic circuitry can be from a simple DC-DC converter to a complex maximum power point tracking (MPPT) circuit with inverter and monitoring of parameters. The BoS also includes battery and wires.

Electronic component installation

This component comes in well-packaged form. In order to have safe installation, one need to find an appropriate place which does not get heated up (there should be good ventilation of the space) and we should also try to avoid dust settlement on these components.

AC and DC cable installation

Cable dimension should be appropriately chosen to carry the current in PV system. In the case of wires that are not designed properly, and carry over current, get heated and they get damaged faster than normally. In the case of overheating, there is also the chance of fire. Design of cables for carrying appropriate current is given in Chapter 9.

Battery installation

Location of battery installation: The battery installation place should be far away from heat source and the place where it is easy to sparkle. The location where the battery is installed should be away from the electricity and electrical switches etc. The distance should be at least 50 cm. Direct irradiation of the sun should be avoided on batteries. Battery installation should be done in area which is not the part of living area.

Space for battery installation: Enough space should be provided for the installation of batteries. The distance between battery sides (or battery backsides) and wall should sufficient and it should not be less than 20 cm.

Interconnection of batteries: The interconnection of battery should be made properly, the connection points should not be loose, else there can be spark and chance of fire. The battery contains electrolyte which contains acid. In the area where batteries are installed, some fumes comes up which is not good for health. Battery are normally very heavy and safety must be taken in carrying batteries. Rolling or throwing battery should be forbidden. We should prevent battery from short circuit and contacting with outside electric conduction while battery installation. While using several batteries, do not put different type and different making of batteries together.

12.3.2
Installing Mechanical Structure and Mounting of PV Modules

In a PV system, depending on the requirement, the numbers of modules are connected in series and parallel combination to make a PV array. The array is kept in a particular sequence according to the number of modules in series and parallel and accordingly, the structure for the array is designed and mounted on that structure. Following precaution must be taken:

- Mechanical structure should be designed keeping in mind the wind load data of the site where the solar photovoltaic system is being installed so that it can withstand that much wind load. There are standard norms that are followed to design structure for given wind load. In solar PV system, structure should be designed to withstand wind loads corresponding wind speeds up to 150 kmph (kilometer per hour).

- The appropriate material should be used for mounting structure. Normally, the PV modules are supposed to last for 25 years, therefore, the PV structure should also be lasting for 25 years. Galvanized iron or aluminium steel structure can be used. Precaution must be taken to use appropriate thickness of galvanization. Normally, galvanization thickness of about 80 to 100 micron is good enough for structure to be rust free for 25 years.

- Solar PV modules are installed either on sun tracking structure on fixed structure. In most cases, solar PV modules are installed on fixed structure. Solar PV modules are installed at an angle (facing southwards on northern hemisphere and facing northwards on southern hemisphere). Precaution must be taken to accurately point the South direction, as well as precise the angle of structure. There are simple devices that are available in the market to give you direction as well as angle. An example of mounting structure is shown in Figure 12.5.

- Stainless steel bolts should be used to avoid any rusting during lifetime of system.

- All the connection should be tightly made to avoid any shorts and sparking.

- Do not install differently rated PV modules together in series and parallel combination.

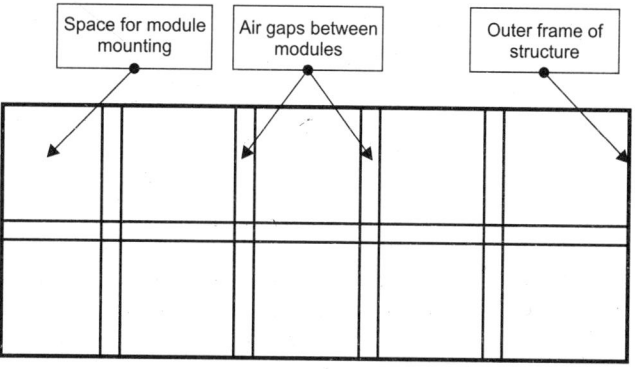

FIGURE 12.5
Example of module structure with air gaps.

12.3.3
Maintenance of Solar PV System

Maintenance refers to fixing any sort of mechanical, plumbing or electrical work so that the component or equipment or system does not become out of order or broken. Maintenance can be of many different types; two of which are mainly employed almost everywhere are mentioned below:

Unscheduled maintenance: Unscheduled maintenance is performed when there is a sudden fault or damage to the system or its components. This maintenance involves repair or replacement of components of the system.

Scheduled maintenance: For any system, it is necessary to perform a routine check up or to maintain the components of a system so that the system and its components have a proper working condition and its life. Scheduled maintenance is done on periodic basis.

The photovoltaic systems and its components require a less maintenance as compared to other power systems although a few periodic maintenance tasks should be performed on the PV system components.

While performing maintenance to the PV components it is must to refer the component specification sheet or the catalogue provided by the supplier so that one is properly familiar with the component and also the necessary precautions to be taken while maintaining the component. Here, let us briefly discuss the maintenance requirement of various components of solar PV systems.

> While performing maintenance, a technician must to refer the component specification sheet to be familiar with the component and to take necessary precautions.

Photovoltaic array

The PV array needs very little maintenance. If the system is in dusty climate then the photovoltaic modules need to be cleaned off regularly. One can use a soft cloth for cleaning the photovoltaic modules where the climate is hot and moisture content is low in the atmosphere. In some places where the atmosphere is little rainy or moisture content is high, the photovoltaic modules can be cleaned with water. Use of mild detergent can also be done to remove the bird droppings. Shadow on PV modules should be checked. It is possible that after installation some tree or tree branches have grown enough to shadow module which were not there at the time of installations. Avoiding shadow is necessary for getting higher energy production from PV system. Connections in the PV array should be checked regularly to avoid loose contact or breakage in wires.

Array junction box

As it is said previously, all the connection should be checked regularly to avoid loose contact or breakage in wires, same way the array junction box should be periodically checked for loose contacts, breakage and also for weather protection.

Batteries

Batteries are the key components in the solar PV systems with battery back-up capability. Batteries require periodic inspections to ensure the proper operation. The battery maintenance depends largely on the battery type. It is recommended to perform periodic maintenance for batteries depending on the type of battery. While performing battery maintenance, it is essential to estimate the state of charge of the battery. One can make the use of a multimeter to check the voltage of the battery (operating a load for several minutes can stabilize the battery voltage). It is recommended not to check the voltage while the battery is charging or discharging. While checking the battery voltage, all the loads and the PV array connected to the battery should be disconnected. The measured voltage readings can be compared with the battery manufacturer's data for the state of charge. For liquid electrolyte batteries, the state of charge can be determined by checking for its specific gravity (described in following paragraph).

Sealed Maintenance Free (SMF) batteries: The sealed maintenance free batteries (Nicad, VRLA etc.) are the batteries which require the least amount of annual maintenance. Even though they are called 'maintenance free' batteries, they require inspections for the casing, terminal connections, wiring, voltage and the venting strategies in VRLA batteries.

Tubular lead-acid (Liquid electrolyte) batteries: The tubular lead-acid batteries are the deep discharge liquid electrolyte lead-acid batteries which are also used in electric vehicles and automobiles, and these are the batteries which require the most maintenance. These batteries have higher amount of gassing than other types of batteries and require addition of distilled water.

Determining status of charge by measuring specific gravity: The batteries can be precisely tested for the state of charge by measuring the electrolyte's specific gravity with a hydrometer. It is required that for proper operation, the specific gravity of battery to be maintained in a certain range. A hydrometer is a bulb like cylindrical syringe having a glass rod inside which is calibrated with the weight of mercury or lead. Figure 12.6 shows the parts of a hydrometer. The glass rod has scale on it, this floats in the liquid electrolyte which is drawn by the hydrometer from the battery. The scale on the floating glass rod gives the reading of the specific gravity where the level of the liquid inside the hydrometer touches the scale of the floating glass rod. The lower the glass rod sinks in the electrolyte, lower is the specific gravity and lower is the state of charge of the battery.

> It is required that for proper operation, the specific gravity of batteries to be maintained in a certain range.

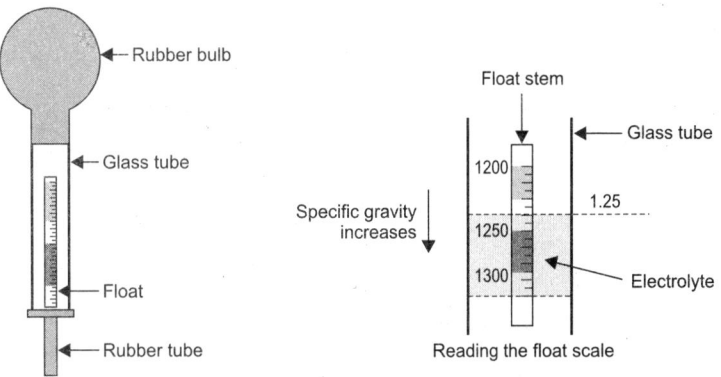

FIGURE 12.6
Parts of a hydrometer.

Adding distilled water in the battery: The electrolyte has a considerable amount of lead-acid and distilled water which, in turn, constitutes the proper specific gravity. Hence after checking the specific gravity of the electrolyte, one can judge to add distilled water in the composition to get the required specific gravity. If the glass rod in hydrometer sinks more in the electrolyte, it indicates high specific gravity, which means that there is need of adding distilled water in battery. After addition of distilled water to the battery, one should not immediately check for the specific gravity with the hydrometer, instead the water must be thoroughly mixed with the electrolyte by charging the battery.

12.3.4
Troubleshooting of PV System Components

> Troubleshooting is a logical and systematic search for the source of a problem or faults so that it can be solved.

Troubleshooting is a form of problem-solving, often applied to repair failed products or processes or systems. It is a logical, systematic search for the source of a problem or faults so that it can be solved, and so, the component or process or the system can be made operational again. Troubleshooting would not be required if the system is working properly without any faults. Proper working of the PV system would be possible if during the initial phase of installation, high quality and properly designed system is installed, and also, by implementing regular maintenance to the system and its components, the faults can be avoided.

The faults in a PV system could be due to cloudy weather, shading of PV modules, dusting of PV modules, blowing of fuses, empty batteries, tripping of circuit breakers and bad connections. Troubleshooting in a PV system can be performed by some visual inspection for the following components:

- Check the PV array for partial shading or dirt.
- Check all fuses and the circuit breaker.
- Check the junction boxes, distribution boxes and wiring for loose connections and/or corrosion.
- Check the PV modules and batteries for proper series-parallel configurations.
- Check system wiring for proper polarity.
- Check the meters installed in the system for proper voltage and current readings.

Let us now discuss how different faults or problems in a PV system can be found out and repaired in a systematic way.

Troubleshooting faults in a PV system using multimeter

A multimeter can be used for measuring and checking parameters like voltage, current, continuity and polarity. If the measured voltage and current is not as per the expectations then it indicates a fault in the component or interconnection of components.

Measuring voltage

For the measurement of voltage of a circuit, multimeter setting should be chosen properly for AC/DC voltage and range of voltage.

We should follow the following steps for voltage measurement:

1. Select the voltage to be measured as DC or AC on the multimeter.
2. Select the proper range for voltage measurement.
3. Connect the multimeter leads to the circuit for voltage measurement.

For DC voltage measurement, some meters have positive (+) and negative (−) values. If meter leads are connected correctly then it will read the positive value for voltage and if the leads are placed on wrong wires then the meter will read negative value. For voltage measurement in alternating current circuit, set the meter to AC voltage. Some meters have the symbol (~) for AC measurements. In the same way, as in DC, if the meter leads are connected on wrong wires, then the meter will read the negative value. The range selection on the meter is important for the meter to read the value, if the voltage value is unknown set the range for maximum voltage scale.

Measuring current

Measurement of current in a circuit is similar to voltage measurement, except that the current flows through the circuit whereas, the voltage is the potential in the circuit and can be obtained at two opposite points in the circuit. Following are the steps for voltage measurement:

1. Select the current to be measured as DC or AC on the multimeter.
2. Select the proper range for current measurement.
3. Plug the red lead in positive (+) jack A, and plug the black lead in the common (−) jack of the multimeter.
4. Connect the red lead to the positive (+) and black lead to negative (−) in the circuit.

For direct current measurement, some meters have positive (+) and negative (−) values. The meter leads are connected correctly then it will read the positive value for voltage and if the leads are placed on wrong wires then the meter will read negative value. For current measurement in alternating current circuit, set the meter to AC current. Some meters have the symbol (~) for AC measurements. Same way as in DC, if the meter leads are connected on wrong wires, then the meter will read the negative value. The range selection on the meter is important for the meter to read the value. If the current value is unknown, then set the range for maximum current scale.

Checking polarity

Polarity of a circuit refers only to DC current circuits. In any circuit, it is important to check for its correct polarity before giving supply to the circuit. There can be many disadvantages and hazard due to reverse polarity. The DC motors may run backwards. In many appliances, overheating may occur, and in many cases, the appliances will simply not work at all and also, the appliances will be destroyed because of reverse polarity. Following are the steps for checking polarity in a circuit:

1. Disconnect the circuit and verify if it is open by using a multimeter.
2. On multimeter, select the type of voltage as DC.
3. Plug the red lead in positive (+) jack V, and plug the black lead in the common (−) jack of the multimeter.
4. Connect the red lead to the positive (+) and black lead to negative (−) of the circuit.

If the value is positive, then the polarity is correct and if the meter reads negative value, it is due to reverse polarity.

Checking continuity

Checking continuity indicates whether a circuit is open or closed. This is useful when checking for broken wires, short circuits, fuse or switch operation. Following are the steps for checking continuity in a circuit:

1. Select the continuity mode in the multimeter.
2. Plug the red lead in positive (+) jack V, and plug the black lead in the common (−) jack of the multimeter.
3. Connect the leads of multimeter to the two points in the circuit whose continuity is to be tested.

The multimeter simply gives a beep if continuity exists; otherwise, if continuity does not exist, then the multimeter will not give any beep sound.

12.4
Safety in Installation of Solar PV Systems

Various safety measures are to be taken into consideration while doing installation, maintenance and troubleshooting in a PV system. Usually, safeties for various categories like electrical, chemical, mechanical, environmental and heath are to be considered.

12.4.1
Electrical Safety

As safety is concerned for the onsite working professionals, electrical safety is considered to be the most important part. Some electrical safety points, while installation and maintenance in PV system, are mentioned below:

Handling PV modules exposed to sunlight: Always a warning on the back side of the PV modules is mentioned regarding handling of PV modules. One should read the warning and cautions mentioned. As PV modules produce electricity when they are exposed to sunlight, precautions should be taken so that the personal carrying or handling the PV modules does not get a shock. Also, the positive and negative terminals of the PV modules should be kept away from each other to avoid the shorting of terminals when the PV module is under sunlight.

Handling batteries in PV system: Always remember to disconnect the batteries before moving or handling them. Avoid shorting the terminals of batteries to avoid severe damage. While checking the battery voltage with multimeter, always check if the multimeter is in voltage mode. If the multimeter in current mode is connected to the battery terminals, then short circuit to the battery terminals will take place which can result in severe damages and also causes fire.

Safe distance from exposed electrical conductors: It is always a good practice to know the location of an exposed electrical conductor so that one can keep a safe distance from it. At the same time, it is necessary to know the potential in that conductor and the safe distance to be kept by a personal.

Understand proper work practices in wet or damp locations containing electricity: Working area selection is must for electrical safety, before working on electrical conductors or equipment, location should be noticed for sufficient space, conducting materials around and also, if the place is wet or damp.

The proper lockout/tag-out procedures for electrical equipment and systems: Lockout/tag-out procedure is always required for electrical equipment and systems. This practice is carried out to ensure that only one person is responsible for the operation of the equipment or system as he himself has the authority to lock and open.

Note to unplug tools and equipment before cleaning, adjusting, or repairing them: Manytimes in many cases, there are severe accidents due to electricity as the working personal forgets to unplug from the electrical mains before doing maintenance work or handling the live conductors or equipment. This should always be kept in mind to unplug from live mains to ensure electrical safety.

12.4.2 Safety Precautions for Batteries

Following precaution should be taken while dealing with the batteries:

Sulfuric acid: The battery contains sulfuric acid that could cause burns and other injury. When battery is damaged, the sulfuric acid will flow out from it. For this purpose, appropriate precaution by the means of wearing apron, wearing gloves and protective glasses should be taken. In case of contact with sulfuric acid, flush immediately and thoroughly with water and go to hospital for a treatment.

Gas: Explosive gas may be generated in the battery, so, combustibles such as spark, flame and fumy materials should be prohibited in the battery room. Fire extinguisher should be equipped in battery room. All the installation tools should be wrapped with the insulated electrical tape in order to reduce the possibility of short circuit while installing battery. It is prohibited that leaving tools, sundries and other conductive things on the battery.

Electrical shock: The system that includes many cells might create high voltage, so, we should avoid the danger of electrical impact while installing battery.

12.4.3 Mechanical Safety

While installation of PV systems, mechanical safety for the onsite working professional is the key point to be considered. The working professional should be equipped with mechanical safety equipments for carrying himself while installing the PV modules on the rooftop.

12.5 Installation and Troubleshooting of Solar PV Power Plants

Installation and troubleshooting of solar PV plant is bit different than the standalone solar PV plant as the power rating of the PV plants is normally higher. In this section, we will see how one can proceed from beginning to end for the installation of solar PV power plants and precaution should be taken in installation and maintenance of the plants.

12.5.1
Preparation for Installation

- Obtain necessary permits from the building and electricity authorities before installation.
- Keep all safety equipment ready to be used during installation.
- Ensure all equipment inclusive of spares is received, tested and available at hand for installation.
- Review installation instructions for each component and become familiar with the installation process.

12.5.2
General Considerations for Installation

- Ensure the roof area or other installation site is capable of handling the desired system size.
- If roof mounted, verify that the roof is capable of handling additional weight of PV system.
- Install equipment according to manufacturers specifications, using installation requirements and procedures from the manufacturers' specifications.
- Observe specifications for external mounting of modules, combiner boxes and DC cabling (IP protection, weather resistance etc.). Pay particular attention to DC installation of PV array.
- Properly ground the system parts to reduce the threat of shock hazards and induced surges.
- Check for proper PV system operation by following the checkout procedures on the PV System Installation Checklist.
- Ensure the design meets local utility interconnection requirements.
- Have final inspections completed by the concerned authority and the utility if required.

12.5.3
Installation of Array Support Structure

- PV array support structure is pre-fabricated and surface treated ready to be installed on the roof or on ground.
- The rooftop support structure is typically embedded into concrete blocks cast on the roof.
- A number of PV modules are installed on one support structure called PV panel. The PV modules in one panel are usually connected in a series string.
- The PV panel is designed for small (1 cm) gaps between modules when assembled. This arrangement results in higher wind resistance.
- Two PV panels are installed in a row with sufficient space (0.5–1.0 m) between them for maintenance access.
- Two rows of PV panels are mounted with space adequate to avoid shadow of one row of panels onto the other. As a rule of thumb, minimum width between two rows is equal to the height of the panel structure.
- The support structure is oriented to south with a tilt angle equal to the latitude of the plant location. This arrangement results in maximum annual yield.
- We should leave vacant space around parapet wall when installing array on rooftop. The minimum width of the space to be left vacant should be equal to the height of the parapet wall.

12.5.4
General Notes on DC Installation

- The modules are electrically live when installed and cannot be switched off. Therefore, modules without shrouded connectors should be covered with lightproof material during installation.

- The level of module DC current output is proportional to the amount of solar radiation, however, the nominal output voltage is attained even when radiation is low.
- The module/array DC current can cause permanent arc if there is an insulation fault. All installations above 50 V DC must be ground fault and short circuit proof.
- The short circuit current of PV module/array is around 20% above nominal current. DC fuses/circuit breakers should take this into account.
- Ensure correct polarity when connecting PV modules, strings, arrays, combiner boxes, DC circuit breakers and DC cables. If the polarity is reversed, bypass diodes and inverter's input stage may be damaged.

12.5.5
Installation of Modules

- Monitor module V_{oc} and I_{sc} and check that they are within specified limits before installing the module.
- Modules with shrouded (touchproof) MC4 connectors are preferred as they are electrically safe to install and convenient to isolate from the string.
- The installation of modules should be done in dry weather conditions using dry tools to avoid risk of electrical shock.
- Use mounting system (clamp/fastener, mounting points) recommended by manufacturer. Use predrilled mounting holes. Additional holes drilled in the frame may void the warranty.
- Modules should not be stepped on during installation. No heavy or sharp edge items should be placed on them to avoid damage to the glass cover.
- Ensure accessibility of roof structure after modules are installed for maintenance. Preassembled and prewired modules may be used for roof areas difficult to access.
- The corners and edges of frameless modules (typically thin film types) are particularly sensitive and are subject to high level of breakage risk during transport and installation. Extreme care in handling these modules during installation is required.
- When installing multiple modules on a support structure, lay out all modules before fastening to ensure they are aligned leaving gaps between them.

12.5.6
Interconnection of Modules, Strings and Combiner Boxes

- To avoid losses due to mismatching of modules, ensure that modules with similar MPP currents are interconnected in a series string.
- Interconnect module connectors under open circuit. Do not short circuit module outputs to avoid arcing and damage to connectors.
- For modules without connectors, use suitable clamp terminals, strain relief and waterproof cable feed-through when connecting cables into the module junction box. Ensure that the junction box cover is sealed and watertight.
- Do not disconnect module connectors under load. Switch off the inverter and trip the DC circuit breaker to isolate load before disconnecting module connectors. The module connectors can be disconnected under open circuit voltage.
- Measure string open circuit voltage before connecting in parallel with other strings. Ensure that string open circuit voltages are matched within specified limits.

- The measurement of short circuit current and insulation resistance to frame/ ground are recommended for safe and secure installation.
- The measurement of string I/V characteristics ensures that string MPP voltages and currents are matched within specified limits.
- The locations of string/array combiner boxes are determined to minimize DC cable lengths. Ensure ease of access for interconnections and maintenance while installing the boxes.
- String fuses, blocking diodes and DC surge/lightning protection devices are installed and wired inside combiner box.
- When connecting DC main cable into the combiner box, ensure that combiner box is isolated from PV string/array to avoid high risk of arc as a result of DC power input.
- For systems using string inverters without combiner boxes, isolate the string at a module cable using DC disconnect switch to avoid risk of DC arcing when connecting DC main cable.
- When connecting DC main cable into inverter DC input, ensure that inverter DC input is isolated using DC circuit breaker.

12.5.7
DC and AC Cable Layout and Connection Guidelines

- DC and AC cables should be installed in separate conduits or enclosures and labelled.
- Careful attention is required to the cable's permitted bending radius.
- For roof mounted installations, fix cables to the roof supports using suitable fastenings.
- Cables should be laid in shadow areas where possible and they should not impede rain water runoff.
- Cables, fasteners and cable ties should be weather resistant.
- Cables should stay away from lightning conductors.
- Avoid sharp edges and mechanical damage to cable insulation.
- Use proper recommended tools and follow cable termination guidelines.
- Cable termination should be either crimped or soldered to suit terminal design. Avoid combination of crimping and soldering the same joint. Crimped terminals are preferred over soldered joints.
- All terminations should use proper terminals, no cable to cable joints should be used.
- Ensure DC and AC circuits are isolated when cables are interconnected.

12.5.8
Grounding Considerations

- Equipment and system grounding is required to provide earth as common reference point for various voltages, to limit voltages due to lightning, line surges or accidental contact with high voltage lines and to provide current path for operation of over-current protection devices.
- The grounding consists of grounding electrode, grounded conductor and grounding conductor. Grounded conductor is grounded at one point via grounding electrode and grounding conductors connect all equipment enclosures to grounding electrode via grounded conductor.
- Equipment grounding provides protection from shock caused by ground fault and is mandatory in all PV systems. The equipment chassis is connected to grounding electrode via grounding conductor. PV array, combiner box, inverter, DC and AC distribution box require grounding. The grounding conductor must not be fused or switched.

- Array support structure should have equipotential bonding and grounding arrangements for safe conduction of capacitive discharge currents to ground.
- All grid-connected PV systems have DC voltage (400–800 V) well over 50 V and require system ground. DC system grounding is done by connecting negative conductor to ground at one single point. The single point ground is located near the PV array for better system protection from voltage surges. AC system can use the same grounding electrode. If two separate electrodes are used for DC and AC systems, they need to be bonded together.
- Jumpers may be installed for equipment and system grounding conductors to maintain ground continuity in the event, one of the equipment is removed from the system.
- Ground fault detector and interrupter (GFDI) is used to isolate grounded negative conductor from ground under ground fault condition. GFDI also isolates ungrounded positive conductor. Most Grid-tied inverters provide built-in ground fault protection. If not, external ground fault protection is required.

12.5.9
Installation of DC and AC Power Distribution Boxes

- The DC and AC distribution boxes are located near the inverter.
- The array output wires from combiner box are routed to DC distribution box along the shortest route.
- Ensure that the installation of wiring to the DC or AC isolator switch and surge protection devices is ground fault and short circuit proof.
- For DC voltages > 50 V, the two pole DC isolator switch must have at least 5 mm gap between the contacts in order to enable safe and reliable isolation.
- Ensure that the type plate of the DC isolator clearly states the DC voltage level of operation.
- The inverter input should be isolated when connecting to DC distribution box and inverter output should be isolated when connecting to AC distribution box.
- The AC distribution box may be combined with Load distribution box. If separate, it should be located near load distribution box.
- The DC PV energy meter is installed inside DC distribution box and the AC PV energy meter is installed inside AC distribution box.
- The DC and AC distribution box enclosures should be connected to ground.

12.5.10
Installation of Inverter

- The inverters should be installed in a location where faultless operation is guaranteed. Factors to consider are ambient temperature, humidity, ventilation, heat dissipation capability, noise emission as well as possible ingress of dust, water and pests.
- The inverters must be easily accessible with sufficient space around for maintenance and servicing.
- The inverter mounted on ground or wall should be at a height convenient for reading its display.
- The inverter for large power application is mounted on ground and is securely bolted to concrete floor.
- The inverter for small power application is mounted on wall and is securely bolted to wall.

- Ensure adequate open space is provided around ventilation panels for heat dissipation.
- The string inverter installed outdoors is IP65 rated. The string/central inverter installed in semi-controlled environment is IP54 rated. The central inverter installed in controlled environment is typically IP21 rated.

12.6
Solar PV Plant Installation Check List

12.6.1
Electrical Testing of PV Array

- Isolate output of PV array from inverter using DC disconnect switch.
- Check resistance from PV array mounting structure to ground is within permissible limits. (typically 0.1 ohm).
- Field Wet Resistance Test (FWRT): Check insulation between PV array positive output and ground within specified limits. Minimum leakage resistance in megaohms should be 36/A, where A is array test section surface area in square metres. The test voltage is limited by system voltage rating of the module. (typically 1000 V DC).
- Ensure that megaohm meter/insulation tester voltage does not exceed surge arrestor voltage rating. Also, ensure that GFDI devices are not damaged by insulation tester. Disconnect surge arrestors/GFDI devices if required before insulation test and reconnect after the test.
- Monitor back surface temperature of the module in each array section with a thermally bonded thermocouple (TC) probe.
- Check open circuit voltage of array is within acceptable limits (typically, 0 to +3%). Open circuit voltage should be checked on a bright sunny day making allowance for the temperature coefficient of the module.
- Check short circuit current of array is within acceptable limits. (typically, 0 to +3%). Short circuit current should be checked on a bright sunny day making allowance for solar irradiance in the plane of array. The disconnect switch used for testing short circuit current should withstand full array open circuit voltage when short circuit is removed. Use clamp-on current probe to monitor short circuit current. It is recommended to disconnect shorting conductor under no light conditions (array covered or in darkness) to avoid arcing.
- Consider a factor of 0.95 to allow for array soiling, misalignment and any other factors when measuring array short circuit current.
- Array *I-V* curve testing is useful in characterizing array performance. String or sub-array *I-V* curve tests are conducted by isolating individual strings or individual sub-arrays by pulling out fuses in string or array combiner boxes. Isolate all three legs (positive, negative and ground) of the array from the inverter prior to *I-V* curve test. Monitor at least 10 *I-V* pairs, solar irradiance in the plane of array and module back surface temperature. All *I-V* curves should have similar shapes (under identical solar and environmental conditions). The fill factor and maximum power monitored should meet system specifications for given solar and environmental conditions.

12.6.2
Electrical Testing of Inverter

- Visual Inspection: DC/AC disconnects, protection components, wiring, enclosures, and grounding.
- Verify operation of emergency stop and other safety controls.
- Turn inverter ON in shutdown mode.
- Connect inverter output to main AC grid via AC disconnect switch.
- Connect PV array output to inverter input via DC disconnect switch.

- Press start-up switch to start inverter operation.
- Double check inverter shutdown and restart operation.
- Monitor MPPT operation. Record MPPT voltage and current and verify maximum PV power produced is within system specifications for given solar and environmental conditions.
- Monitor AC output voltage and current and verify AC output power of the plant within system specifications.
- Monitor AC output frequency and phase and verify that the results are within specified limits.
- Monitor AC output energy produced by PV plant for one complete day and verify that the results are within expected range.

12.6.3 Testing of Islanding Protection

- The purpose of this test is to verify proper operation of the inverter under the loss of utility condition and subsequent restoration of utility.
- In this test, the time it takes for the inverter to disconnect from the AC grid after loss of utility voltage and to connect to AC grid after resumption of utility voltage is determined.
- If multiple inverters are connected to the grid in near proximity, this test should be performed one inverter at a time and then with all inverters operational.
- Remove or shutdown all nonessential loads that are on the inverter side of the 'loss of utility'.
- Monitor AC grid voltage with inverter output connected to grid. Ensure grid voltage drops to zero shortly after utility grid is turned off.
- Monitor inverter output current using clamp-on current probe. Ensure inverter supplies current to load/grid shortly after grid is turned back on.
- A Digital Storage Oscilloscope (DSO) may be used to monitor the line-side AC voltage and the inverter AC contactor status. Determine time delay between the two for both 'grid turned off' and 'grid turned on' operation.
- Inverter should shut down and restart within the time specified in Standard 929–2000 or as required in other national standards or as per the utility interconnection requirements.

12.6.4 Commissioning and System Functional Testing

- Visually check the system after installation is complete. Check that all modules and system components are bolted down securely. Check that all wiring connections are properly made as per diagrams and instructions.
- Ensure all required parts are properly grounded.
- Ensure all disconnects and circuit breakers are turned off and all fuses have been removed out of their holders.
- Check the polarity of all PV strings and PV array both at combiner boxes and at inverters.
- Check open circuit voltages of all PV strings and PV array. The string open circuit voltages should be within specified tolerance.
- Measure the voltage across the circuit where shorting link is to be installed. Only if this voltage is zero, install shorting link across the load side of the PV output circuit while the disconnect is open. Do not close any disconnects, breakers or insert any fuse toward the inverter or the battery while performing these steps. Then insert a PV string fuse in the first string fuse holder and

close the associated disconnect. Measure the short circuit current, then open the disconnect. Repeat the procedure by moving the fuse to each string circuit fuse holder, measuring the current each time. The string short circuit currents should be within specified tolerance.

- The disconnect on the PV output circuit should be open and the shorting link should be removed. All the source string fuses should be installed. The next step is to measure the open circuit voltage of the PV array. It should be close to the lowest individual string open circuit voltage measured and within specified tolerance.

- If the ground fault protection device trips in any of the above tests, ensure there is only one grounding point and follow troubleshooting procedure to find ground fault.

- Connect the inverter to the PV array and the utility source by closing output disconnects/circuit breakers prior to the input disconnects/circuit breakers.

- The inverter will remain off for sometime with its input voltage close to PV array open circuit voltage and AC output current zero.

- When inverter begins delivering power to load/grid, the inverter output AC current as well as DC input voltage and current will reach maximum power values.

- Monitor inverter output current using clamp-on current probe. Record inverter output AC current, voltage and frequency. These should be within specified limits.

- Monitor inverter DC input voltage and current. Ensure they are within maximum power specifications.

Index